The Wheel of Autonomy

Integration and Conflict Studies
Published in Association with the Max Planck Institute for Social Anthropology, Halle/Saale

Series Editor: Günther Schlee, Director of the Department of Integration and Conflict at the Max Planck Institute for Social Anthropology

Editorial Board: Brian Donahoe (Max Planck Institute for Social Anthropology), John Eidson (Max Planck Institute for Social Anthropology), Peter Finke (University of Zurich), Joachim Görlich (Max Planck Institute for Social Anthropology), Jacqueline Knörr (Max Planck Institute for Social Anthropology), Bettina Mann (Max Planck Institute for Social Anthropology), Stephen Reyna (University of Manchester)

Assisted by: Cornelia Schnepel and Viktoria Zeng (Max Planck Institute for Social Anthropology)

The objective of the Max Planck Institute for Social Anthropology is to advance anthropological fieldwork and enhance theory building. 'Integration' and 'conflict', the central themes of this series, are major concerns of the contemporary social sciences and of significant interest to the general public. They have also been among the main research areas of the institute since its foundation. Bringing together international experts, *Integration and Conflict Studies* includes both monographs and edited volumes, and offers a forum for studies that contribute to a better understanding of processes of identification and intergroup relations.

For a full volume listing, please see back matter

The Wheel of Autonomy
Rhetoric and Ethnicity in the Omo Valley

Felix Girke

berghahn
NEW YORK • OXFORD
www.berghahnbooks.com

First published by
Berghahn Books
www.berghahnbooks.com

© 2018, 2025 Felix Girke
First paperback edition published in 2025

All rights reserved. Except for the quotation of short passages for the purposes of criticism and review, no part of this book may be reproduced in any form or by any means, electronic or mechanical, including photocopying, recording, or any information storage and retrieval system now known or to be invented, without written permission of the publisher.

Library of Congress Cataloging-in-Publication Data
Names: Girke, Felix, author.
Title: The wheel of autonomy : rhetoric and ethnicity in the Omo Valley / Felix Girke.
Description: [New York] : Berghahn Books, 2018. | Series: Integration and conflict studies ; volume 18 | Includes bibliographical references and index.
Identifiers: LCCN 2018002589 (print) | LCCN 2018004569 (ebook) | ISBN 9781785339516 (ebook) | ISBN 9781785339509 (hardback ; alkaline paper)
Subjects: LCSH: Karo (African people)--Ethiopia--Ethnic identity. | Karo (African people)--Omo River Valley (Ethiopia and Kenya)--Ethnic identity. | Guji (African people)--Ethiopia--Ethnic identity. | Ethiopia--Ethnic relations. | Omo River Valley (Ethiopia and Kenya)--Ethnic relations. | Differentiation (Sociology)--Ethiopia.
Classification: LCC DT380.4.K357 (ebook) | LCC DT380.4.K357 G57 2018 (print) | DDC 305.8009633--dc23
LC record available at https://lccn.loc.gov/2018002589

British Library Cataloguing in Publication Data
A catalogue record for this book is available from the British Library

ISBN 978-1-78533-950-9 hardback
ISBN 978-1-83695-061-5 paperback
ISBN 978-1-83695-217-6 epub
ISBN 978-1-78533-951-6 web pdf

https://doi.org/10.3167/9781785339509

Contents

List of Illustrations	vi
Acknowledgements	viii
Introduction. How Do They Do It?	1
Chapter 1. A Rhetorical Approach to Groups and Ethnicity	25
Chapter 2. Categories of Being Kara	46
Chapter 3. Ethnicity within Kara: The Demotion of the Bogudo	83
Chapter 4. The Moguji: All That Is Not Kara	104
Chapter 5. The Schism and Other Predicaments of the Moguji	132
Chapter 6. The Regional Other in the Cultural Neighbourhood	148
Chapter 7. South Omo in Kara Terms	166
Chapter 8. The Cleverness of the Kara	194
Chapter 9. Seeing Like a Tribe	226
Conclusion	250
Glossary of Non-English Terms	261
Glossary of Places and People	266
References	271
Index	287

Illustrations

Maps

0.1	Local groups in the Omo Valley	2
0.2	Settlements of Kara	15

Figures

0.1	The initiates of the Ologuita age-set are driven through Dus	9
0.2	Both spears and gun are often left outside a dwelling when their owners gather within	12
0.3	Loxopil, the author's name goat (front), with a friend	19
1.1	Teenage girls grinding sorghum	30
1.2	The Wheel of Autonomy	32
1.3	Three consecutive age-sets join to start a dance	38
2.1	A public debate in Dus	56
2.2	Maide, Oita and Haila: three close friends from the Nyiramalai age-set	64
2.3	Rifles and *borkotto* put aside for a dance at Labuk	70
3.1	At rare times, a sudden flood clouds the river so that the dazed fish can be harvested with knives	85
3.2	Twins are not uncommon in Kara, and their birth order is carefully registered	95
4.1	After the whipping	111
4.2	A Moguji conducts a true Kara (left) and a Gomba towards Kuchur	118

5.1	A young woman in the sorghum fields of dried-out Lake Diba	138
5.2	A Hamar, a Moguji and a Kara jointly wait for the noon sun to pass	141
6.1	Looking across the Omo at the western riverbank, claimed by the Kara but cultivated by the Nyangatom	156
7.1	A Hamar man waits for his speech to be translated into Amharic, Dassanech and Nyangatom during a peace meeting in a Turmi school house	183
8.1	A Kara elder at the height of his influence and competence	216
9.1	The hearth inside the huts blackens the wooden girders, which have to be replaced regularly	230
9.2	The Kara erect shelters in their exposed fields to rest, share food and coffee, and talk	242
10.1	The young men of the Ologuita age-set prepare for their initiation	254

Tables

7.1	Dimensions of being alike and being different	180
9.1	Segmentation in the imperial encounter	227

Acknowledgements

This book was many years in the making; I do hope it was the sort of ageing that wine and whiskey undergo. Since I finished my first drafts, my anthropological life has led me away from the savannah and the Omo River to the golden spires and the tumultuous streets of Yangon, the former capital of Myanmar. Especially to reassure my peers in South Omo research – notably Echi Christina Gabbert, Sophia Thubauville, Lucie Buffavand and Shauna LaTosky – I want to state here in writing that my departure from the Omo was surely not permanent. How could it: while the writing of this book has – to a great degree – been a solitary affair, the years spent in and out of Ethiopia were foundational both for me personally and for my professional work ever since. If anything, research in a Southeast Asian megacity has reminded me just how communal and neighbourly anthropological work in the company of South Omo scholars always has been – and that is doubly true for my life in Kara.

To say 'thank you' is always an odd thing in Kara. So I say *tsalina*. My age-set, the Nyiramalai; my clan, the Gorsbolo; my fellow riverbank dwellers at Chellähte; my mother-brothers and in-laws in Dus, Labuk and Korcho; my hunting-friends Lale and Basso; the Ologuita age-set whose initiation I could witness; all the elders who patiently explained things to me; all the households who fed and housed me again and again; the children who laughed with me, showed me things and helped me out in so many ways; and especially all members of the lineage of Kete who became my family – they all know quite well what I owe them. I hope they will be pleased that this homage to life on the Omo has come out of our shared time.

To be able to work as an anthropologist in Kara was enriching like little else, and I want to thank the people and institutions who have sponsored and supported various legs of the journey. The lion's share of my fieldwork was financed and logistically supported by the Max Planck Institute for Social Anthropology in Halle/Saale (MPI). I had the pleasure of enjoying the stimulating atmosphere of the MPI from 2005 to 2008, and I want to thank Professor Günther Schlee, Director of the Department 'Integration and Conflict', for supporting my research. While the MPI offered a greatly supportive environment at the time, I want to specifically thank Bettina Mann for her coordination, Oliver Weihmann for technical support, Jutta Turner for the two maps included here and Cornelia Schnepel for overseeing the incorporation of this book into the 'Integration and Conflict Studies' series.

Across the street from the MPI, Professor Richard Rottenburg at the Institute for Social and Cultural Anthropology of the Martin Luther-University Halle-Wittenberg gave me theoretical advice and moral support as well as a welcome opportunity to discuss my ideas in his colloquium. Before I came to Halle, I worked with Professor Ivo Strecker at the Department of Anthropology and African Studies at the Johannes Gutenberg-University. Ivo Strecker and Jean Lydall opened the path to South Omo for me, and Ivo has been my most important academic teacher. Together with Christian Meyer, he inducted me into the 'Rhetoric Culture Project', a theoretical enterprise largely founded on fieldwork in South Omo. The insights I gained through my involvement in the project since 2002 have laid the groundwork for my theoretical approach. The resident SFB Research Group 295 'Cultural and Linguistic Contacts: Processes of Transformation in North-Eastern African and West Asian History' financed my first three trips to Kara. At Addis Ababa University, I thank Professor Andreas Eshete, Dr Taddesse Berisso, Dr Shiferaw Bekele and Professor Baye Yimam for support, encouragement and curiosity about my work. In Jinka, I thank the representatives of the municipal and zonal administration, and especially the administrators at Mago National Park, who always allowed me to pass through on my way to Kara without paying the entrance fee. I am also grateful to the many officials from the Hamar District who eventually let me attend all those meetings I discuss in the later chapters.

Other people have in a wide variety of ways contributed to the emergence of this book. The list below is partial and incomplete, but as I write this, and find myself able to recall so many people who supported my work, the inevitable omissions hardly diminish my pleasure.

I am especially grateful for my parents' and siblings' unquestioning support throughout this time. That they always took an active interest in my exploits was a great encouragement.

I thank all the individuals who commented on early drafts or parts of this book: Günther Schlee, John Galaty, John Eidson, Joachim Görlich, Echi Gabbert and Jolanda Lindenberg. Very valuable feedback also came from my audiences in the Colloquium of the Department 'Integration and Conflict' at the

MPI, the Anthropological Workshop, my peers in IDOCO and the participants of Richard Rottenburg's colloquium. Next to Jean Lydall, Echi Gabbert, Sophia Thubauville and Shauna LaTosky, I would also like to thank Tina Brüderlin, Susanne Epple, Hanna Getachew and all the other colleagues I had the privilege to spend time with in South Omo. I thank Steffen Köhn for putting his money (or rather the German Academic Exchange Service (DAAD)'s money) where his mouth was and coming to meet me in Kara for an exciting visit out of which emerged our film *Morokapel's Feast*. I thank the staff at the South Omo Research Centre for providing shelter, helpful hands and company.

Beyond the people already mentioned, I had some other academic teachers whose enthusiasm inspired me especially. Thus, I want to thank Anton Escher from Mainz University, as well as Bill Watson, Roy Ellen and the late John Bousfield from the University of Kent at Canterbury for making me want to become an anthropologist.

I thank the community of South Omo drivers, who were kind and helped me fix my car. The late Halewijn Scheuerman and his staff took me for an amazing boat trip across the jade-green border. In Hamar, I thank Choke Bajje. In Arbore, I thank Horra Surra, the Ginnos and the other people who welcomed me when I first came to Ethiopia.

Two anonymous reviewers understood perfectly well what I was trying to do with my manuscript and encouraged me immensely. Marion Berghahn and her staff were ever-helpful in getting this to production.

Judith Beyer has always made sure that I had time to spend on this project while helping me to trim this to a manageable size. I very much hope that she will be with me when I hand copies of this book over to the Kara, and that Constantin and Felikiss will become fast friends like their fathers did.

Introduction
How Do They Do It?

'How do you do it?'
'*Aga-ni, aga wossa paxalmamo-xa.* (This, this is due to our cleverness.)'

Looking through the sparse material on the Kara, agropastoralists residing on the banks of the Omo River in southern Ethiopia, their relatively low population stands out. When I first read about them, the estimates ranged between 500 and 2,000, whereas other groups in the greater region had as many as 10,000–30,000 members, or even 60,000 if you included the nearby highlands. These low numbers get more interesting if we consider that over the last few decades, the Kara have been involved in perpetual warfare with their much more numerous western neighbours, the quite expansionist Nyangatom. At the same time, the Kara, in terms of culture and language, are extremely similar to their eastern neighbours, the Hamar, Banna and Bashada. These groups also have population numbers several times greater than those of the Kara. 'How do they do it?', I wondered when I first considered a fieldwork project in the South Omo region, 'how do the Kara manage to sustain themselves as a group, being so few people, and having such fraught relations to their neighbours?' Specifically, how did it come about that they had been neither already eradicated by the Nyangatom nor assimilated by the Hamar? Judging from the available material, these were two likely eventualities that just did not seem to be occurring. To my fledgling anthropological assumptions, this hinted at extraordinary goings-on. The sparse ethnographic record did not indicate that there was anything remarkable about how the Kara managed their communal boundaries. The historical record is virtually nonexistent. This intrigued me further.

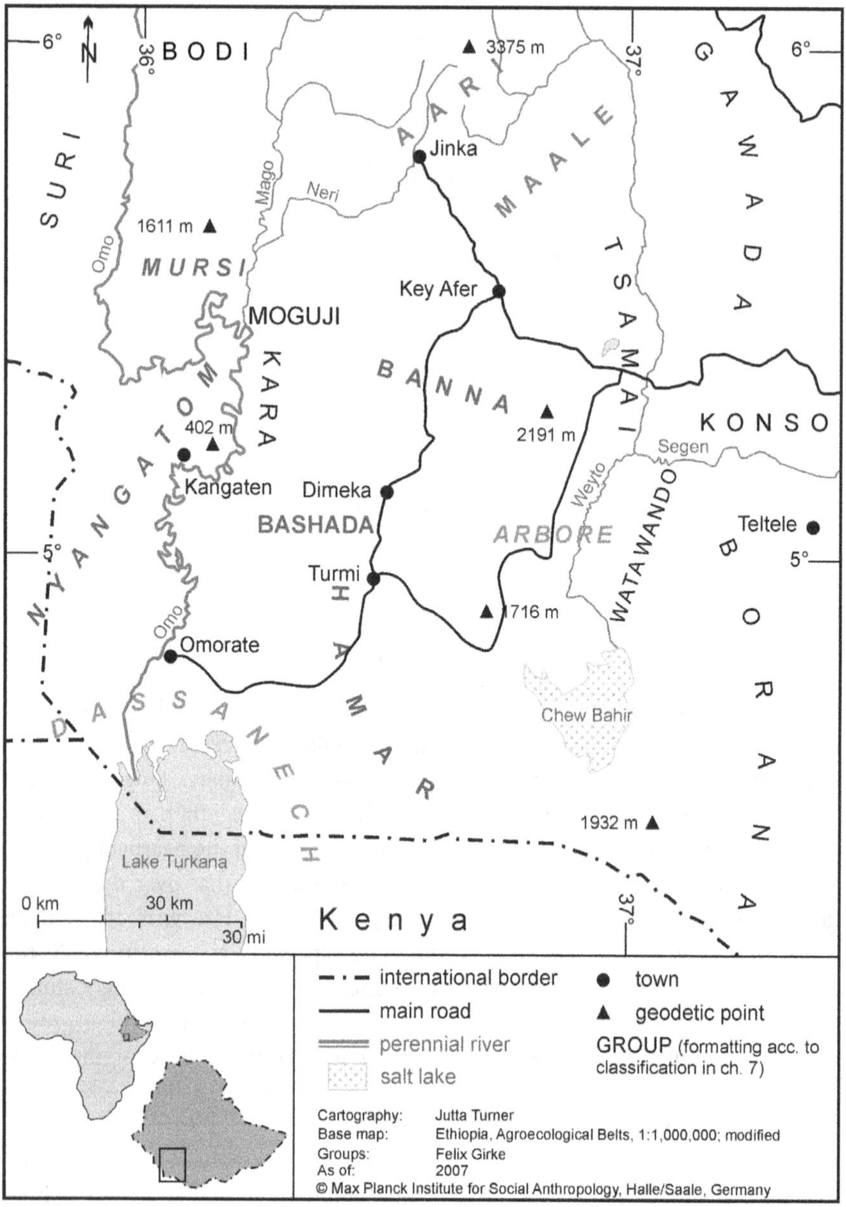

2 *The Wheel of Autonomy*

Map 0.1 Local Groups in the Omo Valley.

In regard to South Omo, many scholars have produced 'heartland' studies. This region, one of the most pronounced peripheries of Ethiopia, surely invites such an approach. A 'mosaic of ethnic groups' presents itself to the visitor. While all still engage in and depend on cattle and/or small stock husbandry and subsistence cultivation of sorghum and maize, the differences between them seem apparent and tantalizing: just a three-hour drive along the dirt tracks of the region opens up yet another distinct cultural world with its own depths to plumb and cultural intricacies to unravel.

Also due to the limited interest of the state in this periphery and the astonishingly late arrival of European explorers in the region – only from 1888 onwards (see Bassi 2011; Girke 2006) – there is little reliable historical material available on any of these populations, whose members are largely illiterate even today, and whose languages are nearly exclusively spoken rather than written (Girke 2018). The for the longest time half-hearted attempts to integrate them into the Ethiopian state proper were quite legitimately sidelined in favour of ever more subtle explorations of culture and internal social organization. Thus, published material on South Omo often focuses on a settlement area where an anthropologist studied the group they had decided upon, working in the one language they learned on site. While most seem aware of the multiple contacts between individuals and corporate groups across the ethnic boundary, few took such dynamics as their focus. With this, I do not only mean anthropological mainstays such as cross-cutting ties (e.g. Schlee 1997), but also linguistic influences, cultural appropriations, mimesis, wilful interdependence and purposive differentiation. But ideally, research programmes founded on the assumption of ethnically separate populations should take stock of how the very people studied are even at the time of research engaged in a constant struggle to negotiate difference and similarity from their neighbours. After all, the most specific thing about any particular 'culture' of group A is that it is not the culture of group B. The case of the Kara made it easy to avoid this pitfall. Looking at their settlements, one finds a string of villages hugging the meanders of the eastern side of the Omo River; Kara even looks more like a line than an area. Its frontier character is obvious (see Map 0.2 below). Kara country, small even from the perspective of its inhabitants, touches on the territory of several other groups. It is a node for many pathways of people, objects and ideas. If any group can be said to form the nexus of Cushitic, Omotic and Nilotic influences, the three major language families of the greater region, this would have to be the Kara. Trying to answer 'how they do it', I found that in order to understand how the Kara viewed their own way of being Kara, it was of the essence to look at how they perceived and dealt with not only one, but also a number of the other groups in their cultural neighbourhood, and eventually with the Ethiopian state to which they have belonged for a hundred years, but that has remained an other to them.

It was this initial moment of wonder and curiosity that led me to the Kara. While some of the specific interests I pursued in my ethnographic work changed over time, buffeted by the winds of contingency, this original fascination has never waned – especially as I discovered that the question of group size bears great relevance to the Kara themselves. One answer to my inquiries was particularly common: 'This, this is due to our cleverness.' To work out the implications of what the Kara told me and to reconcile this with what I learned from other sources, has kept me in a years-long conversation with numerous Kara, charitable colleagues, uncountable texts and myself. *Paxalmamo*, 'cleverness', was a popular reason the Kara were wont to give for their success in various endeavours; this claim proved to be a salient local explanans and a tricky ethnographic explanandum, but relevant on many levels for understanding just 'how they do it'. This book offers a long-form answer to this question. Ethnic categories, social organization and political groups are its main substantive topics, and rhetoric its methodological inspiration in the analysis of integration and conflict. Both discursive and material dynamics matter in facing the even more fundamental problem of just who the 'they' are, which both my initial inquiry and my interlocutors themselves presumed.

Rhetoric and *Ädamo*

Rhetoric and *ädamo* are the conceptual attractors around which my discussion will revolve throughout this book. Both terms require initial clarification, in terms of how they came to acquire such prominence in my approach and what work they are expected to do.

The methodological tool that I bring to the fore in the analysis and also in the structure of this book is rhetoric, specifically, a wide notion of rhetoric that transcends the common use, which equates rhetoric with 'artful speech' or even 'intentionally deceptive speech', as in the dismissive expression 'mere rhetoric'. This is no arbitrary choice. Since antiquity, the concept of rhetoric has undergone much variation in terms of how broadly or narrowly it was conceived by various schools of philosophy, the humanities or the social sciences (see Meyer 2009). My specific understanding derives from Rhetoric Culture Theory (RCT), a venture first launched in 1998 by Ivo Strecker and Stephen Tyler.[1] In its most pithy form, RCT posits that just as rhetoric is founded in culture, so culture is founded in rhetoric. This chiasmus serves to say that RCT proceeds from the axiom that while ways of persuasion and figuration (as the classical Western tropes and speech styles) are culture-specific, culture as such emerges, changes and is perpetuated by persuasive and figurative processes. I give an account of my personal initiation into this project and my subsequent involvement with it elsewhere (see Meyer and Girke 2011). Here, suffice it to say that since 2002, I have been thinking, talking, reading and writing about the constitutive role of rhetoric in the social life of culture. This focus has inspired most of my academic work, having become one of the lenses through which I approach ethnography. This book draws mainly on the persuasive aspect of rhetoric in interaction, and illuminates how this is fundamental for understanding ethnicity, conflict and integration.

A related basis of my approach is the theoretical and methodological work of F.G. Bailey, an under-studied but highly stimulating and prolific political anthropologist. Reading his numerous publications (see Girke 2002), I absorbed his attention on the rules of interaction, the practice of practice, and of how people managed to achieve their goals in this world, often within the rules of the arena, but also by strategically changing the very 'game' everybody thought they were playing. His take on 'the definition of the situation' as the methodologically central site of analysis best encapsulates this stance:

> The phrase *defining the situation* presupposes a plurality of structures in competition with one another and assumes an adversarial encounter in which one person tries to foist his or her definition onto another and so stabilize their relationship. *Foist* suggests the nature of the encounter: it is not simple *homo homini lupus*. Its mode of persuasion is somewhat less than naked force; ego and alter already have enough in common to let them communicate; so there is at least a modicum of civility. But neither is the encounter necessarily sweet reason; *foist* retains a sufficient whiff of nastiness to make clear that defining a situation is not an occasion when both parties want only the 'truth' (even if they say so); they have axes to grind. When someone successfully 'defines the situation' for me, I agree, like it or not, whether I believe what has been said or not, to behave in accordance with whatever conventions the definition stipulates. That agreement structures the situation. (Bailey 2003: 135, emphases in original)

When I embarked on my journeys to Kara, this was the perspective from which I looked at social life, and such was the vocabulary through which I thought about the dynamics of interaction. This focus on claims and attempts to define a situation had the effect that much of my data are not words spoken to me, but words spoken by other people to other people outside of an interview-like situation.

But how relevant are 'mere' words? A central problem in the study of rhetoric is that the link from words, i.e. public claims, to subsequent social action (or even putative inner states) is regularly tenuous. There is no epistemological shame in admitting that one is bound by this problem; so are the actors we are dealing with. People neither have perfect information, nor do they always act in their own best interests. Instead, they sway themselves and others through well-placed arguments, and know they might end up with unforeseen consequences. When trying to understand their choices and actions, one could certainly do worse than humbly accepting that much interpretation is guesswork, impossible to positively verify, and hence to make that shortcoming a strength. Rhetoric incorporates this very human uncertainty, which we always try to overcome in interaction, without ever being able to ensure complete success. It also provides the tools to categorize and differentiate genres of speech, among which ethnicized talk is particularly prominent in and around Kara. People speak 'ethnically', they have special ways to talk about ethnic groups and categories. If we accept that people can speak ethnically or not, and interpret situations ethnically or not, it follows that ethnicity is never a given. People can rhetorically define situations in terms of ethnicity – or not (compare Girke forthc.a). Close attention to situated speech helps us in tracing the cultural models underlying any struggles over defining situations in terms of ethnicity.

Whereas rhetoric provides me with an analytic vocabulary in which to formulate some answers to 'How do they do it?', allowing me to elaborate aspects of this guiding question further, I use the Kara term *ädamo* as a placeholder for certain Kara ideas about being Kara. I came across the term *ädamo* during my second stay in Kara in 2004, when discussing the social practice of bondfriendship (*beltamo*); bondfriendship, a voluntary bond established between two adult men and their respective households, often crossing ethnic boundaries, is a site of unquestioning solidarity, mutuality and even support in times of war between the two groups to which the bondfriends belong (see Girke 2011, forthc.b). *Beltamo*, it was explained to me, was a kind of *ädamo*, which in turn is etymologically an abstraction of 'kin' (*äda*) and links up to 'social person' (*edi*). *Ädamo*, then, is how *äda* act, the ways of *äda*, as it were – and vice versa; acts of *ädamo*, behaviour in the mode of kinship, just might make *äda* where there were strangers before. *Ädamo* entails both privileges and duties, and always demands a subjugation of individual interests to some larger social formation, from the dyad of *beltamo* to the imagined entirety of Kara and even beyond. In later chapters I address the abstracted and yet affective idea here called the 'cultural neighbourhood' that encompasses much of South Omo, which serves as an attentive audience to such creative efforts at crossing ethnic divides.

Learning about *ädamo* alongside the more technical formulas of kinship alerted me to the ways in which people actively and reflexively shaped their social worlds, instead of mechanically falling back on their seemingly natural ties of kinship for support, amity and intimacy. In turn, this semantic usage reveals that while in most instances *äda* refers to consanguinal and affinal 'kin', and would be translated and explained as such if prompted, the Kara routinely subsume other individuals of personal relevance to ego under this category.

During subsequent stays in Kara, I continued to look for other ways in which *ädamo* was constituted, for how, as it were, the Kara 'did' social relations. I found that explicit behavioural norms that were ordained by kinship principles still had to be negotiated, performed and often came to be transformed. Where no template was pre-given, people sought out ways to establish new bonds, proudly embracing the commitments entailed. In the wake of this recognition, I was struck by what I call (in Chapter 2) the Kara's 'proclivity towards differentiation'; the in absolute terms very small body politic is crisscrossed by an overwhelming number of divisions of ethnic, descent-based, settlement-oriented, ritual or interest-directed dimensions. These provide resources for factionalism and could well be taken as a standing challenge to the constant invocations of *ädamo* – alternatively, they provide plenty of illustration why such an ideology as *ädamo* is so badly needed in Kara. All these divisions provided at times a basis for inclusion or exclusion, for escalation or mediation. To focus on these ways of differentiation also suggested the methods of research; the way these social categories were connected in any real sense only ever emerged in interaction, in the larger and smaller dramas of everyday life. My insight into the workings of these categories, how they were opposed to one another and in which way people invoked them to frame, justify and explain their own and others' actions thus only grew by attending to and participating in social action. The plausibility rules for cultural arguments emerged there, notable precedents were established and relevant historical accounts invoked. In such context-rich moments, it became apparent that these numerous social categories were not hierarchically ordered; how should one weigh an affiliation to a settlement against clan membership or membership in an age-set? In observed practice, all these did the same work, in providing grounds on which people persuaded themselves and others to follow a suggested definition of the situation. This is just as true for the ethnic categories within the Kara body politic, and nearly as true for the relation between the Kara and their various neighbours in the South Omo region.

When I turned my eye on arenas where ethnic categories met, I found that they were related in distinctly different ways. In short, ethnic differences were different from one another. A related to B differently than to C, and again differently than B did to C; both the structural models and the social ways of expressing and negotiating them (viz. speaking about them) were markedly dissimilar. While it was usually clear what could be usefully translated as an ethnic category, the activation of these categories was not very orderly. Some only mattered in specific contexts, some seemed to be argued along 'primordialist' lines, others were more clearly 'constructivist',[2] some afforded a certain kind of interpersonal relations and some precluded them. Sometimes opposed categories of people had an ethnic component, which turned out to be only rarely invoked, as the interaction between members from both sides of the divide usually seemed more plausibly guided by another, nonethnic difference. Finally, all of these ethnic relations suggested a formal model guiding the hierarchy and opposition of groups and categories, hinging on ritual and taboo, land ownership and especially the capacity of collective action. These different ways of conceptualizing ethnic group relations are explored in the ethnographic chapters.

The focus of my analysis is on how the Kara discuss, contest, apply, perform and transform social categories, and *ädamo* is an inevitable element in these negotiations: as an oppressive harmony ideology to rebel against, or as a refuge from factionalism, or a rhetorical weapon to coerce others to fall into line. Following on from the last paragraphs, attention to rhetorical action enables insight into people's attempts to make others accept their definitions of the situations, and reveals the different ways in which ethnicity is conversationally and discursively upheld. This approach will unfold over the course of this book, as I turn to the various ways in which belonging and mutuality are created and sustained. *Ädamo* itself is difficult to define due to the polysemic plasticity of its application, and this is precisely why I have to approach it in a tangential manner: Kara ways of inclusion and exclusion shift and change, and words might not mean in one context what they mean in another. *Ädamo* is a social claim people make about how the world ought to be; thus, it has an ideological and political aspect. Even as *ädamo* generally evokes mutuality, it will come as no surprise that relations of domination are sustained in its name. This sort of ambiguity leaves room for rhetorical manipulation, for strategic ways of establishing closeness and distance, for declaring differences significant in one context while gainsaying them elsewhere, for displaying affection and demanding reciprocation.

My interest in *ädamo* also points to the problem of translation. *Ädamo*, by its very nature, requires contextualization when used, and other Kara terms that I learned to use and apply over my fieldwork are similarly complex. As a rule, whenever I introduce a Kara term, I aim at what Michael Herzfeld has called a 'shorthand referentiality', which educates the reader 'into the significance of the term by "seeing" it used in a set of diagnostic contexts, after which its appearance in the text is routinized and assumed to be semantically stable' (Herzfeld 2003: 113). Such use expresses the tentativeness of my understanding. It also reflects my main methodological insight that all these terms, as I encountered them, always stood in their own specific context. They were used as elements of rhetorical claims and were often left intentionally ambiguous.

This ambiguity should not become a source of frustration, not for the fieldworker, not for the reader – ambiguity is a central and, one could argue, necessary and beneficent element of face-to-face interaction.[3] Stephen Tyler goes as far as calling literalness 'odious' (1978: 396), and with good reason. Political positions in communities such as that of Kara are prone to rapid change, alliances are often fleeting, and ambiguity helps people to find compromises, backpedal or simply to forgive, forget and move on. In analysis, this role of ambiguity needs to be appreciated, and any attempts to smooth it out, to achieve perfect translations, are misguided, as the reality is as fuzzy as its rhetorical expression.

All social action can be looked at in terms of its rhetorical aspects. Even a maximally utilitarian action pursued by the most formidable *homo oeconomicus* or *homo politicus* needs to be successfully communicated in order to become social; thus, it becomes subject to rhetorical analysis. My attention to persuasion, then, is intended to demonstrate the potential of the rhetorical approach for the study of interaction across ethnic and other social boundaries.

Figure 0.1 The initiates of the Ologuita age-set are driven through Dus (October 2004). Photograph by Felix Girke.

In the Company of Age-Mates and Bondfriends

I encountered the work of *ädamo* through my own integration into Kara webs of social relations. It is inevitable that any stranger in a given place will be somehow categorized, classified and assigned certain roles along with behavioural expectations and demands, even if they are minimal and exclusionary. This happens in cultural ways, particular to a certain time and place – for example, Kara between 2003 and 2012. Thus, when I now recount my personal 'arrival story', the narrative of how I arrived in my fieldsite, it is not just because it is textually proper to start off a fieldwork-based book with some such authorizing account. Instead, my experiences of 'getting there' and subsequently 'being there' are presented with an eye on methodology; it was the way in which I was persistently being classified in, by and for Kara and other audiences that led me on the path to discover how Kara establish *ädamo*. In other words: how the Kara rhetorically set up and maintain normatively loaded and affectively powerful social relations was a key personal experience throughout my fieldwork.

More than just incidentally, this section serves to establish my position in Kara – where my allegiances lay, what sorts of relationships I engaged in, what demands I was under, and which choices made by myself and others shaped this configuration. As the sections below as well as the later chapters will illustrate more fully, even if one attempts to not take sides, it might well be that one is eventually taken by a side.

I started off from the South Omo Museum and Research Center (SORC)[4] in the regional capital of Jinka in August 2003, seeking out Choke Bajje, an elder from Hamar and a close friend to my erstwhile teacher Ivo Strecker. He, Strecker had suggested, could and would love to introduce me to the Kara, whose territory lay not too far away from his homestead. The formidable Choke, who has brokered not only my but also several other anthropologists' access to their study sites, quickly offered to introduce me to his *bel*, his bondfriend in Kara. While Nukunu, the man with whom he had initially established the bond, had since died, there was still the latter's family. One of the sons, Choke intimated, was around my age. Soon after, guided by a sister-son of Choke, I made my way down from the Hamar mountains into the lowlands of the Omo River.[5] It took us some time to discover a track that led to Chelläte, the settlement where the family of Choke's *bel* was to be found. When we did arrive, most adults had gone down to the nearby river to clear the banks of last year's growths. Only later in the afternoon did I finally met Haila, the son of Nukunu.

While we had no language in common at the time, this did not stand in the way of getting to know each other. Quite surprisingly, there was not much to be debated regarding my wish to work in Kara: people were familiar with (and seemed slightly in awe of) Ivo Strecker and his decades-long work in Hamar, as well as the longlasting friendships he and his wife Jean Lydall had established there. Through his sister-son, Choke had sent word that just as Ivo had studied the Hamar language and culture, so had I come to do the same in Kara. As he vouched for me, I travelled the path of bondfriendship, and that was sufficient for Haila, his mother and his brothers to support my work and to host me.[6]

This first day marked not only the beginning of my affiliation with Haila's core family, then consisting of his mother Mudo, and his brothers Mulla, Nakwa and Nukunu; I also 'began belonging' to the settlement Chelläte, a small assemblage of huts, established for convenient access to the riverbank fields, the site of the main Kara subsistence activity of flood-retreat cultivation (see Matsuda (1996) for details). In these early days, I had no real appreciation of what other categories I was gradually being inducted into: my understanding of Kara social life grew in parallel to the growing number of people I got to know, and who then proceeded to offer relationships to me (compare Girke 2018). Wider exposure meant wider integration. When I got to know Haila's mother-brothers, they addressed me as 'sister-son'; when I met Haila's classificatory grand-daughters, they eventually displayed the joking behaviour to me that was appropriate to the role. With growing cultural and linguistic competence, I reciprocated, and most people who stood in any sort of kin relation to Haila eventually included me in their relationship as if I were his insignificantly younger brother. Initially, this was only manifested in terms of address, but over the weeks and months and years of my various visits to Kara, the interaction with many people became more personal, multifaceted and often cordial.[7] Acting 'as if we were kin (*äda*), people extended amity and the appropriate role behaviour to me, in the spirit of *ädamo*. Had I become their *äda* now?

But back to the early days again: on the fourth day of my stay in Kara, a group of Haila's friends jointly approached me, and even as it took me some time to get the message, they announced that they were of the Nyiramalai age-set and that I would belong to this group as well. Again, it started with the term of address, *hariya*, used among age-mates and their wives. Suddenly, a number of men began calling me 'age-mate'; some of their wives picked it up too, as wives of age-mates use the same term of address towards their husbands' peers. In a few cases, even their children joined in and called me *abba*, 'my father', as is appropriate towards the father's age-mate. Now, I obviously had not gone through the age-set initiation phase with the other Nyiramalai some ten years earlier. I had not alongside them pestered the elders for permission to debate on the public square with the other adults. I had not offered goats to the elders for them to grant 'us' the right to sit on an adult's headrest in public. I had not been whipped alongside the other Nyiramalai for our insolence. Neither had I shared with them the tedious chore of goat-herding, also the source of many valuable skills I had never acquired, nor had I joined the hunting trips of their youth, journeying far into the Mago River valley to the North. Still, since that day, many of the Nyiramalai were true to the initial offer extended to me by this first group.[8] Up until today, the Nyiramalai form my main peer group, my foremost interlocutors, guides and advisers, and my closest friends in Kara. Had I become their age-mate then?

I could extend the list of social categories into which I became integrated in precisely this way by listing settlement sections, clan and, eventually, after his marriage, Haila's affines. Members of all these categories extended the offer of a dedicated relationship to me and consistently acted out their parts. 'How much of this was carnival?' is an obvious question here. My answer is methodological: as long as I was willing to act 'as if' I took a given role or category-membership seriously, people acted 'as if' I belonged. An 'as if'-relation is not tangibly different from an 'as'-relation – whether somebody is 'truly' somebody else's age-mate only ever matters in the moment of contestation. As long as people choose not to press the issue, to not challenge this established definition of the situation, namely that I ought to belong, the point remained moot. That my integration was hardly arbitrary is illustrated by the awareness that I could not switch paradigmatically: my clan, Gorsbolo, is 'my clan', as I belong to it at least in a way that precludes belonging to any other clan at all, ever. The categories in which I found myself were exclusive vis-à-vis the several other similar ones, and to break the emerging pattern would clearly have entailed great social costs for all people involved.

The point I want to make using my arrival in Kara as an example is that if one looks at social relations in terms of interaction, their performative qualities are evident. Age-mates are age-mates as long as they agree that they want to treat

Figure 0.2 Both spears and gun are often left outside a dwelling when their owners gather within (December 2006). Photograph by Felix Girke.

each other as such. The Kara thus demonstrated to me, in a bodily and striking manner, how social relations emerge from will and performance, and that even while I could never quite match the intimate familiarity that might exist between any given Kara, to consistently act 'as if' I belonged was a practically and emotionally sufficient basis for interaction. The Kara and I persuaded one another that it would be desirable, for a number of reasons, if we all defined the situation in a way that integrated me into social life in these dimensions. Until somebody underwent the effort of counteracting this tacit agreement, there existed a shared basis for interaction. Young men of junior age-grades deferred to me; I let older men order me about. To talk about 'fictive kinship' here obscures the methodological point that all interaction is based in principle on such agreements, such semi-stabilized definitions of the situation that sometimes don the guise of perpetuity. The illustrative example, which takes us back to the start of this section, is bondfriendship (*beltamo*), the ethnic boundary-crossing bond that establishes solidarity through war and peace, and in the name of which people have turned against their own polities in support of the bondfriend. *Beltamo* – under various names – is practised and celebrated all over South Omo, and to cultivate a range of successful, enduring bondfriendships, to create one's own significant others in a variety of places rather than just accepting what one is locally born to, is a mark of social mastery (Girke 2011).

I 'came of age' in Kara as I grew more competent in seeing social life unfold, recognizing it as a dynamic arena, where even 'natural' categories came to be contested on various grounds. It is hardly decided *a priori* whether A will aid his brother B or support his age-mate C with whom his brother B has a fight. The categories of being Kara were situationally invoked to justify action or to persuade people towards action. Which category would come to be decisive was often an open question; the benefits of the choices eventually made were in many cases hardly evident. I made these experiences alongside my Nyiramalai age-mates, especially and foremost through Haila, who, even as he knows little about the circumstances of my European life, knows me, with my likes and dislikes, my moods and thoughts, perfectly well. The same is true of his wife Worssa, whom I also have known since 2003. The fact that we got along as well as we did ever since was perceived and appreciated by other Kara. I stuck with him and his family, he was committed to me and my project, and we became friends – these factors made my stay in Kara possible and feasible. When his first son was born, he was named after me. Looking back, it is hard to imagine how it would be possible to do in-depth research with the Kara without travelling the path of bondfriendship. As a cautionary gesture, Granovetter has pointed out that in such a social constellation:

> The local phenomenon is cohesion ... An analyst studying such a group by participant observation might never see the extent of fragmentation ... In the nature of participant observation, one is likely to get caught up in a fairly restricted circle; a few useful contacts are acquired and relied on for introduction to others. (1973: 1374)

He was right in that the friends of my friends became my friends too, but his general statement does not address the emerging counteracting social dynamics. Other Kara saw what was happening – that I stayed in the village Chelläte, that I was with Haila's family and the Gorsbolo clan, and that I belonged to the Nyiramalai age-set – and some of them acted to influence this state, for example, by striking up individual friendships with me. While there certainly was such a 'fairly restricted circle' for me, this was purposive and beneficial for my integration, and did not prevent me from realizing the 'extent of fragmentation', as I show in Chapter 2. Throughout this book, then, it should be kept in mind which categories of being Kara were applied to me: a young man, unmarried at a time when most of his age-mates had already become elders with children, a Nyiramalai of the Gorsbolo clan, who belonged to the settlers at Chelläte and who sat on the Nyuwaya dancing ground for the evening chats of the men. Other categories of me 'not being Kara' of course never quite ceased to matter.

As indicated above, the Kara population is also ethnically divided, with ritual differences, marked commensality taboos and restrictions on intermarriage between members of certain categories. I fit none of the established categories, so I became a person not subject to ethnically marked interaction – people felt no need to invent commensality taboos with a *parang* or *ferenj*, a European. However, through Haila, I was strongly associated with the 'true Kara', an ethnic subsection who are both the numerical majority and politically as well as ritually dominant. Most of my closest friends were also true Kara, and it is still difficult now to assess what impact this had on my role in the field. I will illustrate throughout this book that true Kara are the local master narrators, the ones who define the foundations of Kara sociality as a whole and who can make the strongest statements on what is and what is not according to *ädamo*. My greater familiarity with their perspective compared to that of other ethnic categories of Kara allows me to explore the dynamics of ethnicity and other social categories as they appear to a true Kara, an approach also justified by the sheer social dominance of this perspective.[9] In writing on and indeed in putting a name to the covert category 'true Kara', which goes unmarked in the local vernacular, I seek to make this hegemonic moment, this usually invisible 'prerogative of interpretation'[10] of the true Kara more legible.

Group Size and Community

Imagine 1,400 people living in small hamlets on a narrow strip of land about 20 km long and maybe 5 km wide. These 1,400 people are united in that they share a great many institutions, such as clans that only exist here, ritual leaders who have spiritual power only within this territory, a joint system of landholding and any number of other arrangements. All of these arrangements have in common that they are only relevant for these 1,400 people. Outside this territory, there is hardly anybody who even speaks their language. While this presentation sounds overly dramatic, this all applies to the Kara. To be Kara today means to know all other Kara; some more intimately, some less, but still – there is nobody who is considered a Kara who is not known to every competent adult. Such a spectacular lack of anonymity has significant effects on social life. As of 2005–6, the official population count of Kara was a total of 1,401 individuals. These numbers stated that 1,086 of these lived in and between the settlements of (central) Dus and (southern) Korcho, and the other 315 in the northern section centred around the village Labuk (see Map 0.2). This is, by and large, it. The diaspora population of Kara could at the time be counted off using fingers and toes: two men had joined the Ethiopian army for good; three young men were being trained as short track athletes in Addis Ababa; a small but growing number of male youths were attending colleges throughout Ethiopia; a few more people had taken up employment and residence in the nearby market villages Turmi and Dimeka, as well as the regional centre Jinka. A growing number of boys and girls were seasonally attending school in these places as well. It is noteworthy that the

Introduction 15

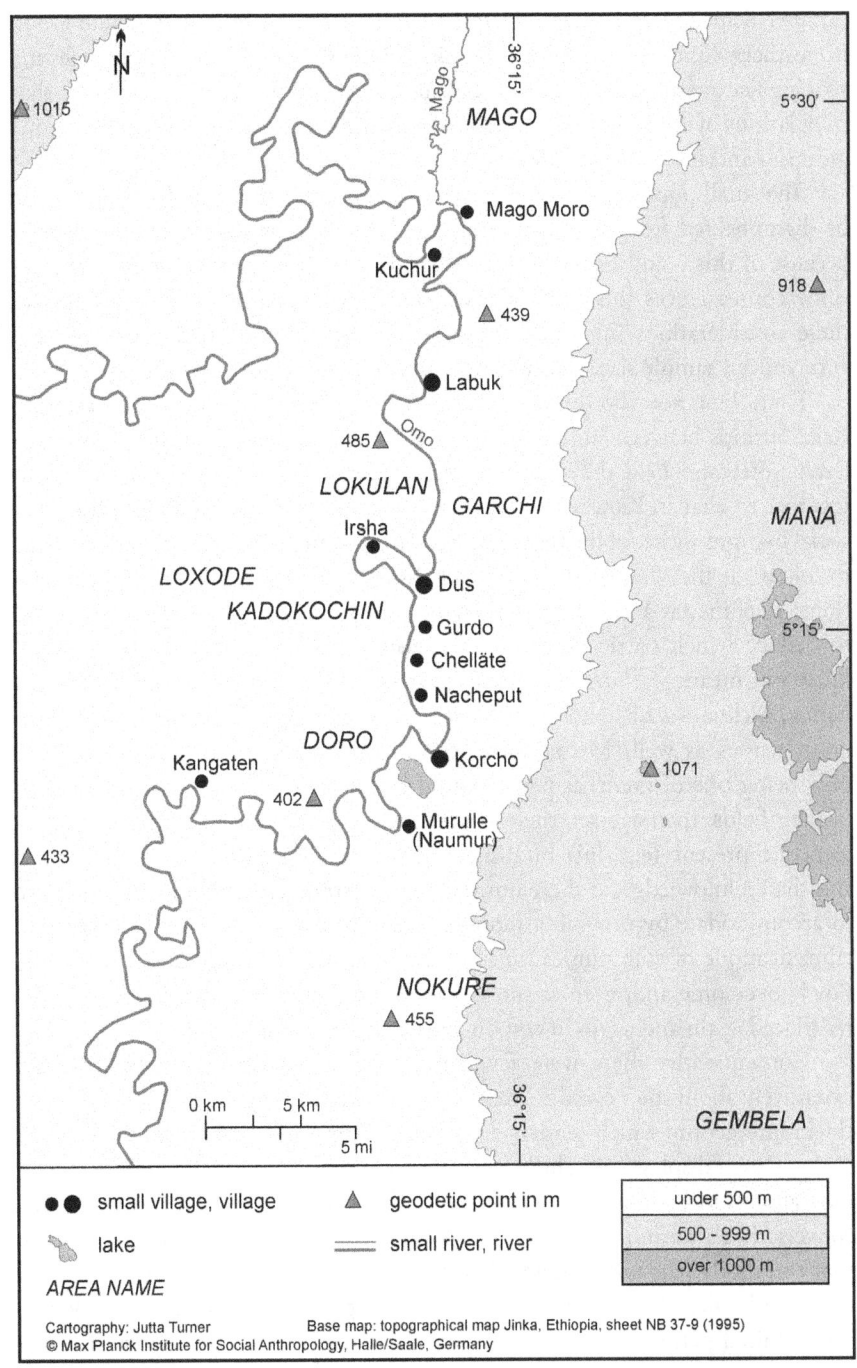

Map 0.2 Settlements of Kara.

number Schlee gives for the minimal population of a viable, sustainable group in northern Kenya or southern Ethiopia is 20,000 (2004: 97), which makes it a striking feature of South Omo, at the western edge of the area he indicates, that populations of around 20,000 already constitute major players among the ethnic groups – and the Kara even more of an outlier.[11]

The small population size is not an element external to the Kara that could be disconnected from who they are; they have become who they are precisely because of this – and not unawares either. Hence, it is worthwhile to point out some consequences this had for my research with and among them. I group these considerations into four blocks, discussing the issues of intimacy (and anonymity), sample size, frontier and heartland, and conflict resolution in turn.

First, then, how did this intimacy of everyday life in Kara affect my research? Relationships between individuals were multiplex because each performed different roles and held different statuses vis-à-vis others. People who sat down together to chat in Kara were always well acquainted and aware of each other's social backgrounds and life histories. Accordingly, many conversations were hard to follow, as they could be elliptic and allusive without violating any conversational maxims vis-à-vis another Kara proper. I, Kara *manqué*, often struggled to deduce which particular 'Lale' of the five or six men called Lale whom I knew was meant – if not someone else entirely. In addition to ritually acquired names, nicknames or honorary names, most people of both genders had several given names as well. Metonymical constructions were common, teknonymy only being one of them, as people could be referred to by way of the location of their fields, their age-set, their in-laws or even a specific, indexical relation to someone present (e.g. 'his hunting-friend'). Conversations assumed precisely this shared knowledge, as there normally are no strangers whom one would have to accommodate by providing more context, so this was both an aesthetic and efficient mode of communication. For me, it created difficulties that were only slowly overcome and, even at the height of my familiarity with Kara, they still resurfaced again and again in certain conversational domains.

Consequently, there were few natural occasions when somebody talked extensively about their own life. Beyond the familiarity engendered through quotidian interaction, which renders dense autobiographies moot, to talk too much about oneself displays just a little too much pride. My attempts at comprehensive biographical interviews led to mediocre results, as I rarely managed to make such conversation a meaningful genre in this face-to-face community. People assume that everybody who was around when they were children will be around forever until death takes them; that there is nobody in-group whom one will know just for a limited period and then never see again; that there is no chance that any event that transpired in one's social life can ever be forgotten (compare Colson 1974: 5). This constitutes how life is lived in Kara. To somehow approximate this familiarity, participant observation was the royal road. 'Hanging around' and 'bringing up a topic' (Helander 2003: 30f) as well as 'ero-epic conversations' (Girtler 1995: 219ff), many of which were recorded, were my main methods. Through such merely partially structured interaction, I slowly acquired linguistic and contextual competence, and also came across a great deal of my ethnographic data. Ethel Albert's suggestion that '[i]t is ... probably a good general rule of method that learning the cultural modes of speech behavior is part of procuring reliable data' (1964: 53) expresses well my initially intuitive and later more deliberate mode of language acquisition and fieldwork, also manifested in the decision to not use the aid of a translator.

This radically mutual knowledge as it is shared among the Kara has direct consequences on the 'worthy anthropological usage ... to obfuscate sources' (Boon 2001: 125). In their attempts to protect their interlocutors from unwanted publicity, embarrassment, intrusion and potential retribution, anthropologists anonymize individuals, research settings and even their own names (see the discussion in van der Geest (2003)). This is a major topic in anthropology today, and I do not want to go into the legal or even the philosophical issues at stake here, but merely point out the practical difficulties for my particular case: barring an intentional distortion of cases and persons in my text, an adult Kara would stand a good chance of identifying the individuals in the situations that I describe and the speakers of the utterances that I quote, no matter how cleverly anonymized. Even outside of Kara, my main interlocutors are well-known; some of them even feature in a short movie I made together with the Berlin-based filmmaker and anthropologist Steffen Köhn (Girke and Köhn 2007). I also feel that there is merit in the demand that interlocutors who possess expert knowledge deserve recognition, let alone praise for their willingness to share it with a researcher. Acknowledging that this must be always a balancing act, balancing the need to protect interlocutors (or people featuring in descriptions or stories) with the wish to praise and commend their cooperation and knowledge, I have assessed risks and thus anonymized (or rather pseudonymized) selectively.

Second, such small discourse communities as Kara present problems for testing assumptions as well as for research methods. In the early phases of my fieldwork, I sometimes tried to ask 'what if' questions in order to get people to provide fitting examples to the issue at hand, drawing on their personal experience and their knowledge of past events. The aim was also to eventually get at the 'workings' of cultural operations, at ritual rules and other such regulated aspects of social life, and of course valid ways of justification: 'So, given this and that, what would happen if ...?' Mostly, I have to say, I got the reply '*hau de*!' – 'who knows, who cares?!' Within such a small group, I was faced with an equally small sample size. People's knowledge about the past usually only extended to their parents' or (rarely) grandparents' generations. This was my sample and, in fact, the sample of the wise Kara elders themselves was also limited in this manner. It is not that people did not know what had happened in the past, it is just that there had not been so much of it. Many imaginable social constellations have actually yet to occur, and I witnessed on more than one occasion people acknowledging that they had no precedent on which to base their actions. Methodologically, this steered me away from the danger of a static view of culture; while one knows this abstractly, the drastic nature of the Kara case made it very clear that social life is emergent, ambiguous and open-ended. My interest in how actors strove to persuade themselves and others of a 'definition of the situation' thus proved especially appropriate – Kara is small enough that one can observe tradition as it is being invented and community as it is being imagined.

There is no reliable information about population numbers in previous decades. Kara accounts on this vary – sometimes it is emphasized that they always were few and sometimes their numbers are aggrandized to emphasize their past might. Consistently, though, the Kara history proclaims that around the end of the nineteenth century, two disasters struck: the *gind'o*, a sleeping sickness that killed many people, and the *tobolo*, a mighty flood of the Omo River that again decimated and scattered the population. The first is consistent with accounts of the wave of trypanosomiasis that swept Africa in the wake of the great rinderpest (see Loimeier 2011), while the second one has found less solid confirmation from other sources. It matters little: no matter how many Kara there were 200 years ago, to be Kara today is to live in a small-scale, face-to-face community. This notion, commonly used and hardly ever precisely defined, applies to Kara no matter how an eventual definition might turn out. They fit Benedict Anderson's imagined 'primordial villages of face-to-face contact' quite well (1983: 6). One might even be tempted to assume that, as the Kara know and experience their actual community every day, they are possibly exempt from the necessity to 'imagine' it. However, much of Kara social life revolves not necessarily around the imagination of the existence of their community, but around persuasive attempts to keep it intact, to keep it relevant, to turn it into a collective actor and to keep up the at least superficial appearance of 'deep, horizontal comradeship' between them (Anderson 1983: 7). In Kara (as elsewhere), community is always an achievement.

The Structure of this Book

This book is about the rhetorical ways in which Kara relate to themselves and to others. In the first chapter, I develop my theoretical approach by discussing some concepts that allow me to trace, in the observation of everyday life, the persuasive processes that promise more material answers to the questions at stake: how do they do it? How do they maintain their autonomy? Who are 'they'? My understanding of why people such as the Kara act in a way that asserts their autonomy in the first place is encapsulated in a model that I call the 'Wheel of Autonomy'. It visualizes the circular motion of how a desire for autonomy creates

Figure 0.3 Loxopil, the author's name goat (front), with a friend (December 2006). Photograph by Felix Girke.

conditions of agency, which is again used to achieve distinction. Distinction, in turn, is a logical prerequisite to autonomy – or, starting at another point, how purposive action, in displaying agency, enables autonomy. Such autonomy then leads to various ascriptions of distinction.[12] Wherever one starts, the Wheel of Autonomy posits that understanding these three notions as mutually constitutive of one another illuminates the political interaction between ethnically marked populations in South Omo. In the following chapters this model is applied to various relations in and around Kara, and rhetoric is shown to be the grease that makes the wheel turn. To talk about relations presupposes elements to be related, so I substantiate my case by analysing classificatory practices in social life. How can distinctions be imposed on an inchoate world of experience? How do categories of belonging emerge? How do they come to matter? The answer to these questions is rhetoric, in its aspect of persuasion, aimed at establishing common ground with others – or, in fact, obliterating it (Girke and Meyer 2011: 17–19). This is where the fundamental importance of the 'definition of the situation' in human interaction comes to the fore. 'Situations', however, are not merely ephemeral moments in our perception; they have very real consequences in that they crystallize categories, imbue distinctions with value, naturalize what was manmade and can be used to suppress dissenting narratives. In this context, I also address the role of power and ideology in the sort of human relations I look at here. All in all, the chapter consists of one extended elaboration of how and why I work on ethnic relations with the vocabulary of rhetoric.

Introducing the 'Categories of Being Kara', Chapter 2 provides an ethnographic overview over the many social categories that divide the Kara just as they unite them. This list takes account of material conditions such as settlements and livelihood, but equally addresses more abstract organizational divides and individually or corporately achieved or ascribed status. Hardly any of these items matter to non-Kara. Hence, the chapter can be read not just as a description of institutions, but as a part of the answer to the question 'who are the Kara?' Explicitly sidelined are internal ethnic differences, which are the subject matter of Chapters 3, 4 and 5. To establish the categories of being Kara in this way lays the groundwork for the rest of the book, which – while more outwardly oriented and focusing on ethnicity – often recurs to inter-Kara dynamics.

Consequently, Chapter 3 still concerns the internal categories of being Kara by introducing the ethnic subdivisions. A spectacular social drama erupted when some members of the Bogudo category decided to relinquish a certain ritual they had up until then been performing. This was treated as a challenge to the *ädamo* of the Kara, and the true Kara re-established their control over the ritual order by recategorizing these Bogudo as ethnic Gomba, lower in status and in fact usually understood as a natural, birth-ordained identity that one could not simply join even if one wanted to.

The relationship between the Kara and the Moguji, a ritually ostracized and politically marginalized ethnic category, is the focus of Chapters 4 and 5, which should not be read individually. This new focus widens the perspective to take in aspects beyond what is Kara in a strict sense: while many Moguji are found in the Kara settlements of Labuk, Dus and Korcho, others live in Kuchur, a Moguji-only settlement further out north, or across the river in Nyangatom territory. Thus, as the Moguji population already is half inside, half outside of Kara, this is even more true for the ritual status of this social category: through a very marked application of metaphor, true Kara constantly 'other' the Moguji, pointing out their general lack of refinement and productivity. Whence this radical othering? The Moguji, I argue, present a problem for Kara. According to myth, they are the true autochthones of the Omo Valley, supposed hunter and fishermen, the ones whose lands the Kara cleverly took over when they arrived on the scene. Today, in most respects, the Kara dominate the Moguji, and the use of metaphor facilitates keeping them in a subordinate position. Unsurprisingly, the Moguji have begun to rally against this situation, engendering ever more drastic response from the true Kara. I analyse how these two groups are forever entwined, as the Kara define the Moguji as what they themselves are not. This provides further insight into how the Kara rhetorically manipulate *ädamo* claims to sustain their autonomy. Thus, this case serves as an ethnographic illustration for the Wheel of Autonomy: by preventing the Moguji from reaching self-determination in any of the fields of economy, ritual or politics, through material as well as metaphorical means, the Kara assert their agency and display their power to define the existence of others (compare also Girke 2014b).

What the Moguji are excluded from in this way is – so to speak – full membership in what I call the 'cultural neighbourhood' (see also Gabbert 2010). The exploration of this notion makes up Chapter 6. I found that there is a horizon of relevance for the Kara, which includes some of the neighbouring populations as significant others. These other groups are at the same level of existence as the Kara themselves: autonomous, territorial, culturally particular polities (see Map 0.1). Important examples are the Hamar, who are so similar to the Kara, and the Nyangatom, with whom the Kara have fought so much over the last decades. These examples indicate that such an equivalence is never a given, as the case of the Moguji already suggested, who were being kept just below this level of autonomy.

As the Wheel of Autonomy turns, groups are engaged in a constant struggle to retain their distinctiveness and autonomy, to keep themselves significant in the eyes of their neighbours. Not all is symbolic, though: there are very material interests at stake, since the Kara and their neighbours maintain not only ethnic but also territorial boundaries. One notable aspect of these relationships is the heavy stereotyping in which groups engage vis-à-vis one another in the narratives they tell. The groups discussed from a Kara perspective in Chapter 7 – specifically, the Hamar, Nyangatom, Mursi, Arbore, Aari, Maale and Dassanech – are specific exemplars of the encompassing category Shank'illa. This term was originally an epithet, employed by the 'Abyssinians' (today: Habesha) of the Ethiopian centre, to designate the 'blacks', the lowlanders, pastoralists and potential slaves at the edge of their sphere of influence (compare Lydall 2010; Smidt 2010). Today, though, the term 'Shank'illa' has been adopted by those very groups to express their relative similarity in their polyethnic field in the lowlands in the face of the Habesha highlander. As such, it is a relevant cognitive and possibly political category, under which the Kara group all the specific groups of their cultural neighbourhood.

Chapters 8 and 9 are committed to the 'cleverness' of the Kara, a salient contemporary charter, under whose banner the Kara seem to prepare themselves for an uncertain future. Even though South Omo has been incorporated into the Ethiopian state in its various incarnations for over one hundred years now, it turns out that there is still an unbridged divide between Shank'illa and Habesha. Instead of seeing this encounter again in terms of ethnic difference, I found that it is the crass imbalance of power and scale that makes these two categories still irreconcilable. Rather than opposing the imposing Ethiopian state directly, the Kara assume an ironical stance towards the narratives of development and national integration. In the face of all appearances, the Kara seem to deny that they, on the very periphery of Ethiopia, are necessarily powerless. Well aware of the predicaments that individual officials face, they turn the tables on those who would govern them, calling attention to incongruities, and generally being shifty and elusive. This sustains their self-esteem where it would be easy to become despondent, and allows them to look to the years ahead, confident that their alleged cleverness will serve them well. Irony is the appropriate trope wherever claims and realities diverge, where (with Nietzsche) 'final vocabularies' such as the high modernist narrative of the state reveal themselves to be as contingent as any others. The stance assumed by the Kara is markedly different from that attributed to other groups of the region, such as the Aari, for whom the conquest was a much greater trauma and who seem to have little confidence in their ability to deal with modern times on their own terms.

The argument thus starts from a narrow focus on processes that have relevance inside of Kara only (Chapters 2 and 3). It then widens, turning to the tricky question of the Moguji, whom the Kara try to keep close even as they metaphorically distance them as much as possible (Chapters 4 and 5). Increasing the scope again, the discussion turns to how the self-determined members of the 'cultural neighbourhood', all categorically similar groups, belong to the larger Shank'illa category, and how they struggle to assert and sustain their autonomy vis-à-vis one another (Chapter 6). The precise relations the Kara maintain to these other groups, through war and peace and less intimate relations, are the subject of Chapter 7. But all the dramatic interaction of the various Shank'illa groups is relativized when (in Chapter 9) they encounter the awesome power of the Habesha, the dominant representatives of the Ethiopian state. Recognizing the ironies inherent in the national project, the Kara refuse to simply accept this definition of the situation.

Finally, I reassess my two main projects: to gain insight into the protean ways in which the Kara use the term *ädamo*; and to develop a rhetorical approach to the study of ethnopolitical group relations. The original interest in group size inevitably led me to not only tactics and strategies of boundary-making, but also the epistemologically prior question of how 'the Kara' even relate to themselves. The conversation on 'how do the Kara do it?' cannot be concluded – it is necessarily ongoing and open-ended, especially considering the incipient transformations of Kara life, and of South Omo in general, through developmental mega-projects such as dams, plantations and oil-drilling, changes that have begun in recent years but whose actual impact can only be assessed in the future.

Notes

1. Several conferences on 'Rhetoric Culture Theory' were held at Mainz University in 2002 and 2005 (financed by the Volkswagen Foundation), in Evanston, IL, in 2012, and in Hannover in 2016 (again financed by the Volkswagen Foundation). The resulting book series 'Studies in Rhetoric and Culture' is being published by Berghahn Books, the series

editors being Ivo Strecker, Stephen Tyler, Robert Hariman, Christian Meyer and Felix Girke (http://www.berghahnbooks.com/series.php?pg=rhet_cult). The original presentation of the project itself can still be found at http://www.rhetoricculture.org. See also the early reviews by Carrithers (2005a and 2005b).

2. In my approach, the two bugbears of ethnicity studies – primordialism and constructivism – are relevant as characterizations of emic views on and expressions of ethnicity. As established by Dereje Feyissa in a work on western Ethiopia, many people are 'playing different games', some of them being more ethnically integrative (which presupposes a certain reflexivity), while others insist on purity and descent (Dereje 2011). The main difference between Dereje's approach and mine is that I would not assign the labels of 'emic constructivist' or 'emic primordialist' to kinds of people in any stable manner, as I found situational circumstances paramount. The self-same individuals could voice a constructivist argument then, and a primordialist argument now, as it suited their rhetorical purposes.

3. Nevertheless, I do provide a glossary (pp. 261–70).

4. The SORC is an established forum for anthropological research and debate in southern Ethiopia, established by Professor Ivo Strecker and long administered and maintained by researchers from the Johannes Gutenberg University Mainz, Germany. Today, it is administered by Arba Minch University, with support from the MPI for Social Anthropology (Halle/Saale, Germany).

5. On that journey, I was also accompanied by Sophia Thubauville, then a researcher among the nearby Maale (and later director of the SORC, today at the University of Frankfurt am Main), as well as by the Ethiopian researcher Tsegaab Kassa.

6. It speaks of the positive image that anthropologists have among the indigenous populations of the South Omo region that such easy access could be found: scholars such as Ivo Strecker and Jean Lydall, as well as David Turton and Serge Tornay, have all sustained their commitment to their fieldsites (Mursi and Nyangatom, respectively) over decades, and my 'cohort' of colleagues, among them Echi Christina Gabbert, Shauna LaTosky and others, have not flagged in their engagement either. Through their example, anthropology has come to be recognized by the resident populations as a normal and appreciated pursuit for foreigners in South Omo, which has enabled a new and more numerous generation of researchers to further enhance the academic understanding of the region.

7. I have undertaken six trips to Kara, starting in 2003. Following on the first stint, when I stayed all of two weeks, I went again in 2004 (two months), 2005 (one month), 2006–7 (one year), 2008 (two weeks) and again a brief visit in 2012. The durations of my respective stays in Ethiopia were longer, but it often took me a week or more to even reach Kara. Mostly in the company of Kara friends, I travelled all over South Omo, with the South Omo Museum and Research Center providing a valuable place to retreat to for rest, to view video material and to discuss recordings together with Kara.

8. To this day, I am grateful to Haila, Nanga, Lale, Arballo and Barke for the faith implicit in this amicable gesture, which was immeasurably helpful and encouraging.

9. Asmarom's attack on 'vicarious ethnocentrism' is well taken, as when a researcher adopts the viewpoints of his most familiar others and then projects their likes and dislikes onto more distant others, creating an unwholesome mess of stereotypes and biased descriptions (1973: 276). Accordingly, my active engagement with stereotypes and the various ways members of ethnic categories maintain their boundaries always explicitly traces the sources of the ethnocentrisms I explore. I discuss this in more depth later (see Chapters 6 and 7; see also Girke 2014a).

10. This is a dissatisfying attempt to render the German word 'Deutungshoheit', also translatable as 'exegetic' or 'hermeneutic dominance' or 'interpretational sovereignty', 'authority' or 'privilege'.
11. Donald Tuzin, writing on the Arapesh of Papua New Guinea, wonders (in a direct reversal of my initial question) how a specific local section 'had managed to achieve and maintain a population size which, at 1,500 persons, was extraordinarily large by Papua New Guinea standards' (1989: 278)
12. I use both the terms 'distinction' and 'differentiation' in discussing such processes. Differentiation highlights the active nature of difference-making. Distinction is more of an achievement than a process. By engaging in differentiation, an actor might achieve distinction.

Chapter 1
A Rhetorical Approach to Groups and Ethnicity

During fieldwork in Kara, my main aim was to understand how the people called Kara sustain their political autonomy and their numerically low population in the face of enemies and rivals in the west, friends and relations in the east, and the increasing incorporation into the Ethiopian state with all the pressures this entails. Initially, I did not even realize the significance of the internal divisions within the Kara population, but they quickly rose to prominence in my fieldwork just as much as issues of exchange, intermarriage, and war and peace with external others. Both can be discussed under the heading of *ädamo*, which in Kara is a protean and very evocative term, and cannot be unambiguously defined. As I use the term *ädamo*, it stands as a shorthand for the assertion of a fundamental equality among all Kara: '*Woti paila Karana* – we are all Kara' is sometimes asserted to express how unity derives from equality. But I also call *ädamo* an ideology, not for entailing a particularly consistent body of precepts and claims, but in the sense of 'ideas in the service of power'. Specifically, speaking of *ädamo* as an ideology refers to my observation that for all the invocations of the term, some very real divisions in Kara did not go away. A key element here is the public claim that ethnic differences should be relevant only in terms of ritual practice and should not shape personal interests. To challenge this maxim is to challenge the community. With this link to ritual, ethnicity becomes spiritually loaded and essentialized, appearing inevitable and non-negotiable. As each ethnic category is bound to a specific ritual practice, and as transgression against these proscriptions brings a risk of sickness and doom, it is risky to say the least to not publically display adherence to the ritual code. Such adherence, though, performatively reaffirms the ethnic divisions themselves. At the same time, this second aspect of *ädamo* allows the 'true Kara' – who form the powerful numerical majority – to gloss over their monopoly on making political decisions, especially about the way in which these ethnic differences themselves are organized. Any challenges to this political power of definition, or even acts that hint to expose that claims of *ädamo* may be duplicitous, are met with reprisals.

I would add a third aspect. These usages of *ädamo* also indicate the Kara's awareness that social relations are rhetorically established, sustained and transformed, with the normative corollary that people are responsible for the upkeep of their social world. In the introduction I have outlined how I found such *ädamo* in ontologically uncertain but interactionally satisfying 'as if' role behaviour. Beyond individual actors, this is equally true even of group relations across ethnic boundaries, and I will go on to explore how such relations are verbalized, conceptualized and practised both within the Kara population and between it and outside groups.

The thrust, then, is two-pronged. On the methodological level, I present a toolkit that is useful both for modelling classifications and for tracing the rhetorical ways in which these systems of classification are enacted, modified or denied. On the ethnographic level, I describe interaction, trace how groups and social categories work in and around Kara, and observe how people struggle over definitions of the situation, bringing to bear ideological constructs such as *ädamo*. My rhetorical approach and the description are co-emergent, as the description substantiates the methodological reflections, while the vocabulary of persuasion gives shape to the ethnographic material.

To make my case, I discuss some more general methodological points under the headings of 'The Wheel of Autonomy', 'Classification and Social Life' and 'Defining Situations through Rhetoric' below. A summary brings together the main theoretical considerations, as they will come to be applied throughout the later chapters of this book.

In anthropological terms, this book is both about social classification and political practice, and rhetoric is the way in which these two fields of interest are linked (compare Brubaker et al. 2004: 36f). An understanding of these links is essential for an understanding of either subject. Prime among these links are what has been called 'languages of claims' (see Bailey 1969: 108). By this I refer to culturally grounded and rhetorical assertions about an 'ought' or an 'is'. There are usually several 'languages of claims' available that will be in competition with one another. In order to reach their goals, actors attempt to persuade others of their version of things. Such versions are hardly ever single, unrelated notions or claims. Rather, they relate back to larger associative sets of classification, which give depth to argument, and suggest implications and entailments. In interaction, then, people seek agreement on one out of many potentially applicable classificatory systems so as to enable joint action. I work from the basis that such agreement is problematic and that social struggle is precisely about competitive attempts to make specific frames count. To be successful in this has direct effects on the interaction, on the actors' positions, as well as on the frame that has been applied. What 'counts', however, is not as a rule decided by the contestants alone: studies of interaction are improved by the understanding that any dyad of actors is complemented by witnesses, by an (at the very least imaginary) third party. With a third party as an audience, interaction becomes performative (see Carlson 1996: 5), because it is inevitably scrutinized, processed and interpreted by present observers. It is such an audience's reaction that gives a culturally valid interpretation to moves and countermoves in people's attempts to apply their preferred classificatory system. Relevant 'meaning' is not hidden within an utterance that we have to decode. Instead, it emerges out of the joint interpretation of the situation by all social persons present. Actors do well to take this condition into account in the way they behave, no matter how genuinely affective or coldly calculating they proceed. It follows from this that I rarely aim at unravelling the 'real' reasons for people's choices, but that I am instead interested in the culturally valid ways in which other people make sense of what is happening. Any analysis of someone's behaviour should be directed at how a given audience reacts to actions and utterances, and should not attempt to discern what the speaker 'really meant'. This is neither possible nor particularly interesting. As F.G. Bailey already cogently argued:

> The best we can do is discover the motivations which are explicitly current in and explicitly acceptable at various levels in that particular culture, and how, when they conflict, they are measured against one another. (1973: 325)

But this somewhat deprecatingly issued 'the best we can do' is in fact very good indeed – Bailey's statement encapsulates for me what cultural anthropology is largely about. To forego 'mind-reading' lets the anthropologist join other local actors, who are themselves constantly busy inferring meaning and attributing intention to action. This in principle ethnomethodological stance is especially well formulated by Jonathan Potter:

> The argument is not that social researchers should interpret people's discourse in terms of their individual or group interests. There are all sorts of difficulties with such an analytic programme, not least of which is that it is very difficult to identify interests in a way that is separable from the sorts of occasioned interest attribution that participants use when in debate with one another … The argument here is that people *treat one another in this way*. They treat reports and descriptions *as if* they come from groups and individuals with interests, desires, ambitions and stake in some versions of what the world is like. Interests are a participant's concern, and that is how they can enter analysis. (2004: 110, emphasis in original)

Of course, this is also the way in which 'participants' constitute (imagine?) themselves in the first place. The argument is even stronger when we take into account that in many cultures it is well recognized that 'authentic motivations' are by and large inaccessible (see Herzfeld 1984).

This book, then, translates observed Kara practices on the basis of local exegesis, the anthropologist's contextual knowledge, and supplemental data. *Ädamo* appears in this translation as a specific ideology, as it is used by actors to remove the realities of power from open debate, just as *ädamo* can plausibly be said to be the very manifestation of power. *Ädamo* is a major argument in the culturally specific language of claims through which the Kara negotiate their dynamic social relations. My approach is based on the recognition of the mutual constitution and co-emergence of social interaction and cultural systems of classification, and grounds them by attending to the internal tensions that arise in the everyday life of a face-to-face community.

Victor Turner has warned interactionalist anthropology not to forget that people are ready to die for 'values that oppose their interests and promote interests that oppose their values' (1974: 140). Exploring the rhetorical aspects of interaction as people reinforce or challenge each other's claims is a way to work out how these tensions come about.

The Wheel of Autonomy

In order to interact meaningfully, actors need to be experienced as different. A 'relation', logically, can only exist between at least two elements conceived of as separate in some way – not necessarily in all ways. As Todorov maintains, it is also not necessary that the existence of the individual precedes the relation:

> There is no point in asking oneself, in Hobbesian fashion: Why do men choose to live in society? or like Schopenhauer: Where does the need for society come from? because mankind never makes this passage into communal life. The relationship precedes the isolated element. People do not live in society because of self-interest or because of virtue or because of the strength of other reasons, no matter what they might be. They do so because for them no other form of life is possible. (2001: 4f)

On the ground, what may constitute an actor is not a given, as conceptions of 'the individual' may vary culturally. Also, legitimacy of action may be denied to certain social categories, and people will always encounter constraints in favouring or even expressing their individual interests at the expense of the group. Recognizing these tensions, I want to preface my elaboration of the question of agency, autonomy and distinction with Gluckman's acknowledgement that even numerically small communities are often 'elaborately divided and cross-divided by customary allegiances' (1973: 1f). Even the Kara population's absolute smallness, and the predominance of multiplex relations and shared knowledge among them, then, does not preclude relative dividedness.

Drawing on a 'wrongly neglected' line of sociological argument, found in the work of Freud, Simmel, Bateson and literary critic Girard, the Melanesianist scholar Simon Harrison (2002: 228) has called attention to processes of differentiation in the face of objective similarity. He suggests that it is the very closeness and the mutual resemblance of individuals (and groups) that can cause conflictual acts of differentiation:

> A problem people seem to face in small, close-knit social worlds is that they can sometimes appear to themselves to resemble each other a little too much. They may be conscious of sharing many deeply held values, goals, and beliefs. But they may not – or some of them may not – always wish to share them. (2002: 223)

I pick up from here. What is it, then, that drives both groups and individuals into differentiation? Numerous answers have been given to this – be it 'face wants' as suggested by psycholinguistics (Brown and Levinson 1987; Strecker 1988, 2006b), the fear of an evil twin or doppelganger (see Harrison 2002: 214), 'identity space' (Friedman 1992: 837), the triangular structure of 'mimetic desire' (Girard 1977; Harrison 2006: 2ff) or Simmel's 'intellectual private property' (1950: 322). I understand these concepts as all referring to similar empirical phenomena: people who share much make much ado over some seemingly minor differences. Familiar examples include regionalism, gang colours, *campanilismo*, youth fashion and innumerable other examples (see Harrison 2006: 6).

Much work in social science has been devoted to this general issue. I want to specifically highlight the work that revolves around the 'narcissism of minor differences', a phrase coined by Freud. Besides Simon Harrison, Anton Blok is the most prominent proponent of this position.[1] A fitting piece of imagery was first supplied by Arthur Schopenhauer in his 'Die Parabel von den Stachelschweinen' and was then picked up by various other authors (see Blok 1998: 34f): porcupines seeking warmth want to huddle together, yet find that they sting one another. They end up maintaining what Harrison calls a 'modicum of mutual distance' (2006: 2). In other words, closeness comes at a cost – the cost of unimpeded autonomy. In an allegory by Fredrik Barth, the logical consequence is illustrated: two neighbours can precisely interact and converse 'in a more carefree and relaxed way' when they have erected a nice straight fence between their two plots. Without a fence, 'entanglements' loom (2000: 28).[2] Predictable relationships, nonpredatory and mutual, then, require the creation of distance and difference – if all were equal, ordered relations would be logically impossible.

Figure 1.1 Teenage girls grinding sorghum (June 2006). Photograph by Felix Girke.

This line of argument understands that (felt) autonomy is a goal in itself for social actors. However, such autonomy is not of the hermetic kind and fully self-sufficient; on the contrary, it emerges from a public recognition of one's legitimate distinctiveness. Having achieved that, the actor can proceed to engage in interaction on their own terms.

As both Harrison and Blok have developed this approach, it applies to groups just as much as to individuals, and aligns with Barthian studies of ethnicity: 'From this perspective, boundary processes are fundamental, irreducible social phenomena. Social groups and categories, in contrast, are merely their epiphenomena. They are just the visible effects of successful acts of differentiation' (Harrison 2006: 8). Accordingly, the position of any given porcupine can only be appreciated if one also perceives the position of the other porcupines and how long their respective quills are.

In symbolic interaction, differentiation often comes to be focused on iconic objects, places or practices. Any encroachment of an other upon one of these diacritical sites can occasion acts of division, even before it ever comes to a material struggle over resources: 'According to this view, an identity is never in some sense self-sufficient, but is always linked to an other – real or imagined, overt or covert – against which it is defined' (Harrison 2006: 38). To stick with the prickly metaphor, this means that porcupines will have very different space demands vis-à-vis birds in the sky, wandering human beings, ants on the ground or their own species. A critical category marker for the relation to one other can be meaningless in a slightly different context, and differences that need to be maintained in one relation can be surrendered in another. This corresponds to the by now classic understanding in anthropology that while distinction is always involved in boundary processes, it is not always the same distinction that is put to work by the same actors (Barth 1969, 2000: 21; Wimmer 2008). So for each kind of actor, group or individual, one needs to find those significant others from which they must at all times be distinct. A self is a self in a community of selves, and an empire is only an empire if surrounded by barbarians (or, eventually, other empires).

We do not choose all these significant others for ourselves. As social beings, we are already born into a world of categories, distinctions and relations. In order to navigate our lives, we 'appeal to identities to make sense of [our] relations' (Otto and Driessen 2000: 11; see also Eriksen 2001: 86). But what happens when relations between distinct beings change – for example, when people engage in mimesis, or its obverse, when people problematize their similarities? This is the problem of the 'minor differences', and Blok credits Pierre Bourdieu with having 're-opened the debate' (2000: 34) with his oft-quoted phrase that: 'Social identity lies in difference, and difference is asserted against what is closest, which represents the greatest threat' (Bourdieu 1984: 479). So it is not the minor differences that are the problem, but the numerous similarities; the minor differences are where distinction can be found and be blown up beyond all proportion. In Girard's terms: 'It is not the differences but the loss of them that gives rise to violence and chaos' (1977, quoted in Blok 2000: 27). As Harrison well realizes, the minor differences are highly contingent, and there is no necessity that the shared attributes might not historically 'have been used to foster some form of common identity or cohesion' (2002: 227). But when push comes to shove, people 'protect their idiosyncrasies jealously' (2002: 212).

To visualize what is going on when actors assert themselves and demand recognition, I have devised a circular model for the social process of differentiation, called the Wheel of Autonomy. The claim is that this model can in principle be applied to all social action. It operates like this: distinction is a logical prerequisite to autonomy. Autonomy affords agency. The exertion of agency effects distinction. These relationships are fairly intuitive even from the common use of these terms. I see all three to be so essentially connected as to mutually define each other. But why is it called the Wheel of 'Autonomy' if the three elements are seen as inseparable? To prioritize autonomy the way I do now is not wholly arbitrary: following the academic line of discussion traced above, I take the existential need for autonomy (as endorsed by the listed concepts from Levinson and Brown to Simmel) as the starting point for the analysis of how actors stay identical with themselves.

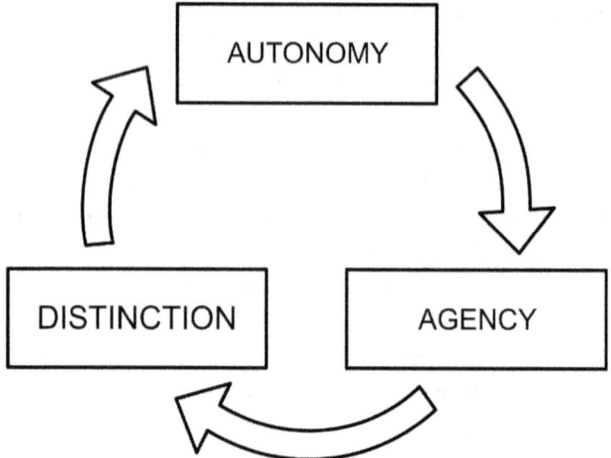

Figure 1.2 The Wheel of Autonomy. Diagram by Felix Girke.

But what can such a perpetual motion machine tell us? Does the process not need to start somewhere? It does, but it does not – we are all already born into a world of categories and relations. Watching a child grow up and struggle with the conflicting desires of autonomy and intimacy is illustrative – or does already the first kick of the foetus set the wheel in motion? Circularity is the very nature of the processes under consideration, which the Wheel of Autonomy models. Starting from autonomy, agency (as the capacity to act) comes to be linked to power and status. Harrison does not quite go far enough when he states (following Simmel) that '[o]ne shows greater respect and deference to someone by "keeping one's distance", allowing that person a larger sphere of psychological privacy' (2002: 216, also 218). I would add that in social action, the relation can be reversed: by successfully demanding greater identity space (i.e. autonomy), we gain in power and status. Agency, then, is our potential to act as a distinct, autonomous actor vis-à-vis other actors. Thus, the Wheel could also be pictured as a gear, constantly locking teeth with other people's Wheels, and thus influencing the ways in which they can assert their autonomy, distinction and agency. Since all three sections of the Wheel are inherently social and intersubjective, there is a corollary to the model: while 'zero degree agency' does not seem not a helpful concept, actors will be able to 'opt out' in certain contexts, when they stop to publicly assert their agency by continually jockeying with the other porcupines. They can also be denied autonomy and they can be prevented from exerting their agency; that distinction is then imposed on them and ought not count as a display of their agency, but of the agency of someone else.

In South Omo, there are several well-known examples of formerly autonomous groups that were absorbed into larger polities as they could no longer ward off other populations who were encroaching upon them. They could not keep their Wheel of Autonomy in motion. When agency became too restrained, autonomy was lost; when autonomy was lost, they were absorbed by the other group, and their distinctiveness was obliterated, or at least redefined by others. Through this looking glass, there are always Lewis Carroll-esque moments in the wonderland of social action – 'who is to be master', as Humpty Dumpty says, is really the question of who gets to define what words mean. More specifically in my approach, it is the question of who gets to define speakers, i.e. actors (including themselves) and their respective relations (see Cohen 2000: 5). David Turton has argued in a similar vein for the contemporary Mursi, the northern neighbours of the Kara. After a particularly crushing defeat, the Mursi expressed their existential need to strike back at the Nyangatom who had massacred about 10 per cent of their population, or – failing to do so – face inconsequentiality and dispersal (1993: 175f). Turton suggests that:

> [For] the Mursi and their neighbours war is a common ritual language by which they make themselves significant to each other and to themselves as independent political entities ... a means by which the very idea of it as an independent political unit, 'free from the normative claims of outsiders' (Harrison [1993]: 215) and therefore *able* to extend or defend its territory is created and kept alive. (1993: 177, emphasis in original)

The Kara also belong to this wider social field, and I have argued elsewhere (Girke 2008) that the warfare between the Kara and the Nyangatom in the 1970s took place in just such a communicative frame. However, I would add the caveat that warfare is not the only way in which autonomy is sustained – groups also make themselves significant to others through exchange, ritual interdependence and stereotypical behaviour.

Elsewhere, Turton also provides a helpful template to formulate the way in which 'the Kara' can be seen as an autonomous unit: 'The particular kind of group I have in mind may be called "politico-territorial", in that it consists of people who have shared interest within a shared territory (Mackenzie 1978) and who conduct their affairs in relative independence from other groups' (2002b: 171). This, combined with a largely subsistence-based mode of production, gives some substance to the collective experience of autonomy. Fortunately, Turton's descriptor 'relative' need not remain undetermined; both for the Mursi and for the Kara, there exist ethnically distinct subsections of their polities (the Kwegu and the Moguji, respectively), who are precisely marked by less independence or who are, in Harrison's terms, less free of the normative claims made by others. There are degrees of autonomy, and – as rendered by the Wheel of Autonomy – social actors, groups as well as individuals, struggle over their freedom from imposition and the power to impose normative claims on others. The issue of 'territory' is fundamental: the ethnic groups of South Omo are who they are *qua* occupation of their own land. Turton argues in a parallel trajectory to Schlee's contention that clans might be prior to and more long-lived than the ethnic groups they make up at any point in time (Schlee 1994a), stating that 'the Mursi' really references several clans that have united some 200 years ago to occupy a certain swathe of land (1993: 173f). The clans themselves transcend the territorial group in the *longue durée*. If the population of the polity were forced to disperse, the clans could live on, but 'the Mursi' would vanish into stories.

This way of identifying political bodies for my area of fieldwork need not mark a return to the term 'tribe', but by and large, as discussed by Fried (1975), Middleton and Tait (1970), the useful essays in the collection by Helm (1968), and Sahlins (1968), it is the old issue of 'tribal autonomy' that we have returned to. The named 'ethnic groups' of South Omo are better understood as polities, bounded, exclusive, competitive and (ant-)agonistic. This is neither to claim ethnic homogeneity within nor to disclaim a host of connections between them; neither the very real effect of their increasing integration into the Ethiopian state administration nor the consequences of development, education, tourism or non-governmental organization (NGO) work. As stated in relation to their clans above, this is also not to suggest that these politico-territorial groups have an uninterrupted historical trajectory. Neither is there no salient differentiation within – there is, and this is precisely the point: at a lower level, there exist a host of institutions that all happen to abruptly lose significance once one reaches the edges of both Kara territory and the people who inhabit it. The cross-cutting ties that exist across these significant boundaries gain their cultural salience in that they are indications that an individual has taken a creative spin on the Wheel of Autonomy, gaining symbolic and social capital by setting up a relation with an other – as 'cross-cutting' demands something to cut across. At the same time, the 'tribal' level gains clarity from the fact that there are the aforementioned 'sub-tribal' ethnic categories, hinting at lost territorial sovereignty and a tumble off the Wheel of Autonomy.

This brings us back to the porcupines: who is it, then, whom we consider significant enough to engage in displays of autonomy towards them? The anthropologist T.O. Beidelman (the prolific ethnographer of the Kenyan Kaguru) offers an overview of the agonistic clashes and acts of exchange between Homeric heroes (1989), which is utterly pertinent to the issue of autonomy, distinction and agency in South Omo.[3] He describes these struggles as not merely driven by the actors' ambition to achieve a specific practical goal. In a much more existential way, the antagonists, by struggling against some other actors and not against other others, assert and defend their version of how social relations should be structured. Consider these excerpts:

> Of course, one vied only with those judged equals or superiors in order to prove that one might actually be their better. Riffraff, slaves, and

> hangers-on had no rightful part in such agonistic choreography ... It was extremely important to recognize with whom one exchanged foods, people, and deeds. Involvement with one's proximate social range insured maintaining rank or its possible escalation at the expense of a competitor ... Contention was inevitably a result of a compromise between need for public approval and need for lowly contenders to be silenced. The public nature of the arena of contention was crucial. If one was confronted by a manifest inferior, contention only demeaned one's standing ... Homeric Greeks drew their personhood, their social identity, from exchange, agonistic and otherwise. (Beidelman 1989: 231)

Interpreting these lines in terms of the Wheel of Autonomy, they give an indication of how a significant other is construed, against whose Wheel one must keep one's own in motion. Beidelman uses 'social identity' as I use 'autonomy': personhood is not an internal state, but an expression of the public acceptance of one's demands for distance or closeness. The movement is again double: one must be willing to assert one's place by engaging with worthy challengers, but the worthiness of the challengers is only created by one's willingness to stand up to them. To refuse or even better to ignore a challenge is to make a statement about social relations, and if this statement passes uncontested, it will lead to a publicly sanctioned transformation of the relations at stake here. Individuals thus encounter incentives to act in ways that support the idea of 'the Kara':

> To sustain a high vision of oneself, one must be able to compel others to accept this view ... When Homeric Greeks speak of honor and shame, of their struggles to maintain or enlarge their respect, they refer to problems of autonomy, and exchange simply asserts and undermines this ... In challenging one's equal or those claiming to be superior, one augments one's own respect. One loses simply by failing to put matters at risk. One cannot drop out claiming to be above such struggles. One must remain agonistically involved ... Respect, dignity, honor, shame, are attributes conferred or denied by others. One needs an audience. Need for others as witnesses characterizes all social phenomena. (Beidelman 1989: 249)

These two sections could be used as a general introduction to the study of interaction: Beidelman emphasizes the need to assert autonomy in front of an audience in order to have any social position at all. He also points out that it can be very difficult to find an exit option to such struggles.

This suggests that porcupines are all about the same size, with quills of similar length, or at least manage to convince an audience of other porcupines that they are. And if one of them really has longer quills, they might be afforded more space. A specimen with tiny quills might be crowded, as they give off warmth without an equivalent sting. At the same time, the porcupines attempt to rhetorically relegate other comers to the category of lesser beings, mere hedgehogs maybe, inconsequential and not worthy of reckoning among true porcupines. Note that this understanding of autonomy is different from 'independence': identity and a sense of self can only derive from relations to other – from mutual recognition.[4] This, I claim, is a universal factor in social relations. For analysis, this means that wherever there is interaction, there will be a struggle for differentiation, no matter how ephemeral and situational, and how much entwined with our simultaneous demand for closeness and intimacy. The unit seeking autonomy, of course, might vary cross-culturally, but I claim that the same principles can apply to individuals and collectives. Accordingly, there must be observable processes that reveal how people assert autonomy, how they display what sort of difference, and who the significant others are against whom actors set their respective Wheels of Autonomy in motion. This also indicates how a collective might establish itself, how people persuade themselves and others that one might want to act as if 'the Kara' or 'the Mursi' were an unproblematic notion. This consideration is another step towards an answer to my initial question: by talking about themselves as a collectivity, the Kara invest in a joint imagination of a 'we', a process that entails the concomitant practical worries of joint action, boundary maintenance and narrative coherence.

So whenever I use 'differentiation', it should be read as an invocation of the Wheel of Autonomy, as some actors attempt to visibly separate themselves from others (achieving 'distinction'), in the process of claiming power and displaying agency. The products of differentiation, and the objects of claims, are 'social categories'. This refers to culturally constructed and condensed types of persons, to which, often in an ambiguous way, specific features are ascribed. Categories are often presented as transcendent and eternal, natural even, but they never are. While some of them might overlap with cohesive 'groups', this is not a given, and it is precisely the striving for 'groupness' that stimulates much of social dynamics (Brubaker et al. 2004: 46f). What the features of categories are, who should be seen as a member of a given category (and not another), and how they are related to other categories – this is precisely what is at stake in the definition of the situation and thus in most identitarian struggles.

Classification in Interaction

Classification of people, ordered claims about their positions vis-à-vis one another, is precisely the culturally crystallized effect of struggles over autonomy. How do social actors, in the pursuit of distinction and autonomy, go about defining their relationships to other, similar or different actors? Such processes of classifying, categorizing and relating are communicative in the most fundamental sense by highlighting a 'difference which makes a difference', to use Bateson's phrase

(2000: 459). They are inevitably cultural and symbolically coded. Following the anthropologically-minded sociologist Richard Jenkins (1997), I want to further develop the understanding that social categories, ethnic and otherwise, are not isolates, not free-floating signifiers. They only exist in contact and interaction. In South Omo generally imbued with political and ritual aspects, ethnic categories stand in various relations to other categories and can be filled with a wide variety of cultural meanings.

Ethnicity, the division of populations 'into "kinds" of people' (Eriksen 2001: 264), is an aspect of interaction, of contested classification, and thus requires persuasion to work. It is not as if ethnicity were something one only did with or for oneself. As Jenkins points out, even 'internal definitions' of ethnic affiliation are 'necessarily transactional and social ... because they presuppose both an audience, without whom they make no sense, and an externally derived framework of meaning' (1997: 53). Even the most genuine sentiment needs to be competently performed. So does ethnicity, if one wants it to matter in a given situation. In cases of 'external definition', when a category is ascribed to people by other actors, Jenkins realizes that there is 'more than one audience involved: the others are here the object(s) of the process of definition, and implied within the situation is a meaningful intervention in their lives, an acting upon them' (ibid.). This sounds, at first, commonsensical. However, it clarifies the questions about interethnic relations in regard to their performative aspect, to the third parties who are also there to witness as an intended or unintended audience. Attempts to define others, seen as a persuasive performance of social relations, have reverberations far beyond the formal act of marking; they are also claims to and an expression of power. To 'intervene' in such a way 'implies the power or the authority to do so ... Power and authority are necessarily embedded within active social relationships' (ibid.). I use this as the cornerstone for my analyses of the interethnic relations within Kara (see Chapter 3).

This leads over to the popular debate about the negotiability of ethnicity – precisely what is it that can be flexibly defined? Are there not non-negotiable aspects that are removed from public contestation? In the context of Kara, the primordial categorizations remain largely unassailable: many people quite literally are A or B. What is negotiable, however, and affords arenas of fierce social struggle, is: (1) whether the fact that an individual is A or B is of relevance in a given situation; and (2) what it entails to be A or B in general. In Elizabeth Colson's apt phrase: 'The categories were rigidly defined; the application of the categories was left flexible' (1974: 27). Such negotiations take place in situational, ephemeral arenas as well as in *longue durée* struggles over classification, ideology and power. This is also how one could reformulate the classical model of ethnic segmentation: as people rally on both sides, they form groups based on categorical equivalence. But this is never automatic or – *pace* Durkheim – 'mechanical': the call to arms needs to be convincing. Never do all people who might be eligible actually join

Figure 1.3 Three consecutive age-sets join to start a dance (November 2004). Photograph by Felix Girke.

the fray. Segmentation remains a useful and applicable model as long as it is recognized that in practice, any segmentary process relies on persuasive claims.

Since Fredrik Barth enshrined the contingency of the 'cultural stuff' within ethnic boundaries (1969), the anthropological study of ethnicity has largely focused on border-maintenance processes. However, instead of singling out one specific boundary, I suggest that all ethnic categories that are relevant in a given context should be addressed in terms of how they interrelate. Such an interrelation is again a cultural construct, which can be used to proclaim both an 'is' and an 'ought', and is often most pervasive and powerful when people manage to conflate both. It will be a rare case where one such construct reigns unopposed: usually, interest-guided actors compete over the different ways in which categories could be systematically linked. Bailey speaks of competing 'structures', which he models:

> neither as objective, quasi-statistical accounts of what people do, nor as an ordering of the rules that guide their actions, but as repertoires or folders that store the *claims* people make to justify, condemn, or in other ways influence actions, opinions and attitudes. (2003: 176, emphasis in original)

I do not want to adopt the term 'structures', but instead refer back to Bailey's earlier concept, the 'language of claims'. Languages of claims are more or less coherent, discursively stabilized ways to make an argument about how the world is, how the categories within it are ordered and how, in consequence, people ought to act. Systems of classification, such as ethnicity, are expressed through languages of claims. In a social environment, they always unite some and divide others. They can be used to proclaim structural equivalence while proscribing formal difference, or they can entail structural difference but formal equivalence. The act of categorizing oneself as different from others, of claiming autonomy, is the original sin that allows meaningful interaction, as it inscribes agency onto distinct actors. With Marilyn Strathern, we can say that 'an agent is one who acts with an other in mind, and that other may in fact coerce the agent into so acting' (1988: 272).

From a socially accepted language of claims, many specific 'rules' can be legitimately derived by the actors and used in explanation and justification of action. It needs to be clear that I have not stumbled across some extrinsic rule-set that reliably guides people who always have to struggle by exerting their 'agency' against the constraining 'structure'. This is not what people do; this is what people say they do. In Kara, this is very striking in ritual. There are numerous claims people make about who has to follow certain ritual rules, such as restrictions on commensality and intermarriage. This language of claims, then, entails well-established but occasionally contested hierarchies. At the same time, the relevance of these ritual rules, and the relations between people that are rhetorically maintained in reference to them, end with few exceptions at the boundaries of the Kara body politic. Thus, the set of rules itself comes to be a focus for identification. In particular, central life-path rituals serve as diacritical markers of distinction for entire populations or ethnic categories, either in self-ascription or in the stereotyping of others.

Individuals often negotiate over the applicability of specific rules and try to define the situation in a way that lets them get away with breaches without suffering sanctions. Being used as arguments, the elements of a language of claims, or even the entire 'language', are situationally reified. In the aftermath of such a situation, these abstractions are then reintegrated into the social world, laying the groundwork for a subsequent contestation, and thus remain emergent, in a constant state of becoming (Meyer and Girke 2011).

Many languages of claims, and the corresponding classifications and normative rules, are sufficiently established to pre-structure communal life in many instances in which they are never problematized. There are of course some sets of more or less established normative claims that generally posit how social categories are connected by and with ritual rules and behaviour, a default people always can fall back on, but that can still be contested and that still need to be invoked and imposed in concrete situations. Hence, in order to engender a 'sense of shared existence as well as determinate boundaries' (Sahlins 1999: 413), formal classification makes use of cultural domains in becoming meaningful and affective. But do people 'believe' in it? Do they 'need' to believe in their system of classifying groups by whichever 'cultural differences are made relevant in interaction' (Eriksen 2001: 263)? The answer is that belief is not necessary. People only need to affirm such systems in action. Such affirmation can well take the expressive frame of 'belief', but can also be noncommittal or even ironical. Classification always needs to be structured as to be persuasive, either aesthetically, intellectually, affectively or symbolically, so that it allows people to go about their lives without constantly hitting their heads on the sides of their pigeonhole.

Importantly, this is a diacritical marker itself: to acknowledge such a set of claims is necessary for claiming membership in a group (like 'Kara-hood') or a lower-order category. Languages of claims are also entangled with material worries, with individuals' or groups' attempts to distinguish themselves, and with issues of power and politics in the widest sense. This is the moment to refer back to the Wheel of Autonomy and also to Beidelman's Homeric heroes: the distinction, autonomy and agency of actors categorized as A vis-à-vis other actors variously also categorized as A, as B or as C are not negotiated afresh in every single instance. The powerful always have a range of means at their disposal that save them the hassle of having to justify their actions, or even provide accounts, to those in a subordinate position. Methodologically, for me to invoke a language of claims serves to connect cases that are on the ground framed in a culturally similar way. While being mutable and hardly codified, languages of claims are practice-based and significant for social action via the specific rules that relate back to them.

It is an old recognition that while there will be cultural 'subpatterns by which men order their lives differently from women, young and middle-aged folk from their elders', there are also more 'fundamental patterns' that act as umbrellas for the entire group (Sahlins 1999: 405). Such groups are again groups precisely because these languages of claims are valid only for their members. As actors frame their actions by reference to rules, they not only suggest that a specific language of claims is applicable in the situation at hand, but they also draw lines, aggregating and disaggregating people and categories in culturally specific dialectics (1999: 411).

In contrast to current trends in ethnic studies, I found a high degree of alignment and boundedness in my field: there is a population that calls itself Kara, that conducts most of its everyday talk in a language called 'Kara' (*kar'appo*) and even now is in the process of physically fighting for a demarcated territory (see Girke 2008, 2013, 2015). The forms and intensity of interaction within what is called 'Kara' are discontinuous from the forms and intensity of interaction across these boundaries. Eriksen points out that social systems have their relevant boundaries 'at the point where interaction decreases dramatically' (2001: 77). This is as neutral a delineation of a social world (or 'community') as one can find, and this consideration would be useful for any attempt to analyse social groups, categories and boundaries. Interaction and the shared classification schemes guiding it come to be a prime criterion for assessing what groups are, even if this means sidelining questions of historical continuity, which, for South Omo with its sparse documentation, are very difficult to address at any rate.

Regarding such boundedness, it is also worth noting that the Kara term for 'boundary' (*maalo*) is common in Kara conversations, often invoked and normatively valued. As Barth (2000: 20f) has pointed out, whenever we insinuate the existence of 'boundaries', it is worthwhile to ground this in both local language and practice. So, notwithstanding their numerous internal divisions, which are not only ethnic but also follow many other social dimensions, the Kara portray themselves as an autonomous actor within South Omo and talk about themselves as a We, juxtaposed to various Theys. In fact, reference to ethnic groups is often linguistically made in the specific singular form of the ethnonym. The category is reduced to one prototypical specimen: talking about what 'the Kara' (as a group) did, one might say *karta*, that is, one definite individual Kara. Thus, while ascription of agency and actor-status to aggregates of individuals remains a fundamental methodological problem, it is much simpler for the people involved. They just do it, even revelling in simplifications and stereotypes, as they narratively imagine the interaction of 'characters' within a 'plot' (Carrithers 1992: 82). So instead of worrying about the difficulty in speaking 'of ethnic groups as collective, active agents' (Abbink 2002: 171), I appreciate Turton's politico-territorial ethnicity precisely because this is a plausible translation of how 'they' themselves talk about 'the Mursi' or 'the Kara' as if these collective entities existed. But never can this status be naturalized; identification is as much the product as the basis of these narrative practices, and it requires work to ride the Wheel of Autonomy.

'Talk' is meant quite literally here. Ethnicity is to a large part an aspect of narrative. Whether people actually 'identify with' certain categories is somewhat secondary to whether they are (by themselves or by others) 'identified as' belonging to some category.

Defining Situations through Rhetoric

No delineation of social categories is particularly insightful without a consideration of the communicative processes through which people make categories count or stick. Any such processes are fundamentally rhetorical. Claims to autonomy and distinction need to be publicly validated in any given situation. All claims to the relevance of certain cultural categories (with their attached entitlements) need to be plausibly and persuasively communicated and accepted. Acceptance is likely facilitated if actors take recourse to culturally familiar templates, that is, the rhetorical commonplaces.

In this book, I use 'rhetoric' to refer to the specific ways of persuading others (and oneself) to accept a certain claim, either normative or empirical, that is, to issuing or resisting challenges to 'definitions of the situation'. These definitions are as powerful as they are dramatic, as binding as they are convincing, as inescapable as they are embedded in social life.[5] The 'definition of the situation' has been introduced into anthropology via the sociology of everyday life (see Heritage 2004: 3). My discussion here by and large follows Bailey's use, which focuses more strongly on the antagonistic struggle between actors than, for example, Erving Goffman's approach to 'framing':

> [Goffman's] players, by and large, seem more concerned with keeping the game and its rules intact than with winning ... My players are different; they are out to win a primary contest that will decide what the game and its rules ... are going to be. (Bailey 2003: 162, fn.8)[6]

In assessing interaction, we find that both (or all) actors are eager to define the situation by claiming that specific aspects are relevant and applicable. The 'definition of the situation' could be seen to rest in the final word that comes to be acknowledged by the involved actors, in explicit agreement, tacit collusion, frustrated exhaustion or mischievous complicity; however, it is the emergent interactional process, more than a seemingly final result, that interests me. As for the rest of this book, this means that I will be talking about 'claims' a lot. Used without further qualification, 'claim' will refer to communicative action that impacts the definition of the situation. People make claims in order to put others in a bind, to assert the salience of specific factors that again preclude certain alternatives. Especially in front of an audience that judges and comments on the relevance of statements and nonverbal actions, claims need to be taken seriously and engaged with. Going back to Beidelman's Homeric heroes and to the porcupines, not only can we define a situational moment, but we can define ourselves by refusing the right of other actors to even interact with us. If we can do this well, by persuading the audience to accept an argument that supports our claim to autonomy, we have not only both gained and exerted power, but we are on our way towards establishing a more durable and less ephemeral positioning of actors and claims, which can be used to bias future action to our benefit.

F.G. Bailey explicitly notes that in such negotiations the deck is stacked if power is too unevenly distributed (1983: 263), if one side is able to act without requiring any sort of cooperation from the other, reminiscent of C.F. Hebbel's aphorism that 'with someone who holds nothing but trumps, it is impossible to play cards'. This recognition does not lead to a limitation of the model. If we reverse this statement, in fact, we arrive at a definition of power: to be powerful is to be able to impose definitions of the situation in interaction. If somebody is able to call a spade a spade even though we insist it is an entrenching tool, we are less powerful than they are. And if one person does it and gets away with it, the next one will surely try to as well. Power is revealed in and emerges from such rhetorical confrontations. In this way, systems of classification are always related to power and politics through what other scholars have been calling 'translation'[7] – in fact, I use the terms 'politics' and 'political' largely to refer to the issue of 'who gets to define the situation? Who can make the rules?' It is clear that political struggles, while involving matters of access and resources and control over bodies, are nevertheless founded on symbolic classification:

> Systems of classification would not be such a decisive object of struggle if they did not contribute to the existence of classes by enhancing the efficacy of the objective mechanisms with the reinforcement supplied by representations structured in accordance with the classification. (Bourdieu 1984: 480)

Exegetes of Bourdieu have criticized interactional approaches to 'the situation' for reducing 'the objective, durable structure of relationship … which organizes every real interaction' to a 'momentary, local, fluid order', whereas '[i]nteracting individuals bring all their properties into the most circumstantial interactions, and their relative positions in the social structure (or in a specialized field) govern their positions in the interaction' (Swartz 2003: 578f). This misses the mark completely. Bailey's use of the notion takes account of the multiplicity of relationships and attends to the methodologically prior question of how 'structures' become durable in the first place. As I ethnographically substantiate later, the institutionalization of ethnic difference and its implementation in ritual and quotidian practice, in divisions of labour and access to material assets is a powerful argument in debates about rights and obligations, as it renders debates moot and ideally even denies the legitimacy of contestation. What better way to exert power than to ritually exclude somebody from the competition? To declare them unworthy opponents on the battlefield? To bar them from the community of porcupines? To deny them access to the Wheel of Autonomy?

Working from the angle that antagonistic social action can best be understood through the culturally valid persuasive language of claims, it becomes clear that the power of definition also works the other way around. Not only can the powerful impose on the powerless by giving them a name, classifying them and assigning them to a category. But to classify, to define, to identify others is in itself a claim to power, especially in situations where it is far from obvious who is dominant and who is dominated. Power is asserted whenever a claim to define others remains uncontested or is sustained despite contestation. This is the same principle underlying verbal abuse. To call somebody names, even when they are not present, gives us a small measure of nearly magical power over them.

People who feel in charge often take action when their subjects attempt to resist the definitions that are imposed on them. Even where the rulers' control over material resources and the monopoly of violence and force is not being challenged, the subordinates' resistance to domination even in its nonmaterial form of rejecting schemes of classification (e.g. naming) often triggers reprisals from above. This understanding of the connection between power and naming, and classifying/categorizing, is not only a pervasive element of folktales, occultism and religion; it is also a central feature of interethnic relations and forms one of the backbones of my analysis of the situation in Kara, where I witnessed numerous struggles over the applicability and the entailments of ethnic categories and how their names were employed.

Considering the more general aspects of classification, it is clear that a domain as salient in everyday life as ethnicity is in Kara will be overdetermined in a 'condensation of meanings' (Colby et al. 1981: 432). It comes with innumerable associations, stories, stereotypes, interactional frames and various entitlements to degrees of autonomy. In correlation with the different ethnicities that matter in and around Kara, I found different ways of expressing them. Specific interethnic relations correspond to different kinds of ethnicity, as ethnicity is situated, relative and relational, and the relations between ethnic groups and categories are complex and often an object of struggle themselves. These differences can partly be worked out from their rhetorical expression. Maybe somewhat iconoclastically, I use this focus on rhetorical struggles over differentiation as the lens through which I present the internal categories of Kara in the next chapter. The idea is that a particularly pointed understanding of social sections, institutions and status distinctions lies in the observation of how they are either contested or brought to bear in a definition of the situation. The theoretical toolkit developed in this chapter will be applied throughout the rest of this book.

Notes

1. It is an uncanny experience to read the texts of these authors who did not reference each other in most of their texts (until Harrison (2006)), while both cite the same sources and

draw similar conclusions. I assume that their avoidance relation was an instance of just such a fear of the doppelganger.
2. There are other viewpoints. Robert Frost's poem *The Mending Wall* (1914) is an indictment of the sentiment of having walls for the sake of avoiding entanglements. It ends with these lines: 'He will not go behind his father's saying,/And he likes having thought of it so well/He says again, "Good fences make good neighbours."' The poet sees this belief as a relic from a presumably less enlightened past.
3. Blok, drawing on work by Norbert Elias, also points out the relevance of duelling and honour to the discussion: 'The duel is an example of stylized and refined violence between equals one of whom has encroached on the "ideal sphere" of another, who consequently gets the chance to vindicate his honor by putting his life at risk' (1998: 41). I do not want to go too far into abstraction when talking about warfare: suffice it to say that due to the nature of communicative action and the above-posited need for autonomy, formal similarities between such expression of individual narcissism and group relations on the Lower Omo are inevitable. 'Honour' is too loaded a concept that I could go into detail here, but the Wheel of Autonomy might well be a helpful tool for studies of 'honour'.
4. This essential recognition of other 'true porcupines' marks my divergence from Nietzsche's infamous 'will to power'. I do not see actors as seeking dominion or the solitude of the tyrant, but much rather the (selective) company of peers. Todorov traces this notion back to Rousseau, whom he credits with 'inscribing a need for the gaze of the other in the very definition of man' (2001: 14).
5. This tripartite valorization echoes Aristotle's idealist division of rhetoric into the genres of pathos, logos and ethos, types that are useful heuristics for analysis, although never present in pure form, and protean in practice.
6. In an earlier work, I have outlined the trajectory of this concept and showed the increasingly sophisticated use made of 'the definition of the situation' by Bailey from 1973 to the present day (Girke 2002: 72–88; see also Bailey 2009).
7. Interestingly, in a turn of phrase quite similar to how Bailey puts it, John Law summarizes that: 'Latour thus rejects the idea that there is a background, determinant, social structure. Rather, what may be observed are sets of different people trying to define the nature of social structure, and then trying to persuade others to subscribe to that definition' (Law 1986: 17–18). Without going into more detail here, this parallel view highlights the possible convergence between rhetoric culture theory and the translation approach as developed by Latour and others (see Callon 1986; Latour 1986; and also Carrithers et al. 2011).

Chapter 2

Categories of Being Kara

This chapter introduces a range of nonethnic social categories of Kara, which are enacted in various forms of relational interaction. There are 'settlements', 'social organization' and 'individual status', and their discussion evokes life in Kara country by including brief accounts of contemporary and past conflicts. The limitation to specific processes within Kara is maintained because, on the ground, there is a clear understanding about which people are 'in' and which are 'out'; as the old aphorism says, while a clear line might be difficult to draw, there is usually no doubt on which side of any reasonable line a specific case lies (see Gluckman 1964: 12). The categories dividing Kara in practice, as discussed here, have little or no bearing on a practically understood 'outside'. Internal ethnic differentiation is treated separately (see Chapters 3 and 4), but is always tempered and modified through the numerous other affiliations discussed here, such as an individual's settlement area, clan membership, political or ritual office, and others. The interminable differentiations within the Kara population can be described as a dynamic, relational co-emergence of emic categories and related practices. In general, these categories carry an oppositional element, so that Kara social institutions afford relational identification and provide arenas for conflict and integration.[1] The categories in which one can be Kara are numerous and interlocking, and instead of attempting to comprehensively describe any of them – say, the age-set system, the settlement structures or the clans – I will portray these and others with a focus on the following questions: how does each category open up an arena for internal struggles over reputation or resources? How do actors plausibly 'perform' these institutions? How can they display their affiliations? And how can they derive further claims from these categories in their attempts to define situations?

My interest lies in how such possible lines of identification are rhetorically activated – on the plausibility of performance, on the claims to a certain way of belonging and on the challenges issued not only against particular processes of identification (from within or without), but also against the moral validity or empirical reality of these categories.

How do people go about finding or, rather, sustaining the 'minor differences' between them? In anthropology, the recognition that conflict provides insight into the workings of identity, as sides are taken and lines are drawn, has become a baseline for many different approaches. Victor Turner has stated early and clearly that it is conflict that is the most efficient eye-opener in regard to social process, because 'disturbances of the normal and regular often give us greater insight into the normal than does direct study' (1974: 34). In conflict, I would argue, one sees both the normal and the abnormal: only through the appreciation of what is counted as a breach and what shape 'redressive action' takes does it become possible to reconcile an abstractly elicited cultural ideology of social categories with practice.

More than thirty years after Turner's seminal texts were written, it is still heuristically viable to start from salient 'diagnostic events' (Moore 1987: 730), which are encountered in fieldwork, and to reconstruct 'social dramas' (Turner 1974). Of such moments, Kara provided plenty. Some events were even locally marked as more significant than others in gossip, group discussions or statements of opinion on specific goings-on; they were considered important or troubling, funny or exciting by the local public. Ostentatious commentary that decontextualized or recontextualized the events was particularly pronounced when conflicts were escalated beyond an initial pair of antagonists. Here, 'escalation' means not progressing from verbal exchanges to sticks and stones, but rather indicates the rhetorical mobilization of certain group affiliations and categorizations out of the wide range available. Such 'action-sets' (Gulliver 1971) become activated out of a sheer need for allies, or even activate themselves as a conflict becomes relevant to more and more people who are no longer content to be merely an audience.

The potential for action in the name of certain social categories is strongest when something materially or affectively valuable is at stake, especially so when the very system of classification, the categories that are invoked by the involved actors, is up for contestation. Logically, identity claims, i.e. statements about social categories, are statements about connections; in such claims, one connects oneself or others to a certain culturally elaborated category within a classificatory system. It follows that people's actions are always interpretable – and usually are interpreted – as intentional, as significant, and as expressive of normative and empirical ideas, of which actors try to persuade others. In regard to conflicts, this means that they can come to be 'about' a much more general social issue than had perhaps been intended by the antagonists.

Conflict, then, allows an observer not only to analyse institutions and identities as relevant for social life, but shows in its dynamics how these categories are transformed by the very struggles in which they are invoked. A setting such as Kara is particularly conducive to such an analysis. On the one hand, a multitude of possible identifications are available and mutual knowledge is considerable. On the other hand, due to its small absolute size, each single act carries more weight for the general understanding and enactment of the categories, as it subsequently becomes integrated into narratives and memory.

Conflicts do not break out because of the division of social categories. This is also the main argument of Schlee (2008). I remain agnostic with regard to whether conflicts do have identifiable root causes. In Kara, I could often only speculate about whether anything was at stake for the actors beyond that whoever 'won' got to define the situation, including the relation between them and those who 'lost'. Accordingly, my aim here is to work out the relations between social categories, collective action, triggers of conflict and their emic justification or rationalization.

A Proclivity towards Differentiation

Already during my first stays in the field, and increasingly as I was working with my data, I gained a sense that within Kara, there were many incidents of conflict in a general sense. Most of these were verbally linked to social categories, whether to group identity or to individually achieved status. Certainly, individuals argued, quarrelled and fought for their own personal reasons. But what struck me were processes in which people asserted not only their own interests, but claimed to be – or, just as often, were accused to be – acting as either typical members of a category ('this is how they are') or as representatives of a group ('this is what they want'). This had the important effect that the categories invoked came to be at stake in the conflict as well. Due to the enormous variety of arenas and the high incidence of such conflicts involving claims to difference, Michael Herzfeld's suggestion that 'segmentary proclivities' existed among the Greek animal thieves whom he studied (1984: 655), resonates with my material. Victor Turner himself has similarly suggested that the Ndembu displayed a 'propensity towards conflict' (1974: 33).

There is little doubt that some communities with which anthropologists work are more ostentatious in their quarrels great and small. However, while the interests and even the personality of the field researcher are bound to play a role in such a perception of dispositions, I follow Herzfeld and Turner in that I want to make specific statements about the Kara way of living in community.

Sometimes, a specific mode of categorization, such as the Nuer segmentary lineages (Evans-Pritchard 1940), leaves its distinct footprints all over the ethnographic record. Often, such a model is copied and exported, and again fairly often it can be shown to illuminate cases in other places. But already Asmarom has noticed that when looking at 'the structural relationships between age-sets and lineages or between age-sets and villages', it is well 'possible for the Nuer to invoke one *or* another of these sociological categories to elicit the support of others' (1973: 230). Thus, the real question in the study of social categories and classification is out of which available options people select a category of belonging to matter here and now, that is, situationally: which classificatory system do they apply? Which language of claims do they use?

It is imprudent to assign primacy to any specific category *a priori*. I found no evidence that would allow me to state a rule for when kinship is stronger than age-set membership or vice versa. For a truly interactionalist, practice-based approach, one needs to allow for any of these categories to become connected or disconnected in rhetorical action if this is what is empirically observed. So when my topic here is how social categories are 'at work' in the social life of a population, I probably could discuss this in the vocabulary of segmentation: as Asmarom makes clear, units of segmentation need not be lineage-based. But rather than use this well-worn model, I present the play of categories in terms of the Wheel of Autonomy, of claims and counterclaims and the definition of the situation: in the drive towards autonomy, people seek to exert agency which in turn induces distinction, which is a logical condition of autonomy.

Accordingly, in discussing these categories of being Kara, I highlight how they were adduced by people as justifications or explanations of social events. This includes the local assessments of the triggers, occasions and reasons for clashes, and the changes in the respective category after breach, crisis, redressive action and reintegration have come and gone. By framing their behaviour in a certain way, people issue claims and invoke their membership in certain categories; the categories, as cultural constructs, are reaffirmed and invoked or, alternatively, challenged, questioned and subverted. In his work on identity, Schlee emphasizes the necessity for plausibility when issuing statements about relatedness (e.g. Schlee 2008: 25). While allowing much creativity, neither are social categories fully arbitrary, nor can claims to inclusion within or exclusion from them be arbitrary.

Some markers of personal distinction for Kara are also listed below – for example, to be a 'killer'. While people do not enter any categorical conflict as a group of killers, even these categories are used to make claims of social relevance, to make persuasive statements on achievement and status. Any actions performed in the context of category-based differentiation provide individuals with the opportunity to present themselves, to work on their reputation, and to display their astuteness in judgement and their strength of character.

The size of the community is of relevance in such processes of choosing categories: to reiterate, Kara in general are intimately familiar with one another, live in centralized villages, hut by hut, door to door, within earshot of most goings-on. People's in-laws, their clansmen, their hunting friends, their age-mates, their fellow initiates – everybody is constantly close. 'Vergemeinschaftung' is at its strongest. Thus, competent adults have a wide variety of affiliations that they can – or are urged to – emphasize in interaction. So when people struggle over external assets or communal activities, the situation always gives rise to challenges to the applicability of category claims, as well as the qualities of categories involved, and their mutual relatedness.

I found that in Kara, hardly a day went by without some public argument, some fight, some scandal of varying levels of drama and physicality. Verbal provocations, reneged deals, petty thefts from individuals and from the community – all this was part and parcel of social life, so much so that people themselves were commenting how it was 'always the same' whenever some trouble arose. Some of the behaviour I observed seemed to follow cultural templates, most evident in the commonplaces of insult, some certainly involved ritualistic elements even, but much of it came across as committed, affective and sincere. Of course, in order to sustain the categories that enable group action in the first place, actors need to plausibly communicate their category membership. These displays of differentiation showed that both for individuals and for certain groupings, there were lines not to be crossed, actions and claims worth fighting over. In fact, to me as an observer, the ease of reconciliation was often at crass odds with the quick escalation of conflict. Even for those individuals who prefer being the audience to such ostentatious acts, this dynamic characterized life in Kara. A few individual elders have the reputation that they do not like this intensity, the constant comings and goings and the hubbub of the villages, the plays of agonistic interaction. They spend large parts of the year in homesteads outside the main villages, on the riverbanks or near a flood plain. While this is in a sense a mute criticism of the Kara proclivities for differentiation, there are also eloquent and increasingly loud criticisms of both of these general tendencies and specific ways of differentiation, which I discuss further below.

Internal Categories and Arenas

Based on empirical data and inductively generated, the following catalogue includes the categories of being Kara I encountered during fieldwork, and represents various intensities and ways of differentiation. Each entry in the list focuses on potentialities of categorization and displays of affiliation. It is uncommon for individuals in Kara to form and act as interest groups that are not structured along the lines of clan, settlement, age or any of the other categories listed below: all these subdivisions have a moral component in that they are 'recognized', even while their applicability might be challenged. Thus, all of the entries and their specific connections belong to the repertoire of a locally central 'language of claims'. To not invoke any of these categories in joint action, to form impromptu factions (see Bailey 1969: 51; 1977), would risk incurring the stigma of anomy and opportunism.

One basic Kara category that cuts across many of the items in the list below is gender. But most of the interaction I discuss is among men, as women are clearly marginalized in many public arenas in Kara. It is also the case that males are from an early age urged to form corporate groups and incessantly practise their presentations of self and competitiveness in general. While young girls are also encouraged to develop assertiveness, and while most women are proud and confident in the practical control of the domestic affairs, they offer few challenges to their exclusion and do not seek to take part in these processes of differentiation in the way that many men do. Empirically, this is apparent in the fact that women rarely form groups for joint action. While such processes are even now being encouraged by NGO interventions, they are culturally nonstandard and have not become entrenched yet. Older women, long past menopause, at times display a provocative sense of humour and can mock or ridicule men as the latter engage in their exclusive (and exclusionary) pursuits, and these women's collectively exercised claims to such carnivalesque licence are usually tolerated. Despite this imbalance in public agency, women are a significant part of the audience to the various conflicts and processes of differentiation. As such, women wield considerable power in that they are witness, judge and jury to the men's performances. To the degree that I am aware of women's involvement, which as a rule tends more to the subtle than the ostentation of men's displays and is more individualistic as opposed to corporate, I will include it in the discussion.

Finally, I want to repeat that nonethnic differentiations in Kara provide categories of joint action for ethnically divided individuals. Most of the categories below are not open merely to the true Kara, but equally to the politically subordinate Gomba, Bogudo, Moguji and Nyangatom-Kara, whom I will address in the next three chapters.

Settlements

Most Kara live in the three villages of Labuk, Dus and Korcho, which lie more or less in a line running north to south on the eastern bank of the Omo River. While this basic set-up has been stable for a few decades, many aspects of the settlement structure of Kara have changed in that time. The northernmost village, Labuk, used to be on the western side of the Omo River. Many families from Dus formerly settled in the Kadokochin area, also on the opposite bank. In addition, some smaller villages have been established close to the riverbank fields between Dus and Korcho. Despite these movements, the settlements are conceptually, ritually and administratively relatively coherent. As a rule, individuals belong to one of these settlement areas for life. Few households migrate permanently from one settlement to another, and in this way, settlements come to be categories that can be operationalized in interaction and discourse. People might say that somebody was 'from Korcho', and this suggests a number of inferences about that person's life and attitude. Even a woman who is married out and moves once across Kara to her husband's compound will often be linked to her area of origin. The most important recent territorial shift has been the massive exodus of children and young adults in order to pursue education. Many stay in boarding houses in Turmi and Dimeka, the market towns in the adjacent Hamar territory, but the presence of Kara youths is equally visible in the zonal capital Jinka.[2]

Mutual comparison with at least implicit competition is quite common, which can lead to explicit conflict between the settlements. Within a small village, or within a defined segment of a larger one, there will be heightened solidarity and cooperation. People have considerable flexibility in terms of where they erect their houses, so usually only people who get along well in the first place will live side by side.[3] Settlements also gain coherence in that many disputes are settled ad hoc and right on the spot. If a public disturbance occasions it, the male elders of the settlement will assemble, assess the case and decide what is to be done. This situational formation is called the *zersi* (see Strecker 1976a; Epple 2007: 250) and, after issuing redress, dissolves (compare Fortes 1969: 245). *Zersi* is an important Kara category, intimately tied to settlement membership and elder status (Girke 2010).[4]

Dus and Labuk

'Dus' and 'Labuk' stand for the two main settlement centres of Kara. Labuk, in the north and closer to the Moguji settlement at Kuchur, is marked in that its population is made up of comparatively few true Kara vis-à-vis the Gomba, as well as a strong group of Nyangatom-Kara, many Moguji and one Bogudo family. It also has a much smaller population, less than a quarter of the Kara total. It forms not only a separate *kebele* (Amharic for the smallest administrative unit; a ward) with its own set of office-holders, but it also has its own ritual leader and 'father of the land' (*bitti*), who is responsible for magical protection against dangers threatening Labuk. Dus, however, is ritually prior as only there can one find the elders' hermetic house (*marmar*)[5], an imposing wooden structure of rows of Y-shaped poles and wooden crossbeams. This is the site for the most sensitive discussions, and the location for the annual *terbi* drum dance. Other than elders of the true Kara and Bogudo, none may enter the *marmar*. 'Dus', in this traditional usage, comprises the old village of Dus proper as well as the more recent southern outpost Korcho, and anything in between, with a population of over 1,000. For significant rituals such as the 'leap across the cattle', the final part of the initiation of true Kara men towards their first proper marriage (see Strecker (1979) for the similar Hamar ritual), people congregate in Dus. The activities of the male age-sets and the installation of new age-cohorts take place separately in Dus and Labuk, but over the last forty years, some efforts have been made to at least synchronize the events if not merge them.[6]

Many young men from Dus seek girlfriends and wives in Labuk, some youths from Labuk journey to Dus seeking excitement and a larger crowd, and some people have moved to the other part of the land for employment in administration or tourism. People tend to live close to their favourite fields along the riverbank and in the settlements of their fathers, a practical as well as ritual arrangement. Most Kara are firmly at home in either Dus or Labuk, which are only a few hours' walk apart.[7] Are there, then, arenas of contention?

Today, the relation seems amiable if distant. Some individuals travel to and fro, while some do not. Talking to teenage girls in Dus, I found they had never even visited Labuk. This serves to show that integration between the two is limited. While everybody has age-mates in both places and many other ties emerge over a lifetime, intimacy and familiarity tend to be focused around one's home. As *kebele*, there is little rivalry, but there is mutual observation. As an example, when in Dus the local self-organized cooperative (the *mahaber*)[8] started on its road to economic success, it was not long until a similar set-up in Labuk got going. But there are, today, few conflicts that are framed in the division between Dus and Labuk.

The Administrative Division of Dus and Korcho

As of 2007, Dus is divided into two administrative parts: Dus itself, and the more southerly Korcho, about two hours' walk away. The division here is of a different nature, in that Korcho is a new settlement. In its current manifestation, no older than fifty years from what I have gathered, it was originally founded by people from Dus. Ritually, Korcho is subject to the *bitti* of Dus. During the time of my fieldwork, Korcho was viewed with distrust, disdain and occasional jealousy by the people from Dus. This was due partly to the special access these southerners had to employment at the permanent safari camp Murule, but mostly to the profits garnered from the steady stream of tourists who alight upon Kara at certain times of the year. Korcho, basically the first stop on the way when descending from the main road crossing the Hamar mountains, receives the lion's share of revenue. Not only are tourists charged for every single picture they take, but each car entering the village is also subject to a parking fee. Whoever is in the village at the time jockeys for their share in photograph-money and whatever else the visitors are prepared to hand out. Some people from Dus actually made the journey and stayed in Korcho for a few days when tourists were coming in droves, to share the bounty as it were. The alleged enormity of the cash acquired in this way both by individuals and by the Korcho community leads to misgivings in other parts of Kara. Suspicions abounded that the Korcho people had deals with tour operators so that no tourist cars would drive the extra distance to Dus, which could be empty on a day when Korcho saw thirty cars.[9] And it was not just tourist cars that only went as far as Korcho: more NGOs had localized projects in Korcho than in

Dus.[10] That the steady cashflow enabled alcoholism in Korcho does not help the settlement's reputation.

For the Korcho people, though, the new *kebele* status awarded in 2007 was a due recognition of their achievements and distinctiveness. They had often felt sidelined because the people from Dus did not forward information on time, and to go all the way to Dus for a meeting was also seen as bothersome: much better to have one's own *kebele*, and own meetings! While calmer minds on both sides stated very pragmatically that the simple fact that now four additional people would receive monthly salaries as paid officials (*kabin*) was enough reason for happiness for all of Kara, others in Dus claimed that this recognition would go to the heads of the Korcho people. This establishment of a new *kebele* would not bring about unity, but rather would spread dissent and distrust. In summary, tensions were visible in that the people of Dus emphasized the 'undeserved' advantages Korcho currently enjoyed, implying that arrogance leading to disunity could be the consequences. 'Our day will come again', people from Dus said, 'when the tourists and the NGOs realize that Korcho is only a small place, and the people there are difficult to deal with.' The relationship between these two centres of southern Kara, as perceived and as enacted, is dynamic. Through infrastructural and political changes, often externally induced, it has changed dramatically since 2003 and will continue to do so.

The Extermination of the Garchi by the People of Dus

In the classic *Altvölker Süd-Äthiopiens*, the map of the Banna territory shows a stretch of land labelled 'Garči' (see Jensen 1959: 313). It took some time until I even encountered this term in the field.[11] Today, people will point out a spot a little upriver from Dus and call it 'Garchi'. However, this only indicates the southern border of the former settlement area of Garchi, which stretched northwards towards Labuk from there. For a long time, Garchi land was largely uninhabited, and there was no permanent settlement to be found. What had happened? '*Ana, Dus-be Garchi-be kinka tsali da* – in the past, Dus and Garchi co-existed peacefully together' begins the narrative about the fate of Garchi, told to me by the late Lowoyo Bordo, one of the most senior elders when I began my research. Both sections were autonomous, much like Labuk and Dus today. The prosperity and security of both lands were in the hands of their respective *bitti* ritual leaders, but, more importantly, the *borkotto bitti*, exclusive groups of respected men who assume the responsibilities of steering the land. The *borkotto bitti* from both sides, so the narrative goes, used to invite one another in order to jointly feast on slaughtered cattle and to discuss affairs in a friendly atmosphere.[12] This relationship went bad when one day, the hosts in Dus hid the best parts of the slaughtered animal and served the less desirable parts to their guests, along with some implausible excuses. Consider this re-enactment of the Garchi's reaction by Lowoyo and my hunting-friend Haila:

Lowoyo: What? Why are they hiding it from us? People who hide food, they think war.
Haila: There is talk among them [the people from Dus].
Lowoyo: There is talk!

'Talk', of course, refers to conspiracy and potential betrayal, so during the return visit, the *borkotto bitti* of Garchi did the same thing, indicating that they had caught on and, being people of perspicacity, should not be trifled with. Offended, the Dus delegation turned back and incited their land against the Garchi, speaking of the hidden thoughts of murder they had discerned when visiting. The Garchi, though, took the initiative and, sweeping into the Kadokochin on the western side of the Omo, they razed a village there. Seeing the smoke across the river, the people of Dus rose as one, and went and 'stabbed' the entire population of Garchi. They only spared the women and children, many of them their own daughters anyway, and brought them home after their decisive victory. Ten Garchi lineages still survive among the true Kara of today, some now based in Dus and some in Labuk. The explanation for their continued existence was that the widows, having been taken away by the victors, still perpetuated their dead husbands' descent lines.

This is, today, one of the least visible partitions of Kara. I only know of one contemporary conflict between individuals in which a person's Garchi-ness was brought up to deny him some ritual rights within Dus. Otherwise, the few survivors of Garchi do not have specific relations just by being classified as such and do not act as a corporate group. The story, regardless of its historicity, is moral in that it demonstrates the dangers of mutual suspicion signified by 'hiding meat' and that the Dus people, still now, when there are hardly any Garchi left, figure as the bad guys. This acknowledges that there are not always fair returns. 'Oh yes, we people from Dus, we were bad', one man said with a satisfied smile, 'the place where we didn't make war, that place doesn't exist!' The kernel of historical truth that I presume behind the narrative is chilling. In one of the earliest records we have about the Kara, the elephant-hunter Neumann reported that the people of 'Kéré' were just celebrating a massacre they had perpetrated on their neighbours in 1896 (1994: 327). Based on the age-sets that I was told were involved in the fighting, the estimate that these events took place around the turn of the twentieth century is plausible. Interestingly, these were also the oldest age-set names I could collect in Kara. The myth itself goes some way to support a Kara self-image of reckless (and ultimately successful) decisiveness.

Dus and the Challenge of an Irrigation Project

A rather recent category of differentiation that people have already managed to turn into an occasional arena divides the Dus people into those who cultivate at the Kundamma irrigation site and those who do not. This *irsha*, as it is called, came into operation in 2005, after long efforts by EPARDA. EPARDA is the 'Ethiopian Pastoralist Research and Development Association', a national NGO that has established irrigation projects in other sites of South Omo as well. The organization, which has since faced political trouble, convinced the Kara of irrigation's potential for cultivation independent of river water level and rain, and especially for crop diversification. A sizeable number of Dus residents proceeded to wrest plots from the forest in the centre of the Kundamma peninsula west of the village. Without going into the details of the techniques of irrigation agriculture, several features of the arrangement are worth highlighting. First of all, the work on the *irsha* is more demanding than the labour for the usual riverbank or flood-plain cultivation. It involves digging and maintaining plots, water channels, furrows and shifting – by means of ropes or hands – the solitary water-pump up and down the riverbank. This sobering experience has caused disgruntlement among the people who had decided to take a risk, believe the NGO's promises and take up this innovation.

The recurring hassles with the NGO workers responsible for the pump use and disagreements about priority in receiving water simply added to this. There were also shortages of fuel for the pump: whenever it stopped working for whatever reason, consequences were disastrous for the growing crops. Some people have dropped out of the venture, but others have developed a dedication to the plots into which they have invested so much effort, and to the emergent

Figure 2.1 A public debate in Dus (October 2006). Photograph by Felix Girke.

community of irrigation farmers. *Irsha* cultivation largely takes place in the months of May to September, before the agricultural work on the riverbanks commences. Already in 2006, a year after the irrigation became operational, much of the social life of Dus had shifted to the new site at Kundamma, around which the river loops spectacularly, about 45 minutes of brisk walking away. Conflict arose about the commitment to the affairs of the community between the people who stayed in the village and those who all but moved to the irrigation site. The accusation was that the *irsha* people opportunistically disregarded pressing issues and instead preferred to sit in their shelters in the shade of the forest, drink *parsho* beer and enjoy out-of-season crops. The last I heard was that the *irsha* was defunct. This development reduces the chances of a new permanent settlement springing up at Kundamma, which would have been to the detriment and anger of those remaining behind at Dus.

Social Organization

The settlements are crosscut by various organizational units, all somehow based on descent, whether traceable or not. The respective affiliation of individuals is largely definite and final, with the exception of the *ball'* (see below), which allow shifting, although usually not without some opposition. To say they are 'definite and final' is to recognize that there is a limit to how much leeway the Kara allow for category shifting; there are, for example, no known instances of an adult male changing his clan belonging. What is relevant for my approach is that what is always indefinite and preliminary is whether and to what degree somebody's formal membership actually matters in an emergent situation. Some of the sections are antagonistic by historical definition, while some provide the segmentary structure for conflicts triggered in another arena.

The *Ball'*: Nyuwaya versus Nyuwariya

A vague distinction runs through the population of southern Kara – a division into two *ball'*, literally two 'open grounds', that is, meeting and dancing grounds: the Nyuwaya and the Nyuwariya section. This is visible mostly in Dus proper, but every household in both Dus and Korcho is affiliated with one section or the other. In Korcho, most people belong to Nyuwariya. Some people in Dus worry that with the recognition of Korcho as *kebele*, the division between the two *ball'* might come to be conflated with the division between Dus and Korcho if the Nyuwariya members attempt and define southern Kara as 'their' land. In this way connected to issues of access, this might engender a real division of Dus and Korcho along *ball'* lines.

Nowadays, the division is largely organizational: within Dus, there is an invisible line running through the village, with a tendency for the Nyuwariya to erect houses downriver of it and for the Nyuwaya upriver of it. When the elders gather on the open grounds to discuss the state of the land, pass on rumours and talk about current affairs, this takes place simultaneously at two sites, not more than a decent stone's throw apart. Also, age-set activities of the two *ball'* are kept organizationally separate, while largely simultaneous. In principle, a man is free to switch and, indeed, the division can even be found within one lineage. But it can occasion anger when the head of a household announces his intention to move 'across'. Linguistically, the division finds expression in *sa* (over there) and *kota* (here), which are used in casual reference to the respective *ball'*. How did this division come about?

The most coherent of the meaning-making stories of the several that I gathered on this division mentions a certain age-set, the Nyuwariya, who quarrelled with another age-set, the Nyuwaya. The Nyuwariya had decided not to beat their sons very much during the installation of a new age-set. This decision led to a division and an end of ritual commensality: 'Having removed their sons from the group of initiates, the Nyuwariya stabbed their own goats and ate them alone!', Lowoyo, an elder who had witnessed this division in his youth, told me.[13] This conflict grew into a real rift, with brawls between the two age-sets. Soon, a second *ball'* was set up. Some people went with the Nyuwariya, some refused to join them, and eventually the names of the two age-sets became synonymous with the two factions. The details of this fight of the age-sets are not well recalled. From my tentative dating, it would have taken place in the 1950s. For a long time after the divide had been established, the whole age-set installation process was separated. In summary, while Labuk is entirely untouched by this factionalism, the divide between the two *ball'* exists and is effective in some ways. However, these currently largely ritual and habitual categories might be mobilized and turned into a political arena in regard to the new Korcho *kebele*.

Clans and the Ears of Livestock
Every Kara lineage belongs unambiguously and in perpetuity to a particular exogamous clan, the *olo*. There are ten distinct names for *olo* in Kara: Gorsbolo, Bitolo, Dirrta, Kalaza and Kogo are individually exogamous; Eshiba, Garshima and Dangarr together form a corporate, exogamous unit; and Dingolo (in Labuk) and Ongosula (in Dus) are treated as one clan. By translating *olo* as 'clan', I follow the established terminology for the Southern Omotic groups.[14] The structural, proscriptive and non-negotiable effects of clan membership are few. 'An *olo*', Kara commonly summarize, 'are those people who "eat" bridewealth together.' However, while an important step in the marriage negotiations is for the suitor to gain the consent not only of a girl's father, but of other elders of that clan as well, this very practice has eroded. In the past, I was told, both the hardship of paying bridewealth and the windfall of receiving it were shared widely within a clan. Today, a man faces the burden of payments alone, but is at greater liberty concerning the distribution of bridewealth received. Still, young men of a clan band together to chase the suitors of their 'sisters' (a mutuality of

arenas between clans), and there is collaboration as lineages of the same clan join together in ritual activity. I did encounter strong, generations-old dyadic bonds between households, which were explained by referring to membership in the same clan. But there were certainly some equally affective relations across clan lines as well. An explanatory reference to clan membership, then, often begged the question. In addition, members of various clans are marked by their claims to specific taboos (especially regarding animals' internal organs) and ritual powers.

In summary, joint clan membership seems to facilitate the establishment of personal bonds, but only in conjunction with other factors such as personal sympathy, and the material basis for clan solidarity was exaggerated in discourse. The subclans of Kara, materialized in the specific pattern in which the ears of livestock are cut (*k'andi*), are adduced in the same explanatory mode in the form of claims: 'Of course they would stick together, they are both from Gorsbolo!' 'Yes, even their *k'andi* are the same.' Between clans, violent conflicts such as stick fights were said to have happened. However, my material suggests that the people who fight are usually acting with the interests of their lineages in mind, and only when escalation ensues is the *olo* is invoked and thereby rhetorically activated. It seems rare today that a situation is successfully defined to this effect.

Moro: Lineages and the Blood between

What I have referred to as 'lineages' so far is locally called *moro*, which also is the term for village or hamlet.[15] A *moro* is a patrilineal family structure with a historical depth of between two and three generations: my father's brothers' families are in my *moro*, and so are my grandfather's descendants in the male line. Beyond that, both genealogical memory and integration into *moro* become fuzzy. The Kara make few claims to a common ancestor beyond the known (great-) grandfather. People were largely indifferent towards the question of whether or not at some point in the past this *moro* and that *moro* had not indeed been one. Operationality of the *moro* always took precedence. *Moro* can comprise several homesteads, often located in different settlements, and there is much integration in interaction. Some ritual duties require coordinated cooperation within a *moro*, such as the annual ritual known as the *kaido*: starting with genealogical priority within the *moro* and going down to the most junior male elder, every head of a household (including widows) ritually chews the first sorghum grains from the riverbank cultivation sites to render the harvest safe for consumption for the people lower in the genealogical order. Such chains of dependency obviously encourage closeness and cooperation. If there are quarrels within a *moro*, people usually try to smooth them over quickly. It is a mark of distinction for an elder if their *moro* is prosperous, quick and efficient in its ritual duties, and if *ädamo* in the sense of 'amity' is seen and felt. *Moro* also jointly organize their land-holdings and cooperate closely in other economic activities, in weddings, initiation, and funerals.

Conflicts between *moro* are common, as this is the most obvious path of escalation when two individuals fight. After a case of homicide, there will be 'blood' (*maassi*) between the houses involved for generations to come. Even when the immediate trouble ensuing after a death is long over, 'blood' entails a prohibition of commensality, marriage, intercourse and even flirting between members. In the event of a breach of these avoidance rules, people are very quick to pick up their sticks and guns again, as I could witness myself: 'It is never forgotten', it was said – even if the heads of the two *moro* have been performing cleansing rituals together for years and years, one should tread carefully.[16] Out of the understanding that commensality between 'blood' enemies will bring sickness and death, the extermination of the Garchi is sometimes adduced as an explanation for the fall of the great Kara of yore from their pre-eminence among all peoples of the Omo Valley. As the survivors of the massacre grew up in Dus, people did not really know whose father had killed whom during the war, and between which lineages there was *maassi*. Accordingly, people were eating and drinking together regardless, and then many fell ill and died.

The *moro*, the lineage, is the kin core of any individual, evidenced by concerted social action both in conflict with others and in daily routines. Even out-married women retain strong ties. In-law relationships connect not only the two *moro* directly involved, but often all the male members of a married woman's clan address her husband as 'in-law' (*baiss*) and vice versa, and his sons as 'sister-sons'. The mother–brother/sister–son relationship is often marked with fair joviality and cooperation. In fact, it is common practice even in a faraway market to address a merchant with this very cordial and persuasive term, 'abiyo!'[17] These relations are by and large dyadic, and thus are of less interest to my discussion here. The character of in-law relationships in general is unpredictable, as in such a multiplex community as Kara, there are always other ties that bind members of two *moro* together.

The 'Roots' and the 'Guts': On Exogamy
From the point of view of any given ego, *chaachi*, 'roots' (compare Schlee (2008: 7) for the metaphor) refers to the people who are marriageable, and *rukunti*, 'guts', refers to the people who – categorically by clan or specifically by descent – are consanguinal kin. *Rukunti* are proscribed not only in regard to marriage, but also to dancing, flirting and sexual relations.[18] *Chaachi* belong neither to one's own clan nor to one's mother's clan, and additionally need to have a certain distance in degree of relation from ego. In Kara kinship terminology, the sisters of a male ego's father are classed as ego's elder sisters, their sons as ego's sister-sons, and finally their sons' children as ego's 'grandchildren' (*kogo-nana*). This degree of distance is the last that is still *äda*. In particular, the female *kogo-nana* stand in a somewhat liminal relation to the male Ego: while *äda*, one is allowed to dance with them, and many such dyads are marked by a lewd joking relationship.

Children are taught early on about who is *rukunti* and who is *chaachi*. At the very latest, they learn the difference when they start joining the nightly dances of the youth that serve as a learning ground in many respects.

These are, then, categories that are indexical for ego: for every Kara, it is this distinction that predetermines their relation to any person of the other gender. There are neither prescribed nor favoured marriage partners, so that any unmarried person of the other sex is either this or that, without ambiguity.[19] The presence of this distinction in everyday life from childhood onwards underlines the immanence of social divides.

Individual Status

The following categories are partly achieved and partly ascribed, and their enactment varies accordingly. They offer guidance to expected behaviour towards and by the holders of the respective status, and can play a role in all sorts of different social contestations. Degrees of corporation are vastly different in this list. 'Status', then, includes office (Turner 1966: 242) as well as individually achieved qualities.

The Fathers of the Land: *Bitti*

In Dus, there are at this point two *bitti*, ritual 'fathers of the land', who wield spiritual powers and whose blessings are of enormous efficacy for the prosperity of the entire land.[20] *Bittamo*, the office, is perpetuated in the lineage, but not always from father to son. In Dus, it is all the men of the Dangarr clan (which does not extend beyond one slim lineage at this time) who are in principle eligible to become *bitti* in the future. There is also a *bitti* in Labuk, of the Dingolo clan, with an equivalent role and capacities, but who is seen as secondary in importance as regards the whole of Kara. In wartime, the *bitti* performs a ritual that bars the ways of entrance into the Kara settlements for the enemy, and he will wash and bless the guns of raiders, who then pass through his ritual gateway (*mul'appo*) – 'then nobody will die'. He chases away locusts and averts other disasters. The *bitti*'s blood should not be spilt on the ground, the 'common folk' construct a house for him, and this house offers protection for fugitives.[21] In principle, there are more *bitti* yet: the Bogudo (of the Eshiba clan) hold the *bittamo* for southern Kara country, and there is a lineage of the Kogo clan that would provide a *bitti* for Garchi if there was anybody living in that area today. In casual use, *bitti* can also refer to the respective administrative heads of each *kebele*. Elders can also be called *bitti* in relation to their own holdings and their own more quotidian '*pehnssa ashka* – the fixing of the land', a task impossible to delegate, since assuming *bittamo* outside one's own domain is inviting disaster. These are clearly subordinate and associated uses of the title.

To belong to a *bitti* lineage is to enjoy a certain protection from quarrels and fights. When a young Dangarr man started an affair with a Gorsbolo girl, the girl's mother drunkenly ran through the village, exhorting young men to whip her licentious daughter – 'but him, leave him alone! Do nothing to him!' – where usually the suitors are the ones to suffer the revenge of a clan for seducing a girl and the 'loose' girl is only a secondary target. When the whipping commences in age-set installations, Dangarr boys are led aside, so that no sacred blood is spilt on the ground.

Many *bitti* are also sorcerers (*arti*) and can send snakes after thieves and other culprits, and work many other charms, but it is neither a complete nor exclusive overlap. There are several known *arti-moro*, lineages whose members regularly are sorcerers, and claiming to be an *arti* demands maintaining some taboos as well. In everyday life, *bitti* act much like other Kara and are neither materially better off nor externally marked in any way. In principle, each *bitti* has his own domain, and who should assume office in the event of the death of the incumbent is usually abstractly discussed long before the need arises. One might wonder what would happen if there was again a Bogudo elder in Korcho to assume the *bittamo* of the south. Would it be easy for the two office-holders from Dus and Korcho to renegotiate their respective responsibilities?

The 'Chair-Men': *Borkotto Bitti*

The *borkotto* is the emblematic wooden headrest found in some variation throughout much of Africa. As an everyday tool, it serves mostly as a seat and to elevate the head while resting or even sleeping, but it can also substitute for a hammer or an improvised projectile at a pinch (compare Abbink 2015). As a symbol, the *borkotto* stands for patriarchy, as one of the most distinguished tasks of elders is to sit in the village square on their headrest and discuss the weal of the land. It is no coincidence that the decision-makers of Kara are known as the *bitti* of the 'chair'. There are separate groups of *borkotto bitti* for Labuk, and for both Nyuwaya and Nyiuwariya in Dus, just as there were *borkotto bitti* in Garchi, as discussed in the previous section. They have taken on the duty of discerning impending problems, to point out transgressions and to suggest strategies for the population to implement. They concern themselves with issues both of morals and practical needs, and they do this – as a committee would elsewhere – first among themselves, before presenting to the public their finished conclusions. In my early fieldnotes, I compared them to Plato's philosopher-rulers: self-appointed thinkers who by dint of their perspicacity always know what is best for everyone. This is insured by way of recruitment: the *borkotto bitti* perpetuate their institution by regularly recruiting young men who show promise in terms of their cleverness and their character. They are judged worthy when they are also known for a peaceful, responsible manner. Some become full members right away, while others become *borkotto bitti* on probation, as it were. The latter are called the 'spear-shafts' (*sugsug*) as opposed to the 'teeth' (*atsi*), i.e. the blades of the spears, as the full members are known. The name 'spear' evokes the ritual spear that is wielded by speakers in public oratory.

Names of the new recruits are announced during a public ceremony (an *osh*), goats are slaughtered and consumed. Later that evening, in a more private setting, the new members host the old guard and are given advice on their duties, their privileges and their code of conduct: never should one *borkotto bitti* voice his opinion without another one being present, and their talk should always be true, never false and flippant. They should look ahead a little more than 'normal people', think about long-term consequences and quietly identify troublemakers. In a way, a group of *borkotto bitti* acts like a hermetic cell, owing no accountability to anybody on the outside, and assuming the right to determine and declare what is right and what is wrong. When any of them violate these prescriptions by publicly speaking in anger, sowing dissent and acting without consideration of the office, members are first warned, then temporarily excluded and possibly even permanently barred: 'What do you have on your foot, B.? It looks like you have put on a child's sandal! Have you not found your own sandals? Maybe you should search for it, at the far end of your granary. Return to us only when you have found it!' Caustic words spoken at an *osh* I attended – some time ago, while severely inebriated, B. had challenged the *bitti* of Dus to a fight. This was inexcusable, 'childish' behaviour, likely to cause spiritual danger to the entire land, and led to B.'s scolding, public humiliation and temporary ostracism.

The claims of the *borkotto bitti* on how certain situations should be defined, and what action needs to be taken, are hard to assail. The institution as such, allegedly based on the virtues of cleverness and 'good and true thoughts only', is also largely immune to criticism unless internal differences arise. In closing ranks, the *borkotto bitti* strengthen their persuasive power, leaving no openings, allowing no alternatives and pre-empting challenges against this united bloc of skilled speakers and respected elders; persuasive skill and authority conspire to shape public opinion. Members who flout the above-mentioned rule of always acting in concert quickly fall from grace – as they need to, lest they demean and besmirch the office as such. The *borkotto bitti* regularly decide over fateful issues, and must be considered the real movers and shakers of Kara, and the ones supposed to counteract all the quite clearly perceived proclivities towards differentiation.[22] But at the same time, by elevating the worthy and sidelining the rest, this on the face of it meritocratic institution carries the seed of divisiveness, as I will discuss towards the end of this chapter.

Age-Sets: *Hariya*
Beyond the general gerontocratic principle in evidence in many social situations, a man's age-set provides his primary peer group and closest circle of friends throughout his life. Age-sets are formed in slightly irregular intervals of six to eight years. After a period of debate and preparation, the local cohort of males in their late teens undergoes a series of rituals that serve to inaugurate a new age-set. The tasks set before them are trying, often painful (as when they are

Figure 2.2 Maide, Oita and Haila: three close friends from the Nyiramalai age-set (June 2006). Photograph by Felix Girke.

whipped) and costly; the preparations also serve as a test of their resourcefulness, so various services are required of them, most markedly communal beer-feasts and the slaughter of goats for members of the senior age-sets. The effect of this rite of passage (and one would assume the intention) is to shape strong solidarity among the age-mates.

This section serves to highlight the many ways in which intimacy among age-mates is expressed and demanded, and the comparatively common occurrence that different age-sets confront each other over slights or differences in opinion. To start with the second point, younger and older age-sets are talked of as respectively 'younger' and 'elder brothers' (*kanna* and *ishemo*), and should act with this in mind: the younger brothers should be respectful and obedient, while the elder brothers' behaviour can run the gamut from confrontational to caring. The division of the *ball* is a case in point of rivalries where responsibility and affection between two age-sets were ignored: in the course of public ritual, or political discussion, the divergent stances of people can be escalated along the lines of age-sets. As one's closest friends and most loyal supporters are usually age-mates, this comes easily.

I witnessed an extended conflict between the Nyiramalai and the Nyichekapus age-sets of the Nyuwaya-*ball*, that is, between my age-set and the one two ranks above, which began over a trivial matter: a certain young man from the

Nyiramalai was told to stop blowing his horn while men from all age-sets were jointly drinking beer. When he and his friends resisted, escalation ensued and the Nyiramalai were – following the principle of seniority – excluded from the event. Subsequently, their opponents attempted to sway public opinion in order to ban them from even sitting on the *ball'* and to have them declared culprits (*d'ebbi*), with the intended effect that they would have to sacrifice goats to the elders towards their reintegration. There was even talk of beatings. However, after weeks of confrontations and mutual provocations, one senior *borkotto bitti* who had been absent from the initial altercation turned the situation around and publicly lambasted the older age-set involved, accusing them of unwarranted pride: 'Where are the scars which marks them as killers? When have they been brave, ever?' The matter was dropped soon after. As this case shows, age-sets also acquire reputations, which add a set of distinctive claims to the fact of distinction. Consider this dialectic: 'All the Nyikuamong have the scars of the killer!' 'But it was easy for them then, they all just stabbed children with spears, this was before the Kalashnikov came here, so that today just one armed defender can turn any attack into a rout!' Challenging such claims can easily lead to conflict as men will often defend their claims and reputation, the face-wants, as it were, of their age-set. When a man's transgressions are unveiled, blame can be assigned to his entire age-set: his peers are expected to discipline him and if they fail to do so, their collective name is at risk. Even collective beatings, ordered by the more senior age-sets, used to be common in the past. The reputations of *hariya*-cohorts are in public display when junior age-sets compare themselves to those of their seniors that they admire (or not). In these narratives, it is most obvious that age-sets come to be described as actors who are in competition with one another.

The conduct of an age-set reflects on the ego of its members, and what one member does reflects on the age-set, so involvement and identification are often high. As youths, age-mates have jointly pressured their seniors for inclusion in the political life of the community, and were put through much indignity and hardship on the way to first acquiring the right to the adult's headrest (the *Kara borkotto*)[23] and later to the white clay body-paint called *selli*. This final step marks their formal acceptance as adults. Purportedly, while they pressure for these rights, they undergo the so-called 'robbing' (*burrma*) several times. This refers to a punishment for their alleged insolence, so in order to put them in their place again and to reinforce the uncompromising hierarchy, all their belongings are stripped away and distributed among senior age-sets. Inevitably, the aspirants persevere and eventually they come of age.[24] The primary age-set names used for each cohort refer to the hide of one of the goats they had to somehow procure and slaughter for their elders. Additional, boastful praise-names are taken voluntarily. Some of these 'become hot' (*oida*) and are used almost exclusively later on.[25]

Beyond the fact that age-mates have been peers for most of their lives and know each other intimately, there is the motto '*hariyassa gebba koleio* – among age-mates, no one is senior'.²⁶ Wives of age-mates are equally addressed as *hariya*, 'my age-mate', and children are expected to call their father's age-mates *abba*, 'my father', and their wives *inna*, 'my mother'. Age-sets, then, are a group within which the gerontocratic principle is denied and in which rivalry has little place. Being alike within, one can present a strong front to the outside and valorize one's name, the specific reputation of a certain age-set. In this way, individual members of the group, who are not politically active, nevertheless partake of the reputation their age-mates have often consciously worked on – and have to bear the fallout of external retribution against the age-set as well. The *hariya* are a focus of much social action, cooperation and integration.

Before the *borkotto* and the *selli* are 'bought' or 'stabbed' (as goats are slaughtered for the elders), before names are laid down, young boys of a similar age cluster together in proto-age-sets, familiar with one another since infancy or the days of collective circumcision.²⁷ Together, they roam around the villages, hunting birds and small game. They will herd together as they grow and start forming peer groups, with the increasing understanding that they will some day in the future be *hariya*.²⁸ They are supposed to push for their recognition as an age-set as they reach adolescence. The group-in-waiting from 2006 to 2008 already had chosen a name for themselves ('Lorianta', a type of cloth) and were referred to as such even as their installation was still years away in the future.

With a wry grin, one old man pointed out to me that if a cohort was slow in demanding their rights to social maturation, their seniors would sometimes perform the *burrma* without technically having grounds for it. To 'rob' the youths proactively served to remind them of their inevitable maturation and that they were expected to assert themselves. The formation of age-sets can become an arena when particularly mature boys are inserted into an age-set ahead of their childhood peers or if individuals are denied integration into the formal installation process due to more political or genealogical reasons. Such a decision can cause intensive debates and conflicts in loyalties even years later.

There also exist age-sets for girls and women, although these are much less elaborate than on the male side: cohorts of girls, starting when they are around ten years old, with an age range of only two to three years, take a name for themselves, and under that name move towards maturity and the inevitable marriage. Such names usually indicate hot topics of the time, be they environmental events (a period of great cold), referring to objects (a popular kind of gun) or outside people (the manager of the nearby hunting reserve and his imagined wealth). When a girl gets married, her age-mates are granted some licence vis-à-vis the groom. After marriage, a woman's own age-set will be recalled mostly when reminiscing about girlhood.²⁹

Personal Initiation: *Bärgitamo* and Becoming *Zonza*

When all of one's own (classificatory) elder brothers – including the younger brothers of one's father – have already gotten married, and if one's grandfather is dead, a young true Kara is eligible for the long road of initiation towards marriage himself. Only upon marriage will a true Kara man's 'great name' be bestowed. In the case of the eldest of the eldest son, this is his paternal grandfather's 'great name'. If the grandfather is still alive, his name is also still in use, as it were, and the grandson's marriage remains forbidden. This is not often an issue, as many men only father children when they are already in their thirties. When the condition arises, though, there is little flexibility in the rules.

As opposed to the comparable initiation in the Hamar-Banna-Bashada cluster, true Kara initiation takes place for groups at a time. These cohorts are the 'people of the rainy season' (*bärgi-ed*). Young men bent on marriage find one another over time, discuss their intents and select one elder to argue the case for them as a go-between (*motalla*, a term also used in other contexts) to convince the *zersi*, the united elders, to allow their initiation period to begin. The initiation period was traditionally over a year long, during which the young men are subject to an extensive list of prohibitions for the various stages. However, the real potential for conflict is at the outset: elders have sometimes denied the entreaties of the group in a roundabout way, for example, in times of war. They will also inevitably require the *motalla* go-between to undergo a gruelling questioning when he makes his application on behalf of the initiates-in-waiting: 'Is everything ready? Are the young men prepared? Is there enough tobacco? Enough honey? There is no chance to turn around once on the path! Have they thought of all the goods they need to provide for their seniors? Are they serious about it? Do you vouch for them?' Note that it is not technically required that the aspirants belong to properly installed age-sets; while this would be preferable, I know of several cases where much younger boys were allowed to become *bärgi-ed*, mostly because their respective *moro* needed somebody to become an 'elder' very badly at the time – and upon marriage, a man becomes a *zonza* regardless of his age.

Once this stage has been passed, the initiates are indeed on the path without return – while there is no anonymity anyway, they are very visible in their liminality: they cluster together, stay away from their age-mates both married and unmarried, use three-legged children's stools again (the *yedda borkotto*) and reply to female or generally unmanly names (*bärgi-nabi*) taken for the initiation time. They have very practical problems to solve to progress in their initiation, and the *bärgi-ed* help one another out in the ritual tasks.[30] The time spent in this long liminal phase creates lasting bonds between them as well. The names of *bärgitamo* are still occasionally used long after the initiates have – as the final step – run and leapt across a line of cattle four times and become elders (*zonza*). When they are called out in the right tone of voice by a fellow *bärgi-ed*, these names evoke this unique period in life very intimately. As it happens, these names can also be used mockingly as a reminder of this liminal phase, as when some young girls call a married man by his *bärgi-nabi*, to which he has to respond, and giggle. Regardless of the relation to the speaker, the response to one's *bärgi-nabi* always has to be 'bargia!' (when being addressed by a man) or 'bärgino!' (when being addressed by a woman), both serving as acknowledgements of the shared liminal experience.

After marriage, the group of initiates only has one final joint duty: to bury one another upon death. *Bärgi-ed*, in summary, are connected by a strong affective bond, but do not form a corporate group after marriage. Once on the path, this categorization is not activated in further arenas. Interestingly, though, it is not uncommon for nontrue Kara who got married around the same time as the true Kara cohort to be addressed and referred to as honorary *bärgi-ed* – even outsiders like Hamar.

However, having become a *zonza*, individuals acquire great autonomy, the privilege to chart their own course in life and to take the livelihood of their family into their own hands. Only now is one truly a part of the *zersi*, the decision-making, responsibility-seeking amorphous body of elders. Only now can one legitimately stand up to others and defy their challenges and only now can one participate in many central arenas of Kara social life.

Hunters, Killers and People of No Consequence

'*Meki zia ukabba*! – I have killed a buffalo bull!' Such exclamations, spoken in various degrees of forcefulness, are assertions of achievements that set the individual apart. Sometimes this in an intentionally silly way, as in response to one's clumsy movement that spills a drink on the ground. How is one's general competence supposed to be reaffirmed by reference to an act of killing a large animal? This is satirical, just as this second example: '*Sobbo ukabba*! ... *bere lemi* – I have killed a lion! ... sometime in the future', as one young man ventured. These joking ways of using the expressive template play with the fact that hunters and killers of men can in fact provoke and humiliate others severely. Who has killed has proven himself, and who has not can be reduced to a person of no consequence (*sünn-ed*). I have seen people fly into a murderous rage at challenges issued by their antagonists, such as '*Edi uidi ukabba*! – I have killed four people!' Implicit is always something like 'and you killed none' or, of course, 'I might well kill another one'.[31] In this way, one's social worth can be condensed into one's willingness to put one's life at stake in the act of assertion, of imposing one's will on the world; in a nutshell, of proving one's autonomy at the expense of others, even terminally so.

Killers of men (or women or children) undergo a purification ceremony with celebratory elements, the *mirt*. *Mirt* in general are the ritual occasions to hand over the archetypical trophy of the hunt to one's mother-brother, which cements one's status as a killer of big game.³² Through a *mirt* occasioned by homicide, one gains the right to have tiny scars cut all over one's arms and chest, one receives a new name often evoking the circumstances of the killing, and one literally gains boasting rights. In the case of killing an enemy, proof must be acquired – either the other's gun, or bloody cloth, or somesuch. In the past, the penis of the enemy was cut off, rendering the body *mingi*, maximally impure. Accordingly, simply killing enemies by sniping across the river does not 'count', nor does it satisfy the need for taking revenge in times of feuding.³³ A killer of one of the locally acknowledged Big Five (elephant, lion, leopard, buffalo and human – the beings that are recognized as dangerous opponents) is as a rule accorded some respect, and he gains the more quaint privileges of wearing certain types of jewellery at dances.³⁴ At any rate, most young men used to put considerable effort in their attempts to kill large game, and many elders seem to delight in the reputation of having taken human life. As mentioned above, such a reputation can become attached to age-sets. More commonly, though, the assertion of one's status is used to shame others, a quick way to escalate a conflict in any other arena. The relation between the sexes link up to this, as women often engage in such provocations as well.³⁵

School Boys and Herders
The Kara boys in Dimeka, Turmi and Jinka are a true phenomenon: numerous, distinct in their immaculate clothes and not shy about their presence in these places far away from their home. During the time of my fieldwork, going to school became an increasingly popular lifestyle choice for youths and young adults, as it offered an escape from the sometimes dreary chores of subsistence in Kara. The one activity that embodies this predicament above all is herding. Even though the Kara have very few cattle, and many do not even have large herds of goats, herding is an important activity in several respects: it is a way of getting pre-teen boys and young teenagers out from underfoot. They have no real duties in the settlements, and herding (though the tedium of it is acknowledged by the Kara) teaches many important qualities beyond the pastoralist techniques proper: patience, observation, subtlety, hunting, area knowledge, endurance and self-sufficiency.

The importance of animal husbandry for Kara subsistence is small, and even the secondary thesis that livestock can provide a 'drought insurance' for agropastoralists (see Turton 1980) in that it is possible to exchange animals for grain in more agricultural areas in different weather zones is untenable: the Kara are too far away from any demand that their supply could meet. True, bridewealth is measured in animals – 127 small stock (mostly goats) are supposed to be handed over to the family of one's wife eventually. Today, though, this number of animals is hardly ever collected. In fact, the going conversion rate of 'one rifle = forty goats' is looking more attractive by the year for the wife-givers. Who should

Figure 2.3 Rifles and *borkotto* put aside for a dance at Labuk (May 2006). Photograph by Felix Girke.

herd all these animals? This is where the Kara see themselves at a crossroads today: women cradle their newborns and quietly ask 'so, will you herd goats, or will you go to school?' When the smart and sophisticated schoolboys parade around Kara during holiday time, fathers cannot always stop their awestruck adolescent sons from absconding to school themselves, no matter what tasks await them at home. Even as money remains a constant worry in town, young boys and unmarried men in their early twenties are confident that they will find ways to make their education pay off. Many try to find sponsors among tourists, and quite a few succeed. Especially for those with many elder brothers, exit options from herding and the demands of cultivation are becoming attractive.

It was a common topic of discussion whether these young men would ever return for good, undergo the long initiation period and marry a Kara girl in the Kara way – or whether they would just stay in the towns, take up jobs in administration or business and discard their fathers' rituals. This has not yet, then, led to an antagonistic arena for clear-cut groups of schoolboys versus stay-at-home herders, but as every new age-set has an increasing proportion of students, lines will become clearer, and corporate interests, tempered by ambition, jealousy and frustration, will be at stake.

There was always distrust among Kara regarding both the schoolboys and the increasing number of young men who came to be employed in the administration. Would they use their training and their influence for the benefit of the community? Would they come back, stay and marry according to tradition? They might not: to be a *bärgi*-initiate for over a year, running around in a leather skirt – this seemed hardly attractive. Such reluctance created daunting problems for the younger brothers at home. The accusation that the educated ones will 'become highlanders' and shed their commitment to their proper home is common and publicly voiced. However, the Kara are already renowned throughout the region for the success of their schoolboys, and it turns out that success in pursuing education is becoming an identity marker for Kara.[36] Recent reports from Kara confirm that the last two groups of initiates, who leapt across the cattle in 2011 and 2014 respectively, were in fact granted a reduction of their ritual duties and especially the duration of their *bärgitamo* by the elders, so that all interests were reconciled.

The Young and the Very Old Ones: *Bersha* and *Yihr*
Beyond male youths being designated as schoolboys or herders, they are *bersha*, a term not applicable to females. This marks them discursively as those with energy and physical strength, but also with a lack of moderation in applying it. Young and rather recently married *zonza* in particular often exploit this and play on their double status, claiming to be both still youthful and vigorous, but also (solely due to the status of being married) wise, responsible and commanding. This is the time when they still go to the nightly dances, to dance and flirt with

young girls, when they still indulge in pursuits that might soon be inappropriate. The interplay of social and physical age occasionally leads to states of both 'neither–nor' or of 'both'; this affords discursive and interactional play, both in the presentation of self and in the designation of others. There are, however, some structural constraints to this.

Consider Orgo of the Nyichekapus age-set, in his mid-forties. His son is grown up, an Ologuita, who has no classificatory elder brothers and who would in principle be eligible for joining the next cohort of *bärgi-ed*. However, Orgo will refuse him: for when an eldest son marries, the parents automatically ascend to the status of *yihr-ed*. While I can offer little in regards to the etymology of this term, *yihr* – physically sometimes marked by certain beads worn around the neck – represents the highest ritual status most people can achieve in Kara. It affords increased respect and ritual prerogatives, including a more conspicuous burial, but at the same time, it imposes severe constraints on its bearers: they are to abstain from longer journeys, from hunting and warfare, from entering houses where dead people lie, and commensality is restricted with certain others – at the risk of debilitating sickness. Now, Orgo is a youthful and assertive, even somewhat educated man – he is not ready to become *yihr* and does not desire this status before the onset of frailty. This leaves him in a tight spot vis-à-vis his son, and my interlocutors hypothesized that at some point in the future, Orgo might accept this unreasonable retirement, because otherwise his own son might threaten and potentially kill him, just so that he himself can socially grow up and marry.

The automatism of *yihr*, then, can cause conflict within a *moro*. At the same time, the discursive conception of *yihr* as the epitome of achievement in sustaining the Kara population glosses over the restraints, which are clearly not in keeping with the times and might well be pragmatically lessened, just as the burdens of *bärgitamo* were. Youth and elderly, as is likely in any community where the gerontocratic principle is cultivated, interact through competing claims that tend to emphasize on the one hand vigour and purpose, and experience and status on the other. This comes to the fore as young men struggle for social recognition while still enjoying the liberty of a lack of responsibilities.

The Triumph of Community

After having dealt with some of its constituent elements, it is time to discuss the 'Kara community'. As has become clear from the previous sections, the various settlements, sections and statuses are interrelated in that they at least contribute to the sense of a coterminous whole. Not that there are no tensions or contradictions between claims and practice, but they are bounded in that they largely have relevance inside of Kara country only. They exert little influence beyond and are hardly influenced by outside developments. For example, unlike other areas of East Africa, the installation of an age-set is not accelerated by a corresponding process among one's inimical neighbours (compare Kurimoto 1998; Kurimoto and Simonse 1998; Schlee 1998).

There is, then, a practical, cognitive and affective context that I term the 'community'. While this resembles ways in which ethnicity is sometimes defined (see Brubaker 2004: 26), the ethnic here takes a backseat in that the ethnic heterogeneity of Kara is structurally tamed, reduced to one of many categories, by the normative and practical organization of the community. According to the claim of *ädamo*, Kara should understand themselves as members of a community that is both internally differentiated and externally bounded. And never the twain shall meet: the internal differentiations are not to interfere, ever, with the unified front presented to the outside. This is mostly visible in terms of population, settlements and when 'Kara' as a discursive and political formation exerts its agency vis-à-vis other similar polities, as modelled by the Wheel of Autonomy.

For individuals, the affective power of all that is Kara is grounded in that it is, quite literally, home. While there is a slowly growing trickle-out of individuals, away from the 'my father's land' (*abba-pe*), the Kara at large are at a loss in terms of how to deal with such decisions, interpreting them as incomprehensible, somewhat crazy or unreasonably spiteful. This autopersuasive nature of community is well expressed by Nigel Rapport:

> In short, 'community' describes the arena in which one learns and largely continues to practice being social. It serves as a symbolic resource, repository and referent for a variety of identities, and its 'triumph' (Cohen 1985: 20) is to continue to encompass these by a common symbolic boundary. (2000: 116)

This context, into which individuals become habituated as they grow up, changes over time, but – following Barth (1969) – its boundaries are actively maintained, with more or less plausible claims to difference. However, as I have shown, processes of identity maintenance that are so familiar from the study of ethnic groups, along and across their boundaries, take place within the community as well, just as Rapport suggests here. The phenomenon of the triumph of community, the fact that such an overarching and immaterial referent can survive and even sustain the constant processes of differentiation within, is what has tempted structural-functionalists to talk of 'equilibrium'.[37] But whatever stability does seem to exist is hardly mechanical. It comes out of the constant persuasive efforts, the hard work of people to keep their community feasible, to, as it were, create displays of equilibrium for themselves and others to see.

Rapport goes on to characterize community 'in terms of: (i) common interests between people; or (ii) a common ecology and locality; or (iii) a common social system or structure' (2000: 114). Common interests can go to the second order:

> it is common interests in achievable things (economic, religious, or whatever) that give members of a community a common interest in one another. Living face-to-face, in a small group of people, with common interests in mind, eventuates in community members sharing many-stranded or multiplex relations with one another; also sharing a sentiment towards the locality and the group itself. Hence, communities come to be marked by a fair degree of social coherence. (Rapport 2000: 115)

This works both ways. When the markers of coherence suddenly go missing, when the agreement falters on what the common interests even are, the entire community founders, and with it the proclaimed *raison d'être* of all interaction. 'To be marked', then, as Rapport says, is perfectly correct: community needs to be marked, people need to mark it vis-à-vis their co-members. 'Not marking' is an intentional activity as well: it is 'unmarking', 'denying', 'subverting' and finally 'betraying'. This is why renegades are so problematic and why challenges against the proclamation of common interests threaten the entire community. In Kara, this becomes manifest in the many invocations of *ädamo*, all of which are reminders of the importance of unity in spite of difference. An action that occasions an arena within Kara is an action that marks 'Kara'; it 'advocates' (Rapport 2000: 117) that people should belong and perpetuates claims about the relevance of community.

I need to mention the alternative to sustaining their community for the Kara, something by and large absent from the structural-functionalist texts about social structure and organization: it is not anomy or chaos or a state of nature,[38] but community on somebody else's terms. This danger of losing all the specific qualities that make a way of life so viable is quite real: in South Omo, several polities have been absorbed, assimilated or even annihilated in the past, and their examples are well-known. This awareness dramatizes the narrative existence of collective actors.

In Kara, the constant public displays of differentiation are not just a strain on the system. They are – but as a byproduct of the small-scale, intimate interactions that at the same time sustain the Kara community. Individuals' Wheels of Autonomy – while seemingly at odds – jointly move the political project 'Kara' forward.

This is not a proposition that purports to explain the existence of the social categories I have listed above. At best, it can serve to show why they are (still) affectively powerful and instrumentally important. The way in which social categories are selectively claimed or disclaimed is not merely an 'in principle' communicative process, as is all of social life. Much more than that, it reflects agonistic, intentional attempts to persuade oneself and others, to create a definition of a situation that always serves to constrain others' agency. But such processes are contingent, since depending on personal competence as well as *kairos*, the rhetorical grasp of just the right moment, they can work well or work badly.

I would not be surprised if some of the categories I discuss above were transformed or even abolished over the coming decades, going into institutional dormancy, or if different ones arose as changing circumstances make it possible and plausible to argue for their (ir)relevance. But there will always be categories that afford affiliation or in fact demand it, and that can become operational through the persuasive efforts of people. As elsewhere, this is an inextricable part of a Kara way of life with all its proclivities towards differentiation, which neither start nor stop with ethnicity. Gezahegn's statement on Kara unity and autonomy remains unsatisfactory: 'This sense of inter-clan solidarity is probably one of the main factors that unites the Karo [*sic*] and helps them to survive in the middle of strong and relatively wealthier neighbouring peoples' (1994: 55). While he understands the role of internal processes for external relations, his view stays firmly in the structural-functionalist camp by highlighting the functionality of institutions in maintaining unity only, disregarding their very real potential to tear apart the population of Kara. So with a nod to Plessner (2002), the radical immediacy of the Kara community is also oppressive and coercive, as it (also in the guise of *ädamo*) puts a premium on the subordination of personal interests to collective demands.[39]

To conclude this section on the 'triumph of community', there is a more general point to be made about a Kara notion of agency, about efficacy of groups, an understanding of how people in concert, be it institutionalized or ad hoc, can achieve their aims. As evidenced by many of the cases above, the Kara realize the importance of solidarity and unity of purpose. Whoever wants to achieve something in the social world needs to display closed ranks and unwavering decisiveness. A group that is indecisive, in that sense, is not even a group: consider the *borkotto bitti*, among whom such an understanding is part of the training of new candidates.

Linguistically, this finds expression as well: I often listened to accounts about groups of people who set out to do something or other, but failed as individuals got distracted. These stories ended unceremoniously with a conjoint gesture and exclamation: 'Zerr! [speaker spreads the fingers of both hands with palms down, moves apart their hands, and shrugs] Lalmo [turning the empty palms up].' *Zerr* is an ideophone, indicating a state of being scattered. For the image evoked, think of somebody scattering a bundle of wooden sticks across the ground. *Lalmo* is the noun-form of *lalma*, 'to be thwarted, confounded, foiled'. It is a common one-word statement and evokes an initially resolute group of (mostly) men dissolving into ineffectuality as each goes his own way. In this simple expression, a statement on the constitution of groups and on agency can be found. This notion is relevant for the rest of the book, when I turn to oppositions that are enacted no longer within a Kara frame of reference only, but vis-à-vis other local groups in the cultural neighbourhood and the (imagined) Ethiopian state. In a nutshell, community is maintained through the various internal conflicts; it is, so to speak, integrated by conflicts. But the unlikely outcome that it is in fact maintained by people's efforts despite all the actions that threaten it does validate Rapport and Cohen's phrase of the 'triumph of community'. Still, as individuals use the categories of being Kara as arenas for their displays of autonomy, some of them worry that the well-recognized proclivity towards differentiation might become too destructive. The next section takes up this sentiment.

The Schismogenetic Moment and its Discontents
I have had several conversations with Kara about the dynamics of their community, and uniformly, they showed an awareness of the constantly enacted differentiations. In part triggered by my own exasperation as I was witnessing yet another social drama along any of the lines established above, interlocutors laughingly or bitterly admitted 'we are a bit crazy like that'. This abstract worry was certainly not the only aspect of their culture and their social lives that people were critical about, but it is revealing that people explicitly said that much social drama went well beyond what was 'acceptable' in self-assertion. Even as public conflict provided much spice to everyday life and was avidly consumed as topics of gossip eventually turned into open drama, the degrees of violence and the contingency of it all had many Kara worried and frustrated. Igor Kopytoff has put it aptly: '*pace* introductory textbooks in anthropology, people do not always consider their culture to provide them with the best of all possible worlds' (1989: 66).

This section, then, serves to undercut a common approach pithily criticized by Michel de Certeau when discussing model-making in the social sciences: 'The unconsciousness of the group studied was the price that had to be paid (the price it had to pay) for its coherence' (1984: 56). But it is precisely the challenge that we need to face: how can whatever coherence there is exist in the face of consciousness and reflexivity? Already during fieldwork, I often confronted people directly with my interpretations of (and at times opinions about) their practices, eliciting their reflections on them. This tactic often afforded rich and extended conversations. Here, I give three examples of specific categories and their respective arenas where Kara voiced their opinion that social differentiation (and the entailed potential for antagonism) was detrimental for the community as developed above.

First, some people stated that the division of Dus into *ball*', the Nyuwaya and Nyiuwariya sections, was outdated, a relic from an earlier period that was no longer functional and thus was not needed: 'When I have a fight with people on my *ball*', said Galappo, 'I just come and sit on your *ball*' at night. It's not a big thing, it has nothing to it.' Others pointed out that young people did not even know the reason for the original division. Individuals had been switching without anyone meeting spiritual reprisals in the form of death or disease, so they said that the *ball'* should be abolished. Everybody should sit together, and there would be one reason less to squabble and bicker.

Second, the practice of celebrating killers was often criticized. While the *ball'* structure has hardly come to the attention of external actors, the cutting of scars, taking of names and boasting about homicide is a well-known feature of populations all over southern Ethiopia. State as well as NGO intervention talk is often strongly geared towards abolishing this practice (see Strecker and Pankhurst 2003; Pankhurst 2006). The somewhat simple assumption behind all these attempts at social engineering is that men kill in order to acquire a higher social status and, as it were, to impress the girls. Accordingly, to delegitimize the marks of a killer and the typical verbal boasts would be a way to make the status unattractive and pre-empt spirals of violence. But the Kara have always been aware of the fateful dynamics through which a killer can provoke an unblooded man into fits of frenzy and are able to disapprove of them without constant outside prompting. Killers' scars have not been cut, as far as I can tell, since 2003 at least. They and other trappings of the killer status have long been denounced as to be merely 'recent' innovations from Dassanech (Strecker 1976a). It is common today to hear disapproval both of killing outside of a legitimate state of war and of boasting about it, no matter how 'the kill' occurred. In a poetic moment, one elder told me that he wished his scars were 'like dirt which I could just rub off'.

However, the most vigorous critical stance I encountered was expressed by some young men vis-à-vis the so strongly entrenched group of *borkotto bitti* – they themselves being junior members of the group. '*Ke shide! Kalun, kalun!* – may it stay behind, fully, completely!' This challenge requires some context. For one thing, the installation of new *borkotto bitti* sows distrust even between age-mates, as some (who feel themselves worthy) feel anger at not having been chosen. Furthermore, one of the rules is that people are not to infringe on *borkotto bitti* who go about their business – unsurprisingly, the new recruits, upon being selected into the club, found that the previous intimacy they had been enjoying with their peers was disrupted. Yet, misgivings towards this self-appointed committee, which prides itself on the oratorical skills and the wisdom of its members, have more to draw on than the hurt pride of individuals who were just 'not good enough'. Around the year 2000, a quarrel from among the *borkotto bitti* of Nyuwaya nearly tumbled that whole section into a fratricidal war. Some old, leading members had called a meeting and chose not to invite three others, all respected elders, and used the occasion to install several young men as new *borkotto bitti*. When the others got wind of this blatant affront, they were upset. Demanding that the newly recruited members be removed again, they claimed that the instigators of this ploy had transgressed. When they were refused, they set up their own *borkotto bitti* group, and themselves installed a group of other young men of the Nyuwaya section. What was left of the Nyuwaya started to take sides in this power struggle. People went armed, with sticks or even guns. At some point, the people from Labuk and Nyuwaria decided to intervene in large numbers and mediate in order to prevent bloodshed. In addition to this dangerous antagonistic potential, I encountered the suggestion that today the institution of *borkotto bitti* had become hypertrophic. There were too many already, and still others were being inducted – obviously, my interlocutors intimated, the selection of members was no longer based on virtues of wisdom and prudence, if in fact it ever had been. This critical attitude towards the claim that the *borkotto bitti* truly act on behalf of the community implied that upkeep of the leaders' elite status had become as important as the public weal.[40] This is why they provocatively (if in a private setting) called for their abolition. According to them, the dangers of elevating individuals over their friends and age-mates – thus inducing both arrogance and embitterment – alongside their growing ineffectuality made the *borkotto bitti* more of a liability than an asset. This was not a universal opinion among the Kara, but it seemed to be gaining ground. The institution does entail a constant flouting of other interactional norms, such as the egalitarian ethos of Kara, and the public nature of decision-making. When Kara reflect about the 'land of tomorrow' (*saxa pe*), they also wonder whether the *borkotto bitti* will lead them well into the future.

So Who Are 'They'?

I initially inquired 'how do they do it?' and intimated that beyond the 'how', the 'they' might be the real issue. This chapter provides a partial answer: the Kara have much to 'feel Kara' about, and the triumph of community is a palpable part of Kara life. The intensity of interaction along the categories of being Kara induces a sense of belonging to some coherent entity, that is very much discontinuous with what lies beyond politically, ritually, territorially, linguistically and institutionally. Beyond this passive sense of belonging, there is an awareness of how one personally contributes to the political project 'Kara', and there are a good number of people – such as the *borkotto bitti* – who visibly labour towards keeping the population united, even in the face of the lamented proclivity towards differentiation. In the best of times, all internal squabbles are immediately moot when an outside threat looms; in the worst of times, a minor issue might lead to a major schism. But not inevitably: the Kara would never absolve themselves from blame if they felt the social equilibrium was endangered. *Ädamo* is one expression of this sense of the manmade nature of community, this emic constructivism. It evokes responsibility and accountability of every person to handle their social relationships well. The 'they', then, is paralleled by a strong 'we', which I understand as an ongoing rhetorical achievement.

In the following chapter, I turn to the position of the Bogudo within the Kara population and how it relates to claims of *ädamo*. The discussion continues with my methodological focus on the Wheel of Autonomy, and various populations' attempts to assert themselves and protect their interests and their capacity for action. The categories that are used in attempts to define situations from here onwards include the ethnic labels used within Kara.

Notes

1. I use 'arena' as suggested by F.G. Bailey, namely: 'When it is necessary to refer to competitive interaction in a general way, the word used will be *arena*' (1969: 88). The term has come into common usage in political anthropology for rule-bound (ant-)agonistic struggles over a prize; however, the specific uses often diverge from Bailey's original suggestion (Bailey 1960: 5; also Lewellen 1983: xx).
2. As these absences are largely seasonal at this point, it remains to be seen what happens when more and more children actually finish school.
3. Jack Stauder's monograph on *The Majangir* (1971) pithily associates hierarchies of social interaction through degrees of commensality with settlement arrangements, which is rather applicable to Kara. Fortes (1969: 236) already had suggested the interactional salience of degrees of commensality.
4. The term *zersi* is also used in the same way as the Amharic *hizb*, as 'general populace'. I have come to differentiate these two uses by checking how agency is allocated: 'Go and tell the *zersi*' points to a different usage than 'The *zersi* have decided', where the latter refers to a proper group of elders.
5. Another term for this house is *galma*, which Gezahegn (1994: 46) points out is an Oromo word indicating a sacred place. There allegedly used to be more *marmar* in the Omo Valley. An earlier one across the river was dismantled when the Nyangatom threat arose, and in the recent and yet mythic past, 'when they were still great', both Bogudo and Gomba are said to have had their own ritual houses. I heard that some fragments of the old Gomba *marmar* could still be seen somewhere upriver in the forest, but never went to check.
6. After the maturation of the Ologuita age-set in 2004, there were some derisive comments in Dus that the Labuk people had included boys who – from their physical development – would not have been included in Dus. The suggestion was that the northern Kara had attempted to artificially bolster the strength of this age-set, for a vague benefit; namely, an immediate rather than staggered increase of the adult male population.
7. Not surprisingly, this was true for me as well. I was a Dus person and never achieved the same degree of familiarity and involvement with more than just a few of the inhabitants of Labuk. While unfortunate from a research perspective, this was somewhat inevitable.
8. This is an Amharic loanword (also spelt *mahabir*). It came into common usage when the Derg regime set up peasant associations all over the country in the 1970s and 1980s.
9. Tourism in South Omo is organized largely through companies based in Addis Ababa, which offer prepackaged 'best-of South Omo' tours. Stops and sights will be 'bull-jumping' in Hamar, the 'authentic' Mursi village, market day in Key Afer, 'traditional Dassanech' in Omo Rate and the 'picturesque village' of Korcho overlooking the Omo. Individual, self-organized tourism is rare and difficult due to the persistent problem of transportation.

10. In my understanding, this was mostly due to four factors: the intermittently horrible state the road from Korcho to Dus, the spectacular panorama across the Omo River and Lake Diba from the cliffs of Korcho, the comfortable Murule lodge and the recently established Gora campsite below Korcho. Individual brokerage might also play a role.
11. As concerns the depiction of Kara country on that map, none of Dus, Labuk and Garchi have been correctly localized. The Frobenius-Expedition, from which the *Altvölker* resulted, never reached Kara.
12. This, then, is obviously a story that recounts the old glory of the Kara. Today, no cattle are slaughtered for hospitality, no matter how important or festive the occasion.
13. The occurrence of the motif of 'one faction decided not to share meat with some others' as triggering a violent separation in both the establishment of the *ball* as well as the doom of the Garchi indicates the significance of this cultural theme. Kopytoff (1989: 49) outlines that mythic clashes in African oral history are often explained by disputes about meat. With similar resonance, the motif of some people wanting to spare their sons a heavy beating also occurred when some Kara told me why they and the Moguji of Kuchur no longer performed age-set initiations together: the Moguji were too brutal (compare Chapter 4).
14. For the Hamar-Banna-Bashada (HBB) cluster, see Strecker (1976a), Lydall and Strecker (1979b) and Epple (2007: 64–67). The equivalent categories are called *gir* in Hamar and *ger* in Bashada, and also refer to moieties, which do not exist in Kara.
15. Kara keep these two meanings of *moro* strictly apart. 'A *moro*' is also specified by names or pronouns, while in the second sense it is a general descriptor of land. Very similar in fact to Mursi language (see Turton 1973: 109), a word pair distinguishes between 'inhabited' and 'uninhabited' places, *or* and *gai* in Mursi, and *moro* and *kau* in Kara respectively. One is tempted to infer language contact here.
16. It is significant that these conciliatory rituals, which consist in the respective heads washing their hands with the dissolved fat of animals slaughtered by both sides, and consumption of bits of meat by every single member of both *moro*, are near-identical to the specific peace-making ritual between Kara and their western neighbours, the Nyangatom.
17. In Kara, *abiyo* as well as the term of reference *abui* are considered to derive from the Hamar language, the closely related lingua franca of the region. However, the fact that the term also exists in Rendille (Schlee, personal communication; see also Schlee 1994c), and possibly among other similarly distant groups, shows how insufficiently the Omo Valley has yet been studied as the cultural node of Omotic, Cushitic and Nilotic groups. Much of this entanglement might be traceable linguistically. A comparison of lexemes indicates surprising distribution of words. I suspect that the 'Korre' (probably Samburu), Kenyan enemies of the Hamar in the nineteenth century, left a linguistic legacy that bridges language families even today, just as they left stone monoliths that also endure (see Epple 2007).
18. There is a way around this in the *baski* relation between a man (married or unmarried) and a widow, where this is not a central concern. As children born of such a union are considered to be offspring of the dead husband, the preferred arrangement in Kara is for a man to take over the wife of a deceased clansman or other *äda*, so that his bodily children would not be his *chaachi*. A kind of levirate where a man takes over the wife of a deceased uterine brother is strictly prohibited in Kara. I only found one case in which expediency overruled this taboo. This is poignant because both sexual intercourse with the elder uterine brother's wife and *baski* relations with the brother's widow are encouraged within the wider HBB cluster. In general, *baski* partners in Kara pursue economic, sexual

and procreational interests, and that such a partnership lacks ritual or legal constraints has the effect that interaction between the partners can be less distant and more casual than within a proper marriage.
19. The rules for marriage across ethnic boundaries in Kara will be discussed in Chapter 3. By and large, there is a tendency for hypogyny in that men will marry girls from ritually lower-placed ethnic categories as second and third wives.
20. Lydall and Strecker provide the etymology of *bitta*, the parallel Hamar institution, as 'the first': the Hamar *bitta* was the first to enter the land and to call people from all the surrounding areas to become his subjects (1979b). In the major Kara arrival story, the *bitti* do not feature. If one specifically enquires about the origin of the *bitti*, one will likely be told that they led the people to the Omo Valley from Arbore (see Chapters 6 and 7).
21. Other eminent rituals are performed by the senior elders in Dus, such as the *gaita-märsha*, the blessing of hand-hoes when the agricultural season starts. When people return to Dus from their cultivation sites, the *kogo-ed*, the 'firestick-man' (not of the Kogo clan) ignites a new fire for the coming year: all fires in all houses are extinguished, and with his ritual drill, he creates a new flame with which the branches brought by every single homestead are lit up. Afterwards, they are carried away, and this very same fire always burns in some hearth until the next year (compare Lydall and Strecker 1979b: 116f).
22. For an extended discussion of the *borkotto bitti* of Kara, see Girke (2011).
23. Before acquiring this specific right, male youths use a simple three-legged stool they themselves cut out of long branches. This is called a *yedda borkotto*, likely from the verb *yedda*, 'to take hold of'.
24. I call this political maturation, as it determines inclusion into debates and decision-making. It has no bearing on qualification for marriage and nor is age-set membership in any way a prerequisite for participation in warfare – 'whoever wants to, can go', I was told. Often, though, age-mates stick together during war, as mutual familiarity from hunting and other pursuits are assets on the battlefield.
25. A comprehensive list of Kara age-sets would require not only attention to the differences between Labuk, Nyuwaya and Nyiuwariya, but would also have to include the different names for the individual age-sets (three to four in cases) and their respective provenience.
26. This is actually not entirely true – when certain information is handed down the age ladder, often those representatives of an age-set are first informed whose fathers belonged to the most senior age-sets. As regards ego, there is also the possibility to praise someone as *hariya-imba*, 'the father of the age-mates', indicating a most prized and most loyal of all age-mates. This, however, is expressed situationally and not institutionally.
27. Gezahegn (1994: 71) claims that such proto-age-sets were called 'nyanyok'. I never heard the word myself, but eventually was told that the Nyangatom word 'nyayuk' is occasionally used by Kara as a term of address or reference to a bunch of children. It does not designate a social category.
28. The Kara recognize childhood friendships that endure into adult life, calling them *yeti*, indicating people who stuck together, hunting-friends many times over, and who helped each other court girls. Such intimacy is rarely achieved with *äda*.
29. Nadine Brückner from Leipzig University has undertaken research that promises to shed more light on female age-sets. In my experience, men acknowledged the existence of the female age-sets, but never took them particularly seriously. Nor did my female informants.
30. Due to the rare and unpredictable occurrence of this initiation procedure, I was only able to observe a few of the activities of the *bärgi-ed* and never the more challenging tasks they

had to resolve for the elders. Nor have I ever attended the initiation-sealing 'leap across the cattle', which also only occurs every couple of years.
31. One curmudgeon in Kara liked to exclaim 'I have killed 99 people!', leaving the interpretation to the addressee.
32. See Girke and Köhn (2007) for the case of a leopard hunt.
33. See Girke (2008) for an example how such an event triggered a war. For a useful overview of boasting, see Meyer (2005).
34. See Degu and Fischer for a slightly different presentation, which only draws partially on Kara (2013: 449–50). Their Bashada informants include giraffe in the list (as did Gezahegn (1994)), which considering that animal's absolute rarity in the region seems to me anachronistic or even nostalgic.
35. E.C. Gabbert's work on Arbore analyses such cases in depth. In Arbore, such provocations have a poetic form and seem more strongly institutionalized.
36. This important development is discussed further in Chapter 6.
37. See Seymour-Smith (1986: 94); Fortes and Evans-Pritchard (1940); Bailey (2003: 69ff).
38. However, the worry about a 'state of nature' that must be actively kept at bay has discursive weight vis-à-vis the Moguji (see Chapter 5).
39. This problematic is further explored in a comparative paper about 'harmony ideology' co-written with Judith Beyer, which juxtaposes the *ädamo* of the Kara with the Kyrgyz notion *yntymak* (Beyer and Girke 2015).
40. Compare the discussions in Epple (2007: 51) on the Bashada spokesmen and Strecker (1976a: 60) on Hamar. In the more dispersed settlements of these mountain dwellers, individual hamlets select single representatives who speak in larger internal arenas on behalf of their sections or negotiate with administrators when required. While she discusses the office only briefly, Epple states that 'the *ayo* [spokesmen] cannot make any decision without the consent of the community' (ibid.). For the Kara, my comparative claim is that the *borkotto bitti* quite consciously try and keep the community in a state where it routinely complies with the fait accompli statements presented by the *borkotto bitti* when they talk the talk of the land in public after having deliberated in private. The *borkotto bitti* are the central topic of Girke (2011).

Chapter 3
Ethnicity within Kara
The Demotion of the Bogudo

Ethnicity can – in one and the same place – be both practically activated and formally conceptualized in quite different ways. The case of the Bogudo of Kara demonstrates this: in this social drama, influential actors rhetorically transformed the ethnic field itself.

Of the various ethnic categories that can be encountered within Kara, the Bogudo are – while numerically insignificant – the ritually highest and especially in terms of land ownership the most important population section vis-à-vis the true Kara. As I mentioned earlier, the 'true Kara' category goes unmarked in speech in the sense that there is a segment of the population at large (within which everybody is 'a Kara') that does not have a more specific ethnic qualifier attached to it. Some people are Kara, but are also Moguji. Others are Kara, but are also really Nyangatom. He is a Kara, sure, but he is actually Bashada. And finally, some are simply Kara. They are numerically the majority, too, but not equally dominant in all settlements. The true Kara hold large tracts of land along the river; they have the strictest ritual requirements; members of this category occupy most of the influential positions; and they have the privilege of embodying the ideal members of the polity. The history of 'the Kara' as it is told in Kara is really the history of the 'true Kara', with everybody else appearing in minor roles or bit parts at best. While there is no distinct label that the true Kara or others use to identify this category, the awareness of who is true Kara and who is not never dissipates.

During the time of my fieldwork, a unique event triggered a complex dynamic that forced me to rethink the relation between true Kara and Bogudo, and that revealed to me the situational nature of social categories. In principle, the ethnic categories of Kara allow no ambiguity. While some liminal and temporary exceptions exist, every grown-up male is firmly located within one category only and will never be able to change ethnicity within the context of Kara: one is a true Kara, a Bogudo, a Gomba, a Moguji or a Nyangatom-Kara. The situation is somewhat different for children and for women who are married out: ethnic exogamy leads to women getting married to men who belong to a different ethnic category. In practice, things get fuzzy at this point, as women occasionally act as if they were both A and B. Children can even be in ethnic limbo for a while until their classificatory belonging has been agreed upon.

The modalities of these ethnic identities do not follow one simple template. 'Moguji-ness' is another sort of ethnic identity than 'Bogudo-ness', and both only gain a clear outline when viewed from within Kara, that is, in the interaction among people belonging to the categories of Kara. The model of ethnic identities that I pursue here does not posit such categories (let alone groups) standing side by side, which are then, in a second step, related to one another. Instead, their relatedness in practice is their constitutive feature at any point in time, and this is always an achievement of often antagonistic human struggles over who gets to impose order on an inchoate world of disorderly similarity and regular difference. Accordingly, actions that threaten (or promise) to change the specific relations between such categories are consequential, in that they challenge the social status quo and the power relations it supports.

As its prime example, this chapter describes the decision by some Bogudo to stop performing a certain ritual. This was treated as a challenge to the ritual order by the true Kara, who – in a move running counter to the default Kara understanding of how ethnicity works – responded by recategorizing the actors involved as ritually inferior Gomba.

The Flight of Uba and the Degrees of Being Kara

In the later months of 2006, when I was staying with the Kara who were cultivating their riverbank gardens near Chelläte, I heard the rumour that Uba had run away from the northern village of Labuk. She was now staying with her brother in the area of Kundamma and, while I had never met Uba personally, she was familiar to me from a kinship diagram that I had constructed some time ago: the third wife and sole surviving widow of Mero, the son of Peysa. She was one of the Bogudo from Labuk.

What had made Uba run away from her homestead in the middle of the farming season? Initially, nobody had a ready answer. Slowly, though, more details trickled in, when people coming from the north visited our fields. The people around me were placidly curious to learn more, and from the visitors we eventually learned that there had been a quarrel within the *moro*, the lineage of Peysa. Nabikolma, the son of Nyaxai Peysa, along with his younger brothers, supposedly had declared that they, despite being Bogudo, would as of now no

Figure 3.1 At rare times, a sudden flood clouds the river so that the dazed fish can be harvested with knives (January 2007). Photograph by Felix Girke.

longer abort or kill *kumbassa* children. *Kumbassa*, in brief, indicates a state of pregnancy that is not ritually sanctioned. The main consequence is that the newborn will be killed upon birth and that over the course of the *kumbassa* pregnancy, husband and wife are submitted to a number of prohibitions, as their spoilt fertility is seen as polluting and contagious. *Kumbassa* comes about through disregard of proper rituals.[1]

Nabikolma implied that Aike, the son of his father Nyaxai's younger brother Mero, should follow him in this regard. This relationship meant that Aike was technically Nabikolma's younger brother. Uba, as Mero's third wife also Aike's classificatory mother (if not by birth), had disagreed and had declared that she would not surrender this custom. She had made a big spectacle out of her disagreement by removing herself bodily from the contentious site where the declaration had been made. With this, she had claimed authority over her deceased husband's branch of the lineage, effectively opposing the offspring of her husband Mero's elder brother Nyaxai.

These events could be framed as a social drama, the model proposed by Turner in Max Gluckman's seminar to afford a 'window into Ndembu social organization and values' (Turner 1985: 5). To assign the typical stages of a Turnerian social drama to the consecutive events: Nabikolma's declaration was the breach, Uba's protest was the crisis, and the ensuing reaction of other sections of the Kara population constituted redress and reintegration. Indeed, to do justice to the drama metaphor, there was an aspect of spectacle present, a sense of rising tension and most certainly an audience that was observing. This audience, in the end, issued a judgement.

I could not observe these first two stages and only gathered first-hand data on the reaction of the audience, but in any case my methodological approach steers away from the analysis of actor- or orator-centred performance towards a rhetorical analysis that works backwards from the reactions of an audience. Both in performative approaches or symbolic interactionism, or in fact Kara practice, public reactions trump the main actors' professed motivations, as in the long run it is the public – here the *zersi* – that decides what actions signify, regardless of what the actors themselves might claim.

The lineage under consideration here is one of two branches of Bogudo still extant in Kara and in terms of members is by far the larger one. Peysa, who is long dead, is considered nothing less than its genuine founding father, which amounts to a rather shallow historical depth, considering that Uba, the wife of his son Mero, is still alive. While there might be some old people who remember Peysa's father's name, it is not general knowledge within the population at large. One common explanation for this, as is so often the case in Kara, was the mysterious sleeping sickness, the *gind'o*, which laid waste to the country, killing off livestock and decimating people around the end of the nineteenth century.[2] Peysa had been an orphan, the sole survivor of his family, and he had been brought up by a specific Gomba section, the Kuldé, a name I never encountered in any other context. Like the Kuldé, Peysa's *moro* is of the Gorsbolo clan, while the second Bogudo *moro*, in southern Kara, belongs to the Eshiba clan.

Now, who or what are the Bogudo and the Gomba? They are among a number of enigmatic ethnic survivals still to be found in South Omo (such as the Murle; see Tornay (1981), (2007)),[3] which are alternately assimilating, co-residing and taking on client status vis-à-vis dominant patron populations. In fact, the Bogudo and the Gomba had already been written off: Ivo Strecker, getting his information from Hamar, thought them lost, absorbed by the Kara. The Bogudo, he claimed, were living on as 'low-class clans and lineages' (1976a: 16). The Gomba, faring even worse, were forgotten, 'only the Kara having some vague memory of them' (1976a: 21). Gezahegn, actually having done research in Kara, realized the Bogudo existed, but found them 'inaccessible ... no informant ... could site me [a household]' (1994: 15). He did, however, talk to some Gomba (1994: 9ff) and collected information on their position within the population of Kara country. In fact, both groups have been 'absorbed' by the Kara, but the nature of this absorption is not seamless assimilation. Matsuda stumbles into the same trap by claiming of the Gomba and the Bogudo that 'neither cultural identities nor languages remain' (2007: 340). While it is unclear what languages the ancestors of either might have spoken, distinct 'identities' are clearly still extant and, as this book discusses, it is a central matter of Kara social life to negotiate their role in the larger community. Bassi (2011: 147) has attempted to reconcile Gomba narratives of their migration to Kara with the early explorers' accounts. As the present case illustrates, their story is not over, and the complex interaction rules between them and other sections of the Kara population indicate that they occupy an important position within the body politic that is Kara.

The late Kolga-imba, one of the Kara elders whose version of the history of the land was usually not challenged, emphatically told me some months before the drama of Uba's flight occurred that 'Bogudo *are* Kara!' The only difference, he said, was that they did not leap across the cattle as the Kara did. Their *zonza* (elders) could even sit together with their Kara peers in the *marmar*, the sacred ritual house in Dus, the political and spiritual centre of the land. Like most true Kara, the Bogudo (and the Gomba) are landowners, but there is no commonly narrated story of their arrival in the Omo Valley. Neither are the Bogudo and Gomba included in the Kara narratives of how their forefathers found the river (see Chapter 4; see also Kopytoff 1989).

What Kolga-imba failed to mention regarding the relation between true Kara and the Bogudo was either too obvious, being so central to the relations of true Kara (like himself) to virtually everybody else, or practically 'unspeakable': never has the daughter of a true Kara been married to someone who had not leapt across the cattle in Kara. That is, even the Hamar, Banna and Bashada in their mountains, who share many rituals with the Kara and who leap across the cattle as well (with some variation in the set-up; see Lydall and Strecker 1979b; Gezahegn 1994: 79–84), are not eligible. Neither are the Bogudo, nor any of the other subsections of the Kara population. This prohibition has to my knowledge never lapsed among the Kara, and it has only been challenged very tentatively (and without success) by non-Kara. I suggest that this fact might be an 'unspeakable' in that it embodies the true relations of inequality, the fundamental failure of reciprocity and mutuality in Kara, which is so stark as to challenge the foundations of the co-residence of the ethnic categories that segment the population. To not mention it, then, conceals protectively the fundamental contradiction between the demands of *ädamo* (that is, positive social relatedness, connectedness, a mutuality of social persons) and the hierarchy of ethnic categories in Kara, which, while practised visibly every day, tends to be downplayed. Thus, this prohibition to marry true Kara girls is not hidden in a way that causes the other groups to be unaware of it, but in a way that excludes it from being publicly problematized. To make it an issue, then, would cast aspersions on the public claim of *ädamo*, which denies domination while being its embodiment, and accordingly would be a challenge against the dominant true Kara. While other sections of the Kara population might grumble about this duplicity offstage, they seem to refrain from articulating their dissatisfaction in more visible arenas. However, the practice of 'true Kara' female endogamy needs to be juxtaposed with another element of Kara marriage rules – how true Kara become 'full Kara'.

'Mullah should leave his studies and come back here to marry', announced one of my elderly classificatory sisters when she was visiting my house in Dus. She was talking about one of my host-brothers, who was then completing Grade 10 in the somewhat distant regional centre Jinka. She continued, '*Kara kimate, edi kimate*! – So that he may become a Kara, so that he may become a person!' Through this harangue, I got an early indication of how defining of male social personhood the ritual leap across the cattle is. Was Mullah, at the age of twenty-something, whose age-set was fully initiated, not yet a Kara, not yet a person? This vivid outburst opened a window on the question of becoming 'full Kara'.[4] Anybody born of a woman married to someone who is already classified as 'true Kara' is also counted as a 'true Kara'. Formally, they will be the child of the true Kara husband, regardless of whether that individual is actually dead or alive. This, then, does not presume that the actual genitor needs to be true Kara. The important step is that a woman has been transformed into a legitimate true Kara genitrix through marriage with a man who has leapt across the cattle.

It is also possible for a true Kara man to marry a non-true Kara woman and beget children before his leap across the cattle. This is often the case when, through the vagaries of birth order and seniority, an individual is blocked from initiation into a *bärgitamo* marriage-group well beyond his social coming-of-age. A single unmarried brother of one's father is enough to disqualify a man from performing the leap across the cattle. Since the wives of a man can continue to bear 'his' children long after their husband has perished, it is relatively common for men to be older than their father's younger brother. However, in the case of a marriage to a non-true Kara woman, which provides an 'out' of the procreatory cul de sac of some genealogical positions, the children begotten through the marriage with such a wife (be she a Gomba, a Nyangatom or even an Ethiopian from the highlands) are not true Kara until their genitor has leapt across the cattle and has become a 'full Kara' himself. If the husband would happen to die before leaping across the cattle eventually, the children would not count as being his, and his wife would not technically be his widow. This is the true implication of the statement of my elderly sister: a man needs to leap in order to gain the legitimacy to swell the numbers of the true Kara. Besides true Kara girls, only Bogudo can be taken as first wives after the leap across the cattle – as Kolga-imba said, they 'are Kara' after all. A wife married before the leap (by necessity non-true Kara) is by default 'demoted' to junior wife after the leap, her children assuming secondary positions in terms of genealogy. This means that all male offspring of a non-true Kara wife who was married by her husband before he made his leap grow up with a disconcerting certainty: they will have to wait for the as-yet-unborn sons of a future 'properly' married true Kara wife to leap across the cattle before they can do it themselves, regardless of their greater age. And so it continues.

Thus, the Bogudo are not Kara, but nearly as Kara as the true Kara themselves. Their girls are occasionally married as first wives by the true Kara, but their sons are not to leap across the cattle and may never marry a true Kara girl. The Bogudo, unsurprisingly, mimetically apply this principle as well: while they have given wives to the Gomba, they would not give wives to a group one ritual tier below the Gomba in the ethnic scaling of Kara: the Moguji (see Chapter 4).

If one now looks at a Bogudo family such as the *moro* of Peysa, and especially considers the provenience of the in-married women, it does not come as a surprise that they have diverse backgrounds. Uba herself is a Nyangatom-Kara, whose ancestors at some point came to Kara, like so many others, and happened to stay. Others are 'true Nyangatom', some are Mursi, some are Gomba, and one of Uba's co-wives was a Bogudo herself, from the southern branch belonging to the Eshiba clan. With that marriage, the two Bogudo lineages have become each other's mother-brothers and sister-sons, and accordingly, for several generations, further intermarriage between Bogudo and Bogudo is quite out of the question.

In day-to-day politics or larger debates on how to handle affairs of 'the Bogudo', the Bogudo branch from the south (based in the village of Korcho and at Lake Diba) does not really figure. Nobody from Labuk went to consult with them, they did not raise their voices and they did not articulate a claim or a competing strategy of how to react to Nabikolma's manoeuvre of rejecting the *kumbassa* practice. The one obvious reason for their inaction is that at the time of the events, there was not a single male Bogudo elder of the southern Eshiba clan alive. The last one, Balacho, the son of Borana (a well-remembered leader and true spiritual 'father of the land'), is survived by his widow and a few children. The eldest son was at this time in training as a short-track athlete in Addis Ababa, and it was far from certain when (or even if) he might return to Kara to marry and to assume the leadership of his lineage. His mother, Balacho's wife, while old and respected, is not a Bogudo by birth, but a Gomba. People acknowledge her competence in the domestic and ritual affairs of the southern Bogudo, but she has little public voice in discussions spanning all of Kara country.

As a Gomba woman, Balacho's wife has been married 'out', having had to leave the northern part of Kara for good. This is another part of the mosaic: while there are really only three Gomba *moro* in Labuk, they do make up a sizeable proportion of the population. In quotidian life, Nabikolma and his family are connected, through multiplex bonds, to the Gomba, so there might be fewer disincentives to become Gomba. But why 'become Gomba'? Because this is precisely what they were doing, according to the opinion that gradually emerged in the rest of Kara country, as Uba remained in her self-imposed exile near Dus.

Adjusting the Categories

Mero, Uba's dead husband, had been very close to many of his Gorsbolo clanmates, especially to true Kara from Dus. In discussions I attended, Uba was portrayed as acting in the spirit of her dead husband when she refused the proposition to give up the *kumbassa* principle for childbearing. Her own 'ethnic' (patrilineal) background, as Nyangatom-Kara, was not considered to figure in the motivation for her actions; according to Nyangatom practice, unmarried women can very well become pregnant and bear out their children, in a way that is rather similar to the procedure installed by Nabikolma and rejected by Uba.

However, as events developed, it turned out that while the wider public speculated about Nabikolma's or Uba's motives, the important response lay in settling on a new modus operandi. But why did the true Kara come to the conclusion that the Bogudo were becoming Gomba? It certainly seemed confusing to me, since – while the past of both groups is shrouded in sleeping sickness-induced mystery – I had assumed that the supposed historical and descent-based origin of the ethnic segments was the defining moment for the set-up of their contemporary relations. Certainly the Kara had not 'meant', I first assumed, that this branch of the northern Bogudo was becoming Gomba, but that they were behaving 'like' Gomba. But soon, I felt more and more that I was asking the wrong question, trying to apply categories prestructured according to my expectations and assumptions. Any relevance of the events lay not in some sort of essence of the ethnic categories, but in the interactional realities. The northern

Bogudo were behaving like Gomba, and so they were turned into Gomba, and it was a categorical problem primarily for me.

It occurred to me then, whereas it had been fully obvious to the Kara from the beginning, too obvious even to point out to me, that what Nabikolma had really indicated when he said that the Bogudo would drop the *kumbassa* practice: not only would his unmarried and pregnant sister give birth to her child and keep it, but that his entire lineage would also give up the *yekinta*, a washing ritual involving the wife, the husband's mother and the husband. In order to underline the magnitude of this step, a few comments on ritual practice are required.

Of the rituals that accompany and mark female fertility, the *bula* and *gori* rituals, postnatal rituals for the newborn, are observed not only by the 'mountain people' (the Hamar, Banna and Bashada), but by most of the sections of the Kara population (see Brüderlin (2005) for the Hamar; and Gezahegn (1994: 61–65) for the Kara). True Kara and Bogudo have both *gori* and *bula*, Gomba and Nyangatom-Kara have the *bula*, and Moguji living in Kara might or might not enact the *bula*. Many Kara I talked to were personally not even sure about which ethnic subsection performed which of these rituals. The *yekinta*, however, is a determining feature of true Kara and Bogudo. Its enactment prepares both new brides and married woman for pregnancy, as it legitimizes conception. It has to be performed at the start of a woman's period, before a pregnancy sets in, and again once or twice in the following months, depending on the seniority status of the wife. As it requires participation of the husband's mother, it entails social control of the mother-in-law over her son and his wife, and several times, from overheard offhand remarks, I gathered that people do pay close attention to their neighbours' *yekinta*. If one knows what to look for, the comings and goings in a mother-in-law's homestead are plain to read. Constant conversations about the legitimacy or illegitimacy of pregnancies show the significance of the ritual. Such gossip takes its extreme form in the glee of having discovered a ritual misbehaviour.

While these rituals – the *gori*, *bula* and *yekinta* – determine the legitimacy of pregnancy, they are, as this case vividly illustrates, also markers of ethnic categories. I will return to this point below. For now, it is important to note that the true Kara started speaking up: if Nabikolma and whoever was with him on this issue, if they truly gave up the *yekinta*, some elders said among themselves, 'we will no longer sit with them to drink *parsho* beer'. This is no small thing. As a reminder of the manifold restrictions of commensality between Kara and Gomba (and Kara and Moguji; see Chapter 4), which are a highly salient feature of ritual practice, this statement referred to much more than just beer. The relative importance of this ritual is indicated by the differing role of the *yekinta*-equivalent among the 'mountain people' (the Hamar, Banna and Bashada). Lydall and Strecker (1979b: 146f) report a near-identical ritual for the Hamar, but neither provide its name nor accord it specific importance in the ritual domain.

However, the true Kara emphasize the *yekinta* because they co-reside with people who do not follow this prescription, whereas the Hamar live in a much more homogeneous social environment, where this ritual does not serve as a diacritical marker of distinction.[5]

In giving up the *yekinta*, which was listed by a didactically-minded Kara friend – along with the male marriage initiation known as the 'leap across the cattle' – as one of the two most important rituals of the true Kara, Nabikolma conjured up an imaginary of the history of the Bogudo, of his own very lineage. He highlighted the image of the poor orphan Peysa (his father's father), the only one left of their entire people, brought up by Gomba: under the Gomba's tutelage and care, the family had again blossomed and grown. An oracle, Nabikolma declared, had revealed to him the reasons for the historical disaster, for the question as to why the Bogudo had been so horrendously struck by the *gind'o* disease: they had become too much like the Kara, that is, too much like the true Kara. They had tried too strongly to emulate in ritual someone who was really an 'other', and for this they had been nearly wiped out. So, following the example of Peysa, who was brought up by the Gomba of his clan, the Bogudo should obey Gomba ritual rules in order to prosper and grow. Such a circular argument – 'our grandfathers died being Bogudo [i.e. acting like true Kara], our father prospered being with the Gomba [i.e. acting like a Gomba], so we should, too, be [i.e. ritually act like] Gomba' – has some validity in Kara, as arguments referring to ritual rules or their infraction are common. Many misfortunes, both between large populations and within families, are – through hindsight or oracular verdict – traced back to rituals that had been wrongly enacted. The *kumbassa* dynamic as described above serves as an example. This quite typical social dynamic can be concisely rendered: misfortune occasions a communal act of thinking backwards to recall possible wrongdoings that occurred in the past. I have witnessed situations where people, engaged in some ritual task, loudly pointed out some ambiguity in a prescribed component and waited for the public to agree that there was a problem, now, on the spot, so one could simply start over, and nobody could come later and bring a possible misstep up after the fact. This social aspect of ritual prohibition is very prominent. Its obverse is obviously possible too: that as long as nobody challenges what you do, you can get away with nearly everything, especially if no diseases or other misfortunes befall the members of your household afterwards. These are common occurrences. If the younger brother has done the ritual instead of the older brother, thus assuming false *bittamo* (responsibility/authority); if people between whose houses is a blood feud (*maassi*) engage in commensality; if an old *yihr* person (someone whose eldest son has married) travels too far from home; if the ritual of chewing the first grains of the harvest (*kaido*) is not performed in Kara but somewhere else – the result was always the same: someone pointed their finger, most often straight afterwards when it was too late to do anything about it, to drag the infraction into the open.

For Nabikolma to argue in this way was a clever and powerful rhetorical move: referring to an oracle's prophecy that identified a past disaster entails a recontextualization, a movement to bring the past into the present. If an oracle has declared Bogudo ways to be dangerous, or if an oracle has told the Bogudo to follow Gomba rituals, then anyone who elected to ignore this warning would be in the public eye. The greater the vehemence with which a potential breach of ritual prescription is exposed publicly, the more people have to mull over and possibly temper their actions. Anyone who refused to accept the oracle, or who blatantly and visibly acted against its recommendations, and then happened to fall ill or have some goats die, would not only have to acknowledge that they were wrong, but would in a particularly bitter turn of the cards also reinforce the oracular verdict they sought to dismiss.

Bogudo Identity and Ritual Practice

To summarize: the true Kara proclaim *ädamo*, mutual positive relations between everybody living in Kara, and deny a relation of inequality with the Bogudo, while maintaining ritual distinction as well as demographic, ritual, political and material domination. Members of both categories perform the *yekinta* ritual as a marker of equal ritual status and superior ritual status vis-à-vis other local populations, such as the Gomba, Moguji and Nyangatom-Kara.

In a move that might have had a variety of triggers and motivation, and so was publicly made to represent a wide range of issues, Nabikolma of the Bogudo from Labuk decided to abolish the *yekinta* and the *kumbassa*, allowing the Bogudo to raise children who under the 'old regime' would have been ritually impure and would have had to be killed. Nabikolma's *imba-kannah-meh* (his father's younger brother's wife), Uba, representing a second branch of the same lineage, decided to oppose the move, and distanced herself from Labuk. The true Kara slowly reacted to the events and declared that they now considered Nabikolma and his supporters to be Gomba, with whom they have many restrictions on commensality. From their perspective, the actions taken by Nabikolma indicated a change of ethnic category for the individuals involved, with a corresponding demotion within the implicit ethnic hierarchy.

Thus, it is difficult, if not impossible, to define what a Bogudo or a Gomba, or indeed a true Kara, would be in positive terms or in fact in any discrete way. A decontextualized description of Bogudo identity might emphasize a common descent, some (few) customs or rituals, a connected kinship pattern and other more or less material markers. It would certainly be possible to assemble a comprehensive list of such diacritical markers, which would, in turn, probably be approved by any Bogudo who might be presented with it in abstract terms. The story of Nabikolma and Uba, however, indicated that pragmatically, the one thing that truly determined Bogudo-ness was their relation to the true Kara.

Through their *position de force*, their unchallenged privilege of definition, the true Kara were able to reset the terms of the relation. This they did. Through their verbal reactions following the incidents in Labuk, they claimed rhetorically, but with quite existential effects, that what made the Bogudo Bogudo, what differentiated them from other sections of Kara and (had) made them a bit like true Kara, was their adherence to a rule of purity that is expressed by *yekinta* and *kumbassa*. 'Purity' is my term, but as the ritual involves washing the menstruating wife's body with water and sand, and as it entails the practice of killing illegitimate newborns and disposing of their bodies in the river, this does not seem an untoward metaphor.

We see that ethnicity in Kara is grounded in persuasive symbolic actions, but this rhetoric of ethnic categories also reveals different cognitive concepts or models. While there is certainly a strong sense of essentialism or primordialism, in that people claim to be bound to their ancestors through rituals only defiable at the risk of disease and death, the rhetorical process through which the Bogudo became Gomba indicates a different sort of model. Bogudo-ness, in one fell swoop, was reduced to one of its distinctive features, namely, to upholding the *kumbassa* rule and performing the *yekinta*. The statements by the true Kara 'that they would not drink *parsho* beer with them anymore' have a symbolic character, in that this constraint on interaction epitomizes the shift to Gomba-ness.

Whereas an essentialist perspective on ethnic groups posits paradigmatically interchangeable bodies with an analogous status, this perspective, apparently, is not what counts in practice for ethnic categories in Kara. Instead, when the *yekinta* was surrendered (a moment that I now use to signify for everything that changed between the Bogudo and true Kara), it was possible simply to say 'they are Gomba, now' and to redefine the relation between true Kara and the renegades accordingly. The argument is, then, that to define ethnic belonging *a priori* in terms of a historical continuity might be missing the point in Kara, and in fact might mean to fall into a conceptual trap. Incidentally, while there are narratives of the past and somewhat elaborate arrival stories for true Kara and Moguji, the history of the Gomba and Bogudo seems to be conveniently blank. Convenient, that is, not for them, but for others who might wish to make use of that underdeterminacy.[6]

When I pressed true Kara to elaborate on the problematic of *kumbassa*, they were dismissive of the other people, such as the Gomba and the Moguji, who would allow girls to simply bear out any pregnancy. To have too few rituals was publicly derided as, literally, 'of the bush, the forest', that is, too close to a state of nature. These other groups, the true Kara intimated, 'they also marry with a hand-shake, just like that', whereas their own marriage procedures are trying, expensive and elaborate. This lack of sophistication or cultivation (in which the personal body is conflated with the body politic) was described as the basis on which the true Kara felt they were on ritually higher ground. However,

Figure 3.2 Twins are not uncommon in Kara, and their birth order is carefully registered (October 2004). Photograph by Felix Girke.

in a reverse movement, they would also apply such a judgement, of essentially personal weakness and lack of willpower, to true Kara men who got their wives pregnant without having performed the required rituals: 'What is it with him? Does he constantly have to screw?'[7] This was said of a neighbour whose wife had become pregnant twice without ritual sanction. The *kelta* ritual, which requires copious amounts of honey-wine upon the marriage of a firstborn true Kara girl, had not been undertaken. Thus, both children were killed upon birth. The husband was called a *sünn-ed*, an ineffectual person who 'is just there'. The implication of these comments was that all the people who were now gossiping about him would – of course! – simply abstain from intercourse with their wives unless pregnancies had actually been legitimized in ritual.[8] Other people who did not wait out the months of the *yekinta* were equally derided.

This example serves to indicate how individuals use the same patterns of distinction when they are talking as representatives of a population section about another section, and when they are talking about an individual within their own section. Despite these given cultural tendencies, the true Kara response to the northern Bogudo's actions was by no means an unconscious reflex or mechanical in any way; in fact, quite the opposite.

Shifts of Interpretation

The true Kara with whom I spoke about Nabikolma were literally shaking their heads. 'What is he doing? It is a bit crazy', I was told more than once. Nabikolma's claim, supported by the oracle, that it was the observation of Kara ritual rules that had killed off the ancestors, upset people considerably. They felt slighted and annoyed that Nabikolma had needed to make his point so drastically. In what I see as an escalation, these displays of annoyance finally grew into discussions in which Nabikolma's motivation, which was still not conclusively known, was no longer relevant. In the sense of Bauman and Briggs (1990, drawing on Kenneth Burke), the true Kara 'decentred' Nabikolma's action from its motivation, whatever that might have been, and proceeded to 'recentre' it as an affront against the true Kara as such.

It was not the case that people had no sympathy with someone who took measures to end the waste of human life. Many, especially but not exclusively younger true Kara, expressed their expectations that their own practice of *mingi* would be abolished in the next few years (correctly, as it turned out), possibly followed by abolition of *kumbassa*, which has long been under heavy discursive attack by state and development agencies as a prime example of 'harmful traditional practices'. During fieldwork, I learned of one current case in which the second *yekinta* washing had been done just one month too late and the pregnancy was accordingly *kumbassa*. This interpretation of the ritual rules was seen as too strict, as not sensible, and as against the spirit of the regulation: 'The first washing, that is important!' However, this discontent remained backstage for some time yet.

So, while there is no evidence beyond speculation either way, it seems that in not wanting to kill newborns, Nabikolma could have tapped into a discursive drift. But in the way the dispute was framed, he lost the sympathies of the true Kara and was not observed striving to regain them. I claim that by linking himself to the Gomba, Nabikolma had backed the true Kara into a corner. Yet if we see this as a struggle in a social arena, a question needs to be answered: what was even at stake for the groups involved? Nabikolma and his supporters could gain the benefit of: a) having more offspring; b) no longer having to kill any infants; or

c) both. Their risk, as it turned out, was a certain degree of exclusion. They were denied the (maybe doubtful) privilege of being allowed to eat and drink with the Kara from one vessel. Also, their daughters and sisters would no longer be accepted as the first wives to Kara men who had just leapt across the cattle, with all the usual benefits of affinity and alliance; they could still become second and third wives. These 'costs' are interesting ethnologically, but apparently they were not grounds for Nabikolma to reconsider.

But what was at stake for the true Kara? Looking at the interrelationship of the ethnic categories of Kara, it becomes apparent that they are all centred on the true Kara. They are the node, the reference point for every definition. Do the Gomba and Moguji have eating taboos together? Having little contact with Gomba, people in the southern section of Kara did not even know, and for them, it hardly mattered. What mattered was their relation to the true Kara. If the Bogudo are marked and in a way exalted as the ones with whom true Kara eat and drink and sit together in the *marmar*, and whose daughters they marry after the leap across the cattle, then the true Kara could not allow a unilateral ritual change to pass unopposed. The *ädamo* of the Kara is sustained by the silent agreement that the rules for ritual supremacy will go unchallenged, that the status quo will be upheld. Everybody is expected to acquiesce to the suggestion that to have many prenatal and postnatal rituals is a mark of distinction, even of being 'civilized', which is a very present claim, especially vis-à-vis the Moguji (see Chapter 4). The rule of thumb seems to be that with more ritual restrictions imposed on an ethnic category, its members enjoy more privileges vis-à-vis the true Kara.

The events described here also have to be contextualized through what I call the 'safety of the second one' in Kara. Above, I have spelt out that a ritual breach is often connected with any incidental mishap that befalls the despoilers or their family, livestock, etc. However, if my elder brother irregularly performs ritual A, for example, eating the first grain of the harvest in the *kaido* ritual before his turn in the lineage order comes around, and I, being next in line after him, eat it as well, the misfortune will strike him and him alone. The first who breaks the rules is the one whom disaster will haunt. But simultaneously, they have blazed the trail for any runners-up. In this case, one needs to keep in mind that with the Gomba, Moguji, and Nyangatom-Kara, there are other sections of the population who are under even more severe constraints than the Bogudo and who were of course closely observing the events. It is fitting that the true Kara did not let that precedent stand, so, *pour encourager les autres*, they reacted to the attempt by Nabikolma to redefine the situation by imposing their own definition of the Kara–Bogudo relationship. The entire situation revolves around power. This power is a diffuse sort of power permeating all arenas of interaction in Kara, and finds its most crucial expression in the way the true Kara manage to define the ritual order. Physical force can be part of such processes as well, but the example of the fall of the Bogudo shows how the true Kara can manipulate their social world through rhetorical means alone: they counter Nabikolma's move, which is a challenge to the central tenets of the ritual order, by coolly asserting their 'power to define' through a display of this very power. Without invoking what James Scott calls the 'troubled terms' false consciousness and hegemony (1990), power relations between the sections of the Kara population need to be viewed in terms of claims and challenges, of collision and collusion:

> The powerful, as we have seen, have a vital interest in keeping up the appearances appropriate for their form of domination. Subordinates, for their part, ordinarily have good reasons to help sustain those appearances or, at least, to not openly contradict them. (Scott 1990: 70)

However, even before Nabikolma, there have been occasional attempts to upset the regime. Some Gomba, for example, deliberated whether they might not copy the *nechauleh* rule from the Nyangatom-Kara. The *nechauleh* posits that whenever a Nyangatom girl becomes pregnant, the genitor will have to pay livestock compensation to her family and her father's age-mates, 'for spoiling' her, it is said.[9] They were, the Gomba intimated, fed up with the true Kara boys coming in, making their girls pregnant and then disappearing again, while no Gomba boy would be allowed to have a true Kara girlfriend. They wanted compensation in the form of livestock.

This was subversive rather than confrontational: instead of demanding the unspeakable, to be allowed to marry Kara girls, the Gomba only demanded a right that others (the Nyangatom-Kara) had by ethnic default. Some true Kara outright dismissed the notion of Gomba claiming *nechauleh* payment when it was informally discussed, thus triggering an interesting dynamic. If the Gomba dared to enforce the *nechauleh*, would the Kara dare to deny them the right to this? A likely tactic would be to point out that 'this is not the ritual of your fathers, you Gomba you!', thus insinuating that one risks spiritual retribution for any breach of the established ritual regime and that, accordingly, the livestock acquired in recompense for the 'spoilt' girl would bring nothing but misfortune. But nothing ever came of this.

Again, this situation can be illustratively framed in James Scott's terms. He discusses acts that rupture the 'cordon sanitaire' (1990: 19) between dominant and subordinate groups. What is at stake in the situations I have described in this section, though, is not anything material, but the power to define what is 'speakable' discourse, basically, from where to where this no man's land of the unspeakable reaches. This is never a given, but always an effect of constant negotiation: the *cordon sanitaire* not only delineates what makes up the public transcript, but the way in which it meanders is also the expression of the very power it represents. Constraining somebody's verbal and nonverbal action needs to be understood in the most general sense as a claim, that is, as the attempt to perpetuate one's influence while instrumentally exerting it.

What would be, one might ask, the most outrageous demand any non-true Kara group could make? What would represent the most serious challenge to the ritual order? A good candidate would be the idea of Moguji wanting to leap across the cattle, i.e. the ritually lowest people demanding access to the most cherished and spectacular ritual. This specific example is not quite unspeakable, only obviously ridiculous, as an anecdote demonstrates that I explore in the next chapter on the Moguji as the quintessential 'other' with respect to the true Kara. To negatively frame this very idea in a moral tale is yet another strategy that limits the potential threat to the *ädamo* of the Kara.

Asking what was at stake, one could also surmise that the true Kara, still by far the majority within the population numerically, did not want to see other sections increase their birthrate and thus become a stronger force within the population, a force possibly less committed to the established ritual and political status quo. But this was not a topic of debate. Neither did the Kara step in to coerce Nabikolma and his hangers-on to 'stay Bogudo'. No violence was exerted, even though it could have been. The true Kara just, in a sense, corrected (with very little lag) the skewing of the categories that had ensued when Bogudo, who 'are' Kara, started acting like Gomba.

The actions of Nabikolma reverberated on ethnosocial relations and their idealist superstructure. The response by the true Kara was not limited to a redress of this breach alone, but ended with a re-alignment of the very definition of the relation between the two categories true Kara and Bogudo. Social relations, be they between individuals or between groups belonging to different ethnic categories, are not something that is simply there; rather, they are rhetorically stabilized through claims, in the form of verbal or nonverbal action. The true Kara were very uncompromising in transforming the ethnic category of half a lineage simply by stating that, in future, they would no longer eat and drink with its members. Especially if one considers that, if Kara were questioned in an abstract way, they would characterize ethnic categories as primordialistically impermeable (for males, that is), this is revealing.

Is it possible to extend the case? For example, what about the rumour that a certain Nyangatom-Kara *moro* had supposedly voluntarily started performing the pregnancy-legitimating *yekinta* ritual? Would that engender any structural responses from the true Kara? Hardly, my friends told me. 'This is an issue of the *moro*, of their lineage; they can do whatever they please.' But obviously, it is not that simple, as the Bogudo case illustrates. What is different between the two cases is that the Nyangatom-Kara are so very clearly immigrants who hold no land rights and who depend utterly on *ädamo*, the goodwill of their lords of the land. They need not be sanctioned for anything they do ritually different: 'They are Nyangatom, they have their own rituals and customs' – including the *nechauleh.*[10] Correspondingly, the Nyangatom way of dealing with pregnancies out of wedlock, namely, that illegitimate children are as a rule raised by the mother's older brother, cannot even be discussed in terms of *kumbassa*. The frame is wrong.

The Gomba, the Bogudo and the Moguji, they are the population sections that belong to the land, since land belongs to them too. Theirs are the ethnic categories that are mutually constitutive with respect to the true Kara in everyday life. There are no eating prohibitions for the true Kara with Nyangatom, Mursi or Hamar, or any of the other 'politico-territorial groups' identified by Bassi (2011) as the 'primary identities' in the Omo Valley. The same is true for highland Ethiopians or foreigners. There is no need to render them emphatically 'other'. Indeed, they are of similar status as the (true) Kara, in that their ethnic categories each align with autonomous polities. This brings us back to the dearth of outside knowledge about even the existence of the Gomba and the Bogudo that was initially mentioned: they virtually do not exist from the outside. These ethnic markers are by and large relevant only within Kara, just as we can assume that a true Kara would not care whether a given Aari (their northern neighbours) he was sitting down with for a beer was a blacksmith suffering ostracism in Aari or not (see Naty (1992) for Aari internal differentiation).

So was Strecker right, after all, when he said that the Bogudo had been assimilated by the Kara? The fact that a Bogudo identity holds no weight for anybody outside of Kara country indicates that it is now, today, located on a similar level as – say – clanship or any another largely intraethnic differentiation. The answer must be a 'yes' and a 'no': an affirmation in purely formal terms, but a firm refutation based on the recognition that the ethnic identity of Bogudo, being conceptualized and handled through its intimate relation to the ritual practice of the true Kara, is a central element of the dynamics of *ädamo* in Kara. Even though there are few Bogudo, 'Bogudo-ness' holds a very special position in the ritual order and the webs of affinity. It not only locates individuals, but also serves as another marker with which distinctions can be made. In this sense, by turning Nabikolma and his supporters into Gomba, the true Kara upheld 'Bogudoness' as an abstract model for ritual behaviour and social positioning over the apparently contingent individuals who embodied it.

The true Kara, the late-coming land-grabbers (see Chapter 4), who have absorbed the Bogudo, Gomba and Moguji, find themselves in a struggle to uphold the moral and ritual order among the sections of the population, which, as one finds, is connected to many conceptions of health, fertility and prosperity, and *bariyo* (blessing and wellbeing). The Bogudo around Nabikolma were, as such, no threat to the unity of the land. Being few, with Nabikolma himself still young, they did not engage in sedition or advocate emigration or usurpation of true Kara privileges. Interestingly, they made the opposite move, which in the local grammar of ritual debased them, rather than exalting them, and still brought about the wrath of the Kara, and their suggestions that Nabikolma was crazy.

This seeming contradiction – that the renegades were excluded for surrendering what is culturally understood as a privilege, not for trying to usurp new privileges – is revealing. As a first step, even though this point was not made by any of my interlocutors, it is simple to create a link between these events and the concept of *ädamo*, which demands positive interaction and entails the understanding that the status quo between the sections of Kara is good for the members of all the ethnic categories. To refuse near-equivalence with the true Kara is a slight to the – so to speak – ritual generosity that true Kara extend to others under the overarching claim of *ädamo*. It is a denigration of the claim of egalitarianism, which then carries the threat of challenging the great 'saving lie'. F.G. Bailey suggests this term, taken from the dramatist Ibsen, to indicate:

> the fiction that people build up about themselves – who they are, what they do – and about how their world works; they live inside the lie. Then the maker of tragedy may not be the one who misrepresents the truth but the honest person, the zealot, who believes that truth alone matters and should be laid open, even when it destroys the life that the lie made possible ... Any idea, any belief, to the extent that it is pronounced 'self-evident' and shielded from doubt and questioning, is a saving lie. (2003: 2)

I find this congenial to my argument. The idea of the saving lie allows me to remain agnostic about what the Kara really believe while I articulate how and why they deal with challenges to *ädamo* in the way that they do: they silence the 'zealots', the ones pointing out incongruities in the public transcript. This 'muting' proceeds by way of othering, and it serves to maintain the true Kara's sovereignty of interpretation in a changing world.

Notes

1. Indications of this can be both retrospective and prospective. In general, certain rituals must be performed in order to legitimate a pregnancy. If there is evidence that these requirements were not met, the pregnancy (and the foetus) are publicly recognized as *kumbassa*. *Mingi* is a diagnosis that indicates, as a rule, a previously undiscovered *kumbassa* breach. In, for example, the rare instance that a child's upper incisors grow first, before the lower ones have pierced the gums, this is taken as an indication that there was a ritual breach before: the child will have to be killed (see also Lydall and Strecker 1979b: 65–66, 147; Brüderlin 2005). This is considered much more problematic by the Kara than the infanticide of a newborn that was already known to be *kumbassa* over the entire period of pregnancy, and several mostly foreign and Christian organizations have tried combatting the 'mingi' in 'Karo', as Kara is often mislabelled. A web search will reveal

the extent of these efforts. One of these has established an orphanage to host unwanted children. In early 2010, I discovered a Facebook page for 'Mingi', while the Wikipedia entry is even longer than the entry on 'Karo People' [*sic!*] proper. This might be partly explained by the fact that *mingi* exists among the Hamar, Banna and Bashada as well. One source uses the term as a metaphoric reservoir and speaks of 'workplace mingi' when 'problem employees' are sacrificed for symbolic purposes (retrieved 29 January 2018 from http://psychicprison.blogspot.com/2007/07/bad-employee-mingi.html). Temporarily, Kara women were imprisoned for the deaths of their *mingi* children. In 2012, the Kara have decided to abolish the practice on their own terms after one hundred years of admonishment by state representatives. The film *Omo Child. The River and the Bush* (2016, http://omochildmovie.com) reconstructs one Christianized Kara man's efforts to bring this change about.
2. The occurrence of a wasting disease is confirmed by the earliest European travellers, who witnessed entire populations being eradicated over the span of very few years. In Kara, the *gind'o* (the 'drooping of the eyelids') is a constitutive part of the story of ethnogenesis. Historically, it appears as if first a rinderpest decimated the local herds and that the wildlife that returned to the areas now free of cattle brought with it the fly that carried the tripanosomiasis (compare Loimeier 2011).
3. Or not to be found: along the Omo, there is still talk about a group of 'forest Mursi' (Numurtuin) who supposedly moved along the foothills down from the Mursi heartland, camped for a while just outside of Dus where there is a dusty place called *murso lit*, the kraal of the Mursi, and then moved on, further south, and perished near where the Murle used to live (compare Bassi 2011).
4. I quote the elder sister here to indicate the emotional weight of the situation in which I first encountered this issue. As a 'diagnostic situation' (Moore 1987), the moment did much to sensitize me to the associations within this semantic domain and its expression.
5. Also different from Kara, among the Hamar, the husband is not involved in the ritual practice, but only wife and mother-in-law, suggesting a possibly even stricter control of the wife.
6. I heard several versions about the arrival of the Gomba. The only thing that was remotely consistent was that one of the two clan groups of the Gomba (who all belong to either Gorsbolo or Garshima *olo*) had ancestors in Mursi, and that in the past Mursi used to come to Labuk to perform certain rituals with the Gomba. These accounts, however, were never presented as charters and never carried any intimation of claims vis-à-vis the other sections of Kara (compare Bassi 2011).
7. In these dismissive expressions, there were certainly no euphemisms employed.
8. A third consecutive infanticide was only prevented by the wife's brother, who, with a levelled assault rifle, prevented the killing and brought the child out of Kara to be raised by a foster family. That this affinal agent felt that it was up to him to change the sad state of affairs of this *moro*, with which the entire settlement was unhappy, reinforced the image of the 'ineffectual man' who would not even save his own child. A few weeks later, the *kelta* was performed. Whether the child will be allowed to return at any point is an open question.
9. The positive revelation that a girl can become pregnant and that she has given birth to a presumably healthy child seems to cancel out any abstract worry about 'spoilage' from the side of potential future bridegrooms. I have not observed that girls who had become pregnant were in any regard less desired as wives than presumed virgins.

10. Serge Tornay (personal communication) has confirmed that this practice exists in Nyangatom as well, but under the name *akamus* or *ngkamusyo*. The etymology of *nechauleh* is unresolved. He emphasizes that the livestock payment is not only for the father, but just as much for the father's age-mates. This is equally true for the Kara-Nyangatom case, regardless of the ethnic category to which these age-mates belong.

Chapter 4

The Moguji
All That Is Not Kara

It cannot be overstated that the Kara, according to their own origin story, became who they were, and are, only as they met and established relations with the Moguji. My discussion of their mutually constitutive relationship opens up with this significant narrative, the one item of mythology that is most readily told by the Kara. It is the foundational charter myth legitimizing Kara as it is today. I have over the years heard about half-a-dozen renderings, all varying slightly, out of which I have now constructed an annotated digest version that would be acceptable for a Kara audience.[1]

The Trail of the Red Bull
It so happened that in the past, when the Kara were still living in the mountains, where they also had their herds, that one big red bull kept on disappearing during the day, and when it came back in the evening, from wherever it had been, it urinated much more than other cattle, and its urine also had a very different smell. 'But where does he drink?', wondered the Kara, and began observing him – but still, he managed to slip away and only come back later. In fact, the bull had smelled the water of the Omo River below – because at that time the Kara did not know the river yet – and that was where he had gone to drink. On the river banks lived the Moguji, who had never before seen such an animal as came to visit them. 'Ah, what a strange buffalo this is!' they exclaimed. 'We should kill and eat it, let us dig a pit so it gets trapped!' However, the next time the bull separated from the herd and went his own way, a Kara followed him and then came to the land of the river, which he looked up and down and which he liked very much. The Moguji,

surprised to see a human being accompanying the 'wild buffalo', called out and greeted him. 'Who are you?' he asked them, after telling them of the domesticated nature of the bull. They knew nothing about domestic animals. 'We are the Moguji', they said, 'we look for the glittering ones with the red fins which go *swish* in the water.' Looking at the fertile river banks, the Kara asked them again, 'So, if you only eat fish, whose fields are these then?' 'Fields? What are fields?', answered the Moguji, who also knew nothing about cultivation. The Kara then returned to the hills, and told his people about the wonderful land he had discovered, with space and opportunity for all. So the Kara and others got up and started following the Trail of the Red Bull, which was very long and difficult. Still up in the highlands, a group got tired and refused to go on. They settled where they were, and became the Bashada.[2] The others then arrived in the river valley, and they all liked it. When the Moguji came to greet them, the Kara asked them for their help, because the former were the fathers of the land then. The Kara then divided up the land on both sides of the river amongst each other, down to Diba and up to Mursi, and the Moguji marked the boundaries between the plots with big wooden poles for them.

Meeting the Moguji

When I arrived in Kara for the very first time in late 2003, I was not only scribbling words and phrases into my notebook on my long journey to learn the language from scratch, but I was also eliciting genealogies from the very beginning, proud for every cumulative level of kin connection I could make. So when Gadi, a young man, pointed out to me that my age-mate Barke was his sister's husband, I was very excited as I felt able to refute him: 'What are you saying? You are of the Eshiba clan, he is Garshima – your two clans don't marry! I know that much!' He insisted, and due to my only rudimentary Kara, we just kept denying each other's claims. I was not actually assuming that he was wrong, but that he was making fun of me. After some increasingly repetitive rounds of this, the very friend who had taught me about Kara clan organization came along. Turning to him for mediation, with me insisting on my data, Gadi suddenly understood the problem: 'Yes, of course, Garshima and Eshiba don't marry – but we are Moguji!' And, to wit, are not as strictly exogamous as the Kara! Only through this did I find out that two of my close acquaintances were Moguji and not true Kara; they belonged to clans that I had learned were Kara clans, they were members of the Kara age-sets, they lived among the true Kara and spoke just the same as everybody else. The tell-tale signs that exist, such as restrictions on commensality and other interaction as well as some material diacritical markers I had not noticed; for example, true Kara elders sport a notch in one of their ears (left ear for right-handed men, right ear for left-handed men), and true Kara first wives wear two distinctive iron rings above their elbow.

I had known of the existence of Moguji among the Kara population from my preparations for fieldwork. In Gezahegn Petros' MA thesis, we find the Moguji depicted as follows (paraphrased from 1994: 13f): They were the first-comers to this stretch of the Omo valley. At the time when other groups reached the area, they were 'hunters and gatherers', and only learned animal husbandry and sorghum cultivation from the Kara who arrived from the mountains in the East. Gezahegn affirms that the Moguji, many of whom live in a separate settlement called Kuchur, with the others partly interspersed with the Kara on the eastern bank of the river and partly on the western bank of the river under the aegis of the Nyangatom, have their own language, but mostly communicate in the Kara language *kar'appo* when not amongst themselves.[3] They join many public activities of the Kara, but young Moguji men in particular often travel together exclusively, to go hunting or trading. This is all very well; the plot thickens when Gezahegn reports the statement by 'Karo elders' that the Moguji living with them 'were not a group forming an independent community, but are a section of the Karo' (1994: 14). He then briefly ponders the related questions of migration, subordination and ecology of both groups, but drops the item short of working out richer political, historical, economic, ritual and (the thrust of my approach) categorial and political implications of what people told him. This claim by 'Karo elders' was not a neutral account of Kara-Moguji relations; it was a rhetorically loaded claim. To determine more analytically what 'the Moguji' ethnic category signifies and in what ways the category relates to group dynamics, I start from the patterns of interaction between true Kara and Moguji that I observed, with special consideration for the power inherent in classifying and categorizing people through ritual practice. The events I witnessed had a deep background that I came to appreciate over the course of my studies, allowing a fuller understanding of the Kara–Moguji relationship, including its rhetorical, material and structural aspects.[4]

The position of the Moguji within Kara is a loaded and dangerous problematic for the 'true Kara', much more than the integration and disciplining of the pitifully few Bogudo (see Chapter 3). Here, the context is thicker, in that the performances of ethnicity refer back to mythical history as well as to recent events, to economic and ritual relations, to the means of production, to cultural claims such as stereotypes and specific metaphors, and to demography, as they are partly entwined and partly conflated inside the boundaries of Kara country. The situation is aggravated as this very boundedness, within which the true Kara maintain their power to define the situation, is constantly threatened: for the Moguji of today, there are other possible affiliations outside this polity. In fact, unlike the Bogudo, they have viable exit options, ways out of Kara country and beyond the categorization imposed by the Kara. This scenario upsets the true Kara, who are aware of 'dangerous' precedents and display perpetual concern about dramatic betrayal, malice aforethought, murder, war and doom. This connectedness of the Moguji's potential flight from the dominion of the true Kara with the true Kara's recurring worry about treachery and its disastrous fallout (which emerges in more detail below), I argue, is one of the focal features of the contemporary relations of the people thus ethnically categorized.

The historicity of Gezahegn's casual statement needs to be recognized: while some Moguji can be said to form a 'section of the Kara' (whatever the Kara term used might have been), there are many who are not, but used to be, who just at that time initiated action to be independent of Kara classification and who denied the claims of mutual amity encapsulated in the term *ädamo*. In Chapter 5 I will go into the details of how this ethnopolitical crisis – here called 'the schism' – came about. First, though, some instances of everyday interaction and differentiation between Moguji and other people within Kara shed light on the practical modalities of the relation. As in the last chapter, I analyse this relationship from the perspective of the true Kara, the ideologically dominant version to which 'hidden transcripts' must by necessity refer. The methodological argument rests not on inner states, but on publicly enacted performances. Accordingly, I present the Moguji's challenges to the true Kara definition of the situation, through which their discontent and the changes some of them desired became manifest.

As with between Gomba and true Kara, some taboo (*kaiss*) restrictions exist between true Kara and Moguji. These have been mentioned by Gezahegn: they 'do not share from the same calabash' (1994: 17). While this is true in essence, it is insufficient to consider one arena of exclusion and differentiation (commensality) apart from a more general perspective on how the interaction between these categories of people is regulated. One could draw up a long list cultural and symbolically loaded items that people say separate true Kara and Moguji, but my approach instead builds on concrete instances of such distinctions being implemented, evoked and contested. Accordingly, I resist the list – but to allow a better understanding of what it entails, every day, to be a Moguji in Kara, I offer these three cases, one playful, one starkly dire and one conciliatory, which arose over the years I visited Kara.

The Calabash Joke: A Playful Moment

'*Zonza sherka! Zonza sherka!* – Elder's calabash! Elder's calabash!', Bero yelled at Bordo, who quickly put down the large drinking gourd full of *parsho* beer he had just been about to drink from. The other young men of the Ologuita age-set, who were also sitting around them, burst into laughter, because there was no *zonza*, no married male true Kara, present among them. But Bero had made his joke confident that Bordo, a Moguji, would react without hesitation. While there are no such restrictions among youths, Kara are strict about one thing: had this been a calabash used by a *zonza*, it would just have been polluted by Bordo's touch and its owner could not have drunk from it any longer. If it had been the personal, decorated *baasal* calabash used exclusively by its owner, it would have had to be destroyed after its contact with a Moguji mouth.

This little episode points to some aspects of the relations between true Kara and Moguji: it is not only that Bero's little prank made Bordo do a double-take that was amusing to behold, but it hints at much more. For one thing, in the eliciting of this response, not only is a habitus revealed, but we also gain an idea of how ethnicity is perpetuated in everyday life in Kara, of how children might learn about these social categories. Now, Bordo is an adult and no longer needs to be told who is a true Kara and who is not. He also knows the rules; he is already conditioned (as all Moguji must be) to control his conduct in the presence of true Kara. What Bero did by means of his practical joke was to provide a commentary on the predicament of the Moguji in Kara, but also of the true Kara: occasions such as this, when these specific individuals, the Ologuita gang of friends, could sit jointly and drink with disregard to ethnic distinction, will become rare in the future. As Bero and some of the others will get married over the next years, will become *zonza* themselves and will stop drinking from the same calabash as Bordo, regardless of whether they still consider them friends or not. The joke, then, highlighted a structural barrier, not a personal one.

Two Beatings and a Headrest: A Dire Drama

The next event revolves around two young Moguji men, Ari and Lale, as well as Galo, a Kara elder. I had not known Lale before, but I had been familiar with Ari and Galo for a long time. I also had not heard about the background of the event, so while I was present when violence suddenly erupted between Lale and Galo, I had to reconstruct what had led up to it afterwards.

The rumours had already been spreading in the weeks before: Ari had reported to Galo that he had tracked Lale's footsteps to both Galo's hut in the village as well as to Galo's shelter on the riverbank. As nothing had been stolen from either site, the fear was great: it must have been that Lale worked sorcery (*ashko*) to damage Galo and his family. Accordingly, people were surprised to see Lale coming down to the riverbank at the site called Gorrente where Galo and some other families were cultivating and where I was also staying. Later, people speculated as to whether Lale had dared to come because he thought the matter forgotten. Or maybe, some surmised, he had thought that as he was sent on his errand by the elders of the southern village Korcho, this might keep him safe from retaliation. Be that as it may, he came. Out of the forest, he walked up to our clearing and shelter, where many people were sitting. We had in fact been waiting for somebody to bring us some news about the upcoming peace conference in Korcho. Lale arrived without baggage and did not even have a *borkotto* headrest to sit on. He crouched down on a log and began to exchange greetings.

Most of us present never saw how Galo slowly picked up his long fighting stick. I only noticed when he entered into my peripheral vision, as if dancing on tiptoe, weaving his pole about and then smashing it in a long arc on the unsuspecting Lale's back. With the impact, and Lale's choking, coughing scream, the scene erupted into chaos. Some people tried to restrain the very physical Galo, who had already been swinging his weapon back for a second strike, others crowded around Lale, who was squirming on the ground in agony, and over it all we heard the shouts by Gorro-imba, the eldest *zonza* present: '*Hagobinnano!* – Don't you run away!' After a few minutes of Galo straining to overcome the people holding him, and of Lale slowly recovering his senses and the control over his body, Gorro-imba managed to assert control and started to sort things out: 'You are safe here, now', he told Lale, 'tell us first what they sent you here to tell, and then tell us some more [i.e. about the witchcraft rumours]! Don't you run away!' Somewhat reassured, Lale grabbed hold of a *borkotto* headrest that had been tossed about and had ended up near him during the fight, shakily sat down and started to tell about the beginning of the peace meeting, and who of the elders from this section of the fields were expected to go there. Before he could end his account, though, Galo managed to tear loose and with a howl of rage again came after Lale, who, however, lost no time in dashing away in an incredible show of speed, across the fields, down to the riverbank, where he leapt into the Omo River and started swimming. Galo followed him, only stopping at the water's edge, heaving and cursing. Meanwhile his son, along with Ari, had unmoored a dug-out canoe (*gaggi*) and started punting it towards the middle of the stream, bent on cutting Lale off. But the fugitive reached the other side of the river unscathed, climbed out and up the bushy slope, and disappeared into the riverine forest.

When people got back from the riverbank, much blaming and claiming ensued. Galo was scolded for spoiling the peace, as people were wondering what Lale might have had to answer to the charges of sorcery. They also marvelled at his running, his swimming and his fearlessness in simply leaping into the river. 'He need not fear! No crocodile would touch a Moguji!', somebody interjected. It was then that Haila, the *zonza* in whose shelter all this had been taking place, realized that the *borkotto* Lale had been sitting on had in fact been his. Having been used by a Moguji, it was now polluted, and Haila dejectedly declared that it might as well be thrown away now. However, in a deliciously ironic gesture, Ari, the other young Moguji who had been so involved in all of this, swept up the corpus delicti, heavily sat down on it and declared, 'so, now that we have spoilt it, I might as well use it, too'.[5]

The most relevant aspect of this drama, which had only just begun, is the juxtaposition of the two Moguji involved, their actions and eventual fates. The drama continued over the following days both at Korcho (where I was present) and back at Gorrente (where I was not). The next day, together with the men from the riverbank fields, I travelled downriver to Korcho, where representatives of many South Omo groups had been brought together as part of the peace effort by AEPDA, a local NGO based in Jinka. To the Kara's surprise, a car that delivered the Nyangatom delegation from nearby Kangaten also brought Lale back, under police supervision. He had, so we learned, come across a group of Moguji on the western side of the river and had been given water to drink, but had spat it out again, bloody. Eventually, people handed him over to the police of the Nyangatom district, saying 'if the Kara beat him this badly, there might well be a reason for it'. Arriving in Korcho, the police ascertained that he had been a fugitive only for his own safety, and so he ended up being escorted away to the hospital in Turmi.

The tail end of the story was what happened to Ari. While Haila and I were gone from the riverbank to work on transcriptions in Jinka, a group of elders and young men from Korcho came to Gorrente. As is the way of the *zersi*, they assessed the events and proclaimed judgment. Galo's 'guilt' (*d'ebbamo*) for having attacked Lale, who had been the emissary of the *zersi*, was quickly established. He proceeded to beg for mercy and, being rich in fields and herds, was allowed to escape physical punishment. Instead, he slaughtered a goat for the *zersi*. Ari, however, was identified as the true culprit, a dangerous liar: how can he claim that he tracked a particular man if he never saw his body proper?, ran the accusations. Just as importantly, is he Galo's son, or why does he report such rumours to him as if Galo was his father?[6] Ari had his hands and feet bound by his age-mates, who took over the responsibility of disciplining one of their own. In a forest glade nearby, they beat his back bloody, all the while admonishing him not to lie and instigate trouble anymore. When we returned to Gorrente, I saw his back covered by crisscrossing welts and pus-leaking wounds, which were just beginning to scab over.

Of course, Ari is not Galo's son. Just like Lale, he is a Moguji orphan, without direct relatives, without any material assets, no fields, no livestock, no gun, no wife and no house. While Lale worked mostly at the safari camp of Murule, Ari had – over the years that I knew him – been attached as a dependent worker to various households, always in the Gorrente area. He was strong, skilled, hardworking and welcome in any workforce. He was great with kids and generally fun to have around – but it was known that he sometimes did ill-considered things too. Had he had any livestock, he might have bought himself free of the charge just like his rich patron Galo did. Ari could not and was beaten bloody. Afterwards, comments on the 'badness' of the situation from various witnesses were not in short supply: what had possessed the *zersi* to inflict such a harsh judgment? 'If it had been a "child of the land", someone with some *äda*, this would be justifiable. But to beat this poor "gathered-up one" [*k'ambi*], who has no place to go, in such a way, that is not the work of real *zonza*' was the gist of several statements I heard. The constellation is truly bitter: one poor dependent orphan suggests that another one who is so much just like him might be a potentially death-dealing

The Moguji: All That Is Not Kara   111

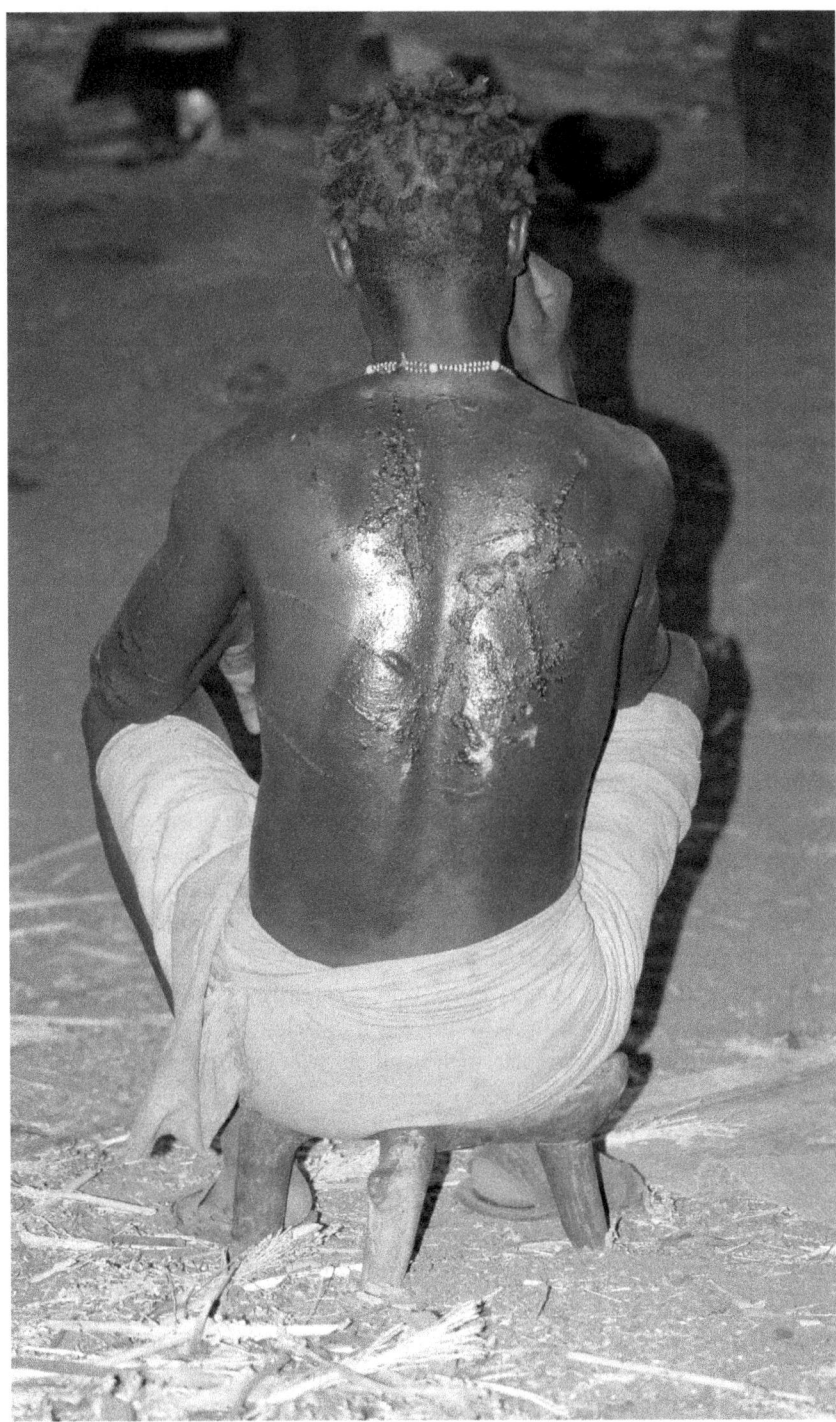

Figure 4.1 After the whipping (March 2008). Photograph by Felix Girke.

sorcerer. As a consequence, one ends up with an injured liver and is handed over to the police by distrustful Moguji, his 'own people', one might think, while the other receives a bloody back and is disciplined – or rather scapegoated – by his own age-mates. Galo, the one protagonist who exerted the physical violence that triggered the events I observed, was able to extricate himself from this mess for the low cost of one goat, sacrificed to the *zersi*.

Interethnic Siblings: A Tale Kinship and Solidarity

Already in my earlier visits to Kara (2004 and 2005), I had met Wole. He is originally from Labuk, but had been ill there for a long time. In order to get better, he had come to live in the southern part of Kara for a change of air. When I met him, he was already convalescent and seemed eager to make both my acquaintance and a good impression on me. Everybody else in the settlement knew him well and nobody felt that it was necessary to explain why he was staying in the household of Haila's mother. I learned that he was a Gomba, but there had been no intermarriage with his family. When I dug deeper, I was told that his and Haila's fathers' fathers, being both Gorsbolo and among the Gorsbolo having the same *k'andi* (goat ear cut patterns; see Chapter 2), had at some point grown close and become personal friends. Subsequently, their sons used to spend much time together, had roamed around together as youths and became hunting friends as a matter of course. This relationship was passed down another generation, and while Wole is an age-mate of Haila's younger brother Mullah, he is a fast friend of all the brothers. They all acted like siblings.[7]

The fact that Wole is a Gomba meant that when Haila became a *zonza*, the commensality restrictions between the two were triggered. For example, when Wole and I were eating sorghum porridge with fresh milk, some sour milk had to be added so that Haila could safely join us. This prohibition had no effect whatsoever on their personal relationship.

Later I met a young woman, Lugo, who apparently was just as *äda* to Haila as Wole, despite being a Moguji. What was the background here? As it turned out, both cases were quite similar, with small but relevant differences. For Haila, Lugo's family was 'his Moguji'. Her father was also called Haila. He had left no other children, he himself dying just before the recent 'schism' (see below and Chapter 5). His elder brother left Kara country along with his dependants when trouble was brewing, but apparently their departure from the fold had not severed the personal relationship with Haila's family. Haila, his wife, his mother and his brothers all act protectively towards Lugo, as is evidenced by the way in which the issues with her husband were resolved: he had not paid any bridewealth and was constantly quarrelling with Lugo, who had also not become pregnant yet – due to the quarrelling, people surmised.

Twice in 2006 alone, Lugo ran away from Korcho, seeking refuge in Haila's house in Dus, and stayed for weeks, while her husband kept sending mediators (*motalla*) to negotiate her return. Haila coolly let them return empty-handed for some time, noting that such things should not be rashly negotiated. Lugo's husband, back in Korcho, was getting quite destitute without a wife to run his household, being reduced to dependence on the goodwill of other homesteads to feed him. Haila stated clearly that Lugo would only be sent back home when he felt it was appropriate and prudent. She also made herself useful, cooking, cleaning, mending, fetching water and wood. Haila's mother especially took her under her wing, urging me to buy Lugo a cloth skirt when I went to town, explicitly pointing out to me the responsibilities of being *äda*. She was eventually sent back; her husband had proffered repeated assurances that he would live in peace with her from now on. It was, however, also made quite clear that if he broke his word, a group of young men with sticks would set off from Dus to set him right, true Kara coming to the defence of their Moguji relative.

These examples show that the relationship between true Kara and Moguji has many aspects, and its workings are far from obvious. In general, I found that the encompassing and often negatively charged ethnic category 'Moguji' was opposed by personalized relations that sidelined ethnic difference. Still, as the case of the two orphans illustrated, there are structural problems: Moguji are under many constraints and as convenient scapegoats, they often bear the brunt in an altercation. This tension between unbiased, mutual interaction between particular individuals and the categorical, largely derogatory differentiation (akin to Gluckman's 'dominant cleavage'; see Werbner (1984)) is not easily resolved, and both these aspects co-obtain in every Kara–Moguji interaction.

Land Rights and Ritual Practice

As a matter of principle, justified in the eyes of the true Kara by the story of the Red Bull, the Moguji own no arable land along the river. There are also individual Kara for whom this is the case, but this is treated as contingent: some have sold theirs, some never had much and when the lineage increased in numbers, the younger sons ended up short, and, finally, some are prevented from access to their lands on the western riverbank by the threat of the Nyangatom (see Chapter 6; see also Girke 2008). All Moguji, however, are by definition lacklands through their membership in the Moguji category. Already the Kara arrival story renders them as fishermen, apiculturalists, as hunters and gatherers, and the Moguji have not been allowed to shed this stigma. By and large, they are depicted as non-cultivators, as the ones of the forest and the flowing water, the savages who are close, all too close to nature.

But the issue of land is complicated. It is in fact not the case that the Moguji lost all their territorial rights in the initial wave of Kara arrival; they are still the 'fathers' of many places inside Kara country, even large tracts of land. Only three generations ago, it is said, a true Kara elder bought the Kadokochin area from them, where a major Kara settlement came to arise. Still now, the land that belongs to the true Kara is quite small – inland, they claim to only properly own small tracts here and there, as well as uninhabited Garchi. The riverbanks are in their entirety divided up between Kara, Bogudo and Gomba, with every plot having its own history of (changing) ownership. None of all these other Moguji-owned areas is reliably arable, at best usable for occasional rain-fed agriculture, a decidedly second-rate quality as compared to the reliably flooded banks of the Omo. Thus, this land ownership rarely matters and, in practice, the claim that a certain spot belongs to Moguji is mostly made when Kara want to explain a reoccurring misfortune like the following one.

An old, respected true Kara widow and mother of four married daughters fell ill and was even briefly taken to the zonal capital Jinka for hospitalization. She was already preparing for her death when a consulted diviner declared that the very hilltop on which her hamlet was located was 'bad land'. It had, so he claimed, previously been held by a Moguji lineage that had since died out. As a consequence, the land had acquired a destructive and dangerous quality. If the people, so the diviner said, did not move away, old people and small children would certainly continue to die. The old woman's house was re-erected promptly a little further north and, rather quickly, she became hale again. Soon after, all houses on the southern hilltop had been uprooted or demolished, as their owners had agreed to relocate the hamlet by just a hundred metres.

The Moguji and the land – this is an indissoluble relationship, yet a worrying one, no matter how disenfranchised the Moguji seem today when it comes to the riverside banks and fields. All land – so the myth proclaims – really did belong to them, and even though they surrendered their claims in the grey past, still, they are its arbiters. I want to refer back to the moment in the arrival myth when the Kara distribute the river banks among themselves. In the story, the Moguji end up being the ones who erect the massive boundary-marking tree trunks, known as *bariyo-maalo*,[8] sinking them deep into holes in the ground, at the bottom of which some ritual items are buried.

This is not very ancient history. Some of these massive markers are said to still be visible. Even now, people occasionally bring up the topic and muse whether one should demand these services of the Moguji again. Demarcation of fields is a constant hassle to people and often leads to boundary disputes: where there is no *bariyo-maalo*, people plant a series of thin sticks into the ground, running straight from the riverine forest's edge to the water, to indicate where their respective fields meet. But such a demarcation is only good for one season and depends on authoritative old people declaring every year where exactly the boundary runs. This judgment, though, is invariably based on memory and some contingent natural feature ('from this tree'), and so not as final and satisfactory as a *bariyo* boundary would be. Thus, as if there was still an ancient first-comer connection to the land, the Moguji were employed as arbiters for disputes between Kara, a neutral 'figure of the third'. F.G. Bailey calls such a role 'tertius numen' (1978). Whoever is placed in such a numinous category becomes neutral and gains the authority to arbitrate, but is simultaneously and visibly excluded from competition in the respective arena. This applies to the Moguji. They are so excluded, in fact, that the very notion of ever selling fields to a Moguji is dismissed with laughter. However, the role of the Moguji here is highly loaded and ambivalent: as they are made impartial arbiters of disputes over the land that used to belong to them, both their ritual potency and their political impotence is displayed. But they are not just neutral, they are neutralized.

The situation of the Moguji in Kara in relation to land-use is one of dependence. As they own no riverbank fields, and in fact no easily arable areas at all, they must in every farming season ask and be granted access by one of the Kara landholders – true Kara, Gomba or Bogudo. This is the most obvious limitation imposed on them and is much more problematic than mere issues of denied commensality and the refusal to lend *borkotto* headrests. This utter, categorical dependence identifies the relationship as domination or patronage,[9] especially considering that according to the true Kara, all their lineages used to have 'their' Moguji, who assisted in the daily work and for this received a share of the harvest. But, as some Kara recalled with fondness, their ancestors used to employ deception (*sudima*) vis-à-vis their Moguji, like boiling the grains they gave them for some time and then laying them out to dry in the sun, so that they lost their germination capacity: the Moguji could only eat, not sow. This perpetuated the dependence of the Moguji on their patrons' continued goodwill and the ritually protected seeds (*benta*) that the Kara set aside after each harvest. Today, the Moguji still living among the Kara are less clearly attached to particular families, even though bonds to the old patrons (which were often cordial, despite everything) are still recognized. They seem be sometimes granted fields (or sections thereof) for their own cultivation every agricultural season. However, this is only ever the case for Moguji *zonza* or their widows. Unmarried men, like the orphans Lale and Ari mentioned in the case above, will likely be attached to one household or other economic unit at any given time.

This sort of dependence used to rear its ugly head in even more dimensions. Similar to how Turton describes the relationship between Mursi and 'their' Kwegu (1982: 11, a description that is probably still valid today), the Kara used to arrange and support the marriages of Moguji. This supposedly came about after the sleeping sickness *gind'o*, when there were (so the story goes) no adult Moguji left. The Kara *zonza* took the surviving children into their households, affiliated them with their own clans and then married them to other Moguji when the time came: 'They are our ritual people, our *gilo-edi*, they mark our fields for us! We cannot let them die out!' The bridewealth, in livestock, was accordingly paid by Kara patrons to Kara patrons. The Moguji were '*kemissada* – made married' (a causative linguistic form of '*kema* – to marry'). So even as the patrons professed benevolence, the relation was paternalistically structured so as to not allow the clients any real choice in the matter.

Such interaction that perpetuated dependence is framed by the Kara both in terms of *ädamo* and also of their cleverness (*paxalmamo*), which above all is a contemporary discourse motif employed to distinguish the Kara from other people. This will be explored at a later point (see Chapter 8). What is important for the present purposes is that the denial of this quality of cleverness to the Moguji is a constitutive part of the way in which they are imagined: docile, not thinking ahead, not cultivators but gatherers, scavengers even, crude, of the forest, not of the fields. The Kara who told me these stories acknowledged that there was much instrumental self-interest in the actions of these old Kara, but did not surrender the accompanying claims to *ädamo*. Instead, this seeming hypocrisy was presented as noncontradictory. The Kara were tricking the Moguji into dependency by giving them boiled grains, but they were also taking responsible care of them. In looking at other aspects of the Kara–Moguji 'social contract' as put forward by the true Kara, again and again I came across the claim that (for an outsider) degrading, dependency-perpetuating practices were genuinely beneficial for the Moguji.

Beyond planting the *bariyo-maalo*, the Moguji used to collectively provide other ritual services for the Kara as well. In the village of Dus there is a site, not particularly marked now, where just a few years ago there used to be a ritual gateway (*mul'appo*). People told me that it was materially identical to those that every head of a lineage has outside his homestead.[10] This one stood apart. It was the *kumbasso mul'appo*, the gateway where married women would deposit their unclean leather skirts after bearing out their *kumbassa* pregnancy (see Chapter 3). To cleanse herself, a woman would put down her blood-spattered leather skirt at the gateway, sprinkle some soil over it and trample it smooth. Finally, ducking under the gateway, she could go home purified. The polluted skirt would be picked up afterwards, at night, I was told, by Moguji, to be washed and used by them. The Kara justified this by adding that it was always difficult for the Moguji to come by leather skirts as they had so little livestock.

In another ritual, now equally abandoned, the eldest son of a recently deceased elder would stab a goat at his father's *mul'appo*, spilling its blood on the ground. Through this action, he assumed the vacant position at the top of the lineage. The sacrificed livestock was then tossed away, for the Moguji to collect and eat the carcass.[11]

These rituals associate the Moguji with unclean objects. Whatever has been cast off by the true Kara was fit for use or consumption by the Moguji, even dangerous, charged items with nothing good or wholesome about them. These practices of the (recent) past were recounted with a sense of benevolence towards the Moguji, as 'beneficiaries', as it were. Both the bloody skirt and the dead goat were part of the *ädamo* relationship of the Kara and the Moguji, a compensation for services rendered. Such acts that played on the sacred and the profane complement the other taboos mentioned above, the specific restrictions of mutuality and commensality between Moguji and Kara *zonza*. I observed ambiguous behaviour by married Kara women vis-à-vis the Moguji. Some would eat and drink with them (mostly with Moguji women), but some apparently did not do so. The views on this matter that I elicited varied, so I have come to the conclusion that to some degree, this is a matter of individual choice. Hence, sweeping statements such as '[t]he Kara share neither food nor drink in the same vessel with the Koegu' (i.e. the Moguji; see Hieda 1996: 149) are problematic in that they only take in the perspective of Kara male elders.

Considered in broad terms, these practices speak of domination and exploitation. The Kara present them as a display of how they extend *ädamo* to the Moguji, as well as of their very special cleverness, which in turn they employ for the sake of all. The aforementioned story of the Moguji who wanted to take part in the most salient Kara rite, the leap across the cattle, exemplifies how the exclusion of the Moguji from a central life-path ritual of the Kara was justified: through the conflation of ethnicity and ritual practice discussed in the previous chapter. The story's character as charter must be seen to take precedence over its historical basis. It was told by Kere Lepel, a Kara elder:

> A Moguji came to the Kara and said, 'this time around, when your young men leap across the cattle, I will leap with them!' The Kara tried to talk him out of it, saying, 'no, leave it be, nothing good will come out of it, this ritual is not for you.' The Moguji insisted, claiming that he was rich, he could bear the expenses, he could endure the ritual, and they wouldn't be able to talk him out of it: 'Where's your problem?' 'Alright', said the Kara, 'if you are really sure, if we cannot dissuade you…' So he joined the Kara initiates, performed all their work with them and prepared for the ritual. So when people were getting ready to leap across the cattle, the Kara told him to wait and to let the Kara boys leap first. He agreed, and so they all leapt and passed across the cattle, one after the other. When it became his turn, he ran and leapt, but when he got down on the other side, his legs gave way and he fell to the ground, the bones in his legs shattered. He could never walk again, and had to be carried off. Since then, nobody else has wanted to take part in our ritual.[12]

This is another example of how everybody's welfare obviously depends on following the lead of the true Kara. They tried, after all, to dissuade the Moguji, did they not?

The question remains what these practices of inclusion-by-exclusion meant to the Moguji. Were they seen as degrading or, more pragmatically, as materially positive?[13] Having no reliable data for the more distant past, it is difficult to tell.

Figure 4.2 A Moguji conducts a true Kara (left) and a Gomba towards Kuchur (January 2007). Photograph by Felix Girke.

My understanding is that since the 1980s at least, the unwillingness among the Moguji to go along with any such imposed definitions of the situation has gained sharper contours. Even if there had been a degree of 'false consciousness' before, which is impossible to assess, a counterdiscourse to these *ädamo* claims of the true Kara has certainly emerged now.

The material presented affords different viewpoints on marginalization, domination and dependence. Do the Kara uphold the ritual order in order to justify the economically dependent position of the Moguji? Or do all the elements of ostracism and othering in the practices described simply combine to mark the Moguji's pre-given marginal position and the structural imbalances? Both views have some salience. Markers recursively mark the act of their marking of difference: they signify in that they function, and function in that they signify. The Kara–Moguji relationship has yet more aspects, though, so I now turn to how Moguji-ness is rhetorically qualified and determined in verbal interaction.

The Metaphor 'Moguji Are Animals'

In Kara, I encountered strong evidence of a conceptual metaphor that I render as 'Moguji are animals'. This is not to suggest that the Kara 'believe' (in any sense of the word; see Sperber 2002) that the Moguji are inhuman or even subhuman. They interact with them on a daily basis, mostly in the same way as with other people. The Moguji are personal friends, age-mates, clan-members, hunting friends or even family. However, the category of Moguji-ness transcends individuals. Sapir (1977: 6) highlights that metaphoric juxtaposition brings together two terms that are 'both similar and dissimilar' – to say of a tiger in the zoo that it is a lion does not do the work of metaphor. The Moguji need to be 'animals' because they are so annoyingly human. Othering is here used to spotlight dissimilarity and thus restore distance, distinction and autonomy (see Chapter 1).[14]

Conceptual metaphors, in addition, are not based on one-on-one similarity or analogy as is often held for verbalized, explicit (but nevertheless ambiguous) metaphors such as when we say 'John is a lion'. While similarly direct expressions such as 'the Moguji are baboons' (see also Matsuda 1994: 54) are occasionally uttered, the specifics of the case lie in how numerous minor claims of association (metonymical, by and large) come to shape, to give a metaphoric gestalt to a category of people (compare Kratz 1994: 66).

In this, I adopt elements of the work by George Lakoff and Mark Johnson. Their seminal contribution to the cognitive work of metaphor, *Metaphors We Live by* (2003), provided evidence of just how much English-language users employ figures such as metaphor and metonymy in everyday classification to think about and act towards processes, objects and people. These authors located many metaphorical operations less at an explicit and conscious level than is commonly held (2003: 1f). Explicit and poetic metaphors, for them, are only the tip of the iceberg. Through many examples from English, such as 'up is good' or 'ideas are food' (2003: 47), they show how conceptual metaphors are part and parcel of the most quotidian semantics, which then come to be expressed and reflected in verbal language.[15]

Images of Moguji-ness are constantly used in the presentation of counter-images to Kara-ness, so regularly in fact that the notion that they are (at least from the Kara perspective) mutually constitutive seems to be right on the mark. This is, then, a selection of the claims I collected. Most are hyperbolical, all are crassly categorical, which leads me to claim that the Kara perpetuate the conceptual metaphor that 'Moguji are animals' for clearly political reasons by means of a verbalized habit. The headings of the following paragraphs are condensations of numerous narratives and comments I encountered; some are actual quotes, while others, as will be indicated, might as well have been. The text blocks following each heading contextualize the abstract claim.

Procreation
The Moguji Marry Just Like That
Since for true Kara the initiation phase, which turns them into full Kara, is such a central part of every male's life, they see the Moguji customs of marrying without much ceremony as telling. I heard the following comparison made: 'just like animals of the bush', 'they agree on a marriage, and that is it'. The bridewealth is low. Another factor is that the Moguji allow the kidnapping of brides, which the true Kara would not have among themselves.[16] Somewhat surprisingly, I have never heard the limited clan exogamy of the Moguji adduced in the disparagement of their marriage customs.[17] But 'promiscuity' is another connected insinuation, and when I travelled to Kuchur in early 2007, stories were afoot that young Moguji men were roaming around, looking for girls to *yedda* ('take hold of', a euphemism for rape) and that, accordingly, all girls were being given away in marriage at a very young age so that their husbands would protect them where their fathers could not. One man I met in Kuchur was called '*alpa ono* – knife sheath' by his friends, because they claimed his 'knife' was never outside a 'sheath' for even one night. This unabashed and crude boast indicated that Moguji are aware of the derogatory claims about them, and some play with and on this, for personal reputation and situational provocation, and a subversive claim to autonomy.

The Moguji Beget Children without Restraint
'*Muina adabba* – those Moguji, have they *ever* given birth!' exclaimed a friend after he and I returned from our trip to Kuchur. We had indeed seen many children and hardly any woman of childbearing age who was not pregnant. Supported by the knowledge that the Moguji have no *kumbassa* and no *gori* ritual, much less a *yekinta* (see Chapter 3) to forcibly extend the period between

childbirths, the Kara found such birthrates impressive, yet appalling. Seen in contrast with the true Kara, who are supposed to abstain from sexual intercourse for long periods at the risk of ritual pollution, this indicates that there are very different behaviour prescriptions for men, with much restraint imposed on and accepted by the Kara, and little to none by the Moguji. Even though the statement 'have they *ever* given birth!' referred to childbirth as such, that is, something that women do, the cultural conception of agency (and accountability) is clearly biased to men. Pregnancies, for the Kara, occur when men sleep with their wives or do not occur when men refrain from doing so, and most of the partial concepts I explore here do refer to activities or traits of men. At first glance, the attributes of women do not seem to be used much in the (especially external) ascription of ethnic identity.

Livelihood
The Moguji Are at Home in the Forest and in the River

Despite the fact that many individual Moguji (such as the orphans above) engage in herding the livestock of their patrons, anecdotes circulate in Kara about the Moguji's disinclination to roam around on the savannah supervising goats and sheep. One of these stories reports that 'the Moguji', having bought some cattle from gains in ivory or bullet trade, were so upset by the tedious task of herding after only two days that they just gave them away to the Nyangatom and did not want to be bothered with livestock anymore. This is diagnostic in the sense that the chores of herding are proclaimed as a touchstone for a young boy's prowess, toughness and cleverness.[18] *Chala* – 'to endure' – is an important theme of adolescence, and the privations of herding are openly acknowledged. '*Chalimma!* – Endure it!' is an often-heard admonishment. The bottom line of these accounts is that the Moguji do not have the mental stamina for herding. Not having cattle and not even sizeable herds of small stock makes the Moguji 'poor' (see Broch-Due and Anderson 1999) in the eyes of the cattle-minded groups of South Omo.[19] This links to the stereotype that a Moguji, after waking up in the morning, will immediately disappear into the cool forest or down to the river. The Kara credit them with the ability to track fish (by species and number) merely by looking at surface eddies in the river.[20] They are said to like the cool shade of the forest, the solitude, and not being observed.

Matsuda also reports an 'uncanny knowledge of the forest and the animals living there' (1994: 52). The Kara, for whom eating game is still a problematic issue and offers opportunities for differentiation (see Chapter 2), conflate this familiarity with an essential affinity of uncultivated beings and uncultivated environments. Due to this affinity, Moguji houses and even settlements are allegedly not well-maintained. This was the one aspect that I personally could relate to after returning from Kuchur: the trails between the field shelters along the river had not been diligently cut, so that one had to constantly duck and watch one's step rather carefully. Huts were not in good repair and hardly any of them had wooden walls as the Kara were building theirs throughout 2006–7. Along with the huge numbers of biting flies and other insects and the cries of large animals at night, the experience drove home to me why Kara evocatively call Moguji country 'the bush'.

The Moguji Are Bad Cultivators

As the Kara origin myth proclaims, Moguji originally knew nothing about cultivation and just lived 'hand-to-mouth' (Matsuda 1994: 51).[21] The underlying claim is that the Moguji are hunters, gatherers and especially fishermen. All these terms refer to categories of people who eat things that are 'just there', who gather the fruits of the forest and the river. The skills required for the apiculture for which the Moguji are equally renowned seem not to be weighed against the strong claim that the Moguji do not shape their environment, neither breeding animals nor raising crops. And when they do plant crops (as most Moguji do, in fact), there are – allegedly – often diseases among the sorghum or the harvest is poor for some other reason because they 'don't know how'. By extension, this suggests that the Moguji are not interested in improving their lot. The claim is that the Moguji do not produce, they do not cultivate, they do not impose their will to change the environment. 'The Moguji, they do not like to sit on the village ground for long to discuss things and to fix the land; they'd much rather leave again to the forest' was a typical comment on the participation of Moguji in community issues in Dus. The abstraction underlying this would be the idea that the Moguji just perpetuate their population, but do not produce any cultural or economic surplus. The expression *galo pe*, a 'land of destitution', was regularly heard in reference to the Moguji whenever somebody had visited Kuchur. Little coffee was to be had there, and many small commodities that the Kara managed to keep in constant supply (such as salt and spices) were often not available.

Personal Character
The Moguji Are Uncontrolled

This is reducible to the claim that whereas the Kara have manners, the Moguji do not – and do not care to acquire them either. A Moguji, in this conceptualization, would just do what they wanted – but without being blessed with much imagination, moral or otherwise. A Kara, however, would consider all their actions well, and especially moderate themselves in courteous social interaction. A corollary to this is that the Moguji are said to be violent. Many stories are told about Moguji brutality, about axe-murders and wild, drunken fights. This suggests a lack of moderation, prudence and restraint.[22] The Moguji were even said to be constantly wasting their assets – they just could not help themselves. An example is the man who in a drunken state fired three magazines from his AK-47 into the Korcho night-sky in 2007, thereby not only destroying his wealth and reducing the defensive capabilities of Kara country, but also endangering other people and making a fool of himself. Still, this is another element of Kara conceptualization that I think has been adopted by some Moguji in their presentation of self.

The Moguji Do Not Suffer as Others Do
Consider the punishment of Ari above – 'others would die, being beaten like that', it was said. It is the assumption of the Moguji's lack of personal cultivation and sophistication that gives rise to the pernicious claim that they can bear pain and injury much more easily than others. After all, they manage to live in this horrid land upriver, getting literally eaten alive by insects, they can recover from the most severe injuries and so on.

The Moguji Are a Source of Sickness
After the journey to Kuchur mentioned above, Haila's arms and legs broke out in rashes, the skin turning white and peeling from his limbs. This condition lasted for weeks and was blamed on the Moguji honey-wine we had consumed. In a weird transferral, the 'excessive consumption' often ascribed to the Moguji had – like a contagion – rubbed off on us, and we were scolded that we should know better than to drink too much honey-wine. The skin condition was also blamed on the (allegedly mouldy) hides of game animals that we had slept on at night: 'In Moguji, there exist sicknesses we don't even know about.'

The Moguji Are Not Clever
This is one of the most salient points that contributes to the image of the Moguji. They do not think ahead, they do not consider the effects of their actions, they care little for 'development' (*lematt*) and they are bad orators.

Animals and Humans, Symbolism and Materialism
I have not yet mentioned that the word 'Moguji' also refers to a certain species of ant. This was not, however, used by the Kara as a source domain for metaphor. Nevertheless, some transient observers (missionaries, NGO workers and tourist guides) take this as the be-all and end-all indication of the derogatory conception of the Moguji by the Kara. Following on from the above discussion, I argue that this item in fact does not carry such weight. The Moguji-ant is neither ghastly nor poisonous, nor aggressive, nor diminutively small. If one engages in the analysis of metaphor, it is a simple fallacy to assume that elements from other people's cultural domains carry the same values there as they do for us – this can never be assumed. Rather, the cultural play of associations should be the object of analysis.[23]

The conceptual metaphor 'Moguji are animals' is constituted jointly by all the individual claims jointly above. To wit: according to these abstracted sentences, all based on anecdotes, public conversation and observed episodes of interaction, for the rest of the Kara, the Moguji are like animals in relation to their indiscriminate procreation, which takes place both excessively and without moderation, as well as without proper ritual. This same sense of a lack of propriety and sophistication comes across in their physicality, their disinterest in improving their livelihoods and their disregard of other taboos. They are also (like) animals in their profound connectedness to river and forest; their hamlets are claimed to be makeshift affairs that are allowed to deteriorate. Their paltry fields and unwillingness to herd livestock show that they are no shapers, no cultivators, no civilizers of any sort. That there are very good reasons why the Moguji might not want to herd livestock is irrelevant for the metaphorical imagination – unless such reasons were put forward by the actors themselves as a challenge to or confirmation of the dominant ideology.

All these elements are highlighted as what distinguishes a human being from an animal in the life-world of the Kara. To summarize this ideology: the Kara are everything the Moguji are not, and vice versa.[24] And not only the true Kara – a young Moguji I knew rather well was also very dismissive of the living conditions in Kuchur and the other Moguji settlements at Galgidda across the river. 'Those *muina* [a dismissive collective term for Moguji]', he said, with a shake of his head, and recounted their limitations to me. Since childhood, he had lived in Kara, and he described the other Moguji in the same way as a Kara might. Was he, then, truly identifying with the dominant discourse or just opportunistically trying to make an impression on me? Was he trying to rhetorically uplift his own lot, as a dependant, persuading me (as well as himself) that his life choices were preferable to the options open to him? Did I witness a 'surrender to the "stronger god"' (Streck 2000: 302)? Would he rather be dependent in Kara than his own man in the allegedly desolate settlements of the Moguji? Or is it proper pride in his own personal achievements? It was impossible to know with certainty, but the possible interpretations I list here illustrate how this young man, in his statement, embodies the predicaments of the Moguji today.

In many real, material as well as affective ways, life in Kara is a good option, affording opportunities and comforts. Even though his social position is not equivalent to that of a true Kara of the same age, the young Moguji, despite being an orphan, a *k'ambi*, has found a place, some friendship, some security. Thus, out of this predicament, the Moguji who have thrown in their lot with the Kara up until today are complicit in the perpetuation of the metaphorical conceptualization of Moguji-ness – the young man twisted the target domain of 'Moguji' so that it was no longer an essentialist marker, not bound to a transcendent ethnic body, but a matter of livelihood, of ready sloth and a careless and in some cases even perversely willing embrace of unsophistication.

It is a simple exercise to extrapolate from the list above *ex negativo* what would be counted among true Kara as virtues and indices of cultivated human livelihood and personal development. Later chapters of this book develop this theme further. Let it suffice for now to point out that the Moguji, through this conceptualization, are not simply '(like) animals', as the trope suggests, not merely 'an other' for the Kara; they are 'The Other', the one other who is not just a stranger, but who allows 'self-defining by opposition' (Taylor 2001: 175). The otherness of the Moguji, from the Kara perspective, is then of a different quality from other othernesses. Consider the Bogudo: I never encountered a single metaphoric claim about their bodies, their ways or their past. Nothing derogatory was said of them. They were never seen as dangerous. Their specific conceptualization makes them an intrinsic part of Kara, whereas the metaphor-based othering of the Moguji indicates that they are the dangerous, twisted mirror-image, even though individuals count as friends and relations.[25] Are they liminal, too, betwixt and between? Rather the opposite: they are within and without, they are part of the body politic while at the same time embodying everything that threatens it.

The Othering of the Moguji

The metaphorization of the Moguji is based on the complex node of livelihood and ritual. It is not simply a response to competition over access, resources and representation, but sets up the basic structure for constructions of pollution, civility and productivity. The way in which the Kara talk about them naturalizes and justifies the ritual order by positing a distinction between those human beings who are (like) animals and those who are not. The category of Moguji presents problems that call out for a strong metaphorization, a 'structural taming' (Kopytoff's (1989: 55) term). This makes them unlike the Bogudo and even the Gomba, who need to be kept in line, but who are still 'proper' people and who are never rendered distinct by metaphor. The tensions emerging in the co-residence between first-comers and late-comers, between cultivators with pastoralist ambitions and purported hunter-fishermen, and the ensuing dissonance afford an extreme form of othering. This othering, performed through displays of differentiation and perfected in the metaphorical imagination, is a justification for why Moguji are marginalized in the way they are. In terms of metaphor, they are the 'pathetic' other (see Strecker 2011), inadequate to such a degree as to invoke pity but also ridicule. Kara use them as the screen on which they project antitheses to what makes Kara morally and culturally superior. But the Moguji are not pathetic: they have been made pathetic or, rather, their way of being has been equated with a lack of sophistication and cultivation.

In Kara, the momentous presence and interactional salience of the conceptual metaphor discussed above indicates that 'Moguji' is a different sort of ethnic category from 'Bogudo' and, most certainly, different from 'true Kara'. Similar to the organization of kinship, the *ädamo* of the Kara effectively posits an ego, 'true Kara', and classifies other ethnic categories in their relation to that node. 'Bogudo-ness', then, exists in a relation of contiguity, which was – when push came to shove – defined solely by the Bogudo's adherence to the *yekinta*. The same is true in principle for 'Gomba', as demonstrated through the transforming response of the true Kara to the renegade Bogudo's attempt at self-definition (see Chapter 3). 'Moguji' signifies a more fundamental difference, sustained and displayed by a metaphor that simultaneously proclaims the animal-like features of stereotyped members of that category and, conversely, the achievements and sophistication of all that is 'true Kara'. Simon Harrison, whose studies of group relations in Papua New Guinea are very suggestive for my cases, has discussed such difference as 'denied resemblance' (2006: 53): a group will differentiate itself from another group by pointing to ascribed properties of either category, and in many of these cases the differences highlighted (and perpetually reaffirmed) mark cultural areas, ideas about culture and personality that are especially valued in the group performing the act of abjection.[26] This suggests that there will be tendencies or regularities in the acts of differentiation that drive the Wheel of Autonomy: acts of differentiation are diagnostic in that they point to values and cultural emphases.

These two cultural operators, the vague association of the Bogudo and the crass disassociation of the Moguji, both shape an understanding of 'true Kara' just as much as they define the Bogudo and the Moguji. This is not a timeless idealist analysis. This cluster of relationships is shaped by centuries of interaction, but the long-dominant definition of the situation by the true Kara, and the sociological and rhetorical forms it employs, are under assault by both a group of Bogudo and the *worba* Moguji, and, tentatively, the Gomba.

In the case of the Moguji, political autonomy was the stake in the struggle, and with the at least partly successful political affiliation to the Nyangatom, I expect that many Moguji hope that the Kara system of landholding will come to an end. The possibilities of an eventual military dominion of the Nyangatom over the Kara, so complete that the latter surrender their hopes of regaining full control over the western riverbanks, or a heavy-handed administrative 'solution', are easy to imagine (see Girke 2008, 2013). This situation has very material reasons outlined above: the question of the riverbanks, of the arable territory in Kara, underlies all. Hence, the origin myth about the 'Trail of the Red Bull' that posits one group as the vital victor and the other as duped dunce requires by necessity a set of rules that validate the story in perpetuity. But the contemporary relevance of the original dispossession is downplayed by claims of *ädamo*.

At one point, Matsuda reports that Moguji told him that the Kara had taken the land by force (2002: 176). People who proclaim this version of the events (as opposed to the one in which the Moguji literally do not know what 'fields' are) will be quite aware that they are actively engaging in politics, are consciously challenging the dominant definition of the situation and are denouncing *ädamo*. Precisely this politicization of ethnic categories, against which the true Kara struggle, will be discussed in more detail below. In a way, this leads us to consider the co-emergence of justifying myth and material relations, to look at how the people belonging to the two categories of Moguji and true Kara came to have such a joint history. The relevant thing to note here is that not only that the claims the true Kara make about the past and the ways in which they define their relations to the Moguji are challenged, but that the structural aspects are also changing. The interaction between Moguji and Kara grows less intense and less multiplex, customary practices fall by the wayside, and the claims to power and the dominion over classification itself are assaulted (see Chapter 1).

But the defiance is not absolute, and it is not always grimly issued. So I conclude this section with an anecdote that marks a return to the Trail of the Red Bull. When I was in Kuchur, to my considerable surprise, a young Moguji started narrating that very story to me, even as my travel companions, true Kara and Gomba, sat by. The rendering was competent and not really out of the ordinary, yet hints of a savage grin could have prepared me that something was to come. Reaching the end of the story, the point when the Kara who had just arrived from the faraway mountains start distributing riverbanks among themselves, he diverged from the standard version by inserting the following: '… and then one Kara said, "This over there, this is my father's land", and then the next said, "Yes, and this is my father's land"…' This comment on the hypocrisy of the myth-making Kara, who inscribed ancestral legacies into the land they were just taking over, was well and cleverly made. Even the true Kara present had to laugh about this clever affront. My presence and inquiries into Moguji history was used as an opportune opening by the speaker. Such ironic renderings of the Kara–Moguji relationship in a nonconfrontational challenge to the master narrative, are rare. Many true Kara would react badly to such suggestions when issued by the members of the rhetorically disciplined subsections of Kara. In a parallel argument, Cohen states that: 'For the British unionist, Scottish nationalism represents an irrational subversion of the integrity of the nation state; while to Scottish nationalists, it is an expression of their right to both national and personal self-determination' (2000: 1f). This approximates the relationship between the Kara and the Moguji, even though the Scots have more legitimate outlets for their protestations. According to the Kara ideology, then, history began with their arrival at the Omo. The relations set up between them and the Moguji at that time have become a charter for eternity, under the rule of *ädamo*.

Returning to 'Moguji are animals', the elements that I have listed to develop this important conceptual metaphor show the complex interrelation in arenas of symbolism, ritual and economy between true Kara and Moguji. In juxtaposing these two ethnic categories, a charter emerges, as the true Kara place themselves at the higher end of a symbolically loaded and hierarchical scale. *Ädamo* provides the ideological commentary on this imbalance. While Kara, backstage, deny neither the patronage nor the domination, the proclamation of *ädamo* lends a moral gloss of general benevolence and justness to their ordering of the world.

Summed up, this complex of figurative imagination represents the view that the Moguji, having given away their land to the Kara, not knowing what to do with it anyway and definitely not wanting to work it, should be happy with their lot in Kara country, just like the true Kara have taken over the burden of responsibility, caring for and thinking for their Moguji clients, who individually are friends and relations. This double-layered view, of the Moguji as a class that needs patronage and as individuals who can be true *äda*, does not seamlessly cover up the basic inequality between the true Kara and the Moguji. Out of this basic dissonance, challenges have emerged and keep on emerging, which then engender redress.

A dramatic and most salient political schism between the Kara and the Moguji occurred in the late 1980s and early 1990s, and its impact continues to be felt today. The key event here is an attempt by a specific group of Moguji, the Worba,[27] to challenge the Kara's claim of benevolence and *ädamo* through a provocative display of a shift in loyalties.[28] These events and their consequences, reconstructed through a variety of sources, form the corpus of the following chapter.

Notes

1. The story has also been told, in varying degrees of elaboration, to other researchers of the area (e.g. Gezahegn 1994: 5f; Tornay 2001: 114f; Epple 2007: 57). The variations mentioned have no bearing on the argument except for one, an ironic twist added by a clever young Moguji, which I will return to at the end of the chapter.
2. The ethnonym Bashada can be translated as 'the defeated ones', in this context, the ones overcome by the hardship of the way (see Chapter 6 and compare Epple 2007).
3. The language spoken by the Moguji is classified as 'Nilo-Saharan, Eastern Sudanic, Eastern, Surmic, South, Southeast, Kwegu' with the code *xwg* in the linguistic catalogue *Ethnologue* (Gordon 2005), with 'Muguji' being a supposed dialect that may not be 'inherently intelligible with Kwegu'. The *Ethnologue* also emphasizes the lexical similarity with Mursi. From the word list I collected, the surprising feature is the occasional lexical similarity to the Eastern Cushitic languages Dassanech and Arbore (*dsh* and *arv* in the *Ethnologue*, respectively). The linguist Osamu Hieda, who has worked with the Kwegu/Koegu in the late 1980s and early 1990s, has apparently not noticed this fact (Hieda (1991) only indexes similarity with the Kara). That the Koegu numerals for 7, 8 and 9 (*gaitsobba, gailonkai, gaisell*) are seemingly loan words from the Omotic Kara, who use *tsobba, lonkai,* and *sell*, was a source of great amusement for Kara who taught me some Moguji: 'They never knew how to count beyond six before they met us!' Etymologically, though, a numeral like *tsobba* (seven) must be linked to the equivalent term *tusba* in again the Cushitic languages of the greater region. Fittingly, Matsuda reports meeting an Arbore man (probably in Kuchur) who 'insisted that the Muguji and Arbore had been one people historically' (2002: 183). On the other hand, I met Arbore youths who firmly believed the Moguji to be cannibals.
4. Again, Marco Bassi (2011) has sought to unravel the various claims about the origins of the Moguji (or 'southern Kwegu', as he calls them), finally arriving at an image of a

composite group shaped by several waves of migration, which more or less converges with my data. However, comparing his strictly (oral) historical approach with my attempt to assess current relevance of social categories, there is less overlap: many of the narratives he collected had no effective political weight on the social dramas I recorded.
5. In the end, I asked Haila for the *borkotto*, because even though it had been spoilt, it was still his. I later installed it with an explanatory note at the SORC permanent exhibition of headrests from the various ethnic groups of South Omo.
6. This is related to the issue of hidden instigation in times of tension between groups by a third party (*kantsi*), which is just one of the things the Kara fear from the Moguji (see below and also Chapter 5).
7. See the film *Morokapel's Feast* (Girke and Köhn 2007), in which Wole features: in a scene filmed in Labuk, Wole's mother-brother points out that 'Haila is of this family as well' in the sequence in which he explains the *mirt* ritual to me. This brief reference is grounded in the deep context of the closeness of Wole's and Haila's lineages, and the fact that Haila's mother was a girl from the village of Labuk as well, and of the same clan as Wole's mother, even though she belonged to a different ethnic category.
8. Lydall and Strecker have identified the field of reference for *bariyo* (or the Hamar *barjo*) as 'fortune, God, fate, luck' (1979b: 228). It is the central positive term in Kara cosmology as well.
9. See Seymour-Smith (1986: 219) for a concise entry on 'patronage' that addresses the connection of ideology and ritual-based patronage well. A classic study is Wolf (1966). For my discussion of domination, Turton (1982, 2002a) is particularly useful.
10. Until their eldest sons marry, widows take care of the *moro*'s ritual gateway. Even people from southern Kara, who spend much of the year in the smaller settlements closer to the fields, north or south of Dus, will have their *mul'appo* next to their main house in Dus. As Dus is the ritual centre, any other living arrangements are viewed as temporary. Such a *mul'appo* also featured in the film *Morokapel's Feast* (Girke and Köhn 2007).
11. It was also said that in the 'good old days', it was taboo (*k'aiss*) for the Moguji to spill the blood of livestock; that they must have been happy about getting tossed impure carcasses follows. Bernhard Helander reports virtually identical practices and attitudes in faraway Somalia (2003: 176).
12. The 'leap across the cattle' (see Strecker (1979) on Hamar), the dramatic climax of the initiation of men towards marriage, offers much depth for symbolic interpretations.
13. Considering the striking parallels to the Kwegu case as discussed by Turton (1982; see the discussion of Kwegu in Chapter 5), I tend to accept the claims put forward by the Kara about this earlier state of affairs as having a kernel of truth in tendency, but including exaggeration and denunciation.
14. Another, more specific argument about avian metaphors of the Moguji is found in Girke (2014b).
15. See Quinn (1991) on 'models' that pre-structure metaphors.
16. The Kara are the odd one out in this regard. Marriages of such a type are documented from the Hamar, Banna and Bashada. One might suggest that it would be more difficult for a population living in closely clustered villages to deal with the frictions caused by kidnapping (and the potential rape that can go with it) than for these 'mountain people' who mostly live in more scattered hamlets and independent households. On the other hand, this does not stop the Moguji. True Kara would readily participate in the abduction of a girl if their Moguji friends and *äda* ask them for assistance; this brings out the contrast of 'this is not something we do' even more sharply.

17. The Moguji *chaachi* (see Chapter 2) are not as restricted as for Kara. While the joking relationship exists just as much, a *kogo-nan* (that is, a father's father's sister's son's daughter, or FFZSD) is *chaachi*, marriageable, whereas in Kara this is the last degree before *äda* turns into *chaachi* again.
18. This is changing: the Kara themselves have trouble maintaining their herds, as many young boys prefer a life of schooling to the chores of tending the goats. However, the definition of cleverness seems to be changing appropriately (see Chapters 8–9).
19. At the same time, it makes them quite safe as far as raiding by greedy neighbours goes. Matsuda's account (2002: 176) that the Moguji had some cattle that their Banna bondfriends were taking care of up in the hills to the east is already challenged by Hieda (1996: 146). Gezahegn reports meeting a Moguji who told him he had forty-four cattle with his Hamar friends (1994: 101). It is common knowledge in Kara that the individual in question has at no time possessed any cattle. Apparently, in this domain, hyperbolic claims are common.
20. Matsuda, in his work on riverbank cultivation, mentions the term '*managura* (meaning unknown)', but states that it refers to the outmost edge of the slope of the riverbank (1996: 13). However, the meaning is apparent when the word is spelled more phonetically accurately as 'muina gura', literally, the 'beaten path of the Moguji'. The Kara laughingly claim that the Moguji create that very path through their ceaseless wandering up and down the riverbank, as this ridge affords them the best view over the river, allowing them to spot their ichthyic prey already from far away.
21. See Hieda's discussion of loanwords from Kara related to agriculture used in the Koegu language (i.e. Moguji; Hieda 1996: 148f, also 1991, 2003). His helpful contribution is unfortunately limited in scope due to his lack of a wider, more regional knowledge. As an example, he claims that *ruubu* (sorghum) is an indigenous word and not adopted from Kara – but he does not know that the Cushitic-speaking Arbore have an extremely similar term and that there might have been entirely different influences still. The trajectories of vocabulary across South Omo are striking and appear relevant in that they might reveal a history of cultural contact and material exchange.
22. Once I was told that the Kara had stopped initiating their age-sets together with the Moguji because the latter had been beating their own young men too brutally. I consider this a post hoc rationalization (geared towards differentiation) that was spawned by the conception of Moguji as brutal. Since an identically structured anecdote was narrated to me as having been the trigger for the division of the *ball'* (see Chapter 2), that one side wanted to spare their sons from the most severe beatings, I see it as more of a moral tale than a historical statement.
23. There is also a ghastly insect called the 'Garshima scorpion'. Should this indicate that the Kara consider all Garshima, one of the largest clans, to be disgusting and poisonous creatures? Regarding the etymology of 'Moguji', the matter is complicated by the fact that the Nyangatom call them by the name Ngimucu (Tornay 2001), obviously a variation of 'Moguji'. The trajectory of the term remains uncertain.
24. Kopytoff points out that late-comers such as the Kara will go to extreme lengths to discredit the first-comers and legitimize their conquest. His rendering of a typical 'getting there' narrative (1989: 49) bears an uncanny resemblance to the story about the Trail of the Red Bull. The two generally very common elements that (a) the act of cultivation of an uncultivated area legitimizes conquest (1989: 25), an indigenous *terra nullius* doctrine, and (b) the late-comers often confess to trickery are borne out by my findings.

25. Compare Leach (2000: 330) and Lévi-Strauss (1966) for alternative ways of linking animal (species) with human categories.
26. Another related concept is 'dissimilation' as introduced by Geoffrey Benjamin, who found in the 'Malay World' a 'story of continued complementarity between the tribal communities themselves and between them and the neighboring non-tribal domain' (2002: 34). Interaction causes groups to mutually assimilate and dissimilate, occupying different niches in mainly ecological but also cultural regard.
27. Bassi (2011) uses the transcription *worpa*. From my (longer) engagement with the Kara language, I find this harder consonant unwarranted.
28. Somewhat similarly, Wood has discussed the Gabra 'spheres of ethnic identity and loyalty', which can be seen as growing and shrinking opportunistically. In contrast to his examples, the shifts in the 'moral and geographic insides and outsides' (Wood 2000: 77) seem to be rare and more dramatic in South Omo.

Chapter 5
The Schism and Other Predicaments of the Moguji

This chapter explores the 'schism', the most dramatic series of events when matters between the Moguji and the Kara that were partially discussed in the previous chapter came to a head. The schism is significant as a historical referent for Kara–Moguji relations today, but it is also a prime illustration for the Wheel of Autonomy and provides insight into more general questions of ethnicity and rhetorical action.

The Moguji who speak the Koegu language on a daily basis are by and large the ones who live in Kuchur and are sometimes referred to as Duyu. Many others whom I met had *kar'appo* as their primary language and did not understand Koegu to any appreciable degree. However, as Matsuda remarked (2003: 464), the Moguji themselves claim to have reached the Omo Valley from five different directions, a claim not given great currency among the Kara (see Bassi (2011) for a more granular perspective). Matsuda fails to address in which way these divisions within the numerically diminutive Moguji population are actually relevant in interaction and material relations. Briefly, the Moguji designated as Worba (which is also the name of a certain area a little south of Dus village) are not seen as the autochthonous Moguji, the first-comers, the legendary hunter-gatherers-fishermen of the forest per se, but largely as the descendants of immigrants, and they are the ones who are most inextricably bound up with the true Kara today: the Worba grew up in Kara, they have been *äda* to specific families of the true Kara and many of them – due to their migrant background and upbringing in Kara country among the true Kara, Gomba and Bogudo – never learned to speak Koegu.

One narrative even severs their biological roots completely: after the *gind'o*, the Moguji had all died. Only the women and children were left. 'Oh no!', said the Kara, 'we need them, they are our ritual people, they cannot be allowed to die out. But we do not have intercourse with their women, that is *k'aiss* [taboo].' So a man called Bala, as near to a mythical hero as Kara has to offer,[1] went to the Nyangatom and announced that he had 'a task' for them. As I was told this story, the punchline was 'and what man has ever refused a free vagina?'[2] This story, as it circulates now, sees the Nyangatom as the genitors of the Worba (and not of the Duyu) and was adduced in the context of wider debates of the schism, the dramatic shift in the allegiance of the Worba.

It was Matsuda (1994, 2002) who first wrote about the schism between the Kara and the Moguji from the latter's perspective. He explained it in terms of the bigger picture on the Lower Omo, that is, by pointing to shifts in the balance of power. After the Nyangatom had been the first group in the region to acquire automatic weapons, and after their display of their newfound power by massacring around 600 Mursi in one fell swoop in the early 1990s,[3] it fell to all the neighbouring groups to show that they still had agency, were capable of action and were capable of keeping the Wheel of Autonomy in motion. This development, according to Matsuda, offered a new option for allegiance to the Moguji. However, the predicament of the Moguji as he describes it, between 'annexation' (by the Kara) and 'assimilation' (by the Nyangatom), needs a thicker conceptualization than he provides. Thus, I first discuss his interpretation of what happened and then turn to events that followed the schism proper from the Kara perspective.

The First Challenge to *Ädamo*

Matsuda starts by asserting that when he came to the Lower Omo, the Moguji were in a state of 'annexation' by the Kara. He claims that 'Muguji' is the exonym while 'Koegu' was the endonym (2002: 175). This raises questions about the relation to the Kwegu, a group known to stand in a similarly complex relation to the Mursi (and who are called 'Nyidi' by the Mursi; see Turton 2002a: 149), and the other population called 'Idinitt' by the Bodi further upriver. I personally cannot even confirm that the people referred to, living in Kara, Nyangatom and Kuchur, do use 'Kwegu' or 'Koegu' as an endonym, for the simple reason that many of them who are categorized as such grew up in Kara, speak only Kara and not their supposed mother-tongue, and would accordingly only use 'Moguji' in conversation. Some Kara know the term 'Kwegu', while some do not, similar to the Mursi (Turton 2002a: 150). Visiting Kuchur, which he originally thought was a Kara settlement, Matsuda only realizes later that nearly everybody there was actually Moguji (1994: 48). He sees the relation at the time as one of political unity, with the unit being called 'Karo', which in the early 1990s proceeded to break down. There is some value to this, as the exonym 'Karo' is commonly used in an administrative context to refer to the people of the (today three) *kebele* of Kara country, but the suggestion that the people living in Kara country would also call themselves 'Karo' is quite false.[4] This unity allegedly broke down because the old ways of reciprocity were no longer feasible: at the time, the Kara had no automatic rifles to protect the Moguji from attackers, the ivory trade that made the Moguji so important for the Kara was closed down by government intervention, and economic conflict entered the picture, as some Moguji had started building up herds. He mentions the issue of arable land as an afterthought (Matsuda 1994: 61). As he describes it, the Moguji elected to shift their allegiance to the Nyangatom who had been moving closer to the Omo after clashes with the Turkana way out west. The Nyangatom were better armed, more numerous and needed an ally in their attempts to displace the Kara from their extremely productive niche on the riverbanks of the Omo (1994: 60f).[5]

For Matsuda, the dynamics of the schism are clear: first, there was friction (leading to violence) between the Kara and the Moguji, and then the Moguji and the Nyangatom realized their common interests, just as the Kara and the Moguji realized that they no longer shared. The schism, in this understanding, was not about territory, 'since the Koegu are not seeking to expand' (1994: 49). What they sought, in his view, was protection. This point (made repeatedly by Matsuda; see also Matsuda 2002: 179) is puzzling, since before the schism, there were no reports of the Moguji being much in need of protection. Indeed, other authors have emphasized that the Moguji had never been raided, and only went on raids or joined wars alongside the Kara. I am not disclaiming that a 'need for protection' might have been felt in these insecure times, as it was apparently a high priority for individual men to acquire automatic rifles themselves (see Matsuda 2002; Turton 2002a), but since the purported threat to the Moguji is not apparent, the statement as such seems unfounded. What the Moguji were willing to provide in return were economic services, while at the same time the relationship satisfied identity needs. As suggested in the case of the Koegu and the Kwegu, another function served by the ties formed between such minor groups and their larger and more powerful neighbours might be to reinforce the ethnic identities of both partners. These relationships are based on the 'consent', as Turton (2002a: 158) has put it, of the smaller group to be stigmatized and subordinated. In return for their subordination, they receive protection. Such a relationship can last only as long as the underlying reasons for it exist. The Koegu–Kara union disintegrated because it no longer had this *raison d'être* (Matsuda 1994: 49).

To summarize the events as reported by Matsuda: in May 1988, the Kara denied the Moguji their share of emergency supplies, people quarrelled, and the Moguji were told to move to Kuchur (1994: 57), in effect denying them access to the valuable fields in Kara country proper for the upcoming farming season (see also Hieda 1996: 149f). In February 1989, a Moguji was killed near Dus in another dispute with a Kara, and the Nyangatom, who had been moving towards the Omo recently and thus had come into opposition to the Kara, offered to support the Moguji. After a mediation session with a regional administrator, it was suggested that in fact the Moguji of Dus should move to Kuchur in order to reduce the friction, but they ended up in Galgidda, on the western bank of the Omo River, where they could better herd their small stock and would be even closer to the Nyangatom. A bad rainy season in 1989, which resulted in a comparatively small floodplain usable for agriculture, aggravated the tensions. After some other minor incidences, a young Kara was killed at Lapa ('inside Nyangatom territory' (Matsuda 1994: 60), a dangerous claim),[6] which ends the narrative as reconstructed by Matsuda.

To sum up the discussion, while I cannot determine when and how the gradual diminishment of the ritual services provided by the Moguji for the Kara took place, I tend to agree that there probably was at some point during the mid to late twentieth century a moment when the amity between the two co-resident populations started to decline.[7] The Moguji of Kara began to act as a corporate group instead of politically mute individual clients to individual patrons. As has been my argument so far, I support the notion that the Kara gain some clarity of identity and strength of purpose from their domination and their multimodal othering of the Moguji, in ritual, in kinship, in metaphor and in discourse. I do, however, challenge some of Matsuda's propositions, which also serves to focus my claims: 'The Kara … were formerly more like brothers of the Koegu rather than neighbors. In fact, a bond partnership between families of both groups was often compared to brotherhood by themselves' (1994: 53).

Here, Matsuda fails to keep his levels of reference apart. The relations between individuals are conflated with the relations between the ethnically marked groups: individuals may be close, but I doubt that the two categories under discussion ever were. Additionally, the 'bond partnership' between Kara and Moguji, as it existed and still exists in part, named *beltamo* by the Kara and *belmo* by the Moguji (the term of reference and address is *bel* in both cases), is not of the same order as other bondfriendships in which the Kara engage. Instead, it seems a gloss on a very specific patron–client relationship.

The simple linguistic fact that there is no term for 'brother' in *kar'appo*, only for 'younger' (*kanna*) or 'elder brother' (*ishemo*), indicates that there is something wrong with Matsuda's statement. This mistake becomes more pronounced in the following: 'I would like to note that *belmo* is not a relationship of equity' (1994: 54). But this is precisely what *beltamo* is claimed to be, more than any other relation on the Lower Omo (except maybe for age-mates), and quite explicitly so. In fact, people who want to establish amicable relations with others might well address them tentatively as *bel*, indicating perfect mutuality (see Girke 2010). That he found the interaction of Kara and Moguji *bel* in practice unequal might have alerted Matsuda that he had fallen for a euphemism that in fact allows both partners to pretend they are equal.

Calling one another *bel* means to aspire to the glorious examples of bond-friendship known from among the 'more pastoralist' groups in the cultural neighbourhood (see Chapter 6), whereas the Kara extracts the labour of 'his Moguji'[8] and often enough his entire family, working the Kara's land. The salient distinction that I want to express here, between *äda* (as it exists between individuals and families) and *ädamo* (the ideology of domination in a discourse of amity), is not appreciated by Matsuda (but see Freeman and Pankhurst 2003: 1f). In a later publication, he rephrases the issue more adequately: 'Under the pretence of *bel* a Kara man would use Muguji man as a labourer to clear and cultivate the land' (2002: 176). But where is the 'pretence'? Even a clever Kara could not keep a purported bondfriend in the dark about the actual inequality of their relation. This suggestion that people would only cooperate in relations of inequality when not aware that they are colluding with their oppressor is absurd. Matsuda, in being oblivious as to what the *äda* aspect of the relationship entails, also wonders why the Moguji had been given eleven rifles by the Kara, 'their immediate enemy' (2002: 181). To realize that relations between individuals are not necessarily affected by the perturbations between their respective political bodies, one of the bases of bondfriendship, clears up this misunderstanding. Hieda assumes a stance that is similar to Matsuda but subtler in claiming that '[the Moguji] would never admit' that they were subordinate to the Kara in this 'bond-partnership' (1996: 149).

An interesting perspective is provided by Gezahegn Petros, whose fieldwork in Kara took place between August 1993 and February 1994. He reports on some of the fallout of the schism, worth quoting at length here:

> [T]he Moguji of Karo made a movement some six years ago to build their own settlement independent of the Karo within the territory of the latter. The desire of the Moguji resulted in a strong objection from the Karo. Having been prevented from founding their own settlement, some Moguji households left Dus and first moved to the Moguji of Kuchuru, to the people whom they refer to as their relatives. There, they were not accepted by their own people because, as one informant put it, 'the Moguji of Kuchur did not want to rupture their relationship with the Karo'. Thereafter, they moved to Nyangatom, to the people with whom the Karo often came into conflict. They had been accepted as refugees by the Nyangatom and had been allowed to found their own settlement there. I observed in the field that some of these households had been returning to Dus one by one. Remarkably, the returnees were not seen by the Karo as deserters, but rather accepted with cordial hospitality. (1994: 18)

Gezahegn, doing research in Kara, picked up on what Matsuda failed to notice: the divisions within the people categorized as Moguji, many of whom individually chose to stick with the Kara, or return later (see below), some of whom even fought alongside the Kara during the schism itself. In a nutshell, the Worba Moguji (who are supposedly of a different origin and not actually descendants of the primordial Moguji of the Trail of the Red Bull myth) are seen in Kara as the troublemakers, the ones who truly shifted allegiance to the Nyangatom, and those who are even today seen as the traitors to *ädamo*, and in some cases to *äda* as well. The Worba families who still now live in the Kara villages are by and large exempt from this accusation. The Moguji of Kuchur, on the other hand, are the ones who – while viewed with occasional distrust through their affiliation with the Nyangatom and their administrative structures – have not denied the ties that oblige and probably never were so intimately entangled with the Kara in the first place. Something resembling egalitarian *beltamo* a little better might have grown between them and the Kara over time.[9]

The entire affair constituted a challenge to the claim that ethnic categories within Kara had no bearing on political matters, which is so foundational for claims of *ädamo*. Whether strategically (as Matsuda claims) or through a contingent conjunction of circumstances, many among the Moguji defied the Kara. In the process, they further weakened formerly defining and presently declining ritual practices, in that the services they provided to the true Kara fell by the wayside. This process found a culmination in the early 1990s (Matsuda 2002: 173, 182) with the establishment of a *kebele* for Kuchur, first as a section of the Kuraz *woreda* (a district, at that time assigned to the Nyangatom and Dassanech) and, since 2006, when the older district was divided, a section of the Nyangatom *woreda*.

The narrative form that 'the schism' takes today does not render it as a process with a gradual build-up and an eventual climax, but as a sudden rupture, a rupture that was fully blamed on the Worba. According to the true Kara, the Worba Moguji, 'having become clever', had claimed the fertile land of Lake Diba right next to Korcho as their own and reformulated the terms of the relationship between them and the Kara accordingly.[10] According to my informants, Korcho was established by a group of mostly Nyuwariya-Kara as a permanent settlement precisely in order to better control these southern cultivation sites, with an eye on both the Worba and the Hamar, who intermittently had been invited to cultivate at Diba alongside the Kara (see Strecker 1976a). Distrust ruled the day: people worried that someone else might entrench themselves overnight and lay claim to the land through occupation. Plus, the strategic location of Korcho on its windy hilltop, offering a unique overview in all directions, cannot be overstated.

Thus, the Worba had transgressed: by politicizing ethnicity, by connecting it to participation and resources, they opened up the Pandora's box of belonging and issued an explicit challenge to the question of land rights. The Kara objected to this in word and deed: for them, under *ädamo*, ethnicity only provided the (ritual) rules of interaction and nothing else. They claim that it has no import in

Figure 5.1 A young woman in the sorghum fields of dried-out Lake Diba (April 2005). Photograph by Felix Girke.

the world of politics, and whoever challenges this claim attacks the very basis of the community. One needs to understand that these Worba are a small group of probably no more than a few dozen people. The ringleaders, as the Kara see it, the ones who 'write letters' to the administration, the ones who instigate against the Kara, the ones who provoke and make a fuss are a handful of men. Hieda reports an assertion made by Moguji in 1989 of their 'right to own the land' they had held before and now were leasing from the Kara. They explicitly contested the Kara's naturalization of their territorial gains (Hieda 1996: 150). In a way, the Moguji Hieda spoke to wanted to retroactively renounce that their ancestors' rights to their land had ever been alienable, a truly complex legal conundrum.

One example from an NGO-sponsored peace conference between the Kara and the Nyangatom, which took place in Gembella in Hamar in early 2008, illustrates what it is that upsets the Kara. During the talks, which centred on the question of the fields of the Kara on the western riverbank over which Kara and Nyangatom had been fighting, a well-known Worba spokesman who had come as a member of the Nyangatom delegation got up and drew all attention to himself by declaring that the discussion was missing the point: 'The Kara have no land', he said, 'in the beginning, we were only three: the Murle, the Moguji, and the baboons of the forest.'[11] This was dismissed as *garro-delak*, unfounded provocation, by the Kara. The Kara denied not only the specific claim of the Moguji, but also denied them the right of inserting their own concerns into the affairs of their betters, as it were (the Kara and Nyangatom), and accused them of political opportunism. This dynamic differentiation of autonomous groups from subordinate categories such as the Moguji is modelled well by the Wheel of Autonomy.

The Price of Reintegration

I now retell a narrative that I heard from my age-mates: so it came to pass that some Worba Moguji, older rather than younger people, moved back towards Kara, after they had originally left when the *siamo* (lit. the 'badness,' i.e. the schism) occurred. These Moguji had, the Kara said, originally claimed that they were turning their backs on Kara for good, that they would become Nyangatom. This was what had upset the true Kara no end – it is a well-known occurrence for individual homesteads to move away for some time, such as after a homicide, and it is tacitly understood that time heals many wounds. Even murderers might be allowed to come back home at some point. So this explicit disclaimer of *ädamo* was felt to be deliberate betrayal. Others, who had returned earlier, had slaughtered goats for the community as ritual conciliation, and so they had been welcomed again: '*ke shide* – may it [the disagreement] stay behind!'

These, I assume, were the ones who Gezahegn mentioned had returned to Dus previously (see above; 1994: 18). Those who came back now refused to submit to this procedure. Faced with this refusal, the Kara then said amongst themselves, 'well now, is that the way it will be? Do they think it will be this easy? So let us not do anything rash, let them get settled, and when they have "slowed down" and become complacent, we shall act.' One Kara man had given the Moguji access to fields at Lake Diba, without consulting with the *zersi*, the elders, and so the Moguji started cultivating. 'Why had they come back at all?', I inquired. My interlocutors expressed their conviction that over there, in Galgidda and these other places where they had been staying, it had been 'suffering only', as the Nyangatom of course would not give them anything for free ('either', it was tempting to add). Then, the tale continues, the Kara *borkotto bitti* discussed the matter among themselves. Having come to an agreement, they started confidentially recruiting younger people down the age-set ladder, taking care that no word about the plan would get out. The day of reckoning approached and the young men were ordered to start cutting long, slender whipping wands, and to get some of their friends to help them. One morning, then, two young men were sent as scouts (*doya*) to the riverbank opposite Lapa, to keep a lookout and convey their observations. The rest of the posse waited in hiding.

When one of the scouts then reported that the Moguji had set across the river, the Kara swarmed into Diba, only to realize that the Moguji had instead entered the village Korcho, which overlooks Diba. This was just as well; because of the special sacred status of Diba, nobody should be beaten within its confines at any rate. The group reassembled and entered the village, where they found all whom they sought in the homestead of a (still now) respected Moguji elder. The Moguji were grappled, bound and severely beaten with the freshly cut whipping wands – 'may they die!' went the cries. Their bodies, it was said, were 'white' from all the punishment they had to endure, while blood was running across the ground. Then nine goats were taken from the offenders, stabbed and consumed by the *zersi* as compensation for the Moguji's transgression, their *d'ebbi*. When this was all done, the Moguji were freed – '*magidina, derkimmateh!* – it is over, you may sit now!' and thus were offered reintegration into the community. The beaten Worba refused this offer, though, and went back to the Nyangatom, where they have been staying up until now, and resumed their plotting against the Kara.

The story, however, did not end there: a short while after, a young Moguji walked unseen from Korcho to Dus. At night, he leapt into the water, cut the ropes holding the most prized boat of the Kara, an aluminium-hull vessel donated by the missionaries of the SPCM,[12] and guided its drift downriver. Making landfall on the eastern bank, other Moguji came to assist him, and dragged and carried the boat to their settlement in Galgidda.

The next morning, the Kara found the boat gone and were very puzzled – until a Moguji woman, cultivating on the other side of the river, had a slip of the tongue and gave the theft away. Some men then went off and finally managed to cross the river from Uala. Reaching the other shore, they managed to find the tracks of the boat and six people, and followed them to Galgidda. What now? 'Don't shoot', said one older man, 'they do belong to us after all!'[13] The Moguji had meanwhile gotten wind of their pursuers and some, along with a number of Nyangatom, were approaching the Galgidda settlement. One of the Kara, in order to initiate negotiations and not to scare anybody, rose from hiding and raised his hand, but the Moguji and Nyangatom immediately started shooting. The bullets were returned and – over time – reinforcements arrived on both sides. Then the Kara decided to retreat, not wanting to start a full-blown war over the boat. One Moguji was injured in the firefight. This happened around March 2003. In August 2003, I arrived in Kara for the first time. In between, the situation was tense. When I left Kara again for a brief excursion after just a few days, the wife of a man from my eventual age-set was killed near Korcho. This triggered a state of more or less continuous warfare between the Kara and Nyangatom that lasted for years.[14]

The beaten Moguji elders, in the Kara interpretation, had refused their due punishment and had not acknowledged their guilt. This is problematic and engenders escalation: normally, accusations in Kara are direct and must be acknowledged initially at least. The accusation '*Ya zerbona!* – you are bad!' requires a humble, affirmative *eh-e* reply ('yes, I hear you/I agree') even before one is told what one is supposed to have done wrong. Trying to get access to the resources of Kara country, without submitting and paying the price of reintegration, was unacceptable under the rule of *ädamo*.

The moral end of the story – for it is yet again a story, and this narrative character drives it forward, the identification of protagonists and antagonists lends it meaning, gives it context and provides motivation – is that the Moguji are instigators (*kantsi-ed*) who stir up trouble between two others, between two larger groups who might otherwise live in peace. But in the end, they have nothing to show for it.

The Moguji did in fact suffer insult and injury, because the Nyangatom carried off the lightweight boat and brought it to their settlements at Aiba. Some individual Kara then proceeded and raided a few cattle from the Nyangatom, in that way settling the score between these two groups. Even though there are surely several versions going around, this narrative has since come into its own right as a moral tale. As such, it throws light on the conception of *ädamo*, and on the basic principle that to live in Kara demands complete subordination to the rules of the *zersi* and the decisions of the *borkotto bitti*. Even if the story as told is inevitably partial – in Clifford's useful double sense, incomplete as well as committed to a position (1986) – it illustrates the strains on the relations between true Kara and Worba Moguji.

Other Marginal Groups: Steps towards Comparison

The predicament of the Moguji is not unique. As my argument on the rhetorical processes of differentiation builds on the appreciation of the underlying material

Figure 5.2 A Hamar, a Moguji and a Kara jointly wait for the noon sun to pass (November 2004). Photograph by Felix Girke.

basis, I want to widen my scope by briefly comparing this relation with other similar relations both from South Omo and greater East Africa. In comparing the relationship between the Kara and the Moguji to relationships elsewhere, what can be achieved? The objective cannot be to develop a historical typology of marginalization as such, as I am interested in interaction and practice. However, a look at cases with a specific 'family resemblance' brings out what is like and what is unlike, where conflicts occur and where not, and in which dynamics of othering and in which conceptions the exclusion of marginal groups finds expression nearby but elsewhere. This allows me to develop some suggestions about what makes the Kara–Moguji relations so particular.[15]

Among the various marginal groups on the Lower Omo, the Kwegu are arguably the most extensively discussed in anthropology (see Turton 1982; Woodhead and Turton 1982; Lydall 1982; Brown 1983; Turton 2002a). While the ways in which the Kwegu are marginalized and ideologically dominated are near-identical, the material basis of the relationship is different. According to Turton, the Mursi patrons are dependent on services provided by the Kwegu, such as ferrying them across the Omo and providing them with game trophies that the Mursi can convert into cattle. Turton states that the Kwegu identify with the status quo to a large degree (2002a: 158), suggesting that there are no strains on the system, no struggles about who is allowed to categorize whom. We learn little about symbolism and possible use of tropes (such as metaphor) in the interaction between the Kwegu and the Mursi. He also claims with not really corroborated conviction that the two linguistically related populations of Kwegu and Moguji 'have no contacts' with one another (Turton 1982: 11). In the light of the material from Kara, it would be valuable to see whether in the last thirty-odd years since Turton collected his material, the Kwegu have issued any challenges to Mursi domination.

Another possible comparison lies in the relationship between the Dorobo groups of Kenya and their pastoralist neighbours.[16] The Dorobo are, as Kenny evocatively puts it, the 'mirror in the forest', the true 'other' of the pastoralist (1981). He goes furthest in my sample of writers in pointing out how the cultural opposition between hunting and herding is totalized: the hunters are everything the pastoralists are not. However, this othering, so similar to the conceptual metaphorization of the Moguji, is fundamentally different. The Dorobo and the pastoralist populations are separated by a 'permeable membrane' (Kenny 1981: 480f), which allows individuals to 'shift' between the categories and the corresponding livelihoods and ways of subsistence.

The assumption is that everybody wants to be a pastoralist, for reasons of prestige and autonomy. Thus, while pastoralists can pragmatically become Dorobo to avoid starvation after losing their livestock, they would constantly strive to recover herds of a sufficient size to rejoin the pastoralist category. Through such shifting, cultural features such as clans, age-set organization, etc. come to be shared across populations (Berntsen 1976: 7, see also Schlee 1994b), and those self-same features facilitate the shifting in turn. So despite the similarities between the Moguji and the Dorobo in terms of their marginalization and metaphoric conceptualization, the agriculturalist Kara need never shift through the dense forest of bodily and ritual symbols and become Moguji who are (despite their reputation as hunters and fishermen) equally agriculturalist.[17] The idea of becoming a Moguji would be dismissed by true Kara as absurd – unthinkable.[18] John Galaty contends that 'an adequate explanation for continuing Torrobo social autonomy must account both for their apparent separate origin and for their periodic incorporation of pastoralists. Their uniqueness today appears primarily economic, with cultural and linguistic differences being secondary' (Galaty 1982: 8). Accordingly, as the economic difference between the Kara and the Moguji is best characterized by control over the means of production rather than different modes of production, and the ethnic difference seems fundamental, the shifting of individuals is excluded from their relationship. Is it perhaps that pastoralists are more at risk of losing their livelihood than the agriculturalist Kara, who can afford to maintain impermeable boundaries between them and the Moguji, as individual households would be unlikely to be rendered as destitute as a pastoralist whose herds are decimated?

Yet other comparisons could be drawn – specifically regarding Ethiopia – through consideration of the study of marginal hunters and craftsmen (see Freeman and Pankhurst 2003; Pankhurst 1999). Briefly, a parallel exists in that segregated groups such as tanners, potters and blacksmiths occasion a division of labour within a population between the numerical and ideologically dominant group and the marginalized artisans, and that ostracism, restrictions on commensality and intermarriage, and numinous ritual duties are common, in principle similar to the Moguji's services to the Kara. However, the relationship as it is emically understood seems to have less of an ethnic component. While these marginalized groups are often seen as former immigrants from a more specialized centre (see Amborn 1990; Levine 2000), they are mainly characterized by their occupation, not by their ancestors' specific provenience.[19] While the mechanisms of marginalization are similar, their symbolic conceptualization as expressed in interaction is markedly different.

A special case, and relevant due to proximity and association, are the Bajje, a specific category found among the Hamar, Banna and Bashada, the 'HBB cluster' occupying the hill ranges east of Kara. Little has been published on the Bajje. As Ivo Strecker and Jean Lydall's old friend Baldambe from Hamar put it, a Bajje is someone who 'observes no rituals himself but performs the sitting ritual for the Hamar, Banna and Bashada people' (Lydall and Strecker 1979b: 149; also Epple 2007: 55f). These peoples consider the Bajje late-comers, as migrants, and trace their roots, so common in Africa for similar groups (see Kopytoff 1989: 55), to the outside. Some individuals are said to have come precisely from the Moguji down in the Omo Valley. Even today, the Bajje of the HBB cluster marry girls from Aari or the Moguji (Lydall, personal communication). Conversely, I have learned of cases of Bajje from 'the mountains' who migrated to the Omo Valley and there joined the Worba Moguji population. There is, then, a permeable membrane between the Moguji and other marginalized people. Whereas a Bashada man who lives in Kara is not subject to restrictions or ostracism beyond not being allowed to partake of the true Kara's central rituals or to marry a true Kara girl, Bajje coming down from Bashada would be included in the 'Moguji' category of the Kara ritual order, as people would impose a familiar local ethnic label due to the fact of the Bajje's ritual exclusion among the Kara's neighbours.

This way of practising ethnicity, then, cannot be reduced to the materialist needs of the Kara to secure the services of the Moguji, even though it is inextricably bound up with the historical account of how the Moguji lost their land to the Kara. The question of whether or not the Moguji have any such figurative or stereotypical view of the true Kara has no bearing on the ideology expressed here in terms of *ädamo*: the power relations in Kara country deny the Moguji the privilege of making effective counterclaims against the proper order. While the Kwegu, as presented by Turton, seem dominated to such a degree that their identification with the proclaimed order is complete, the struggle of the true Kara to suppress challenges to the rule of *ädamo* is the dominant feature of the Kara–Moguji relationship today. On the Lower Omo, some ethnicities are denied relevance in the political arena, even as their ritual aspect is constitutive in the legitimation of the larger, political body. The Moguji are not granted their own Wheel of Autonomy. Individual shifting as in the Dorobo case is impossible due to the primordialist conception of the ethnic differences – even though this very primordialism is sidelined in the inclusion of the Bajje into the category of Moguji, just as it proved of little weight when some Bogudo were turned into Gomba.[20] Such cultural 'translations' are common in South Omo and not only shed light on the interplay of practice and ideology, but also on the configuration of groups and boundaries here called the cultural neighbourhood (see Gabbert and Thubauville 2010), discussed in the following chapters.

The comparative data on other marginal groups and their relation to more powerful (affective) 'pastoralists' suggest that there are structural reasons for these dominant populations to exert symbolic and rhetorical effort in suppressing people categorized as low-status hunter-gatherers, fishermen or in some places rather caste-like craftsmen (Amborn 1990). The result is that there is a regional understanding that there are 'proper' and autonomous groups as well as those who simply do not have what it takes to assert themselves in the cultural neighbourhood. Ethnicity seems to be the idiom for these processes of subjugation, and especially their legitimization, but we can already see from the examples here that the mode of production is also an important aspect. My conclusion is that if the Moguji did not exist, the Kara would have to invent them: the Kara's sense of collective self and many of their cultural values are strongly stimulated by having those others to point at. The subsequent discussion of the Kara and their neighbours shows the Wheel of Autonomy in its ideal type – egalitarian actors engaged in an ongoing process of proving to each other and themselves that they are all worthy contestants. But these contestations are possibly better performed if one is assured that there are people lower on the rungs of the ladder of civilization and accomplishment.

Notes

1. Bala was also the one who united the clans of Garshima, Eshiba and Dangarr, which form a corporate exogamous group today.
2. Between the lines, this is a claim of distinction and ritual purity: the true Kara have in fact 'refused'.
3. See Turton (1994) for an account of the events and (2003) for his personal struggle with this for South Omo unprecedented act of violence. But he also indicates that in the conflicts between the Mursi and the Aari, the acquisition of automatic rifles by the Mursi did not lead to higher casualties among the Aari. Regarding Kara-Nyangatom warfare, I was told that the presence of automatic rifles, which allow one or two hidden defenders to fight off a raid, discouraged people from open battles and attempts to slaughter entire villages, as had been done on both sides in the 1970s with little more than spears, knives and ancient bolt-action rifles.
4. Matsuda's contention that the Moguji would introduce themselves to outsiders as 'Karo' (1994: 50) fails to appreciate that when they did that, they were using the terms they could safely assume this outsider would understand.
5. The anthropologists Jerome Lewis and James Woodburn, neither being a regional expert for South Omo, wrote a report on 'low-status tribal groups with a history of hunting and gathering who live on the lowland plains of South-Western Ethiopia', solicited by the Christensen Fund (Lewis and Woodburn n.d.). Their research took place in December 2007–January 2008, just subsequent to my longest fieldwork visit. They reproduce some further accounts on the relations among 'Kwegu', whom they divide into southern, central and northern, and between them and the more powerful groups such as the Mursi, Kara and Nyangatom. From their report, the item that the 'Moguji' allegedly migrated to their present locations from a hill called 'Mugunya' in Hamar was new to me; I had no opportunity to crosscheck this with my informants. The claim is as likely to be a post hoc explanation as to provide an etymology of the ethnonym. Lewis and Woodburn, working exclusively through sometimes several translators, realize that their work is only a 'starting point' for further research (n.d.: 7).
6. Galgidda and Lapa are two of the numerous areas on the western side of the river that are claimed by the Kara but controlled by the Nyangatom and Moguji. This issue is explored in other publications (Girke 2008, 2013). Here, I only want to mention that scholars should be careful about casually representing one area as 'belonging' to one group and not another, when it is exactly these issues that people are being killed over on the Lower Omo.
7. Kara interlocutors told me that it was the time of the Derg regime, the thirteen years of repressive military junta government, 'when everybody started doing things by themselves'.
8. Turton found neither in Kwegu nor in Mursi a translation for 'patron' and 'client' (2002a: 154). His informants referred to their partners as 'my Kwegu' and 'my Mursi',

respectively. I have found the same euphemistic usage among the Moguji and Kara. In address, the relation is not marked beyond the use of *bel*.

9. Many Kuchur households seem to be habitually cultivating fields 'owned' by Kara, but much remains unknown about the dealings between Kuchur and Kara proper.
10. The name Diba (elsewhere Dipa) refers to a large depression due southwest of Korcho that completely floods in years when the Omo River rises particularly high. As this occasional lake dries out over the next year or so, very valuable farmland emerges, while children catch the catfish and other unfortunate water-dwellers that did not manage to escape while the lake was still connected to the river. As outlined in the chapter, there are ritual rules applied to Diba.
11. This story came up repeatedly in conversations when I visited Kara in February–March 2008. For an extensive historical discussion of the case of the Murle, a formerly powerful and rich group on the Omo Valley today assimilated by the Nyangatom, see Tornay (1981).
12. The SPCM (Swedish Philadelphia Church Mission; see Matsuda 1994; Alvarsson 1989: 18f) worked both in the Kibbish area of Nyangatom and in the Kadokochin for several years. Even today, the Kara very much revere a near-mythical female missionary they call Gimbort (really Gunborg Molin) as 'a friend of the Kara'. Her merits in seeing to the education of Kara boys are unrivalled. This is in stark contrast to other members of the SPCM, who are dismissed as 'friends of the Nyangatom only'.
13. The Kara claim that it brings misfortune to kill a Moguji. This ties in with *ädamo* and ritual practice, but is not a killing taboo based on ancestral kinship, as in the case of the Arbore and Dassanetch (see Chapter 6).
14. See Girke (2008) for a first account and analysis of what happened in Kara between that time and 2007.
15. This follows Dumézil's understanding of the comparative method. He observed that 'it permits the recognition and a clearer view of structures of thought but not the reconstitution of events' (1966: 8, quoted in Needham 1970: lxxxiii).
16. See, for example, Berntsen (1976); Broch-Due and Anderson (1999); Distefano (1990); Galaty (1982); Kenny (1981); and van Zwanenberg (1976). Writers show different biases in the prefix they attach to the 'Dorobo' stem: 'wa(n)'- is from Swahili, 'il-' from the Maa (where 'torrobo' is also found), and 'n-' from Kikuyu (Distefano 1990: 41). The etymology of the word stem itself, while often handwaved as meaning 'poor/without cattle' or 'hunter' in Maa, is also disputed. Kenny lists three versions, all with a range of scholarly supporters (1981: 478).
17. I choose this point in my book to admit that technically, the Kara and other populations cultivating along the Omo should be considered horticulturalists, as they use the digging stick rather than a plough. However, in the regional discourse as well as established academic usage, this distinction is usually glossed over. To boot, the more correct term 'horti-pastoralists' is entirely awkward.
18. As is familiar from East African groups, a perpetrator of homicide will leave the settlements of the Kara and stay 'in the forest' for some time, until negotiations can slowly be initiated by a middleman. However, such a person would most likely go and live with a bondfriend outside of Kara, and thus would neither be dependent on hunting and gathering nor forced to join a marginal group for their protection.
19. The discussion sometimes blurs when it comes to hunters, who are just as marginalized, but as a rule are said to be autochthonous. This distinction, which is central to the Kara case, is not always accorded relevance in other studies. Alula Pankhurst recognizes this

when he claims that the processes of differentiation in southwestern Ethiopia are 'so complex and varied that no simple unitary explanation of the origins and persistence of marginalized groups is tenable' (1999: 492).
20. This shows how my approach differs from Dereje's study of the Anywaa 'emic ethnic primordialists' and the Nuer 'emic ethnic constructivists' in eastern Ethiopia (Dereje 2011): the Kara sometimes are primordialist and sometimes not. Their cultural understandings of ethnicity are not set in stone but opportunistically adapted to the situation and rhetorically enforced.

Chapter 6

The Regional Other in the Cultural Neighbourhood

This chapter steps away from the struggles within Kara. The perspective widens to encompass the relations between the Kara as a political group (now including the Moguji, Gomba and Bogudo) and other similar polities. Metaphor was a central aspect of the blatant othering of the Moguji, with their subordinate position at the edge of the Kara polity, but the relations between the Kara and the populations they consider to be equally autonomous are framed quite differently. The Kara see it as a structurally egalitarian relationship, and people often express the basic analogy between the various polities of South Omo: they compare them and talk about them as autonomous and distinct agents. This relationship portrays each of these politico-territorial groups as an instance of a specific type, and allows the Kara (and others) to aggregate at the scale of the wider cultural neighbourhood:[1] in order to establish a categorical opposition to the Habesha, the generic and collective Ethiopian highlander, the Kara self-consciously employ the term Shank'illa (see Smidt 2010). This particular term has thus inadvertently switched sides. It was originally an epithet used by highland Ethiopians in reference to the potential slaves, the 'blacks', the 'lowlanders', the 'pastoralists' at the 'natural fringe' of the Ethiopian centre (Levine 1965; compare Donham 2002a; Markakis 2011; Strecker 1994). It has become more ambiguous today.

Use of the term Shank'illa allows people to make empirical claims and normative statements about themselves or others, but the underlying relationship between the specific Shank'illa groups always remains problematic. The overarching category never erases the differences between its elements; the Wheels of Autonomy keep the separate social agents tangible, even as in specific arenas the claims to difference are muted vis-à-vis an overarching commonality. In order to meaningfully relate to one another, the groups of South Omo require such a common frame, as Sahlins points out: '[S]imilitude is a necessary condition of the differentiation. For, in the end, culturalism is the differencing of growing similarities by contrastive structures' (1999: 411, emphasis removed). Harrison (as if echoing Sahlins) admonishes us to keep in mind the 'deeply ambivalent nature of relations of resemblance' (2002: 228). In Chapter 1, I have outlined the history of such an approach to identity, from Simmel onwards, which not only acknowledges the difficulties of difference, but that especially emphasizes that people have to reconcile with similarity just as much or even more. This can be ethnographically substantiated particularly well for the case of South Omo.

In this chapter, then, I trace the relations between the various Shank'illa groups as seen from Kara, and show the necessity to understand social action in this arena as strategic, performative and rhetorical, in the face of an audience composed of both Shank'illa and Habesha, of insiders and outsiders, respectively. While many of the arenas in which such claims and contestations are issued can ultimately be connected to concerns of political economy, what is primarily and irreducibly at stake in these processes are questions of power, domination, resistance, autonomy and self-esteem. What results from these dynamics is that nearly everything happening on a supraindividual level in South Omo is rendered in ethnic terms and, often enough, in terms of ethnic groups as collective actors.

Similarity and difference are constituted in very different ways between and among the various groups. As stereotypes are strikingly common at this level, I discuss this pervasive social practice in some detail, as it is often underappreciated and undertheorized in anthropology (see Rapport and Overing 2007: 391–97). Half a century ago, Beidelman stated that:

> to the best of my knowledge, there have been no accounts of the beliefs and abuse which define and separate various Negro-African groups in any particular area of the continent. This is surprising since intertribal enmity has, especially recently, been a matter of considerable significance in explaining social and political affairs in many parts of Africa. Insult terms and ethnic stereotypes would seem to provide especially useful clues to explaining such conflicting attitudes. Neglect by social anthropologists of these various problems is difficult to understand or excuse. (1964: 33f)

Current anthropology might not assign to stereotypes the facility to 'explain' conflicts; it much rather works from the understanding that stereotypes are expressions of other aspects of a relationship. Still, this admonishment remains relevant and revealing, but not quite in the way Beidelman intended: while 'the beliefs and abuse', that is, the content of stereotypes that people hold of each other, is surely pertinent, the more pressing questions in the rhetorical analysis of interethnic relations are 'who is talking about each other in stereotypes?', 'when do people use stereotyping?' and 'what does this sort of talk achieve?' The argument pursued here is that the phenomenon of stereotyping talk is closely linked to a specific sort of ethnic status enjoyed by the recognized politico-territorial units of South Omo. This leads to the idea of the 'regional other', the template around which all stereotypes revolve, which is a means to and an expression of a balance of power and relations of interdependence throughout the region. To look at where we find stereotypes tells us much about which relationships are relevant in interaction or imagination for the constitution of localized narratives.[2]

The Rhetorical Evocation of a Region

It is remarkable how certain services, features or material objects can become iconic for a group and its role in the narratives of South Omo. When a Kara elder blesses a household by expertly spraying a fine mist of atomized coffee from his mouth, the chances are that he will designate the coffee as 'Aari coffee', regardless of where the coffee husks were actually acquired.[3] Such a behaviour is no mere liturgy, but encapsulates a narrative. It nostalgically evokes the (good) old times when Aari people travelled on foot to Kara country leading donkeys loaded with coffee to exchange for the locally available salty soil called *muutsi*.[4] The invocation also regretfully comments on the (bad) present times in which the cultural neighbourhood has deteriorated through the 'great transformation' engendered by the increasing presence of administration and market (compare Girke 2010).

In terms of sociality, intimacy and community, size does matter. Consider Donham's perspective of the regional particularities: 'Southern Ethiopia is a structuralist's delight. Here are dozens of cultural groups, many small, in historical interaction for millennia, all different in one way or another, but all resembling one another as well' (2000: 21). Even without thorough documentation and a comparison to prove the special status of the South Omo region in containing extreme cultural and ethnic diversity in a small area, as evidenced by the size of the various populations and their territories (Schlee 2008: 38f), a positive argument can be made: looking around them, the Kara recognize several neighbouring populations as part of the region, as extant elements of a social landscape. This landscape has a horizon beyond which it gets very difficult (and really largely irrelevant) to make out any details. This (changeable) horizon has been established over time by means of individual journeys, trade routes, warfare and intermarriage, a community of discourse and experience – in brief, through Donham's 'historical interaction'. For this social landscape, which is not only a cognitive but also an affective anchor for members of the various groups that are entwined in this way, the term 'cultural neighbourhood' has been introduced (compare Beidelman 1964: 34).

Beyond the indicated mutual familiarity and mutual imagination, this notion serves to highlight how much the cultural and linguistic diversity of South Omo is appreciated not only by the tourists in their land-cruisers and the itinerant anthropologists, but also by many of its inhabitants. Many local people love travelling the region, and I have found numerous interlocutors highly interested in and very knowledgeable about their neighbours' customs and multilingual to a surprising degree. The delight in other people(s), who are in so many ways just the same, but different, comes out very strongly in storytelling about bondfriendship, and the travels, exchanges and adventures it involves (Girke 2010).

This is what the term 'cultural neighbourhood' is intended to evoke. But this use of 'neighbourhood' does not fully align with other usages. As an example, the contributors to the volume by Konings and Foeken (2006) apply the notion quite exclusively to the urban context, where a neighbourhood is an entity, of which a plural is possible, synonymous to an urban quarter or a ward. In my usage, neighbourhood is a singular, and has a different referent, and indeed two main applications: it indicates the spatial fact that culturally differentiated populations live close to each other, with recurrent interaction of individuals, and that they conceive of each other as being relevant, as being 'people, too', and especially that each collective neighbour within the neighbourhood can be made to take the role of a coherent actor. Rogers Brubaker has said of ethnopolitical entrepreneurs that '[b]y invoking groups, they seek to evoke them, summon them, call them into being' (2004: 10, emphasis removed). For South Omo, this plausible claim can be generalized, as it is not always a strategic purpose that underlies the presentation of other populations as collective actors. To invoke ethnic categories as groups, to narratively frame interaction between individuals in terms of their ethnicities, is the default way of people to talk about others, at least if these others fulfil certain criteria. The groups have been 'called into being' a long time ago, and it usually does not take much rhetorical effort to plausibly define a situation not just in terms of personal ethnicity, but also in terms of ethnic groups. Hence, the cultural neighbourhood is not an entity; it is a way of ordering relations. 'Neighbourhood' denotes the mutual awareness of neighbouring populations, understanding themselves and each other as groups or communities, with all the comparative and schismogenetic and mimetic moments commonly occurring in interaction with a familiar other. The cultural neighbourhood is a perspective, and it has a horizon, beyond which similarity (and relevance) is no longer necessarily assumed.

This in some ways is closer to Appadurai's usage (1995: 208–11), who sees the 'context-generative' character of locality and neighbourhood. In his terminology, however, neighbourhood still refers to given segmented units that then interact within a wider territory. For my purposes, it seems more promising to focus on the use of the term to the application spelt out above: for each centred, ethnically anchored perspective, there are neighbours who live this side of a cognitive and practical horizon, neighbours who matter and who 'belong', even where violent conflicts occur. The cultural neighbourhood is context-generative, in that it provides an entangled history. Cultural neighbourhood is not only a forest of symbols (Turner 1967), but also an oasis of admiration, a lagoon of belonging, a savannah of claims, a swamp of stereotypes, a mountain range of mimetic appropriation and a jungle of tropes.

In being so fundamental to the constitution of ethnic identity, cultural neighbourhood is a matter as much of narration as of interaction. Here, the Wheel of Autonomy is set in motion in different ways: not only do people resist encroachment on their material territory, thus asserting agency, but they also imagine and negotiate sections of symbolic territory as means to maintain difference. This is most visible in the numerous stereotypes people hold about their neighbours (and, at least implicitly, about themselves), both positive and negative, which are mainly used for internal consumption. Far from being merely pejorative dismissals, stereotypes:

> are a stable and widespread discursive currency, and they provide significant points of initial reference. They afford bearings from which to anticipate interaction, plot social relations and initiate knowing – and from a safe distance, too – however far removed their biases become from the manifold elaborations of social relationship and being which eventuate. (Rapport and Overing 2007: 394)

I address particular stereotypes found in Kara and the significance of the cultural practice of stereotyping in turn.

As I mentioned at the beginning of the chapter, 'full membership' within the cultural neighbourhood is not an unproblematic given for each ethnic category in the region: some are more equal than others, and in the recent history of South Omo even, several ethnically categorized polities have risen and fallen. Some still struggle now to sustain their positions as significant, relevant and autonomous political actors. The cases of the Moguji and the Bogudo have been developed above (see Chapters 3–5). I have also mentioned the Gomba with their echoes of historical autonomy, who allegedly used to have their own ritual house, who retain fragments of arrival stories and ritual particularity, but who have otherwise been wholly integrated into the Kara body politic probably more than a century and a half ago.

In this sense, today's internal divisions are yesterday's group boundaries. One could see this as a nondramatic feature of the cultural neighbourhood, acknowledging that separatist clans or mutinous age-sets or other renegade factions have always been absorbed by another group. But this view is opposed by the recognition that in their respective here and now, people in South Omo by and large do not want to become members of other ethnic groups. This is well illustrated by Turton's description of the Mursi's worries after their crushing defeat by the Nyangatom (Turton 1994; see Chapter 1). The Wheel of Autonomy supports collective identity but also carries individuals along, since an individual's place in the cultural neighbourhood is always predicated upon their belonging to one exclusive category and their group's political ability to defend the interests of its members (compare Kopytoff 1989: 23). Concomitantly, a group that becomes too small to assert itself is on the road to dissolution, as individuals or whole sections will begin seeking affiliation and protection elsewhere (see Schlee 2008: 27, fn. 3).

Cultural neighbourhood, then, is usefully understood as an ongoing, depersonalized, positioned narrative of ethnogenesis and interaction (compare Dereje 2009: 125). Oral historical accounts, as told by Kara, are generally reductive in that they posit integrated collective actors, who then engage in clearly motivated and morally evaluated activities, having interests, resources and characteristics. Narratives and their defining aspect of sequentiality are today recognized as essential features of human consciousness and identity: 'Our conscious lives constitute dramas in which our selves, our societies and our reference groups are central characters, characters whose significance we interpret even as we live out their stories' (Rapport and Overing 2007: 320; similarly Carrithers 1992: 82–84). All social occurrences are integrated into such narratives as we already inhabit. But this entails that familiar elements or characters can drop out as they lose significance to the story. The Murle, Gomba and Bogudo have lost their relevance to anybody in the cultural neighbourhood other than the Kara, Nyangatom and maybe Mursi. The Moguji are trying to become a more significant part of certain stories, an actor in their own right. The Kara, Mursi, Nyangatom and all others are vying to remain free of the impositions by other distinct and autonomous actors in a narrative they are jointly telling, a narrative to which all sorts of people are listening (see Kratz 1994: 59) – while working hard to keep the Moguji (and Kwegu) in the position of narrated rather than narrator (see also Girke 2014b). Thus, while it is more or less an empirical claim when I talk about what 'the Kara' like, or prefer, or say (as I am then generalizing across many instances and individuals, drawing on my personal experience), in many other ways to talk of 'the Kara' is a central ontological problem: a population is not really a collective actor, the people so presented do not unproblematically have (let alone pursue) collective interests. But many Kara act as if they were and as if they had (and did), especially as they tell stories about themselves and others, to themselves and others. Thus, my initial question of 'how do they do it? How do you do it?' reveals itself as an ethnomethodological echo of a problem faced not only by the observer, but by the individual participants as well. That there are contexts in which Kara talk about 'the Kara' is thus a function of a social environment in which to *not* talk about oneself in terms of a collectively acting polity is an invitation to others to take away one's capacity to do so in the first place: basically, it would constitute an active slowing down of one's Wheel of Autonomy, with likely detrimental results.

Furthermore, cultural neighbourhood, as a social landscape, is not merely functional in providing templates for the imagination of the self and interaction with other people, nor is it merely a byproduct of other, wider historical processes: it is an extension of this principle of community across regional ethnic boundaries, the recognition (embodied in narrative) that notwithstanding all differences and conflicts, there is a commonality of tradition, history, livelihood and increasingly political interest between the member groups and the Great Ethiopian Other. This very contrast, that such a blatant 'They' is provided by the Ethiopian Highlanders, the Habesha, makes any conceptualization of a 'We' much more plausible.

As I will further develop in this and the next chapter, the social dynamics in South Omo need to be understood as more than yet another example of the 'tribal zone' (Ferguson and Whitehead 2000). Not only have the differences and conflicts between the resident groups become exaggerated and aggravated through the presence and encroachment of a powerful political centre, but in parallel to that narrative, another narrative, speaking of a regional community of all Shank'illa faced with the predations of the Habesha centre, has also flourished. Not without reason do we find the word *gal* (the enemy) used for the Habesha as well. The Habesha is too nonsimilar, his power too far beyond the local scale, to become an equal actor in the narratives of cultural neighbourhood, in what Corinne Kratz calls the 'regional rhetoric of ethnicity' (1994: 52) in reference to a similar constellation in nearby Kenya. The Habesha in large part provides the contrast that makes it possible to establish the category of the mutually similar Shank'illa. To investigate the cultural neighbourhood is to attend to periphery–periphery cultural contact, which in the face of a dominant (postcolonial) concern with centre–periphery relations with the concomitant themes of 'hegemony', 'resistance' and 'appropriation' has been neglected in recent social science and, as Beidelman's cited complaint (1964: 33f) indicates, in not so recent social science as well.[5]

In the South Omo region, as a rule, most such practices and discourses are informed by what the neighbours are doing. From such a perspective, some similarities to Leach's description of Highland Burma are apparent. There as here, a focus on seemingly internal processes, without taking account of what 'external' factors might have been influencing and shaping them, occludes the nature of cultural particularities:

> The significance of particular features of particular tribal organizations cannot be discovered by functional investigation of the more usual kind. It is rather that we come to understand the qualities of 'Tribe A' only when we measure these qualities against their antithesis in 'Tribe B'. (Leach 1964: xv)

Before discussing the embeddedness of the practice of stereotyping in the cultural neighbourhood, I will first delve deeper into the relations of the various Shank'illa groups to one another. They all co-exist and interact in what was called in comparatively little regarded or at least little-quoted sections of the otherwise ubiquitous *Ethnic Groups and Boundaries* (Barth 1969: 16f; Izikovitz 1969) – a polyethnic system.

The 'Regional Other'

To speak of the regional other is to make a statement about classification, generalization and analogy, from the perspective of the classifying inhabitant of South Omo. For the Kara, but likely in revealing variation in other places too, there exists a certain cultural category through which the groups of the region and the individuals making them up are conceived: some fit better, some worse and some do not fit at all, and are thus assigned to a different category. Just as Kratz says about the Kenyan Okiek and their neighbours, 'the regional system of ethnicity is not just a matter of style; it is also a matter of hierarchy, power, influence, and inequality' (1994: 52). I trace this for South Omo as it is relevant for Kara below.

The specific ethnosociological category (Galaty 1982) under consideration here has grown out of the realities of the interethnic dynamics of South Omo. My term for it is the 'regional other'. I suggest that it is founded on the following features, all of which facilitate personifying such a regional other in narrative and turning them into a collective actor: (1) an ethnically marked claim to cultural distinction; (2) the occupation and cultivation of a specific territory in a subsistence-oriented mode of production (not necessarily pastoralism); (3) the political autonomy to govern a wide range of internal and external affairs of the group; and (4) the willingness to defend the members of the population and their territory through violence.[6] I discuss these four features in turn.

Claims to Cultural Distinction

An ethnically marked claim to distinction emerges out of a group being itself and not any other. Only a sense of and especially an assertion of a self can afford inclusion in the regional narratives. In the cultural neighbourhood, this finds expression when people tangibly cultivate their differences and highlight certain allegedly distinguishing features in conversation, always with an eye on the audience. In this sense, there is a revealing and sufficient way to answer the one question all visitors to South Omo inevitably ask: 'Why do the Mursi women wear round clay discs in their lips?' This answer would be 'because this distinguishes them from the Surma and the ancient Murle, who use differently shaped lip plates, because the Aari have no lip plates at all, because the Nyangatom and the Turkana women wear metal jewellery, because the Kara women only insert a nail under their lower lip, and because some Hamar and Banna already imitate

Figure 6.1 Looking across the Omo at the western riverbank, claimed by the Kara but cultivated by the Nyangatom (January 2007). Photograph by Felix Girke.

the Kara nail' (see also Tornay 2007). Cultural practices gain their significance in the face of contrast, or even through contradistinction, and not some hermetic substance. At the level of contact, the Mursi lip-plate is the perfect Batesonian 'idea', as a 'difference which makes a difference' (Bateson 2000: 271f): adorning the lip was and is commonplace in South Omo, but the 'how' affords distinction. While imitation and appropriation are real enough processes in South Omo, they are constrained precisely in that displaying too much similarity is problematic.[7] This is again an instance of the Wheel of Autonomy in action: distinction needs to be achieved to plausibly claim autonomy.

But at the same time, the Wheel of Autonomy requires a fundamental translatability, a cultural commensurability across social divides, so that it is clear who the people are who qualify as significant others – porcupines, in the imagery introduced in Chapter 1. This is clearly in evidence in the region discussed here. In nearly all respects that matter in interethnic contact, a Kara *bitti* is a Mursi *komoru* is an Arbore *kawot* is a Hamar *bitta* is a ritual leader (see Chapter 2), and I have witnessed people using just these shorthand referentialities to all participants' satisfaction. The specific duties and powers of each manifestation of ritual leader will vary, maybe even greatly, but they are all understood as variations of one prototype. One can compare lip decorations, ritual office and ways of blessing because in South Omo, they act as the formal syntax for the cultural paradigms. As the populations see each other, their most basic institutions are fundamentally the same, and this is the basis of the template of the 'regional other': by and large, they all have age-sets, a division between ritual and political authority, clans, livestock husbandry, agriculture, eating prohibitions, exogamy rules, life-path rituals, etc.[8] But the ways in which these human concerns are expressed are different and specific, and even as such distinctions play their part in the Wheel of Autonomy, many people in South Omo take an interest in these contrasts in a noninstrumental way.

The Occupation and Cultivation of Territory

Collective identity in South Omo is predicated on territory. In Kara one finds rather clear-cut understandings of territory and both moral and spiritual rights to land, applicable both to Kara country proper and the immediate surroundings (see Chapters 2–4), regulating ownership both for individuals and groups. Regarding populations further away, it is common to find people eagerly listening to travel accounts and memorizing place names mentioned. Such attempts to establish a catalogue of cross-referenced settlements, locations and group sections indicate the centrality of territory for the conception of groups. The fact that populations are struggling over access and control of territory, and that people (or their ancestors) might not have been residing where they do live now for a particularly long period, does not invalidate the underlying notion that people and their land are claimed to be quite inseparable at any given point. In Kara, many stories of 'land gone bad' after its masters perished can be found (see e.g. Chapter 4). In another example, it is said that the Hamar still perform their 'leap across the cattle' initiation only east of the Käske riverbed, as the land adjoining the western bank used to be ritual Murle land and was vacated by the latter only some hundred-odd years ago – and so is clearly unsuited for a ritual so central to Hamar identity.

Connected with this understanding is the stipulation that all groups in the cultural neighbourhood are agriculturalist and pastoralist, that their mode of production is fundamentally subsistence-oriented. Accordingly, a great divide is established – the *katama*, a loan word from Amharic used for the market towns, about which Kara complain that 'you have pay for everything', and the regions within the cultural neighbourhood where you can find *äda*, kin, friends and relations, who will host you and care for you (see Girke 2010). If individuals leave their fields and abandon their herds, and try to make a living off trading alone (or other professions), they risk severing their ties to their communities. This is a fundamental marker: whoever relinquishes their herds and fields also takes a first step towards surrendering their membership in the cultural neighbourhood – a mirrored analogy to the people like the mythic (and contemporary) Moguji, who never quite attained herds and fields, and have a tenuous position in the cultural neighbourhood as well.

Political Autonomy

As Donham asserts, at the utmost periphery, 'the Abyssinian state never really penetrated to the level of local communities' (2002a: 39). Commentators on styles of imperialism in general (Sahlins 2004: 7) and the Ethiopian kind in particular (Donham 2002a) furnish a background to the contention that the imperial reorganization of local conditions in South Omo 'entailed little change in the basic structural and cultural premises of the conquered populations, and, over time, "little restructuring of the relation between center and periphery in the new unit"' (Almagor 2002: 96f), even as the imperial regime was 'based on centre-periphery distinctions and thus predatory by its very nature' (Dereje 2009: 127). Accordingly, especially groups such as the Nyangatom, Dassanech, Kara and Mursi, in their unwelcoming, hot and disease-ridden lowlands, 'retained a large degree of local autonomy', while developing 'little orientation, let alone commitment, to the Ethiopian centre' (Almagor 2002: 96).[9]

Whereas similar populations that – after the late nineteenth-/early twentieth-century scramble for empire – ended up on the Kenyan side of the Ethiopian–Kenyan border were more thoroughly subject to administration, governance and the *Pax Britannica*, these influences were not much felt on the Lower Omo, even at the beginning of the twenty-first century. To claim, as the Kara and others do, the right to handle what amounts to legal issues internally, to not feel bound by Ethiopian law, has come to be an identity criterion and a feature of the groups that make up the cultural neighbourhood. But with current macro-development projects transforming the physical landscape, this situation is undergoing significant change, and it is hardly clear to what degree the Kara and their neighbours can maintain their erstwhile (relative) autonomy. They will, however, continue to struggle for it.

The Use of Violence

In South Omo, year after year, Ethiopian citizens were picking up arms and jointly attacked other Ethiopian citizens, and as long as things remained 'orderly' in that only small arms such as assault rifles were used, police and the administration seemed little inclined to intervene.[10] This is in a sense prudent, because it is hard to tell what sort of intervention would not aggravate matters further. Having said that, the basic principle on which South Omo warfare operates is that acts of aggression perpetrated by or even on a single individual fairly inevitably trigger a collective response, where this collective is a bounded politico-territorial group as outlined above. Anything done to violate a single body necessitates a reaction by the whole body politic – which in itself is a subtle form of integration of a community, a striking manifestation of community, of a 'We' against a 'They'.

For the purpose of this list of features, it is sufficient to note as an empirical tendency that groups do react this way, and that to not react with violence against violence would be a surprising turn of events and a risky one: in the blind spot of Leviathan, what is to hold violence in check, if not counterviolence?[11] The ethnography of South Omo provides ample evidence of this general principle (see Turton 2003; Tornay 1979; Alvarsson 1989; Girke 2008). The willingness and ability to exert violence is one feature of what makes a polity relevant and significant: in terms of the Wheel of Autonomy, it is a display of agency that enforces boundaries and claims autonomy. Once people jointly fight and kill, often with a ritually marked beginning and a ceremonial conclusion to a period of intermittent violence, they also come to be seen as a collective, autonomous actor (and narrated as such) by the observers to these actions.

These four points provide a perspective on what people in South Omo assume about one another in the most general terms and, accordingly, what they take into account when devising their own strategies. The next chapter will substantiate ethnographically how these features are manifested in the interaction of the Kara with their neighbours. But first, in a necessary step, I discuss the general significance of stereotyping, to show how relevant the analysis of such 'folk belief' is for an understanding of interethnic relations.

Stereotypes and the Narration of a Social World

Doing research in Kara, I was constantly exposed to stereotypes. Already on my very first evening, arriving in Chelläte on 15 August 2003, the Hamar guide who led me to my future host family not only triggered comments on what was 'typically Hamar' as he unabashedly ate an entire bowl of honey on his own (when it was meant to be shared), but also led the group of young Kara men present in a parody of Arbore prosody. From that day onwards, such talk about kinds of people and their attributes never stopped during my fieldwork. The work of other scholars of South Omo rarely indicates how prevalent everyday talk about other groups is among the Kara's neighbours. Living in Kara, though, it became indispensable to learn the language of stereotyping, and so to map the Kara perspective of the cultural neighbourhood (Rapport and Overing 2007: 395). Throughout my stay, such knowledge, ranging from references to specific Nyangatom spokesmen to the question of which South Omo group consumed tobacco in which way, via the question of who of the Kara's neighbours were the most notorious thieves, was a perpetual element of conversation.

Even there and then, it was apparent that many of these conversational commonplaces were not assumed to hold much truth value even by the Kara.[12] At any rate, truth proved an irrelevant criterion: people were creating resonating stories and provided situational orientation through moral narratives. Indeed, I found that stereotypes were always 'relative to performance settings' (Chock 1987: 351), as people could choose from a wide reservoir of such generalizations in any given situation. Having recognized this performative aspect, I am aware that as a participant in these contexts, I was an intended audience to such attempts to define the situation just as others were. As I have discussed in the case of the metaphorical othering of the Moguji (see Chapter 4), this again drives home the importance of a contextualized interpretation of such positional utterances.

Stereotyping and the narratives that invoke and perpetuate cultural neighbourhood are less accessible as raw data than other elements of this book: I got to know them through a long, slow, observation-based and participation-based process, listening to contextualized narratives that led me to an understanding of certain reference points in conversations. Thus, the tales people told only ever gave hints towards an emplotment of relationships. Talk about the cultural neighbourhood, I found, was based on narratives that reduced ethnic categories and populations to cohesive actors, guided by intent, motivated and with recognizable attributes, who were in turn entangled in plots and often at cross-purposes.

There are numerous attempts in the social sciences to salvage stereotyping as a worthwhile object of study.[13] Stating the point more comprehensively than Michael Herzfeld in his discussion of the role of stereotyping in the realm of bureaucracy (1998), Nigel Rapport and Joanna Overing (2007) provide one of the best perspectives on this topic within social or cultural anthropology. While explicit on the point, they are not alone among anthropologists in pointing out that to discard stereotypes as bad or wrong sort of data (cf. Asmarom 1973: 277) is premature (see Barth 2000: 33; Streck 2000: 301). Casting the net wider, I found that MacKie (1973) presented a thorough analytical approach, especially in her refutation of positions that see stereotypes as simply mistaken (1973: 432ff) or that equate stereotype with prejudice (1973: 438). The definition she suggests is this: 'A stereotype refers to those folk beliefs about the attributes characterizing a social category on which there is substantial agreement' (1973: 435). I would add that stereotypes are always implicitly comparative, even where they are not negative. When I discuss stereotypes, I do so in MacKie's sense, which dispels any notion that stereotypes might be individual cognitive defects. They are more or less collective representations, which 'provide a social group with collective explanations as to why different social groups act as they do' (Hinton 2000: 158).

For my argument, then, 'folk beliefs' are important both regarding the question what sort of social categories seem to call for stereotyping and to the way in which such 'agreement' is reached and expressed. If stereotypes are explanatory devices (Bateson 2000: 38–58), what are people trying to explain? One must not assume that stereotypes override other aspects of social relations (Streck 2000: 301) or that they inescapably prestructure interaction. Instead, as collective representations, they not only reveal something of the worldview within which they flourish, but also allow a more pragmatic analysis: who uses what sort of stereotypes in which contexts about whom? How collective are they really and how grounded are they in a 'bodily experience of the environing world' (Rapport and Overing 2007: 46)? MacKie's definition, in using the word 'agreement', points to this persuasive nature of stereotypes: to use a stereotype, to set it in motion, as it were, is an attempt to rhetorically define a situation by invoking images and icons of otherness, triggering chains of cultural associations and ideally assent, and providing us with anchors to our social landscape. A stereotype tells us what is important about a given other, allows a metonymical intensification of our focus and, as a conversational commonplace, will often simply trigger assent. We might choose not to use such generic categorization ourselves, but the stereotype is always there, beckoning us to increase situational relevance by reducing complexity.

Thus, stereotypes are as a rule evaluative, as well as of pragmatic use. But are they not 'wrong'? MacKie cuts to the heart of the matter: 'The symbolic interactionist finds the stereotype validity issue quite meaningless. He asks, "Since the stereotyped group's behavior is *determined* by powerful groups' beliefs about it, how can one speak of the accuracy of perception?"' (1973: 440, emphasis in original) In analysis, then, one needs to assess in which way the stereotype comes to be employed, abused or resisted. How does it shape, or even determine, interaction? But this is an empirical question and has to be addressed as such. However much we might wish for it, there is little point in showing stereotypes to be 'false' if we strive for an understanding of how people actively relate to each other through their competing definitions of the situation. What Asmarom derisively labels 'native ethnocentrism' (1973: 276) is important data, even as he makes a valid and nearly prescient statement in claiming that when scholars unreflectedly reproduce stereotypes, the 'net effect on the cultures under study is that their submerged, ritualized, and carefully regulated hostilities have appeared in print and in time will become a bone of contention for the Western-educated native elite' (ibid.). This contention cannot be casually dismissed: just like many other fields, the study of stereotype requires methodological clarity and sensitivity.

These language games, as Eriksen calls them in Wittgensteinian terminology (1991: 134f; see also Dereje 2011), are not wholly arbitrary. It would be odd to accord academic validity to political presentations of identity (what people say about themselves), but to deny it to 'folk beliefs' in the form of stereotypes (what people say about other people). Perception of cultural difference cuts both ways: '[H]ow can one have his "identity" and deny his "difference"? ... The rhetoric of stereotypy is shared by both bigots and cultural integralists' (MacKie 1973: 443).[14]

In summary, I argue that stereotypes, in being expressions of perceived cultural difference, should hold a prominent place in the study of identity and, specifically, ethnic identity. As 'group relations' are not as such accessible to our observation, one cannot afford *not* to assess what work stereotypes are made to do in observable interaction, especially as they shape and naturalize power relationships (see Meyer (2008: 152) for the methodological argument). I suggest that the main function of stereotypes in the cultural neighbourhood is to tell better, more coherent stories. They are also used in a historiographic function. This emerges from the cascading processes of people denying the differences between individual members of a wider category, then creating (out of such 'types') named stable collective actors with distinct attitudes and attributes, and finally bestowing relevance on such actors for the plots of narrative. Jonathan Potter phrases it similarly: 'The social world is imbued with stories, versions and representations whose topic is the social world itself. Moreover, these are not merely free-floating images, they are both highly organized and highly consequential; the characterizations are there to do things' (2004: 42).

The eminent cognitive anthropologist Roy Ellen has stated, in pointed simplicity, that '[w]e cannot think about the world unless we assign it to categories' (2006: 31). Applied to social categories, it is clear that we are born into a world where a host of categories jockeys for pre-eminence in our perception. The first section in Chapter 2 gave an overview of salient categories of being Kara, and the discussion touched on the power of the actor to – in any given situation – define one or more possible categories as relevant in the now. Is it decisive that A is B's mother-brother or is it more important that they are neighbours? In the realm of the social, Ellen's proclamation needs to be amended: people can make demands of us in terms of how to categorize them or others. Once this is achieved, role expectations and role demands are inevitably encountered. 'Role' corresponds to stereotype in that both entail such expectations and both provide blueprints for action. Through such cognitive operations, actors come to assert that all members of a given category have so much in common with one another that the category they belong to comes to appear inductively established rather than deductively. To paraphrase, a speaker W might (deductively) ascribe all sorts of features to an individual X because X belongs to a certain category, but then W might also claim that it is X's behaviour (and that of all those like him or her) that led W to establish this stereotype in the first place.

To stereotype is to act as if any individual was a more or less faithful representative of a larger category. In South Omo, the traits that are purportedly shared will likely be physiological, cultural or character-based. In Chapter 4, I summarized the Kara claims about the Moguji, which centred on procreation, livelihood and personal characteristics. There, the stereotypes happened to be shaped through a particular metaphorical reservoir, but this need not always be the case. Still, the ascribed traits can be affectively powerful when stereotypes are used to assert and sustain difference, and to highlight one way of identification over others. To point out that X is from Hamar (an identification that in this moment can override age, gender, class, occupation, interests, religion, etc.) is affectively less powerful (and rhetorically less effective) than to jump ahead and say that X is 'a thief like all Hamar', a phrase often encountered in Kara (see Chapter 7). Note that this not only makes the identification of X as Hamar more evocative and memorable. In addition, it seeks to reinforce existing views of the 'Hamar' by pointing to yet another individual whose example (inductively) supports the stereotype. Another affective aspect is that such stereotypes render individuals more familiar than they would otherwise be. In that sense, stereotypes actually heighten intimacy, even when based on spurious assumptions (see Herzfeld 1998: 72).

This interplay of type, individual and ascribed features is difficult to escape. Any stereotype sets up a synecdochical relation between an individual and their 'type' or social category (see Tyler 1978; Schütz 1982), and is not as such a falsifiable proposition: somebody who ostensibly does not exhibit the trait typical of their category need not encourage a revision of the stereotype. The exception can easily sustain the rule, as when we say that somebody really is a remarkable specimen of their type for not being like we know that they all really are (Hinton 2000: 98).

To reiterate: such stereotyping, while universally prevalent in narrative, is regularly overridden by people in interaction. While it informs and while it is – as a commonplace – of rhetorical efficacy, it cannot be seen as determining people's choices. As Michael Carrithers, in his discussion of narrative thought, has emphasized: 'We need to know what to do in this conversation with this particularly difficult colleague, not just what to do with people we call "colleagues" in general' (1992: 83). In practical terms, a stereotype will hardly ever satisfy all interactional requirements.

It still provides a starting point for interaction, in that when not pressed by somebody making claims to their individuality (or their autonomy), people will attribute certain attributes to an individual assigned to a familiar 'type'. As is particularly evident in South Omo, people's narratives of the cultural neighbourhood might also make of the 'type' a 'character' in a 'plot' (Carrithers 1992: 82–84). This is how ethnic categories become actors with intentions, propensities, features and individual accountability, specifically how 'the Kara' become a 'we' or a 'they' with interests and needs, which then proceeds to act and be acted upon by other similar (or dissimilar) actors as modelled by the Wheel of Autonomy. Logically, stereotyping and the narrative creation of a category-as-an-actor need not go together. It is not, however, far-fetched to establish a connection between pervasive stereotyping, considerable individual anonymity, routinized forms of interaction and the notion of groups-as-actors as mutually supporting one another. Carrithers claims that humans principally create meaning in that they 'understand characters, which embody the understanding of rights, obligations, expectations, propensities, and intentions in oneself and many others; and plots, which show the consequences and evaluations of a multifarious flow of actions' (1992: 82). Humans 'perceive any current action within a large temporal envelope, and within that envelope they perceive any given action, not as a response to the immediate circumstances or current mental state of an interlocutor or oneself, but as part of an unfolding story' (ibid.). This story is the plot. The various events of social life do not stand unconnectedly, but come to be meaningfully related or, here, emplotted: 'Plots embody what a character or characters did to, or about, or with some other character or characters, for what reasons, how people's attitudes, beliefs, and intentions thereby changed, and what followed on from that' (1992: 84). For a proper understanding of interethnic relations in the case of South Omo and for the general conversational competence of an ethnographer, locally perpetuated stereotypes are far from irrelevant, as they hint at these much larger processes of people imagining and narrating their personal and their groups' social environment. Such narrative construction of social categories impacts all processes of inclusion and exclusion, enmity and amity. The result is not merely an ethnic patchwork map, a static, cognitive ordering. The result of narrating a world of collective actors with stereotyped attributes is that this world comes into being as a plausible and near-tangible experience, in which culture and ethnicity are facets that help the inhabitants of that world better express and understand the particularity of the respective actors.

Notes

1. As a notion, 'cultural neighbourhood' was developed under the direction of Ivo Strecker by the members of the E2/C7 project of the interdisciplinary research project SFB 295 'Kulturelle und sprachliche Kontakte in Südwestasien und Nordostafrika' at the University of Mainz. My early fieldwork was facilitated by the SFB 295. The edited volume *To Live with Others* (Gabbert and Thubauville 2010) contains work from several members of Strecker's team. Focusing on the South Omo region, it offers a thorough exploration of the 'cultural neighbourhood'.
2. I make the general argument for the study of stereotypes elsewhere (see Girke 2014a).
3. 'Coffee' in Kara today is made by roasting and then boiling coffee husks, and drunk in large quantities out of calabashes (*sherka*) throughout the day. The word for coffee, *bunno*, is clearly derived from the Amharic *bunna*.
4. *Muutsi* was prized throughout the region as a source of salt, especially for supplementing the food of livestock. Even today, people in Jinka say that *muutsi* was better for their animals than the salt they buy from traders today.
5. For a relevant discussion of anthropology's interest in 'culture contact', see Brandstetter (2006) and Brandstetter et al. (2004, in German). Anna-Maria Brandstetter makes the point that Franz Boas himself and other early scholars on acculturation already did deal with the interaction of 'local cultural orders'. Gregory Bateson (2000: 64) pointed out that one could legitimately study cultural contact even within a given social configuration. However, as Brandstetter adds, the colonial and postcolonial moments diverted interest from periphery–periphery relations, in thrall by the prospect of the new centres to which the spellbound subaltern reacted with syncretism and mimesis, but also the ever-fascinating 'resistance'. The subtler processes going on regardless of the centre's attraction were little addressed in comparison (2006: 30).
6. For now, I intentionally exclude (5): being marginalized at the edges of state, as this requires the extension of the system by including the additional actor category of 'the State'/the Habesha. But setting up this opposition here would do little to illuminate the ways in which the various Shank'illa groups are 'different, yet the same', each other's

'familiar strangers', since the Habesha is not specifically opposed to the Kara or Mursi, but generally to all Shank'illa.
7. Beyond this example of the Mursi lip-plate, I have excluded discussion of material culture from this chapter, even as it is an extremely important site of identity maintenance, of the negotiation of distinction and similarity. Both objects and the ways to produce and handle them are ethnically categorized. When Kara girls tentatively load jerry cans on their heads as they have seen their Nyangatom counterparts across the river do it, other Kara react to this with ridicule or sneering dismissal. For a Kenyan example, Kratz states that 'ethnic categories are used to identify styles of beadwork, ceremonial performance, song, and various other activities and products. My own use of ethnic categories as adjectives … follows this practice. So I may write of Maasai color sequences in beadwork, Kipsigis initiation songs, Okiek baskets, and so forth' (1994: 52). I follow this methodological and textual lead.
8. Compare Tosco on 'areal cultural features' (2005).
9. Parallels to James Scott's work on 'escape populations' and their flight from the manpower-hungry centre (2009) are explored in other publications (Girke 2013, 2015)
10. The heaviest weapons I have personally seen were some light machine guns, but I tend to believe people's claims that there are caches of hand grenades (*bombi*) around. Reportedly, in a spate of argument in 2006, some Nyangatom threatened to attack Kara villages with a flamethrower.
11. E.C. Gabbert studies how one community of the region refused this principle: the Arbore at one point decided to forego violent retribution in their quarrels with their neighbours. Already the fact of this decision is astonishing, but that the Arbore managed to restrain themselves in this way over many years is even more so. This counterexample shows the general level of awareness the people of South Omo have over the systemic features of their interactions. How sustainable this policy of the Arbore 'rhetoric of peace' will be, as Gabbert calls it, remains to be seen (2012, 2014; compare Sagawa 2010). Clashes between the Hamar and the Arbore in 2016 especially challenge the status quo.
12. See Herzfeld (1998: 80) on truth claims in stereotyping.
13. An earlier draft of this section provided the basis for my introduction to the edited volume *Ethiopian Images of Self and Other* (Girke 2014a: 16–19).
14. This of course undercuts the strategic essentialism in which reductive identity politics are seen as a legitimate tool in oppressed people's struggle versus hegemonic power, which is at times propagated in subaltern studies.

Chapter 7
South Omo in Kara Terms

It is an empirical question to what degree people will simplify a dynamic and plural life-world into plots and characters. One aspect of this turns out to be linguistic. In the Kara language, it is common to talk about an ethnic group in the specific singular form of the ethnonym: all the Nyangatom are encompassed when somebody says *bunta*, consisting of the generic term *bume* (the Kara name for Nyangatom) and the specific singular suffix *-ta*. '*Bunta shuindidina* – the Nyangatom has [sing.] grown bold' would be a sample expression. But even where a plural form is used, in narration, people often imply a significant coherence and unity of actors. It is obvious how such a reduction parallels stereotyping, which seems to be based on the same cognitive and rhetorical processes. From the hyperbole so commonly found in stereotyping, Rapport and Overing suggest that 'clarity and definiteness are to be derived' (2007: 394) precisely for the people using the stereotypes to characterize actors in a plot. Stereotypes are used as much for persuasion of the self as of the other, and the causal connection between stereotype and modalities of interaction is far from determined.

Regarding the following discussion of the specific relations between the Kara and their variously categorized neighbours, my approach remains Kara-centric, as I cannot in the same measure present the complementing perspectives of the Kara's neighbours. Still, when studying stereotypes, the critical aspect is less the substantive content of the stereotypes themselves than the practical modalities of their use.

Also, due to the little-recorded history of South Omo, I cannot discount the possibility that I am missing out on historical or cultural factors that simply never arose during my fieldwork. I include other authors' work in the discussion where possible. As was mentioned earlier, in the past not many South Omo scholars have attended to interethnic relations beyond the discussion of warfare and exchange. Basic information about all these populations can be found in the *Encyclopedia Aethiopica* (edited by S. Uhlig), but the ease of comparison is hampered by the tendency in South Omo studies since the late 1960s for individual scholars to write into being a near-monopoly of knowledge on particular ethnic groups.[1] I have inserted short text excerpts both from this encyclopaedia and other sources to preface each section. These serve the purpose of showing how stereotype interplays with academic description even where stereotype is not the topic.

Yet another aspect of interethnic relations in South Omo has so far been little addressed in my description of how groups view groups, and of the 'culture of contact' that has emerged between them: this is the important point that the relations between groups, be it enmity or even warfare, are no obstacle to individual cordial solidarity. As I discuss elsewhere (Girke 2010), the institution of bondfriendship (*beltamo* in Hamar and Kara) is a prime socially acceptable way in which individuals can transcend group relations and engage in individual reciprocity and mutuality.[2] In Simmel's terms, what unites the Kara with the members of all the categories below are the 'possibilities of commonness' (1950: 41) that make them all Shank'illa – lowlanders, vis-à-vis the Habesha highlanders.

My argument starts from the recognition that the different Kara ways of negotiating their relations with their neighbours are driven by the irrefutable and obvious cultural and linguistic similarity between them and the groups of the Hamar-Banna-Bashada (HBB) cluster. The rest of the chapter follows from this.

The 'Mountain People': The Hamar, Banna and Bashada

> The [Hamar] engage in a mixed economy of pastoralism (goats, sheep and cattle), slash-and-burn cultivation (sorghum, maize, various kinds of beans, squash, lettuce etc.), gathering (wild fruits, leaves and roots of trees, various kinds of greens during the rainy season), and apiculture.
> —I. Strecker, 'Hamär Ethnography'

The case of the *gemeri-ed*, the 'mountain people', is the obvious choice to commence a description of the intergroup relations between the Kara and others, as the four groups, one by the river and three up in the hills, are usually seen as forming a cultural and linguistic cluster – the HBB cluster (note that the Kara are not included in the designation). Of all the Kara's neighbours, the mountain people are the ones with whom there is in sheer quantity the most interaction today. Hardly a day passes in Dus without some Hamar herders dropping by for a chat or Hamar women coming in from their cattle camps to sell milk or goat hides.[3]

While intensely aware of them, the Kara often disregard the distinction between the three populations of the Hamar, the 'Atula' (the Banna; see Masuda 2003), and the 'Banno' (the Bashada; see Epple 2003, 2007) in everyday talk.[4] The three categories share much of significance, and in many instances of interaction there is little difference for the Kara whether they are talking to (or about) a Banna or a Bashada, even though often enough Banna and Bashada act as independent political groups. The label 'Hamar' is often used interchangeably with 'the mountain people' at large. Their languages lie closely together on the same dialect continuum and all belong to the South Omotic sub-branch of the Afro-Asiatic family.[5] While they are mutually intelligible, the local diglossic situation is remarkable in that there are few 'mountain people' who can speak proper Kara, but that many Kara will usually switch registers from speaking Kara to speaking Hamar (the regional lingua franca) whenever interacting with a non-Kara from the HBB cluster.

In terms of kinship and ritual, there are many powerful parallels, but there is hardly any cultural dimension in which the Kara and their Omotic-speaking neighbours follow wholly identical practices. Still, their practices can be very readily translated without being quite equivalent. The story of the Kara man who leapt across the cattle in Hamar illustrates this. While the reverse would be quite impossible (see Chapter 2), he was welcome to do so, finding a Hamar bride and living (mostly) among and like the Hamar. However, it turned out that as far as the Kara were concerned, this man had not properly married, with the consequence that his juniors within the lineage were in turn not allowed to leap across the cattle in Kara. The suggestion that he might leap across the cattle again in Kara in order to satisfy the ritual demands was also rejected: he already had performed a ritual, it was said, and one cannot do 'the same' ritual twice – but of course, it was not 'same enough' in order to be truly acceptable. That he was considered unmarried and yet married meant that his younger male relatives were barred from marrying as long as he was alive. This predicament was only solved with this man's not entirely accidental death.

This bizarre dilemma is not adduced to make a point about the differences and similarities in Hamar and Kara culture. Instead, what emerges here is that both groups pursue very different agendas in the maintenance of their group boundaries. The people of the larger population in this dyad, the Hamar, seem to be rather casual about allowing both cultural features and social persons from elsewhere to become Hamar. In fact, their origin myths emphasize their divergent origins. In this sense, they could be labelled expansionist (see Schlee 2008: 35–42), as naturalization is not particularly problematic, but this tells only half the story. The Kara, the numerically far inferior side, also allow integration into the body politic as such even for male outsiders, as they seek to absorb manpower. However, they do make it difficult for others to properly acquire their language and also watch the various arenas of interaction carefully and suspiciously. One of the most striking features of Kara 'foreign policy' thus holds true even for the seemingly so closely related Hamar: true Kara girls are not given in marriage to anybody else than other true Kara, but true Kara men do marry 'mountain people' girls, at least as second and third wives.[6] This practice of enforcing female endogamy is an expression of a highly regulated stratification that in effect keeps the true Kara lineages aloof from all others, even as they are willing to accommodate immigrants.

While in political speech, especially in times of war, all the groups from the HBB cluster might emphasize their unity, the Kara make fine distinctions: they are 'somehow' related to the Banna. The Bashada, as the ones who were left behind on the migration that led the Kara to the Omo Valley (see Chapter 4), are relatives too, but these claims to *äda* are only weakly voiced. Most markedly, the Kara emphatically disclaim any descent relation to the Hamar proper. In any internal discussion of the topic, they are more likely to bring up some old stories that tell of how their respective ancestors waged war on one another (see Lydall and Strecker 1979a: 253).[7]

This contemporary tendency in Kara to emphasize the differences between them and the 'mountain people', rather than the unquestionable similarities, is the real explanandum of this section. It is necessary to add that this is only thinly veiled in the interaction with the Hamar. Regularly, Kara will say that 'we are one, there is no difference between us' when holding council together with 'mountain people' (e.g. Gezahegn 1994: 105f), but such claims of allegiance are gainsaid by a host of contradictory narratives and emphatic statements they issue when they are amongst themselves again. This ambiguity is possibly part of the reason why the Hamar talk about the Kara as the 'snakes by the river' (Lydall and Strecker 1979a: 229f), a trope that again shows the importance of stereotyping and metaphorical imagination for interethnic relations.

As regards stereotypes, the 'mountain people' are all grouped together in Kara conversations. Their land up in the eastern mountains is seen as poor, rain-dependent and drought-prone, and this ecological perspective carries over into the Kara stereotypes of the Hamar as people who are driven to other people's lands by their needs. This view is then tied to the condemnation of Hamar warmongering, of Hamar thievery and of Hamar begging, a truly dismissive accusation: 'Their land is one of suffering, this is why they come here to us' was a typical comment, highlighting again the extremely lush and fertile banks of the Omo. The Hamar are acknowledged as great herders and fighters, even if these qualities come at the cost of insufficient cleverness: the notion that Hamar men have spent so much more time outside of settlements in pastoral pursuits than their Kara contemporaries was adduced to support their presentation as supposedly unrefined and unsophisticated. Their personal grooming is also a topic of conversation: while many Kara youths and adults today prefer a minimalist style, keeping their hair shortly cropped and largely forgoing wearing traditional braids and clay caps in everyday life, these fashions are still very much in evidence among the 'mountain people'. This provides yet another arena to depict them as out of touch and out of time. Great respect is usually accorded to the old Hamar; it is the current youth that is often discursively rendered with some disdain.

Beyond these more interpersonal arenas, the sites of interaction between the Hamar and the Kara as political groups today are threefold. First, they fall under the same administrative structure, the Hamar *woreda* (district), which besides them also includes the Arbore (see below). I had a first indication that this administrative structure was already a conflicted arena during one of my first visits to Kara, when I was witness to a debate about the name of the district: some young men concluded in their discussion that just the fact that the Hamar were the biggest group encompassed by the district did not justify naming the whole *woreda* after them. In fact, they argued, this was demeaning both for them and for the Arbore. The Hamar would already incur numerous benefits, since the administrative centres Dimeka and Turmi were within Hamar territory, and that most 'development' (*lematt*, from Amharic) also took place in the mountains.

I encountered this attitude again and again, not in direct accusations of corruption, nepotism or systematic negligence, but when Kara admonished other Kara to be alert for possible trouble, and encouraged one another to assert their rights under the district administration especially firmly. Concomitantly, the Kara often talked about their young kinsmen who had joined the force of clerks of the administration, wondering whether they were investing enough effort to help the homeland. It is worth noting that the Arbore never figured as rivals in the 'district narratives'; it was all about the Hamar.

As I see it, this widespread attitude of distrust derives from the underlying worry of the Kara that the Hamar might want to take over their land at some point. To provide some context: over the last few decades, the 'mountain people' and the Kara have been allies in many aggressive raids as well as defensive wars, mostly against the Nyangatom. The Kara, while having been displaced from their settlements on the west bank of the Omo River, were by and large able to hold their own militarily on the east bank, especially since they could often mobilize adventurous Hamar to join forces. The Hamar profit from this close alliance in that they – especially in times when they are at war with the Dassanech further south – can lead their livestock to the Omo for pasture and water. The large herds of cattle seen when driving down from Hamar, after crossing the Kizo gorge and proceeding through the Nokere plains towards the riverland and finally the Kara settlements, are not Kara livestock, but belong to Hamar herders. These cattle range from the southern tip of Kara to the edge of the Mago National Park in the North, and often enough encroach upon park territory in such numbers that the park wardens issue threats of violent retribution against the Hamar herders. Simultaneously, there are many joint camps for cattle and small stocks, where Kara and Hamar families have teamed up, pooling manpower and other resources for a more efficient pastoral practice.

While both sides profit from this arrangement in a number of ways, it turns out that among the Kara, murmurs of discontent are growing louder. They claim that the Hamar, their self-imposed guests, spoil the land in a number of ways. As is regularly brought up in meetings with NGOs and government representatives concerned with conservation, the Hamar are blamed for killing off all wildlife in the valley. Not only is there the charge that they trigger-happily shoot at any animal they come across (and thus have extinguished for example the hippopotamus population along the Lower Omo); no, in addition, their herds are said to displace the formerly plentiful gazelles and antelopes. This leads over to the second point – desertification. I have little visual data on what Kara country looked like in the 1970s or 1980s even, but both Kara and visitors of previous decades have told me how high the grass used to grow everywhere and how plentiful the vegetation was. Today, grass, used both to construct one kind of hut and to thatch another type, can be very difficult to come by, as more and more stretches of land turn dusty and fall prey to erosion. For this perceived desertification, the Kara blame Hamar cattle, suggesting that while the increased car traffic also contributes to the destruction of the topsoil, it is really the incessant tread of hard hooves that is ravaging their lands. Every now and then, to add injury to injury, Hamar cows will stray and rampage through a Kara field, trampling and eating the crops. While this is a nonissue for the 'mountain people', among whom it is *k'aiss*, quite forbidden, to complain about damages wrought by livestock (personal communication with S. Epple), the Kara are righteously upset about the property damage. Among them, compensation is paid for such incidents, but they could never receive any reparations from their Hamar 'guests' as they would from fellow Kara. When, on top of that, opportunistic thefts by Hamar herders plague the Kara villages, which are largely unsupervised during farming season, people find colourful ways to express their opinion that the Hamar have in some ways overstayed their welcome.

This exasperation was most strongly expressed by the accusation that 'the Hamar are all thieves', a conversational commonplace throughout my time in Kara. Notwithstanding their perpetual internal discussions about this predicament, it is very difficult for them to do anything about it: to deny the Hamar herds access to the low-lying pasture and the waters of the Omo River would amount to a declaration of war. The Kara could only lose in any sort of conflict with the 'mountain people' – their backs to the perennial river (and to the Nyangatom, their perennial enemy), greatly outnumbered, they would be easy victims of a Hamar assault. Even to regional specialists it might sound initially unlikely that such close allies would resort to violence without a more blatant provocation. But consider the following episode.

Together with a youth from Kara, I was driving from Dus to Turmi in Hamar territory, the closest market village. Turning the car at the roundabout, I heard the shrill sound of a police whistle. Stopping as requested, we talked to the policeman who had approached the car after recognizing me. He had, he said, 'an assignment' for us, namely to ascertain whether it was true that the Kara had killed some Bashada herding boys down in the valley. We were quite nonplussed, as we had just arrived from Kara where no bullet fired goes uncommented upon, and thus told the policeman that the information he had received was certainly false. We got annoyed when he insisted, as his claims seemed too outlandish for both of us to consider. However, upon returning to Kara some days later, we found out what had happened in other places in the meantime. As far as people could piece together the story, a Banna (or Bashada) man, in his cups during a *parsho* beer party somewhere near Dimeka, had suddenly leapt up and announced that the Kara were killing 'our boys down there'. A posse had been assembled and a number (with estimates varying) of Hamar, Banna and Bashada men trooped down the mountains and set up camp in the savannah to discuss how to attack the Kara. Fortunately, one of the Kara *bitti* was herding his goats nearby and went over to investigate what all these 'mountain people' were doing there. He was then able to convince them that no incident had taken place and that certainly nobody was dying along the river. The would-be invaders went home.

I had to reassess the situation. It had been inconceivable for me that the Kara would kill any visiting herders, but I had not considered that it might be of the essence to be able to counter any emerging rumour of this sort as quickly as possible.

Such instigative action is not unusual. The Kara have a word for it, *kantsi*, which refers to what is called a 'false flag' operation in (post)modern warfare: to create false evidence in order to set two groups against each other. There seems to be a serious risk of unexpected warfare breaking out in the Omo Valley through *kantsi*. I cannot judge whether the danger of this has increased over the last few decades, but I have collected stories indicating that it has been a constant worry throughout human memory. This is the final point of tension between the Hamar and the Kara that bears mentioning: after a long and painfully protracted war, the Kara and Nyangatom made peace in early September 2006, reaffirming it with a joint meeting just after Christmas 2006, which I attended. Only a few days later, some Hamar men ambushed a Nyangatom in his fields on the east bank of the Omo, opposite of Kangaten, killing him and escaping with his rifle. Collectively, Kara country held its breath, worried that this event would spoil the land again, as it was not out of the question that the Nyangatom would blame the Kara as complicit in the ambush or that some the Nyangatom would retaliate before realizing that the attackers were Hamar, not Kara. The collective breath was released when some Nyangatom (while keeping a safe distance) shouted across the river that they knew well who had attacked them and that the Kara need not react hastily. But in everybody's book, it had been too close a call.

To sum up, I was surprised by how these contemporary worries dominated talk about the relation of 'the Kara' and 'the Hamar'. Even if individual friendships, the numerous *äda* relations cultivated by particular lineages, seem unaffected by this, the Hamar today are seen more as a part of the predicament of Kara than as a way out of it. I heard the two Kara ideophones *ənch* and *chip* used to describe their situation – these utterances indicate crowding, being squeezed in (see Tedlock (2001) on ideophones and Lydall (2002) for the Hamar data). The Kara have recognized that their strategic wiggle room, created by keeping their neighbours not only culturally but also spatially at bay, has shrunk. With the Hamar encroaching from the east and the Nyangatom beleaguering the Omo in the west, they found themselves between a rock and a wet place.

The 'Distant Relations': The Arbore and Dassanech

> The [Dassanech] are a pastoral people of south-west Ethiopia and north-west Kenya ... The D. belong to the cattle-complex like their neighbouring pastoral peoples, but they practice agriculture ... and fishing.
> —M. Tosco, 'Ɖáasanač Ethnography'

For both the Arbore and Dassanech, a growing corpus of anthropological literature is available, some of it stemming from the 1970s, and due to the efforts of younger scholars, it currently keeps growing.[8] They are in a way the odd groups of South Omo, speakers of Cushitic languages separated by a wedge of Omotic language groups (see Map 0.1).

While there are cultural similarities and very complex interrelations between the Arbore and the Dassanech, and while acknowledging that they have managed to maintain positive ties over time, their joint inclusion in one category as seen from the Kara perspective is solely warranted by the fact that the Kara declare them to be their 'true *äda*', their actual (blood) relations, within the region.[9] This entails a commitment to peaceful relations. I have collected a few stories in which Kara decided to not injure or kill Dassanech who had wronged them. Whenever a Kara conversation turns to either the Arbore or Dassanech, the assertion is regularly made that to kill a member of either group would lead to disease and death.

One of the Kara's two 'arrival stories' (complementing the Trail of the Red Bull) recounts their migration from somewhere to the far west, the direction of the Ugandan Karamojong escarpment. Minimally told, it reports how the ancient Kara came from the southwest. Reaching the Omo Delta, they left behind a section of their group who became the Dassanech. Moving on, they travelled further east, circumventing the Hamar mountains, and when they reached the

Woyto Valley, another group stayed behind: the Arbore. The remainders of the original group then turned counterclockwise. Crossing the mountains in Banna territory, they reached the Omo lands. I want to note that this story was never explicitly reconciled with the 'Trail of the Red Bull'. My attempts to goad people into addressing the lack of fit between the two failed: the stories are simply not relevant in the same narrative context and thus do not need to be reconciled (cf. Bassi 2011).[10]

The Kara regularly invoke this ancient kinship. Now, considering that there is not much evidence (linguistic or otherwise) that supports the story's truth value, and rather more indices that the Kara might at some point have split off from an Omotic proto-HBB cluster, what is one to do with this claim of primordial relatedness?

Looking at the forms of interaction between the Arbore and the Kara on the one hand, and the Kara and the Dassanech on the other hand, no obvious pattern emerges. No traditional intermarriage is on record. Today, the Kara have little interaction with the Arbore in any regular or regulated way. Knowledge is minimal: the Kara could neither name the Arbore 'clans' (see Ayalew 1995), nor do any speak the Arbore language. Even though they belong to the same *woreda*, contact is largely indirect, being mediated by the Hamar who settle on the hills dividing the two valley dwelling populations. Due to the unequal demography and the central location of the numerous Hamar (the 2007 census has them at more than 40,000) between the two smaller populations (there are about 7,000 Arbore), the Kara and the Arbore are far apart, and it is rare for individuals from either side to go visit one another. While I was told by the Arbore that the Kara used to come to their cattle gates to pay their respects to the Arbore *qawot* (the ritual leader and *bitti* equivalent) in the past, the Kara did not offer any such stories (see Girke 2010).

Talking about the Arbore, the Kara varied between hilarity and admiration: people depicted the Arbore as sophisticated, introverted, fundamentally honest and steadfast. They would never steal. There was not one rascal among them (or rather, exactly one; see Chapter 8). But Arbore ways of speaking are a staple joke among the Kara, who love to imitate the long-winded start of an Arbore speech. Additionally – and this is somewhat damning – the Arbore are seen as not sufficiently outgoing or extroverted to be unreservedly impressive or politically consequential.

Between the Kara and the Dassanech, however, relations used to be very close even within living memory. While Dassanech land is some ways downriver from Kara, only around two decades ago, it was very common for young Kara men to go to Dassanech for a few days of dancing. There was also always exchange: the Dassanech, like many other groups in the Greater Lake Turkana area, desired the clay pots made by the Kara and Bashada, while the Kara had a great demand for metal tools and especially the ancient, large glass beads so well-known from

Kenyan pastoralist groups (Sobania 1980). Bondfriendship was a decisive factor here: individual men established ostentatiously egalitarian friendships across an ethnic boundary, visiting and hosting one another, caring for the *bel* partner's family in times of need, shielding them from the vicissitudes of war, and offering goats or grains when times were rough. Many Kara men who are in their fifties and sixties today speak Dassanech well, appreciate the Dassanech people and still remember the time they spent there nostalgically. Even if the relationship has deteriorated somewhat today, as the traditional exchange of pots and beads has been substituted by the less 'moral' one of bluntly commercial gun and bullet trade, I observed some fondness whenever Kara met Dassanech.

As an example, in late 2007/early 2008, a group of Dassanech reached Kara, led by a respected Kara elder from Korcho. They sought 'spotted hides' for an upcoming *dimi* ceremony (see Almagor 1978). Roaming around Kara land, they were happily received and hosted, bought eight skins of leopard and some smaller spotted cat called *loxoll* by the Kara (possibly a serval), and departed again, practically begging the Kara to go and hunt some more. This, it must be understood, is life as it should be. Having guests from afar, exchanging with them and sharing a joint 'base', that is, 'locally defined values – embodied in goods, services, and ideologies – [which] express identity in community' (Gudeman 2001: 8), brings out the moral component of the cultural neighbourhood most clearly. Now that such visits are rare, they are doubly appreciated.

Regarding stereotypes, I found a relative paucity: the Kara remarked negatively on the fact that the Dassanech 'ate crocodiles' and how they and the Hamar never could keep the peace, but little more. Still, an immanent change in tenor was noticeable. Triggered by events I describe elsewhere (Girke 2010), people in Kara tended to highlight the bad influence of the city Omo Rate in Dassanech territory, as it 'spoilt' people and made them forget the value of *ädamo*. Still, they phrased their words deploringly rather than accusingly. Thus, recent stories of anomy and thievery are balanced out by positive narratives, such as of the wars of the 1970s when some Dassanech travelled north to back up the Kara after a particularly horrific defeat that the latter suffered at the hands of the Nyangatom (see Girke 2008).

Both the Arbore and the Dassanech apparently confirm the Kara claims of ancient relatedness. I find it rather pointless to look for corroboration of assertions such as 'we are one, if we spill each other's blood we shall perish' in an archaeological record of migration. Instead, the Simmelian approach to identity seems more promising as an explanatory device of why the claim of kinship is rhetorically powerful and effective. As quoted by John Wood, Simmel suggests that it is precisely a 'lack of similarity in these cases [that] becomes a strategic sign of relation' (Wood 2000: 60). The joint occurrence of the striking lack of similarity between the Kara and the Arbore or the Dassanech and the claims of relation, of 'blood identity' even, only makes sense if we include the 'mountain people' as discussed above in this picture: their case is an exact mirror. Between Kara and the HBB cluster, there is much greater individual familiarity and contact, and a wide-ranging cultural and linguistic similarity, but an outright denial of kinship.

I argue that the Kara emphasize their fundamental difference from the 'mountain people' in the face of a similarity that has led Strecker to comment that the Kara seem to be 'a variation' on the HBB cluster (1976a). This is just what they do not want to be. Instead, the Kara insist on a shared identity with and relatedness to groups that are more distant and that exhibit (in direct comparison with the HBB cluster) no specific similarity with the Kara. This is an instance of the Wheel of Autonomy in action: to maintain autonomy where it is not evident that such autonomy exists (in the eyes of the cultural neighbourhood), the Kara exert their agency to differentiate themselves from the 'mountain people'. Simultaneously, the Arbore and Dassanech are not close at all in terms of the 'cultural stuff' (Barth 1969) or as regards sheer proximity so as to offer a challenge to Kara autonomy or distinction.

The creativity in this chiasmic opposition is readily apparent. While it will not be possible to determine a point when this way of presenting interethnic relations was introduced, we can see how once established, these claims could come to be meaningful and pragmatically useful for the Kara. The very real competition over material resources in the Omo Valley takes place not only through violence and demographic or migratory processes, but also through rhetoric. Struggling to live largely in amity with the Hamar, in by and large cordial mutuality and cooperation while carefully maintaining a certain distinction, allows the Kara to remain a group apart, a small population in an ecologically rich niche. This is also what allowed them to style themselves the masters of the Omo Valley (see Chapter 4).

At the same time, they manage to establish ties of both *ädamo* and historical *äda* with the more distant Arbore and Dassanech. Through this, it becomes possible to deny any – at first sight very plausibly imputed – roots within the HBB cluster. Regarding this 'ancient relatedness', a more general point can be made. During an NGO-hosted conference at Kangaten, where Ethiopian, Kenyan and Sudanese groups met, the Kara suddenly heard bestowed upon themselves kinship with the Sudanese Toposa. As far as I could reconstruct, the Toposa claimed that there was a killing taboo between them and the Dassanech, and the latter willy-nilly extended this as well to their respective relatives, the Kara and Arbore. This is peculiar as the Toposa are occasionally enlisted by the Nyangatom to join their eastbound raids against the Kara and Hamar. But beyond the surprising casualness of this identification, which was bemusedly discussed among the Kara later, this incident points to a much wider, and more complex web, less of kinship and affiliations, but of kinship claims, rhetorically set into motion and occasionally socially effective.

Some enthusiastic young Kara one day confronted me with their hypothesis that the Karamojong of Uganda (*Nkaramajong* in Kara), of whom they had heard, must be their ancient relatives as well, a hypothesis happened upon by way of etymology: 'Kara' and 'majong', meaning, as they said, 'old' in the Nyangatom language, which belongs to that same language group. The Kara of old, then! An especially enterprising young man had through some channel acquired a music cassette of what was purportedly Karamojong music. People listened eagerly to pick out words that resonated with the Kara vocabulary.

I suggest that the tales of the varying proveniences of clans and group section so abundant in South Omo (as elsewhere) ought to be interpreted in the same vein. Schlee has called them 'raw materials for political rhetoric' (2008: 49f), which emphasizes that such tales do not necessarily reference historically traceable connections, but must be seen as ways to highlight or sideline distinction and autonomy in the definition of the situation, as attempts to establish or disclaim alliances, and to keep the Wheel of Autonomy spinning.

The 'Respected Enemies': The Mursi and Nyangatom

In any categorization of societies into 'peaceful' and 'warlike', the Mursi would have to be included in the latter category. (Turton 1993: 165)
Often described by highlanders and government officials as pastoral nomads, the M. in fact depend heavily on cultivation, mainly of sorghum and maize.

—D.A. Turton, 'Mursi'

I group the Mursi and Nyangatom into one category since from the Kara perspective, these Nilotic-speaking groups engender similar sorts of interaction: nearly all Kara warfare since the mid twentieth century has been directed at one of these two neighbours, while at the same time, there exist considerable mutual respect, admiration, intermarriage, co-residence and – so far unreported in South Omo ethnography – adoption, at least in one direction.[11]

I start with this last item. While still in the process of figuring out categories of being Kara, and Kara assumptions about the behaviour, attitudes and bodily attributes of these categories, I met a young man who was introduced to me as an age-mate, a Nyiramalai just like me. Having the chance to spend time around him, his physiognomy began to strike me as odd. While there is considerable variation in facial features within Kara, Appa Chaula stood out. Observing more closely, I noticed two incongruent features about him – the notch in his ear, which unambiguously identified him as a married 'true Kara' elder, and the scarification on his arms and upper body, shapes and patterns created through lines of tiny, raised welts. This is I had come to know as typical Mursi body decoration. As he himself seemed shy and reluctant in my presence, I approached some closer friends and demanded clarification: was he a Mursi? As far as I knew, even though he looked like one, he could not possibly be one. The notch in the ear clinched that he was true Kara: nobody else was allowed to leap across the cattle in Kara and marry a true Kara girl. Resignedly, my interlocutors conceded that he was, in fact, Mursi. He had been adopted. Starting from that day, I was able to piece together an understanding of this regionally quite unusual practice.

Today, there are two elders in Kara who began their lives firmly in the category of being 'Mursi'. At some point, well beyond their adolescence, they were each formally adopted by Kara widows who had no living sons. The sample size is a little small to make general statements about the procedure, but my Kara interlocutors put it in a striking way: 'They were bought.'

This was said inevitably with some embarrassment or chagrin. I never had the occasion to converse with Mursi relatives of these men about what this practice meant for them, but for the Kara, it was quite straightforward. The following paragraph paraphrases an explication given to me by the elder Mirja-imba, whose sister had attempted to buy a Mursi boy once:

> It occasionally happens that a man has no son, but only daughters. After he has died, and as his wife also grows older, it is clear that she will not bear a son anymore. Then the brothers of the man will travel to Mursi, and there, they will seek out a young man, maybe an orphan, and they will say, 'look, come with me to Kara. There, I have a mother for you, and some mother-brothers, I have fields for you, livestock, I have age-mates for you, I will find a wife for you.' Then the Kara talks to the youth's family, and he gives them some goats, and takes the son of his brother home.

Such an offer was presented to me as an exciting prospect for Mursi orphans, who at home could not hope for anything other than growing up as dependants in some household whose priorities would not be their autonomy, wealth and status. However, in Kara, after the infancy rituals of *bula* and *gori* were performed upon their adult bodies, they would become 'true Kara' eligible to join the next batch of young men who were preparing for their initiation, their *bärgitamo*. This would in turn lead up to their leap across the cattle and their achievement of the status of 'full Kara'. All that these young men would have to do to receive a head-start in life was to go to Kara, become Kara and stay Kara. This is easier said than done, as the record shows: just a few years ago, another young Mursi 'turned back on the way', that is, he died of some illness during his *bärgitamo*. Another Kara elder of Mursi descent was killed over a decade ago by an in-law over a quarrel. One young man ran away about a decade ago, returning to Mursi for unknown reason.

Of the two current adoptees, Appa Chaula spends most of his time outside the major settlements, preferring to have little company. He also has not yet fully mastered the Kara language. The other adoptee, a highly extroverted, brash, physically powerful man who can be very abrasive, constantly gets into disputes and even physical conflicts, such as when people challenge the sincerity of his allegiance to Kara. Incidentally, by way of his adoption, he had become the wealthiest landowner in all of Kara. He sees his predicament, and suspects that people try to provoke him into a fight during which they might get away with killing him, so that the Kara body politic would be cleansed again. This suppressed and in Kara discourse quite unspeakable topos that runs counter to all claims of *ädamo* reminded me of a Frazerian corn king, enthroned to ensure fertility and killed off (in a convenient and symbolic 'hunting accident in the bush') when an ancient Kara lineage is sufficiently refertilized. This second adopted Mursi-turned-true-Kara man was certainly justified in suspecting some hostility. Not only did certain people consistently chide him whenever he spoke Mursi with Appa Chaula, but they also conspicuously sought occasions to provoke him, and his in-laws themselves repeatedly expressed their resentment over his personality, sometimes connected to the public declaration that all would be served better if he went back to Mursi.

I have described this at length because not only because of its ethnographic novelty, but also because it is relevant to the identity politics of Kara. I can hardly overstate my astonishment to find out that there was a way in which somebody who was not legitimately born to the wife of a true Kara man could become a true Kara. This was doubly surprising as this practice so specifically targeted Mursi men. Inquiring further, I was told that Nyangatom boys also could be adopted in the same way, but never found an actual contemporary case of this. Despite these assertions, no publicly acknowledged reason was ever given as to why it was possible to adopt Mursi (and possibly Nyangatom) but not Hamar or Dassanech. In order to contextualize the practice, I can merely point out several formal characteristics shared by both the Mursi and the Nyangatom vis-à-vis the Kara.

In the past, both Mursi and Nyangatom girls were sometimes abducted and brought back to Kara from raids. After being integrated into a household, they were later married off as second or third wives to other Kara. Numerous contemporary Kara have mothers or grandmothers from either group, many more than have female ancestors from among 'the mountain people'. I heard that there used to be consensual intermarriage as well, but not even this is the case today. In a stereotype possibly linked to the practice of adoption, Mursi and Nyangatom women are renowned for their fertility. Despite this pervasive integration of these women into the Kara body politic, nobody ever claimed that the Kara and either group stood in a descent relation. Their entire interaction is based on contingently established practices, but remains mutable as a result.

All visible cultural and linguistic similarities between the Kara and the Nyangatom are apparently evidence of Kara appropriation of features considered attractive. For example, the Kara use numerous Nyangatom words in all sorts of contexts. Such appropriation does not take place vis-à-vis Mursi.

Table 7.1 Dimensions of being alike and being different

	Obvious cultural and linguistic similarities	Claims of historical identity and kinship (*äda*)	Possibility of integration into the true Kara
Mountain people (Hamar, Banna, Bashada)	Yes	Few (Ban., Bash.) No (Hamar)	No
Distant relatives (Arbore and Dassanech)	No	Yes	No
Respected enemies (Mursi and Nyangatom)	No (Mursi) Few (Ny.)	No	Yes (Mursi) Allegedly (Ny.)

Mursi and Nyangatom groups are considered warlike, both groups sharing a strong pastoralist ethos and ideology, and, as has been mentioned already, the Kara have exclusively fought against these two groups in the last few decades. Both are also direct neighbours of the Kara, but until rather recently were not engaged in conflict over material resources with the Kara. Today, the Nyangatom's territorial encroachment is the major interethnic arena that most strongly impacts Kara social life.

These paradigmatic features allow me to follow up on the opposition established between the 'mountain people' and the 'distant relations' by adding this third category of the 'respected enemies' and another variable to the model. The 'mountain people' and the 'distant relatives' were opposed in that the former were rhetorically distanced while obviously similar, and the latter were enshrined as primordial kin despite a lack of evidence for such a relation. Now, the Mursi and Nyangatom are neither markedly similar to the Kara in terms of culture, language or social organization, nor are they said to be ancestral relations. But for members of this last category, it is comparatively common to be individually integrated into the Kara body politic and into material kinship relations.

This simple table shows the problematic of being different and being similar by tracing three discourses and their social validity in Kara, as well as indicating the interactional entailments. Other variables (such as warfare, interpersonal intimacy and economic interdependence) could be added, but need not be. The table as it is sufficiently sharpens our understanding of how these paradigmatic dimensions relate to the more abstract question of Kara 'identity'. In brief, there are a number of different ways, both in discourse at a distance and in observable interaction, for groups to deal with the often conflicting desires for distance and intimacy in the face of competition and conflict. Note that a fourth column has been omitted: 'Possibility of integration into the Kara body politic' would likely apply to all, as it seems unproblematic for refugees from anywhere (even Toposa and Turkana) to set up new lives in Kara.

The Mursi, for one, are probably the most strongly stereotyped neighbours of the Kara. Their 'warlike' nature is proverbial, no so much in that they are reviled as raiders, but in that their skill in stalking and tracking enemies is admired. Their spectacular stick fighting contests stimulate the imagination, while their ostentatiously 'casual' dress code, which occasions more male nudity than elsewhere, along with the notion that the Mursi vastly prefer vomiting over defecating, sometimes elicits indications of embarrassment from their disconcerted neighbours.

In the Mursi case, there has been no fighting over the last fifteen years at least, but early raids and counterattacks are still vivid in people's minds and visible on their bodies. In Labuk, there are several age-sets whose members acquired scarifications for killing Mursi. Still, there is no hate or even dislike on the Kara side. The Mursi are even respected for being unpredictable, assertive and sometimes uncooperative. Even as Kara commented somewhat condescendingly on the unrestrained droves of Mursi descending on hapless tourists at the Jinka market, demanding to be photographed (and get paid for it), they acknowledged that the Mursi were just being 'Mursi'.

The Mursi, then, are seen as fierce and brashly unsophisticated, but equipped with a forthright demeanour appreciated in Kara. This applies equally to Mursi men and women. I never came across Kara commentary on the one Mursi feature that has garnered them worldwide publicity – the females' lip-plates (see Turton 2004; LaTosky 2006, 2014). And despite the Mursi triggering Kara imagination, I found no evidence that the Mursi were in any way othered through metaphor, as was so typical of the Kara–Moguji relationship.

During these times of peace, the most common mode of interaction I noticed was that Kara journeyed to Mursi to barter cattle for firearms. Such groups usually contained someone from Labuk, the northern part of Kara, which is rather close to Mursi territory.[12] Quite a few Kara can communicate in Mursi, and I did sometimes come across Mursi conversant in the Kara language. All in all, I gained the impression that the Kara would like to have more interaction with the Mursi than they did, that they would like to increase the degree of familiarity and intimacy, even as the Mursi who had become Kara were suffering from the ambivalence of their special status.

The Nyangatom, for their part, have to be understood as the most significant neighbour for Kara, even granting that this is truer for Dus and the southern areas of Kara than for Labuk.[13] Over the last forty years, there has been an unstoppable Nyangatom incursion towards the Lower Omo. Without going into too much detail, some points need to be stated.[14] Due to this 'encroachment' (Tornay 1979: 114), the Kara have abandoned all their permanent settlements on the west bank of the Omo River. Many of my Kara age-mates, who were born around the mid 1970s, grew up herding goats on that side of the Omo. In particular, the Kadokochin, a settlement area west of the Omo, was a centre of Kara land, ritually, economically and politically. Today, areas such as Loxode, Doro and Lokulan (see Map 0.2), claimed by the Kara as their 'fathers' land', were first occupied by the Nyangatom and eventually became part of the Nyangatom district. In the 1970s, the Nyangatom annihilated the Kara settlement at Kundamma, probably killing over a hundred people. The Kara reciprocated by laying waste to several Nyangatom hamlets at Aiba (also Aeba; see Tornay 1979; Alvarsson 1989). Tit for tat, every raid occasioned a counter-raid. The imperative to never let a provocation go unanswered, as posited by the Wheel of Autonomy, surfaced very blatantly in these recent Kara–Nyangatom relations.

Today, the unresolved issue that engenders constant tensions is the effective Nyangatom occupation of the fields on the west bank of the Omo. In earlier, better days, Kara used to grant their personal Nyangatom friends a lease to cultivate one of their spare fields – but the ownership was never in question. Today, through an administrative decision that effectively granted the Nyangatom the entire land west of the river, many Kara households have been deprived of what they consider their very own land, riverbank fields that metaphorically belong to the body of their lineages. Come each farming season, they are reduced to dependency on the goodwill of others, while having to watch 'their' land on the other bank cultivated by the Nyangatom. Disgruntlement never rests for long and opportunistic violence – mostly sniping – was common throughout the time of my most regular fieldwork (2003–8).

Despite this, many Kara are fond of the Nyangatom. While they do want their lands back and do feel that the Nyangatom have betrayed them, while they both shoot and shoot back to kill, they would much rather live in a more neighbourly, more regulated and slightly more geographically distanced relationship. Remember the example of the fence between neighbours mentioned in Chapter 1: while seemingly separating them, the fence still provided rules that allowed both sides civil conversation across it. No fence, no mending wall, and the squabbles about where each plot began and ended would be neverending. The Kara also want a proper fence again. The one drawn by the administration, simply taking the natural feature of the Omo River as a dividing line, would not fairly separate the two gardens, all to their detriment rather than to that of the Nyangatom (see Girke 2013). They might find Barth's example most apposite, with its pragmatic as well as its moral component.

What is it about the Nyangatom that attracts the Kara? For me, the most noticeable item was the guttural, harsh-sounding language that many Kara know to perfection. At a peace conference in Turmi, the young Nyangatom man who was translating from Amharic to Nyangatom was occasionally at a loss how to express a certain 'big word' in his own mother tongue. When he hesitated, inevitably one of the senior Kara present would tell him which Nyangatom word to use, a situation that confused the administrator, embarrassed the Nyangatom youth and made everybody else chuckle. But this display of intense knowledge

Figure 7.1 A Hamar man waits for his speech to be translated into Amharic, Dassanech and Nyangatom during a peace meeting in a Turmi school house (July 2006). Photograph by Felix Girke.

and intimate familiarity only seemed incongruous at a meeting devoted to the issue of reconciling these two warring groups. Even today there is a man in Kara, a true Kara at that, who refuses to speak the Kara language. Now around fifty years old, he grew up in Nyangatom and is more conversant in that language than in his supposed mother tongue. That he gets by in Kara with such behaviour is remarkable. I have also witnessed Kara men who had to fall back on their young wives for translation of more complex Nyangatom utterances. Due to the perpetual state of war, I witnessed little contact between women from both sides,[15] but it is obvious that not so long ago, there was an interethnic community of women with a high degree of intimacy and familiarity.

Regularly, Kara elders speak Nyangatom even when there are only Kara present. Evidently, they revel in the memories and associations triggered and in the expressive opportunities provided by Nyangatom prosody, syntax and vocabulary. To list some other sites where the attraction of Nyangatom culture is visible: there are many material objects in Kara that are only called by their Nyangatom name, while an equivalent Omotic term does exist for them elsewhere in the HBB cluster. Kara age-sets mostly take their names from Nyangatom. Personal goat-names (usually denoting the colours and patterns on a goat's hide) are from the Nyangatom, but this practice extends eastward well beyond Kara. Many Nyangatom songs are sung and, by and large, women's ornaments are as similar to Nyangatom style as to Hamar. Regarding behavioural ethos, I found that the Kara cherish stereotypical Nyangatom conduct, raucous, provocative, with little regard to face-saving strategies in interaction (see Strecker 1988; Brown and Levinson 1987). The recent spates of violent conflict seem not to have engendered a re-evaluation of these cultural elements.

There is also a sizeable resident (and well-trusted) Nyangatom population in Kara, who practise, for example, life-cycle rituals largely in their own way. But even across the river, back and forth, there are many individual friendships and highly involved mutual histories. Until the troubles were aggravated throughout the 1970s and 1980s, and still during that difficult time, many people who are today elders (both female and male) grew up together. Kara households took in Nyangatom orphans and often cooperated with their Nyangatom friends or affines during farming season. In early September 2006, I was walking with a delegation of Kara through Kangaten, today the administrative centre for the Nyangatom, on our way to a meeting point from where cars were to convey us to the Kibish peace ceremony. On this brief trek, I witnessed how every few minutes one of the Kara I accompanied quite emotionally greeted or was greeted in turn by a Nyangatom whom we met on the way, as old relations and friendships were recalled.

This all serves to emphasize that today, in a very different way as compared to the Moguji, the Nyangatom are an extremely relevant other for the Kara. While there is no dearth of negative stereotypes, as they are constantly said to be liars and thieves and unreliable, they are the main source of cultural innovations, a still fascinating focus of imagery, desires and mimesis. Two topoi have to be mentioned where negative stereotyping surprisingly is not strong. First of all, while the ethnonym 'Nyangatom' is rarely used in Kara, who instead mostly say 'Bume', the latter name should not be considered an epithet. Tornay calmly states that *bume* is their 'nom ethiopien' (2001: 209) and already von Höhnel, in 1888, addressed the (putative) ancestors of today's Nyangatom as 'Buma' (1968: 207). While it is a common claim of people only superficially familiar with the region that *bume* means 'the smelly ones', no one has been able to name the language in which this is the case. The issue of the variation of ethnonyms is much more complex than that. The second item is male circumcision. Kara are circumcised, Nyangatom are not. Yet circumcision in Kara is not part of a lengthy and ostentatious initiation, but is performed more perfunctorily in the establishment of proto-age sets among herding boys. Thus, to be circumcised is a marker of adolescence/adulthood, and it might at some time have been a marker of *not* being Nyangatom, and possibly the presence of the foreskin might somehow be associable with 'smelliness'. But, as it turns out, unlike other places in Africa (compare, for example, Beidelman 1964: 41), I did not find circumcision to be rhetorically exploited to emphasize difference.

The very pressing material-territorial rivalry and the ensuing bitter grudges cannot be ignored, but one needs to realize that they are tempered by a deep desire to reconcile them. Many people on both sides would prefer not that the other would simply disappear, but that one might live together with regulated, peaceful contact.[16] People described a positive, ideal state of relations in terms of 'our boys should cross the river and dance with their girls, and they should come to us, so that *äda* might farm together and eat together', even as many have lost the belief that this might be possible.

To relate this discussion to Table 7.1 above and my more general statements about social relations and identity: while the Mursi and Nyangatom are closer to the Kara in sheer geographical proximity than the 'distant relations' Arbore and Dassanech, this would be too simple an explanation for the interplay of the paradigms of similarity, relatedness and integration.

I would suggest that a key to understanding the way the 'mountain people' are distanced lies in the Kara's worry that too close a relationship might lead to being eventually absorbed. Seen rhetorically, however, a straight-out denial of common descent in the face of fundamental similarity is not very convincing if there is not an alternative available on which to project descent. After all, everybody needs to have come from somewhere. Thus, I understand the Kara claims of relatedness to the Arbore and Dassanech as implicit disclaimers of descent from the 'mountain people'. Take note that this creates an A-B-A pattern on the map (compare Schlee 2008: 53): the Hamar have regularly fought both the Arbore and the Dassanech, and the Kara's claims to kinship with these groups also allowed the latter not to be drawn into these conflicts, while still being able to enlist the Hamar in struggles against their 'common enemy', the Nyangatom.[17]

Regarding the Dassanech, the mutually recognized kinship also facilitated visits and regular trade expeditions, but one should be wary of reducing the relationship to this aspect: as I have argued above, all social actions have an audience. By introducing the last category of the 'respected enemies' Mursi and Nyangatom, I want to make the point that for intensive interaction and even intermarriage and adoption, cultural or historical (mythic) closeness is not a necessity and might in fact be a liability. Both the Mursi and the Nyangatom are so distinct that the relations between them and the Kara are evidently manmade, created through choice and guided by attraction. Consider this brief episode: after the inauspicious slaying of a Nyangatom in the early weeks of 2007 (mentioned above), an angry Hamar man who had come to Korcho tried to stir the Kara into solidarity with the Hamar. He spoke at length about the necessity to stick together and assault the Nyangatom again, jointly, to pre-empt their inevitable counterattack. Eventually, one of the Kara elders present slowly shook his head, as if in exasperation, and told the visitor, as if trying to make a slow child understand: 'Our *ädamo* with the Nyangatom – it is *ädamo*.' In effect, he was saying that the Kara only fought the Nyangatom when there was absolutely no way around it, and not on behalf of anybody else, not even the Hamar. To call the relation *ädamo* in this context emphasized the will to mutuality.

I have repeatedly argued that social relations are not exempt from the requirements of (good) performance. People are not only brothers, they also must act like brothers if the relationship is to have any motivational effect. *Äda* and *ädamo* are understood by the actors themselves to be manmade, even as they use naturalistic metaphors of 'blood', 'guts' and 'roots'.

The structural conditions of demography, administration and resource distribution force the Kara to manage their relationships with their neighbours very deliberately. To assert that some are collectively ancient *äda*, while defending the practised *ädamo* (mutuality and intimacy) with others, while again trying to keep the – to an observer's eye – rather obvious relatives at arm's length in the face of a plethora of relations is an expression of this deliberation (compare Schlee 2008: 52).

There is no interpretative need to posit a secretive masterplan devised by the Kara *borkotto bitti*, the council of elders, but as far as their actions and competences are known, there might well be one. Issues just like these, establishing procedural rules of how to interact as members of a political group ('the Kara') with members of other groups, have been discussed by the *borkotto bitti* before and guidelines have been proclaimed: 'Don't sell them bullets' or 'Don't allow them to farm your fields'. It seems that the problematic of closeness and distance is well understood by Kara elders.

In terms of the notion of the 'regional other', these last sections served to highlight that within a larger cognitive category, which has also come to be political, there are different ways to establish similarity, closeness and distance, and these can be tools of political action, just as they are fed by desires, imagination and other contingent factors.

The 'Harmless People': The Aari and Maale

> There are occasional conflicts between the south-western [Aari] and the Mursi, but for the most part the A. live at peace with their neighbours, who do not consider it bravery to kill an A. because of the A.s' non-warring, agricultural life style.
>
> —C.M. Ford, 'Aari Ethnography'

The Aari are included in the discussion of the 'regional other' of the Kara even though they, as indicated by Ford's entry quoted above, are both affectively and economically much less 'pastoralist' than the already rather agriculturalist Hamar, Kara, Dassanech, Nyangatom, Arbore and Mursi, who at least make an effort to display their participation in the East African cattle complex. They are included because they belong to the South Omo region not only administratively and in terms of historical contacts, but also in terms of imagination and cultural neighbourhood.[18] Precisely the fact that they are so sedentary and nonpastoralist, rather overwhelmingly agriculturalist, makes theirs a useful stereotype that brings out the 'warlike' nature and the pastoralist bias of others.

First, it ought to be said that most Kara today know little about the Aari and next to nothing about the Maale. The former is somewhat surprising: even in the twentieth century, Aari traders wandered down rough forest tracks to Kara, leading donkeys laden with coffee beans, to exchange the coffee for *muutsi*, the salty soil that the Kara collected in the flats around Mt. Lokulan. Since then, coffee production has been turned into state-controlled profitable cash cropping, and new sources of salt have become available. It took only a few attacks by Banna and Bashada raiders on Kara-bound Aari to finish off this trade (Girke 2010). So while the interaction between the Aari and the Kara effectively ended, the icon of Aari coffee is still invoked in Kara ceremony. Today, contact is rare, limited to the times when individual Kara visit Jinka town. There, the Kara experience the Aari as strange little folk: as a rule less tall than the peoples of the Omo Valley, with quaint behaviour (men kissing each other in greeting) and costume (groups of girls dressed uniformly in very colourful outfits), leading horses with gaudily decorated tails. While the phrase 'harmless people' is mine, it is fair to say that the Aari and Maale have come to be the epitome of inoffensive, deferential and inconsequential people for the Kara. That their land is lush and fertile is registered with admiration and a little envy.

The Maale are basically assumed to be another instance of the same type of people: 'Aaribe Maalebe – The Aari and the Maale' are regularly mentioned in the same breath. There is even less contact with them, but the Kara are aware where the Maale live, that they belong to the same *woreda* as the familiar Banna, and assume that they, as well as the Aari, are more influenced by urbanization, missionary activities and administrative measures than the other groups in the Lower Omo. Those Aari and Maale who have become 'ethiopianized' in this way are, as is true of any group in the cultural neighbourhood, no longer viewed as proper Aari or Maale and would not be measured accordingly.

An unresolved question, which I cannot further pursue here, is whether the Aari and Maale are perceived as 'harmless' only today, in the reproduction of a stereotype current among the Habesha. Among the Hamar and Arbore, the Maale were renowned as fierce fighters as late as the 1970s, who 'killed off everybody with their poisoned arrows (Lydall and Strecker 1979b: 24). But as I will develop in Chapter 9, following the work of the late Alexander Naty, it is striking that the Aari themselves maintain a stereotyping discourse that portrays them as 'powerless'. This has emerged out of the imperial conquest and the institution of the *gebbar* system of landholding, which turned the Aari into subservient workers serving their Habesha landlords (see Strecker 1994; Donham 2002a). All this goes to show that the work of stereotype is not unidirectional. The imperialist Habesha conquerors considered the Aari less fierce and accordingly less impressive than the lowlander groups, and unfavourably compared the Aari in whose country they set up camp with these others (Naty 1992: xx). This has, as I will discuss later, possibly influenced Aari views of themselves. In turn, the Kara and others have been exposed to such Habesha stereotypes of the Aari and have possibly integrated them into their own views.

The Aari and Maale, as seen from Kara, live at the very horizon of relevance. They present the outer edge of the cultural neighbourhood. In a sense, this is not only social and geographical, but also in terms of historical teleology: a Kara friend once wondered loudly 'whether the Kara would one day be as the Aari are now'. It was not that the Kara would become the Aari, but that over time what was characteristic of the Aari would become characteristic of the Kara too. They might become as structurally tamed, and as compliant with outside forces, less in control of their Wheel of Autonomy. As he saw it, Aari-ness loomed in the Kara's future. The lifestyles that are attractive in the cultural neighbourhood today will recede into the past – either as fond or as embarrassing memories. The 'harmless people' of today are just similar enough to warrant inclusion into the category Shank'illa, even as they are far from perfect examples for the 'regional other', and do not serve well for projection, desire and mimesis.[19]

Ädamo in the Cultural Neighbourhood

The argument underlying the last four sections was that obvious cultural similarities, public claims of descent, and intimacy of interaction are wholly independent variables in the relationships between the Kara and their neighbours. This 'raw material for political rhetoric' serves to emphasize that there is a strategic element in this, as there was to the other ways in which *ädamo* has been discussed so far. I find it plausible to acknowledge the Kara's own, emic understanding of the politics and rhetoric of belonging. They do know why at times they pay only lip service to the unity of the Hamar and the Kara, and some surely realize the rhetorical need of having a different category of people to call their true relatives when they perpetually deny their descent from the 'mountain people'. Finally, the close interaction with the Nyangatom (and, in some arenas, the Mursi too) is certainly facilitated by the geographical proximity as compared to the Dassanech or Arbore, but can hardly be reduced to this one factor. And all strategic awareness does not preclude occasional disasters, since – in these times and places – it just takes one man with a gun to spoil the best-laid schemes. The complexity of such situations, and the demands they impose on actors, is spelt out by Wood:

> We get tangled up in relations that maintain differences, or differences that maintain relations, or similarities that call attention to differences.

> These verbal tangles are not surprising, if one considers that when people negotiate similarity and difference across cultural divides they manage the real but paradoxical problem of maintaining relation, if not similarity, and difference *at the same time*. They keep the borders between people meaningful, not arbitrary or accidental. They connect and distance at once. (2000: 60f, emphasis in original)

I argue that especially the ways of interaction between Kara and their 'respected enemies', which include mimesis and allow intermarriage and adoption, even in the face of intermittent warfare, are indices that speak of cultural attraction, of imagination and desire, of people trying to enshrine meaning in their social practices. F.G. Bailey, in a surprising move to repair reputations, points out that initially, the structural-functionalist notion of equilibrium did not refer to a naturally occurring phenomenon, but to something 'intended ... something that is valued: people attempt to resolve and regulate conflicts. It is – apparently – a norm in the moral sense of the word, not only a statistic, and it is likely to be both supported and contested' (2003: 71). Only later could some proponents no longer distinguish between these two distinct senses. For me, this serves to highlight again the basic message of the notion 'cultural neighbourhood': that sentiments of community can be extended along trajectories of familiarity, facilitated by narrative thoughts and the inevitable plots and stereotypes.

As an aside, to put warfare next to intermarriage inevitably conjures up the old phrase 'We marry those whom we fight' (Radcliffe-Brown 1952: 20; cf. Brown 1964). This association with structuralist logic does not, however, bear out application to my case: that the Kara marry the Nyangatom and fight the Nyangatom are again independent variables, emerging out of the historically contingent interaction of these groups. Even within Kara, the brother-in-law is not as a rule or a role particularly assertive towards his sister's husband. This is especially visible in that the true Kara are such dominant wife-takers rather than wife-givers. The adoption practice I described above also is unidirectional. All this points towards a deliberate demographic strategy and away from underlying structural(ist) reasons. It also challenges the assumption that Kara might see social categories as fundamentally natural categories. This somewhat deviates from Galaty's argument about the naturalness, species-like character of social categories in Maasai ethnosociology. Still, his subsequent suggestion translates well into my stereotype-oriented discussion of South Omo. He argues that to posit an ethnic category is 'not ... problematic for Maasai. As a *name* it designates specific persons and groups; as a *concept* it embodies specific values and qualities accepted and manifested by all' (1982: 3, emphasis in original).

In this chapter, I have returned to themes first developed much earlier. The view from Kara showed how the Wheel of Autonomy can be used to model interethnic interaction. Kara ways of relating to their neighbours can only be addressed from a regional perspective, by taking into account the strategies pursued by these neighbours as well (see Schlee 2008: 41). Concomitantly, the examples supported the methodological recognition that all such interaction is rhetorical, being performed with the intention of convincing or persuading, thus, in full awareness that there is always an audience that observes, interprets and finally judges. This audience is recognized as relevant. As Barth has argued (2000: 30), when boundaries are drawn, the resulting 'social forms' are not determined. But the recognition that an other exists is necessary.

This, in fact, offers a definition of the territorial polities of South Omo: they are constituted through their ongoing success in being recognized by each other. They do not struggle and display agency necessarily in order to achieve any additional, extraneous goals. To be recognized as a group entails to be included as an accountable actor in the narratives that make up the interethnic imagination in the cultural neighbourhood. To be a group is to display agency, distinction, power and vice versa. As I outlined in Chapter 1, I understand agency and autonomy and distinction as dependent variables, which constitute one another and that are impossible to define without recourse to the other. In some ways, this turns on its head simple intentionalist models: as observers, we might say that an aggregate of individuals such as 'the Kara' would at best 'behave' and not 'act'. But in narrative, their behaviour is understood as action and thus rendered meaningful, and this is what allows me – in the first place – to ask 'how do they do it?', a question that the Kara even ask themselves of themselves. In the same way can a population come to be considered a group.

My discussion so far traced other conversations that I witnessed in the field and abstractly referred back to plots, actors and commonplaces in the narrative of cultural neighbourhood. In such emplotment, stereotypes matter: stereotypes allow casting characters, which in turn are required for plots. Stereotypes are transmitted, they 'rub off' on other groups (Wood 2000: 71) and 'they are used by the very people they encompass' (Chock 1987: 360). They can also get turned around, as when a negative connotation is recontextualized in a more positive light (see Kratz 1994: 67). Michael Herzfeld has convincingly shown how stereotypes reflect emergent political relations: 'Their efficacy lies not in their recognition of some unchanging reality, but in their appeal to the conventions of collective self-representation' (1998: 72). In the face of an absence of effective central authority and institutionalized historiography, the agreed-upon plots of narrative thought, which Herzfeld calls an 'idiom' (1998: 73), are important for communal orientation and transmission of knowledge.

In that regard at least, the cultural neighbourhood of South Omo is not on the wane: up until today, no official narrative threatens to overwhelm and displace local understandings of just what was going on in the region throughout the twentieth century and since. The interpretation of the transformations caused by the arrival of the Habesha and the conquest is not relinquished to the dominant outsider. Chapter 9, in particular, picks up on the local versions that seem in no danger of being supplanted.

I want to end this discussion of the 'regional other' by returning to the Moguji, who, as I argued in the last chapter, are excluded from full membership in this category. What is different in the relationships described here vis-à-vis the relationship between the Kara and the Moguji? In a nutshell, the latter are supposed to remain a disaggregated category, not a group with interests, engaging in collective action. Their attempts to achieve this status are denied naturalness and legitimacy by the Kara. The Moguji are rendered different because they need to remain an other. This is not to say that they do not belong to the cultural neighbourhood or are not Shank'illa – they do and they are. Their fate is entwined with that of the Kara, they are part and parcel of Kara social life, and they feature in numerous narratives, even playing central roles in some. However, just as they have been denied the status of 'pastoralists' – recall the taboos imposed on the Moguji in Kara regarding livestock, this most condensed of regional symbols – they are still denied the right to issue their own versions of the existing narratives. Their attempts to make this last step towards gaining autonomy as a collective actor, to be a narrator and not only a narrated, to emplot and not only to be emplotted, is counteracted by the Kara, who instead insist on telling the story for the Moguji (compare Girke 2014b). After all, in the spirit of *ädamo*, this ought to be sufficient.

The Moguji, by demanding recognition of their status as a group with the same degree of agency, disclaim this integration. By working towards autonomy, they want to become recognized by the Kara on the same level as the Nyangatom and Arbore are. The Kara resist this move not only for material reasons, but also because a successful emancipation of the Moguji would subvert the Kara's narratives and their power to construct narratives of interethnic relations on the Lower Omo. This might undermine their own claims to autonomy and consequently erode their own ability to define themselves, and to effectively keep the encroachments of others on both their distinction and autonomy at bay. Specifically, the way in which they have managed so far to keep themselves bodily and politically distinct from the 'mountain people' might be at risk if they would have to deal with the Moguji on equal terms.

The Wheel of Autonomy rumbles ever on.

Notes

1. This is only now slowly being broken up by a new generation of anthropologists, mostly through the efforts of the Hamar expert Ivo Strecker, who has encouraged numerous students at both the MA and the Ph.D. level to start their research in the region, and of Günther Schlee, director of the MPI for Social Anthropology (Halle/Saale), who has enabled them to finish it. One of the cornerstones of my argument is precisely that in South Omo, it is both necessary and – due to the closeness of the groups and the many sites of interaction – actually feasible to maintain a comparative perspective.

2. As this is not particular to the relationship between the Kara and any of their neighbours, but instead a general feature of the cultural neighbourhood, and since it is in fact the one aspect of interethnic relations that has been extensively dealt with by other scholars (see Tadesse 2000), I have left it out of the subsequent discussion. For a full appreciation of the cultural neighbourhood, though, these bonds need to be considered.
3. Here, the rapid transformation of the Omo Valley forces me to add a cautionary reminder that this was true at least until 2011. I am not certain how much, for example, the range of Hamar cattle has been constrained by the industrial farms that have been established in Kara since.
4. These Kara terms muddle the already-puzzling field of ethnonyms even further. In the following, I use the terms 'Banna' and 'Bashada', which are in wider use. As far as I could gather, Atula is the name of a riverbed and the corresponding area in Banna territory. The etymology of Banno is unclear and the parallel to Banna seems misleading.
5. The *Ethnologue* database classifies Kara as 'Karo' (kxh), stating a 'lexical similarity of 81% with Hamer-Banna' (Gordon 2005); 'Hamer-Banna' is listed as (amf). Both are classified as 'Afro-Asiatic, Omotic, South', often rendered as 'Aroid' (after the Aari; see below). Jean Lydall states that the Hamar, Banna and Bashada speak 'one language ... in variants with a few lexical differences' (2005: 983), while the Kara 'speak a dialect of the same language' (ibid.). Being accustomed to Kara, I find spoken Hamar generally intelligible. Not having made a linguistic survey, I am not certain about the extent of the grammatical differences. In terms of prosody, differences are noticeable, and in terms of vocabulary, differences are both striking and at times etymologically puzzling. Hayward declared in 2009 that there was very limited linguistic material available on Southern Omotic/Aroid languages; Petrollino's recent *A Grammar of Hamar* (2016) is accordingly particularly valuable.
6. The term 'girl' is used advisedly. In Kara, *anza* designates all unmarried females. Considering that remarriage is virtually impossible, one can by definition only marry girls. Grammatically, I would add, men marry and girls get married, clearly shifting the agency to the husband's side of the alliance.
7. The Kara are atypical of the populations of South Omo in particular, but also for Northeast Africa in general, in that narratives about the origins of their clans (*olo*) are not particularly salient. In direct inquiry, some notions regarding clan origins can be found, but people do not use them to make any sorts of claims. In contrast, the elaborate ethnogony of the Hamar highlights the numerous directions from where the sections and clans entered the land (Lydall and Strecker 1979b: 2; Strecker 2005). I have collected a few tentative statements linking Kara clans to Hamar clans, but my interlocutors presented these connections more as quaint and curious folklore than as historical ties that could be effectively invoked in interaction to activate alliances.
8. For the Arbore, there is primarily work by Yukio Miyawaki, Tadesse Wolde, E.C. Gabbert, Ayalew Gebre and Alula Pankhurst. For the Dassanech, I would list Uri Almagor, Claudia Carr, Peggy Elfmann, Yvan Houtteman, Toru Sawa and Neal Sobania.
9. Unfortunately, no scholar so far has explicitly explored Arbore–Dassanech interrelations from 'both insides', as it were, even though this seems to be an eminently feasible research design.
10. Some earlier versions have also included the Bodi as a group left behind. Today, the Bodi barely register in the Kara's cultural neighborhood.
11. Of the four categorizations made in this chapter, this one and the next one (the 'harmless people') are least explicitly made by the Kara: while 'the mountain people' is an oft-heard term and while the Kara's similar relationship to the Arbore and Dassanech is commonly

invoked, to call the Mursi and Nyangatom 'respected enemies' is my term rather than that of the Kara. The existing parallels justify formalizing this covert category.

12. I have heard it said that the Gomba of Labuk have specifically close relations to a Mursi section, who would come and perform some specific rituals as their 'mother-brothers'. I could not confirm this so far.
13. As an illustration: the *bitti* of Labuk is in charge of the rituals of peace-making with the Mursi after a period of warfare, just as it is the *bitti* of Dus who will perform the equivalent ritual with the Nyangatom. Similar arrangements exist in other groups (see Turton (1999: 146ff) for the Mursi).
14. I have addressed recent violent episodes in an earlier text (Girke 2008), presenting an overview over the dynamics of escalation and de-escalation. A more recent text (Girke 2014b) gives an account of a Kara–Nyangatom reconciliation meeting. Finally, the conflicts over land between these two groups are discussed in Girke (2013).
15. Women are particularly vulnerable in the sort of warfare that was common at the time of my fieldwork, as one of their main tasks is to fetch water from the river, which exposes them to snipers on the other bank.
16. This general statement could be qualified by disentangling the specific relations between the Kara and the different sections of Nyangatom (see Girke 2008, 2014b). The various sections among the Nyangatom each have their own distinct stance towards and history with the Kara – a proper study of these differences from within Nyangatom might well reveal aspects of the relationship that I never came across.
17. The triangular relationship between the Hamar and the Kara and the Arbore/Dassanech is structurally similar to how Schlee describes the constellation between the Borana and the Gabra and the Somali: the Gabra and the Borana are visibly similar, entangled in ritual interaction and political alliance, yet the Gabra say that the Borana are 'of different blood' – while claiming that the visibly dissimilar Somali were of the same 'blood'. 'Blood', here, has the same entailments as in South Omo, namely that spilling the same blood will lead to misfortune and death. Schlee (2008: 61–75) explains this in reference to interethnic clan relations. This does not bear out in my case, as there are, as far as anyone can tell, no interethnic clan relations between the Kara and the Arbore or the Kara and the Dassanech.
18. In South Omo, there are also the Tsamai, or Tsamako, who live north of the Arbore in the hot plains. The only way the Kara ever spoke about the Tsamai was in terms of the latter's feared sorcery – no other group, apparently, was believed to know as many eldritch secrets as they. A few times I heard rumours about people who had gone to the Tsamai to buy some sort of sorcery, and most people found this a genuine reason to worry. Since I also have not visited Tsamai, I have left them out of this discussion even though they clearly belong to the cultural neighbourhood.
19. I do not reiterate Table 7.1 from the last section: for the Aari and Maale, all answers would be 'no', the linguistic and cultural parallels between the Aari and the other groups speaking Southern Omotic languages not being obvious or even well-known to many Kara.

Chapter 8

The Cleverness of the Kara

A young official of the Hamar *woreda*, the administrative district that encompasses Kara, Hamar and Arbore, arrived in Dus on 1 February 2007, and had the elders and some select women assemble. He had come to bring news about recent policy and to assess the local moods and attitudes. The news, it turned out, came not merely from the district administration, but from the customarily conflated chimera of government and ruling party (EPRDF), in Kara simply known as *mengist* (compare Taddesse 2006: 214). At some point, the meeting turned into an admonishment to order, civility and loyalty. The visitor sternly inquired whether anybody had been criticizing the EPRDF government, colloquially known as 'Ihaddik' in Ethiopia: 'And when you heard somebody speak badly of the Ihaddik, and when you heard him praise the Derg government, did you call him to order and show him the right way again?'[1] In reaction, a Kara elder (whom I will call Goiti-imba throughout this chapter) languorously got up from his *borkotto* seat and announced with expansive gestures and firm voice: 'No, no, we don't have anything of that sort here in our land. Such problems only exist up there in the mountains. When the Ihaddik came into power, we all welcomed it.' That was all; Goiti-imba sat down again. The official nodded somewhat grimly, gave no reply and proceeded with the meeting.[2]

Now this is a rather brief vignette. What weight can it have? It does not induce much ethnographic dissonance to resolve away; the incident seems trivial. However, one can read from it the key elements that shape the relationship between 'the Kara' and their 'Great Ethiopian Other', the Habesha highlanders – in every way unlike the 'regional other' as discussed previously. Over the course of this chapter, I outline the Kara way of performing this relationship, which is an active and creative engagement rather than reaction or passivity. As was the case with this episode, meetings of various kinds and degrees of involvement were central sites of such interaction. In the quotation given above, the salience and oppositional use of 'highlander' and 'Kara' (as a special case of 'lowlander'/ Shank'illa) comes out well. This dualism is commonly found both in everyday interaction and in less ephemeral conversation and imaginaries. The vignette gains its significance through the ironical attitude displayed by the Kara side. This attitude has to be seen as a distinguishing feature of how the Kara conceive of their relation to 'the highlander', represented and embodied by the young official.

Central is the concept of *paxalmamo*, 'cleverness', as it is used by the Kara in reference to themselves or less commonly to others. I argue that today, the Kara are engaged in rhetorically perpetuating 'cleverness' as an important diacritic marker of their identity. This appears as such a concerted effort that I call it a charter. It certainly is more consciously pursued than a mere cultural commonplace or leitmotif to which conversation keeps on reverting. The distinction to be achieved in this way consists in a discursive denial of the Kara's apparent marginality and powerlessness, there at the Ethiopian periphery, a denial that is as such ironic.

Departing from this acknowledgement of how appropriate a charter of cleverness shot through with irony is to the times, the second section of the chapter focuses on the 'Great Ethiopian Other', the Habesha highlander. Notably diverging from the relations to the 'tribal' groups in the cultural neighbourhood as discussed in the last chapter, the Kara relations to 'the Highlander' is not fruitfully described in terms of cultural difference. Within the cultural neighbourhood, as I have argued, the interaction between groups is horizontal, marked by a constant struggle to maintain a general power balance between fundamentally symmetrical and familiar actors, who themselves point to paradigmatic 'culture' to explain and describe their similarities and differences. The Habesha, inseparable from conceptions of state apparatus and administration (compare Tadesse 2006: 305, fn. 12), are *a priori* more powerful than any or all of the Shank'illa groups. Thus, the relationship between them is inevitably vertical and needs to be analysed accordingly (see Schlee 2005: 38). The similarities as they obtain between groups of the cultural neighbourhood do not apply here.

It is not that there is no communication: the unfamiliar Habesha are not only the stereotyped objects of Kara discourse, but are also simultaneously the main addressees of the Kara claims to cleverness. The relation between them, which combines colonial features with assertions of equality and citizenship as issued by a modern state, is fundamentally incongruous, as such claims and tangible social facts diverge in a pointedly obvious way. This incongruity is enhanced by the fact that not even the defining feature of the Weberian state, the monopoly on violence, was being fairly and reliably enforced in South Omo. Accordingly, the matter of domination and subordination is far from resolved and, even today, much interaction between the Kara and the Habesha is marked by constant negotiation of power, specifically the power to define (discussed in Chapters 1 and 3). The stance the Kara assume in the respective arenas, I argue, is fundamentally ironical. The relationship between the Kara and the Habesha can only be understood by taking the subtle and often humorous ways into account in which people ironize the other, themselves and the incongruous relationship. Even as this discussion veers away from a 'social problems oriented sociology' (Zijderveld 1995: 342), by highlighting irony, fun and humour, it investigates 'an important weapon in the armoury of civil society' (Obadare 2009: 244).

It has been argued that within anthropology, the capacity for irony was rarely accorded to the 'native', even where the reflexive anthropologist, observing from betwixt and between, could afford to take in all the incongruities and contradictions of social life:

> But if anthropologists are ironists to a degree, they have sometimes distinguished themselves from their subjects by implying that the latter are not. We anthropologists often portray our subjects as earnestly committed to specific ways of life, to realizing and affirming certain truths that they 'hold self-evident'. (Lambek 2004: 4; compare Friedrich 2001: 232)

Others have suggested that the study of irony 'both cross-culturally and across contexts invites investigation' (Hill and Irvine 1993: 20). In Kara, I met people who constantly took on distanced positions that allowed them to ironize, and who then cast doubt on the 'final vocabularies' (Rorty 1989: 73f) with which they were confronted. To me, this seemed most prominent in arenas where power was at stake, where claims to equality met with stark hierarchy and where the mantle of authority was worn by undeserving individuals. This understanding allows an aspective description of the Kara–Habesha relationship, which focuses on irony and power, offering a methodological counterdiscourse to approaches that assume that domination and resistance are clear-cut issues. Irony denies this; ironists perceive their own implicatedness in the situations they comment upon, and even where they are in a subordinate, marginal position, they realize that their rulers are entrapped in demanding roles and constraining discourses just as much, if not more so.

I began my ethnographic discussion with the internal categories of being Kara, then extended my perspective to encompass the outside-on-the-inside position of the Moguji vis-à-vis the true Kara, and again stepped away to look at how the Kara broadly stereotype themselves and their Shank'illa neighbours. Whereas these earlier chapters presented social configurations in which the identity categories of the actors always had mutual relevance, the encounter between the Kara and the Habesha pits a merely regionally salient ethnic identity against a social category that is at an entirely different level of scale, organization and power.

Exploring *Paxalmamo*

As I have done before when addressing Kara terms, I want to briefly explore the semantic field. After initially becoming aware of the term, I started inquiring more directly and was then told that the three terms *paxalmamo*, *maltamo* and *asaabamo* all referred to the same human faculty. As I only ever encountered *asaabamo* by virtue of its inclusion in this very list, I leave it out of the debate. Regarding the other two, especially the use of the respective adjectives *paxala* and *malti*, I found distinct differences in tenor that allow me to highlight what *paxalmamo* is all about.

With a strong tendency, *malti* and the noun *maltamo* were used to refer to mischievous trickery, to a roguish and somewhat malevolent cleverness. *Maltamo* is best embodied through the trickster figure of the squirrel in the Kara fables of animals, which regularly has one of the larger, powerful animals (baboon, lion, leopard, hyena, elephant) falling prey to a fiendish scheme set in motion by their mother-brother or sister-son, the squirrel. These animals go about regular Kara activities, such as visiting each other, preparing food for themselves, but as they beg tobacco of one another, ask fire from a neighbour to get their own hearth going or engage in some other all too human interaction, their human-animal nature always lets it end cruelly: the leopard kills his own mother by mistake, the lion eats faeces, a leopard skin is tied to the tail of the sleeping hyena who, upon awakening, runs himself to terminal exhaustion out of pure fright.[3] The squirrel, however, is the main protagonist, setting both physical and social traps, provoking incidents and accidents, and laying false trails. To call someone a squirrel (*kubuni*), or simply *malti*, is a reference to these tales and a denunciation – albeit usually playful and somewhat admiringly – of intelligence directed at the wrong ends: too selfish for its own good, too clever by half, with a generous helping of schadenfreude. The imagery is grounded in the actual behaviour of the animal – it flees into one hole in the ground and you never know where it might emerge again.[4]

Paxala was used more neutrally, mostly in comments on a display of competence. It refers to foresight, to thrift, to success in avoiding trouble, to knowing when to make a departure, to being able to deal with other people's demands and neither snubbing them too obviously nor having to surrender one's last shirt. Someone who is *paxala* is successful in their wheeling and dealing, shows skill in handling their private affairs without interference from other individuals or the community at large, and can trick game animals when hunting.[5] *Paxalmamo* indicates 'cleverness' in a wider and somewhat more positive sense than *maltamo*.

The term that is mostly used as an antonym is *malgintamo*, which can be translated as 'weakness', from the adjective *malgimi* ('puny', 'feeble').[6] The rhetorical question 'is this *paxalmamo?*', which in political oratory often follows the description of a certain attitude or incident, implies that 'no, it isn't: it is *malgintamo!*' This opposition indicates that 'cleverness' is more than a common theme in judging action. It is also more than just a luxury to indulge in: cleverness, even opportunism, is a pragmatically necessary element in political life, without which action will be half-hearted and inconsequential. This makes it moral again, as the good of the community requires *paxalmamo* to avoid inadvertent *malgintamo*. The contemporary situation of the Kara population does have a certain 'urgency' to it (see Matsuda (2007), as cited below), which must stimulate reflections over morality and expediency (compare Bailey 1977). In the face of existential worries, one might not need to have to weigh pragmatism against principles so very scrupulously, as whatever works comes to be legitimate.

Looking at how *paxalmamo* is used in speaking and at its antonymic oppositions, it becomes evident that it is not only about cleverness in a narrow sense: 'cleverness' always contains traces of 'confidence' and 'self-assuredness'. Mostly from attending conversations about children, I have come to understand this cultural domain to operate in the following way: if someone is clever, they will also be confident, talkative, entertaining and not shy in interaction. To be quiet, subdued and introverted largely precludes the label of *paxala*. While it can be very clever to not say anything in a specific situation, a 'cleverness' that was largely internal would be of little value for Kara. To be quiet is also called 'being slow', a negatively valued insinuation of indecisiveness and passivity. As this is also reflected in practices of childrearing, which reliably encourage precocious insolence, this semantic field provides some insight into the local ethnopsychology and the cultural values of certain dispositions.

In summary, I want to re-emphasize that 'cleverness' goes along with competence and confidence, that it is usually diagnosed from the ways people act verbally, and that it (in the form of *paxala* rather than in the form of *malti*) shares the positive moral value of such terms as 'prudent'. It is only prudent to be smart, just as it is moral to embrace expediency. Occasionally, there is a semantic shift towards outrageous audacity and overconfidence, touching the semantic boundary with *maltamo*.

At this point, I want to supply a first layer of interpretation to the vignette that opened the chapter. Cleverness is displayed in the self-assured and well-chosen reply by Goiti-imba that left the official speechless: Goiti-imba was being morally clever by asserting the closed ranks of the Kara to this outsider, who had hoped to find (and presumably exploit or even aggravate) latent factionalism.

In the following section, I will give some examples of Kara displays of cleverness. My ethnographic material is complemented by another conversation from antiquity: there is a striking affinity between *paxalmamo* and *mētis*, the ancient

Greek concept eruditely explored by Detienne and Vernant (1978) under the title of 'cunning intelligence'. By highlighting the similarities between these two notions and the uses they were put to, I show how despite cultural and historical particularity, there are quite universal processes discernible in the Kara claims to cleverness.

'Cunning Intelligence' in Kara and Ancient Greece

Below are two instances of behaviour that were either commented on as *paxala* on the spot or labelled as such upon later reflection. Such a minute selection of displays cannot be representative, only illustrative. I found the notion applied in many more contexts. To diagnose the actions I recall here as 'displays' is warranted, as in each case other Kara saw the behaviour as performative, i.e. they put themselves in the position of addressees.

The case of 'Mero Roba' is notorious: when a group of Kara was hassled and finally arrested by a group of policemen in Omo Rate in Dassanech territory in the late 1990s, they were all asked to give their names to be entered into the records. One by one, they proceeded to faithfully gave their names, until one of them – utterly deadpan – offered the plausible pseudonym 'Mero Roba'. This was an audacious bid with an uncertain benefit. Nothing ever came out of the arrests anyway and intimidation (and bribery) was at issue rather than legal persecution. But that he was the only one to even have thought of giving a pseudonym and then had the presence of mind to follow through with a convincing delivery was greatly applauded and has become legendary. He is still hailed with the name 'Mero Roba' on occasion. Such deception (*sudima*) is often legitimized and appreciated, especially when it is directed at state representatives or other outsiders, and when it makes for a good anecdote. Ethel Albert's words, reporting on cultural speech patterning in Burundi, fit the Kara case like a glove: 'There is a premium, practical and esthetic, upon rapid, graceful, and more-than-plausible falsehood' (1964: 47).

In the realm of divination, Kara is short in skilled and acknowledged practitioners. The preferred method of divining, casting sandals on the ground and reading their positions, was thus largely the monopoly of one specific man, an unreliable but highly entertaining curmudgeonly figure. He has since died. Over the years, I have become aware of two other people using 'sandals'.[7] One of them, I was told, revealed his sandals after his return from an extended journey and consulted them in open sight, providing unsolicited advice to others about what they ought to do or not to do, what the weather would bring and the like. His actions were considered somewhat grotesque. The other one, in contrast, never made a big production out of his divination. It was known that he consulted them before going hunting, and he had been seen occasionally using sandals when sitting by himself. In his case, people were more cautious about labelling his performance as either 'genuine' or 'phony'. It was possible, after all, that he did have some skill in reading the sandals. Especially the fact he (to my knowledge) never gave advice based on alleged divination was effective in causing people to wonder whether he just might not know something after all.

Here, cleverness lies not in consulting sandals or not. It is *paxala* to use knowledge in a way that people are never quite sure how much you know and how much you hold back. To tell all, straight out, is not the mark of the cunning man, but that of a child. But if people suspect that you might be making a display of *not* making a display, cleverness ascriptions are bound to follow. The work on 'suspicion' as the fundamental principle in art as proposed by the media theoretician Boris Groys (a spin on the hermeneutics of suspicion more generally) has relevance to my attempts to get at ways of meaning attribution in the most basic sense. Groys argues that it is only the suspicion of something hidden behind the surface that holds our gaze in the first place (Groys 2000). Similarly, in the terminology used by Linda Hutcheon in her treatise on the 'edge of irony' (1994), the 'unsaid' behind the 'said' is fundamental to and not peripheral to meaning construction. Furthermore, the recognition that the unsaid will remain forever elusive, intrinsic to the act of displaying cleverness, 'epitomizes an ironic attitude' (Lambek 2004: 8). Potter sets up an opposition that is good to think with and that applies well across cultural contexts by referring:

> to discourse which is constructing versions of the world as solid and factual as *reifying* discourse … In contrast, we will refer to discourse which is undermining versions as *ironizing* … I will treat ironizing discourse as talk or writing which undermines the literal descriptiveness of versions. It is the opposite of reifying discourse: it turns the material thing back into talk which is motivated, distorted or erroneous in some way. (2004: 107, emphasis in original)

These statements illustrate why I discuss Kara claims of cleverness as ironical. The examples I collected of *paxala* behaviour do not offer themselves to easy summary, but three elements can be usefully distilled. First, there is the quality of mobility, shiftiness, of reversing the situation, by confounding others' expectations or (subtly) violating conversational norms and interactional frames. Second, there is the sense that *paxalmamo* allows the physically weak to overcome brute force or allows the underdog to persevere in face of social convention. Third, the cases I found were narrated or commented upon by the audience with admiration, amusement and feigned indignation, and they lent themselves to narration well, having distinctive characters and plots. The actors in such stories are not merely contemplative even where they pretend to be, but are instead successful in their struggles with practical predicaments, even if their concern is merely impression management.

Having thus established the position of *paxalmamo* in Kara social life, I turn to the concept *mētis*. My main information on this derives from the work of the classicist scholars Detienne and Vernant (but see also Scott 1999: Chapter 9). Drawing from a range of sources, they investigate this 'master value in the Greek world' (Harrison 1986: 16), which in a way offers a counterdiscourse to the more prominent theoretical Greek philosophy: *mētis* is 'a type of cognition which is alien to truth and quite separate from *epistēmē*, knowledge' (Detienne and Vernant 1978: 4). There are no ancient treatises on *mētis* as there are on logic (1978: 3), but looking at a wide range of sources, the two authors do not find it difficult to sift out the textual presence of this 'intelligence', which draws on 'forethought, perspicacity, quickness and acuteness of understanding, trickery, and even deceit' (1978: 44). These qualities allow its bearers to turn the table on the powerful:

> Cunning, *dólos*, tricks, *kérdē*, and the ability to seize an opportunity, *kairós*, give the weaker competitor the means of triumphing over the stronger, enabling the inferior to outdo the superior rival ... To bring about a reversal of the position *mētis* must foresee the unforeseeable. Engaged in a world of becoming and confronted with situations which are ambiguous and unfamiliar and whose outcome always lies in the balance, wily intelligence is only able to maintain its hold over beings and things thanks to its ability to look beyond the immediate present and foresee a greater or lesser section of the future. (Detienne and Vernant 1978: 27)

Through all this shines the notion that *mētis* is an adaptation to conditions that require it, conditions that necessitate 'elusiveness and duplicity' (1978: 44). Cleverness is always (ant-)agonistic, if sometimes playful. It is a claim to and expression of agency, and even as a quality of a seemingly autonomous actor, it affects the observers as they find themselves wary of the protean individual endowed with *mētis* – or, as I suggest, with *paxalmamo*.

The point I want to make with this comparison is that the contemporary Kara might very well recognize their own ways in Detienne and Verdant's (and the ancient Greeks') 'cunning intelligence' and that by comparing *paxalmamo* and *mētis*, we might gain insight into how such elusive notions can be practised as 'master values' in a given cultural context. The examples from Greek antiquity also indicate how the pursuit of 'cunning intelligence' or 'cleverness' reveals conceptions of power, agency, the capabilities of the individual, and the connections between morality and self-interest. For the Kara, *paxalmamo* is a charter that provides both a pragmatic way of dealing with 'a world of becoming' through the cultivation of deliberate elusiveness and a moral agenda. As a current site for the identity-management of the Kara, it is effective both towards the inside (in auto-persuasion) and the outside (in a more traditional instance of rhetorical effort). *Mētis* and *paxalmamo* are both geared towards an audience, both give rise to definitions of the situation and both purport to have a significant effect on power relations. Even where they do not visibly overturn extant power relations, one can argue that – as is generally the case with indirect communication – they create 'room for free action, joy, resistance or at least fugitive behavior' (Torres 1997: 20).

How does such 'cunning intelligence' figure in the initial vignette about the visit of the young official and his admonishment? For one thing, the reversal in the situation achieved by the Kara elder Goiti-imba is obvious. The visitor, attempting to speak from authority, ended up confounded. His charge that some of the Kara, backwards Shank'illa to him, might be harbouring dissident thoughts was turned right back not at him, but at the imperial centre he represented and that had sent him forth. The Kara know fully well that the main opposition to the current government and to the ruling party comes from other groups that are Habesha, which also belong to the distant centre. They also know that they themselves by a huge majority did in fact vote for the EPRDF at the last election. Even where in other places there had been accounts of rigged ballots and the like, most Kara do appreciate that despite all its shortcomings, the current administration has done more for them than any other before (compare Matsuda (2002) for the Moguji case).

In effect, Goiti-imba, when giving his reply, revealed the duplicity of the official paternalistic discourse: 'Before you go and try to shame us, or try to divide us, look, it's your own house that is divided.' This is what I understood Goiti-imba as saying, and the official could hardly escape considering this interpretation as well. He did not have an answer to that, so he passed his chance to turn the tables again and, in the way the game is played, had to concede this point. As Bailey has stated, this sort of '[c]ombative irony challenges the victims to look at what is being done to them and to acknowledge that they are helpless ... To challenge ironic mockery with anything but a counterirony is exactly that – an admission of defeat' (Bailey 2003: 167). In his original admonishment, he had probably just reproduced what he had been instructed to say on his visits to the outlying *kebele*. Instead of being accorded sincere deference, he had been shown in no unclear terms that the Kara were not willing to let the administration manoeuvre them to the receiving end of a conversation on morality (compare Abbink 2006: 162f).

The Kara, in terms of my methodology, were able to define the situation through the reply by Goiti-imba so that their loyalty became quite unassailable. They rejected the insinuations with which the official's question had been so ripe and imposed some of their own on the visitor, which he could impossibly refute, since they were uncomfortable truths in the face of his 'saving lie' (Bailey 2003): the God-given and history-proven superiority of the Habesha over the Shank'illa. Already here the similarity of Goiti-imba's action to the self-deprecating ways of

Socratic irony can be noted: Socrates, too, underplayed his perspicacity to let his interlocutors deconstruct their erroneous discursive positions themselves. If we follow Lambek's contention that '[w]e think of irony as a stance that gives ambiguity, perspective, plurality, contradiction, and uncertainty their due' (2004: 3), it is quite apparent how Goiti-imba's statement is fruitfully understood as ironic. While we cannot know what he thought, we do know that he is a competent elder versed in oratory and must have fine control over the space he left for ambiguity in interpretation. Definitions of irony that hold water when applied outside formal speech situations are hard to come by, but this scene would fit most of those that are on offer.

Irony provides us with an interpretive screen for what people do when they engage in cleverness and, simultaneously, following the rhetorical displays of cleverness leads us to arenas that seem to invite irony, first throughout the cultural neighbourhood, then in the encounter between the Kara and the Habesha. *Paxalmamo* serves as a charter for the Kara and, as far as they are concerned, only for them. I provide a range of examples of how this notion is reflected upon and rhetorically brought to life, from the primordial arrival myth that highlights the cleverness of the land-grabbing Kara across the centuries to the most recent efforts in cultivating a reputation for excellence in education throughout South Omo.

The Charter of Cleverness

The entry for 'Kara' in the usually solemn *Encyclopedia Aethiopica* ends with the excited phrase '[h]ow to recreate a new identity is an urgent issue for this group' (Matsuda 2007: 341). Context is conspicuously absent. The general usefulness (and shelf life) of such a remark in an encyclopaedia is debatable. But instead of debating it, I take up the matter in a more constructive way by showing how the contemporary Kara are already engaged in doing just what Matsuda diagnosed as problematic. It is their very claim to a particular cleverness that increasingly serves as an identity marker. 'Cleverness' is the banner under which they rally. I describe this as a joint charter that draws on the ways of being Kara as I have discussed them so far.[8]

Following up on Chapter 4, which noted the alleged disparity in sophistication that allowed the clever true Kara to usurp the riverland from the naïve Moguji of legend, it is important to point out that this greater charter integrates all members of the population vis-à-vis outsiders. No matter whether one is a Moguji, Gomba, Nyangatom-Kara, Bogudo or true Kara, interaction of members of the Kara polity with the Habesha and other Shank'illa is often shot through with displays of *paxalmamo*.

By calling *paxalmamo* a charter (beyond its function as a value, discussed above), I want to pursue how Kara use the term consistently in reference to themselves and their relations to others, be it for identification, explanation or justification. Such use is always political. As a social practice that impacts on both their relations to others and to their conceptions of self (just like the stereotypes of Chapters 6–7), it is worthwhile to trace how they express and sustain the theme of *paxalmamo* in interaction amongst themselves and with others. Now, the last sentence begs the question about intentionality. Do I suggest that the Kara are engaged in a conscious effort of making everybody think that they really are clever? Putting it in such strong terms is daunting. I have settled on the understanding that the Kara of today immensely enjoy the current discourse about their cleverness, especially as it has come to be perpetuated by others, too. Many Kara have clearly turned this discourse into a personal project and perform 'cleverness' whenever they can and wherever there are witnesses. This is certainly to some degree instrumental, as they realize that for every single individual who does so, all of the Kara stand to gain. I also propose that Kara who act 'cleverly' do so not only for the fun of combative irony (see Bailey 2003: 167; Huizinga 1994: 166ff; Beidelman 1989), but also act upon the above-presented discourse-as-charter, infusing their actions with morality. The more individual Kara are recognized as 'clever' and concomitantly as confident and generally competent, the better for everybody. As noted in Chapter 6, stereotypes serve both through opposition and hyperbole (Rapport and Overing 2007: 394): as the Kara make outrageous claims about themselves as if they really believed in them, they are quite consciously acting as members of an ethnic category as well as members of a politico-territorial unit, and thus propagate these stereotypes of Kara. Sometimes it seems as if in real life, everybody subscribed to the 'culture and personality' school (see Eriksen 1991: 127f).

Whereas the last section re-created some displays of cleverness, this section presents Kara reflections on their own 'cleverness'. This meta-discourse (while it is in its own way a display too, and a salient one to boot) is where the charter-aspect of the cultural topic of *paxalmamo* comes to be elaborated and propagated. The 'cleverness of the Kara' is not an exclusively recent topos. Contemporary claims to cleverness point back to the accounts of 'the old days', that is, before the imperial conquest in the late nineteenth/early twentieth centuries, as well as to the constitutive arrival myth. Only their 'cleverness' made the Kara who they are today: coming down the Trail of the Red Bull, they tricked the Moguji and took hold of the uncultivated riverbanks.

Complementary to this mythical narrative, various Kara have presented the following standard account of the 'old days' to me, in much the same way: 'We were very few even in the past, but we were *paxala*. All our neighbours looked at us, admired us, and came to live with us. Turkana, Nyangatom, Dassanech, all came and stayed, or got married here. We had the sorghum, we had the calabashes, we were rich in cattle. The Nyangatom were few and weak, and they did not know how to wage war. They only learned that later from the Toposa and Turkana.' My age-mate Nanga, a firm proponent of the cleverness of the Kara, provided further imagery: 'We used to travel all over the land, in order to trade – we knew all prices and had access to all things, and nobody could hide anything from us.'

The claims that a role as regional brokers was held by the Kara 'of old' in their special geographical and ecological niche is confirmed by the few writers who give evidence of those times, either by being direct witnesses (Neumann 1994: 341; Stigand 1969: 237) or through historical data (Sobania 1980: 102–13). The settlements by the Omo River were a resting place for Somali and Swahili caravans. The Kara introduced coffee, bartered from the Aari, to the neighbouring groups, and they were important middlemen in the ivory trade. One of the more recent 'secrets' they claim to have first brought to light was the way to disassemble and reassemble the modern rifles (i.e. AK-type guns) that were introduced into South Omo in the early 1990s. The people selling the rifles to the Shank'illa did not provide the knowledge necessary for their maintenance, and the Nyangatom, early adopters of the AK through their connections to the Sudanese civil war areas, also held on tightly to this hermetic craft. But this secrecy was allegedly bested by Kara cunning.

Such recollections form the basis for the Kara claims to their relative cleverness: it was always there, it always distinguished them from others. But where did it come from? Again, Nanga was the one to school me: 'Our cleverness, where does it come from? We really do not know. Is it from the river water? Others drink of this as well. But when we look around, we find that we understand things better than other people, and they also say the same about us.'[9] I have already mentioned that the small size of the population was sometimes adduced in the narratives that aggrandized the attraction of Kara country in the olden days, and Nanga also used this notion as a tentative explanation: 'The cleverness, nobody knows where it comes from. But probably it comes from *bariyo* [here used as creator/God], who gave it to the Kara because there are so few of them.' Clever himself, he managed to restate the underdog position of the Kara in South Omo, while taking it for granted that they were indeed cleverer than the rest.

But there does not seem to be a master narrative of 'why' or 'whence' the cleverness had come. On the contrary, according to the way Nanga put it, this, basically, was the *only* thing they could not comprehend: '*Woti bashadidi* – [by this conundrum,] we are defeated.' These constant self-deprecating boasts, hyperbolic in their understatement, go well with the numerous claims issued about the Kara's capabilities. Such humble disclaimers are common in Kara conversations, both within (often with a wink) and without (mostly with an utterly straight face) – as was the case with Goiti-imba and the *woreda* official.

Linguistic competence is a good example of this. Numerous Kara understand the national language Amharic, that icon of schooling, and many of them also speak it decently, even if they cannot read or write. Still, that knowledge of Amharic is often hidden or flatly denied, even in interaction with the Habesha. When witnessing Kara play dumb for any number of situated reasons, Hobsbawm's contention that '[t]he refusal to understand is a form of class struggle' (quoted in Scott 1990: 133) often came to mind. To underplay competence can also become a cultivated habit. During my fieldwork, it came to the point that I grew distrustful every time somebody innocently said 'oh, we don't know this sort of thing'. As often as not, I was being set up for a punchline.[10]

The performative nature of the Kara claims to cleverness was hardly obscured: when talking about cleverness, people often took higher-order intentionalities into account, i.e. they reflected on what other people would assume about what they were intending by their actions. When I was told by a group of my agemates about the naming of things, they were exuberant as if they had just played a practical joke on someone: 'Look at this – the *borkotto* [headrest], the *gaggi* [dug-out], the *woh* [an edible plant], we call them *kara-borkotto*, *kara-gaggi*, and *kara-woh*: even though they also exist elsewhere, we call them with our name!' This account most likely derived from some post hoc reflections, from their personal puzzlement as to why in the Kara language these utterly non-Kara-specific things were named after the Kara themselves. The answer that my interlocutors gave framed it as a delightful act of insolence against virtually all their neighbours to pretend that the dug-out canoe, the *borkotto* and the *woh*-plant had come from Kara, or had been invented or discovered by the Kara.

As far as I know, no other group is using these specific designations. But this did not reduce my friends' glee. Cleverness, then, lay not in actually having discovered these things, but in assuming the power of naming, in insolence, chutzpa and partly in doing something that purports to be meaningful, but remains impenetrably opaque. Kara reflections on the sources of their cleverness simultaneously hint at transcendent essential qualities and acknowledge that 'clever is as clever does', two prima facie contradictory assertions. To me, this was yet another display of the shiftiness and fluidity that is so defining of *paxalmamo* and that I found people were very engaged in perpetuating.

Comparing Cleverness across the Cultural Neighbourhood

Some of the above-mentioned 'sources' imply reasons why others are not as 'clever' as the Kara. This is an inbuilt feature of a claim to cleverness: like other stereotypes, it must be relational and contrastive, so there must be someone who is portrayed as less clever if the claim is to have any value. A distinguishing feature must distinguish. While they readily offered estimates of their neighbours' cleverness, in this arena the Kara were mostly stereotyping themselves for internal as much as external consumption.

Cleverness, it sometimes seemed, was not just one stereotypical feature of the Kara: the ubiquity of their claims to cleverness went towards overdetermining them. What greater success can be achieved in impression management than a stereotypical reputation for cleverness that is so dominant and pervasive that it can hardly ever be falsified? As the next section will show, this battle is not fought everywhere with the same intensity, as it is not the entire cultural neighbourhood that serves as the arena for these displays. So, how about those others? I provoked people to offer comparisons quite explicitly, basically saying: 'If you guys are so clever, what about them? Or them?' As it turned out, the opinions about the others' cleverness that I encountered were fairly consistent and congruent with the more general stereotypes for the peoples of the cultural neighbourhood as developed above. What came out clearest was that *paxalmamo* was relevant and discursively elaborate only for the neighbours with whom the Kara cultivate the most intense interaction: the Hamar (and Banna/Bashada), Nyangatom and Moguji. This confirms that 'cleverness' is not just a discursive category, but that it is first and foremost a rhetorically practised charter that regulates interaction with and reflection on current, pressing sites of encounter.

Accordingly, regarding the Mursi and Dassanech, people were fairly non-committal. The fact that many Ethiopian Dassanech go to school in Kenya was mentioned, as people assumed that quite a few of them were getting a good education these days. The notion that the Dassanech were exploiting the possibility of crossing state borders, being accepted on both sides, was acknowledged as clever as well. For the Mursi, little was brought up: they were able to track enemies who intruded into Mursi country all the way back to the attackers' homes, where they would extract revenge and head home again unseen. This paucity is not surprising: considering the stereotype of the Mursi as depicted above, 'cunning intelligence' and the subtlety that goes with it are a near-antithesis to the iconic reckless physicality for which they are renowned.

The Arbore, again in alignment with the more general stereotype, were depicted as wise and competent, but fundamentally lacking in the fields of duplicity and elusiveness. In a way, they were seen as too serious, too straight and too introverted to be truly *paxala*. An example illustrates this. One day in Jinka, sitting in a café with schoolboys from Kara, they pointed out to me a young Arbore nearby, whom I knew as well: 'All the Arbore', they said, deliberately loudly enough for him to hear, 'all the Arbore are decent people. Except for one, he is a *duriye*!' In Amharic, the *duriye* are the anomic ne'er-do-well boys spoilt by city life who avoid actual work – especially the subsistence production of their homes. So in terms of Kara discourse, the one Arbore who was indubitably endowed with *paxalmamo* presented a categorical deviation – he was a 'bad' Arbore. I do not want to make too much of this episode. Still, it is worth noting that while the Kara boys were in a joking mood, they could not have made this same statement about a member of any other ethnic category. Only the stereotypical image of the Arbore made it possible to suggest that someone would be better off by forgoing the benefits of 'cunning intelligence'.

Regarding the 'harmless people', the Aari and Maale, their cleverness was largely denied. Partly, this came from the understanding that they were (even) less pastoralist, more sedentary, closer to the city, more changed by the Habesha ways, and partly it was based on a view that saw them as people with a hierarchical social organization, lacking in individualism and assertiveness.

As an afterthought to this, I recall a hot afternoon in the riverbank fields of Kara in late 2006. A working party had assembled, and a score of young and old men had cleared the land in all directions, hacking and slashing the brambles. As the sun began to sink, the reward for the willing helpers was dished out: as is customary, bowls and bowls of *parsho*, sorghum beer, had been prepared. While some of the men eagerly sank down on the cowhides that had been spread out for them, others continued finishing off little tasks such as gathering up tools, chopping away at a last stubborn tree-trunk and throwing some of the uprooted bushes onto a smouldering pyre. Ameriken, a particularly extroverted elder among those already reclining, took this slow petering out of activity as an offence: 'Hey, you Konso!' he called out, 'will you come over already?' To jeers and laughter, the 'offenders' sheepishly joined the party. I have not mentioned the Konso before: they figure in Kara experience and imagination as the people who do nothing but work. This is a recent development, as over the last few years, many construction projects both in Kara and nearby places have been manned by labourers who supposedly come from Konso, to the east of South Omo.[11] To call someone a 'Konso', then, is a derogatory way to indicate an absence of the Kara master value of *paxalmamo*. Not knowing when to stop working (namely, as soon as possible without losing face) or maybe even enjoying physical labour simply has to be distasteful for a self-respecting Kara – or rather a Kara who knows that they have an audience. This attitude is being reinforced by the fact that the administration keeps sending such labourers down to the Omo Valley, who are, in a sense, working for the Kara – or at least, they are doing work from which the Kara stand to benefit and that they are really happy someone else is doing for them (compare Beidelman 1964: 49).

These recent developments connect to the narratives of the servants (*k'aissi*) of the Kara: it has been a stable topos in Kara history that to have people come to your land and work for you is a clear mark of your superiority. Such *k'aissi* used to be mostly Nyangatom, who alongside the Moguji took over the chore of chasing away birds in exchange for some grains come harvest time. Conversely, to offer your labour to someone else hoping for money in return will elicit derisive comments. It was a staple joke to talk about the serfdom (*k'aissamo*) of those Kara who had found employment with local tourism operators. While people readily laughed at their friends who constantly had to run off and do the dishes for some rich white people, and inquired of these usually proud elders as to the 'sweetness' of serving, many people of course were still eager for these jobs.

This instance unfolds the duplicitous work of stereotype very clearly: at one level, it is good and right and moral to work, and to work hard at that. Still, one can be put on the conversational defensive if anybody makes the rhetorical connection to images of Kara-ness, as Ameriken did in this instance. The transfer of an originally ethnic stereotype to a pattern of activity, i.e. engaging in physical labour without complaint, detaches the label ('Konso') from its original referent in a metonymical operation, as is common in stereotyping. There is nothing any Konso can do to change this notion – it is only over time that it might lose relevance, or perhaps 'Konso' gets replaced by some other categorical label.

The situation as described above is far from exotic. That one's deserved rest does not taste so sweet anymore when others keep on working, insinuating that the work is not done yet, is a familiar sentiment. We can also sympathize with the Kara who finished off a few more little tasks, who 'while they were at it' found it difficult to desist from cleaning up the place. They found their innocent bustling derided and labelled as 'unworthy of Kara'. Ameriken loudly interpreted their activities as performative, where they had probably not even been thinking of their potential audience. This example shows how 'cleverness' as an identity marker of the Kara can come to be invoked and made relevant to actors who had not been making a conscious display of anything. It had not even crossed their minds that the way they were working could be interpreted in terms of their particular category of being Kara. As regards Ameriken, he likely only wanted to start drinking with his friends and he saw the little scene as a chance to add yet another anecdote to his already extensive personal dossier as an entertainer. The reference to what ought to be a standard for all Kara was a convenient way to elicit a few laughs and to make the others finally stop working. The stereotype of Konso-ness had its effect, and people were reminded that they were supposed to be more *paxala* than that.

For Ethiopianists, this description might recall Levine's classic study of the Amhara (the core element of the Kara's Habesha category), as when he claims that:

> Status considerations keep the Amhara of making a fetish of work as such ... He avoids when possible unskilled manual labor, for traditionally that has been relegated to slaves or servants from 'inferior' tribes. Work for wages is likewise deemed undignified. (1965: 81)

One reads this with a growing appreciation of the irony of the contemporary political economy: the Habesha (i.e. the Amhara) sends the Konso to do the 'dirty work' he himself will not do, and the Kara proudly and happily reclines and watches the Konso building roads and school houses for him. Meanwhile, the Konso labours and earns money.

In reference to the three other neighbours listed above – the Moguji, Nyangatom and Hamar – talk about *paxalmamo* was significantly more common and more involved. My interlocutors hardly needed prompting here. To reiterate, the 'mountain people' are acknowledged as invincible and unsurpassed in their own country. The Kara attributed to the Hamar considerable cleverness in herding and hunting, saying that 'in this, nobody will best them'. The image these narratives evoked was of the young Hamar men who spent virtually all their youth and early adulthood out in the savannah, herding cattle, learning the lay of the land and the ways of the beasts. But of course, in the contemporary world, the ever-shifting place that requires the Shank'illa to be clever, elusive and duplicitous, such reclusive contemplation must have opportunity costs.[12] Seen from Kara, then, regarding modern affairs (administration, tourism, trade and meetings), the Hamar were clueless. As one elder said: 'If there is a meeting in which both they and we take part, the Kara will always win the day.' This point will be developed further below when I discuss 'arenas of cleverness'. In many contemporary arenas, such as tourism and education, the Kara and Hamar are in incessant contact as they share the same district, and it is quite inevitable for them to compare achievements.

Regarding the Moguji, they have been fixed throughout time as the ones who are the antithesis of cleverness, in a way the inevitable dupes of manipulation in Kara narratives. However, this imagery is crumbling. The events following on the 'schism' indicate how Kara is permeated by the worry that Moguji who truly 'wised up' could create tremendous problems for them. 'Wising up' here stands not only for an understanding of the way things really are, i.e. seeing through the guise of Kara-Moguji *ädamo*, but also for the concomitant recognition of one's self-interest, and for the display of one's agency through deliberate action that is so fundamental of *paxalmamo*. So both for ideological and practical reasons, from the Kara point of view, it is the 'cleverness of the Moguji' that can never be allowed to flourish, which must be denied and opposed. Not only would the Kara's own charter of *paxalmamo* lose its most potent and empowering mirror image, but it could herald the end of *ädamo* as the ideological foundation of Kara social order (see Helander (2003: 173) for a comparable Somali case). I will return to this fundamental point later.

The Nyangatom, to conclude this list, are problematic. On the one hand, they are explicitly described as lacking *paxalmamo*: 'They constantly fight against and antagonize everybody; they have not embraced development; they do not know how to profit from tourists.' These were statements I heard over and over again. On the other hand, the Kara are very aware that some Nyangatom have climbed to influential political positions, that due to the activities of Swedish missionaries (the SPCM), Nyangatom got a head-start in education (and 'development'; see Tornay 2009), and that their elders and leaders are as astute in talking the talk during meetings with NGOs as the Kara themselves. People on both sides of the Omo River know each other perfectly well; many of today's elders from Kara and Nyangatom have been friends since childhood and their youth. But these familiar others are the very same people whom the Kara, according to their oral tradition, have uplifted from a wretched life in the forest and whom they have installed at Nakwa (Kibish), giving them fire, and telling them to stay and cultivate there. In the 1960s and 1970s, they were the ones who were prominently the *k'aissi* serfs of the Kara, as they flocked to the Omo during the agricultural season, offering their services as unskilled workers to the owners of the riverbanks. This dissonance between mythic charters and undeniable realities is well recognized when Kara grudgingly say, nodding towards the other riverbank, '*ena paxalidina* – they have become clever'.

Thus, *paxalmamo* is not a yardstick that is applied to all the world equally. Especially as it has come to be a charter, it gains its full significance only in reference to those people with whom the Kara see themselves in competition, be it in terms of symbolic action or more material struggles over riverbank use. The Wheel of Autonomy of Kara as a polity really gets into motion vis-à-vis the Moguji, Hamar and Nyangatom. They are those regional others whose own Wheels of Autonomy can at times be impeded or stimulated by the Kara efforts to assert their autonomy and display their agency. In contrast, while the cultural stereotypes and the experiential knowledge of the Aari, Arbore and any others also make it possible to formulate statements about their alleged cleverness, this is not so salient for the identity construction of the Kara at the beginning of the twenty-first century. The cultural neighbourhood has different zones of intimacy, it turns out, which are rhetorically delineated and affirmed, in this case through comparisons of cleverness.

For the Kara, to talk about their respective *paxalmamo* is a way to define the situation of intergroup relations in somewhat stable terms. Such relationships can then be reduced to this one aspect of an actually much more multiplex interplay, an aspect that would even be difficult to falsify. This helps to bypass the full picture and to instead conjure up a vista in which the Kara alone are prepared for the demands of the contemporary world. In this section, I have already indicated some arenas where 'cunning intelligence' can be profitably displayed. I will now discuss what it is that makes these and other arenas relevant for the Kara imagination and rhetorical practice of claiming *paxalmamo*.

Contemporary Arenas

The Kara claims to cleverness are particularly geared to the perceived demands of the contemporary world. To be the greatest warriors or even to have the largest herds – these are not the proving ground on which the polities of South Omo find themselves today. In this section I focus on those arenas to which the Kara point today, the sites where their *paxalmamo* is applied, displayed and acknowledged by others.

First and foremost, this is the field of schooling. Education began to gain relevance for the Kara in the 1970s when the SPCM opened its schools first in

Kibish, deep in Nyangatom territory, and later, more accessible for the Kara, in the Kadokochin (see Map 0.2). Several Kara received an education there as young boys decades ago, and some also more recently. To put this in perspective, there is hardly anybody above the age of forty-five who has received schooling of any kind. Talking about these early days, people emphasize what lengths fathers went to at the time, 'carrying their sons all the way' to Kibish, taking the gamble of valuing school higher than herding, in the hope of doing the right thing. One of these early adopters became extremely successful. After going to Teacher's Training College, he found employment in tourism and finally secured an administrative position and NGO sponsorship. While not everybody is convinced that his loyalties still lie with Kara, and while many people are unhappy about the way he chooses to handle his domestic affairs, his has become a prime example of what can be achieved through education. Still today, it proves quite irresistibly tempting to many young men. The sheer numbers of students who enrol, some even eloping from home, is said to reflect the ambition his example stirs in youngsters.

Today, there are primary schools in all of the three major villages. Habesha teachers seasonally live on site and are in constant negotiations with Kara elders in order to fill quotas, especially for female pupils. Further education is available in the market towns of Turmi and Dimeka, both in the Hamar part of the *woreda*. At the time of my research, classes there went up to Grade 7 or 8; it was only in the zonal capital of Jinka that Grades 10–12 and the 'preparatory' training for college and university were attainable. Walking through Dimeka or Turmi during term time, with a knowing eye, one could see many Kara students populate the streets. They constantly showed their presence, as if to obscure the fact that they were few in absolute number, in this place a good distance from home. With this visibility, though, it hardly matters how proportionally represented the Kara are in these schools that cater to the Arbore, Hamar and Kara. By taking up space in the street, by being present, the young Kara men assert that they are to be reckoned with.

In Jinka this was even more pronounced. This impression was enhanced by the extreme care many of them take in terms of their clothing and general appearance. Another anthropologist I talked to in Jinka was quite surprised when he realized that all these polite, impeccably dressed young men he had been seeing were Kara. These Kara relish the fact that they do not fit the local categories and expectations, as it were. Their physiognomies betray them as Shank'illa, but their dress code and adaptation to city life goes against the 'country bumpkin' stereotype many city dwellers hold vis-à-vis the Mursi, Hamar or even more familiar rural Aari. The Kara boys attending higher grades seem to effortlessly find employment as assistants for NGOs and researchers. Often, they have some money to spare and do not mind splashing it around in the more uptown cafés near the old airstrip where elites, tourists and aid workers mingle. Many project teams in the region who require a translator from English to Hamar will hire a Kara. There is an explicit discourse in Kara that expresses their pride that they, being so few in number, produce more and better translators than the numerous Hamar themselves. An anecdote I heard in early 2008 illustrates this.

There was, so the story went, a public meeting of Hamar elders up in the mountains. Also present, but sitting unnoticed in the shade, was a Kara clerk who had come as a delegate from the administration. At some point, one elder got up and started haranguing the others: they were not sending enough of their kids to school. When he was walking through Dimeka recently, all he saw in the streets were those Kara boys! In Hamar! At this point, the Kara man in the back was pointed out to him, and some embarrassment ensued. The Kara, however, simply praised the words of the speaker and added that yes, he could not agree more, the Hamar should send more kids to school. The anecdote is ironic: the inadvertently maligned (and somehow trespassing) Kara man ended up validating the initial utterance made by the Hamar elder, which, while directed against the Kara, constituted an acknowledgement of Kara prowess – and at the same time, he could still belittle current Hamar efforts at schooling.

In these and numerous other ways, the Kara find their claims to cleverness affirmed by a wide range of people. It is salient that the schoolboys have apparently taken the charter of *paxalmamo* to heart, striving to combine personal confidence and educational competence.

It goes on in relation to tourism. The Kara are convinced that they understand the ways of tourists better than other Shank'illa, that they can draw the highest financial profit from it and that they have a good reputation with both visitors and the tourism operators. There is no space here to discuss Kara notions of tourism and their interaction with tourists at length. Still, it is worth pointing out that success in these arenas depends on individual creativity and enterprise. What will make a tourist pay attention? What will make tourists part with their cash? Whereas the wealthy visitor comes to find authenticity, Kara constantly seek innovation in their poses, their ornaments and their enthusiastic attempts to push aside the linguistic barrier.

It is considered only somewhat demeaning to pose for a photograph and take money in return. People from all age groups participate, even as some individuals remain aloof; for youths, it is completely normal to have tourists around. While there is usually no direct competition between Kara when it comes to the resource that are tourists, people do pay attention to each other's loot after the land-cruisers have come and gone. In addition to these opportunistic encounters, two permanent safari camps exist in Kara country today, and there are talks of an additional eco-lodge to be built in the future: this is, then, the most material marker for the Kara that they have considerable appeal as a tourism destination. However, there is a comparative moment even here: the Kara of course wonder how other people in the cultural neighbourhood 'do tourism'. The iconic Mursi offer a direct comparison, being equally remote and even more renowned.

By and large, the Kara assume that the Mursi deal as aggressively with tourists as they do with everybody else. Many shared the story of how a young Kara accompanying some tourists upriver was thrown into the Omo by upset Mursi who felt that he was constraining the cash flow. So when tourists tell them on arrival in Kara how much better they like the peace and quiet of Dus or Korcho as opposed to the hassle and stress that they experienced in Mursi, this is noted, chalked up to the workings of *paxalmamo* and strengthens the Kara efforts to conduct themselves in contrast to those dramatic Mursi they keep hearing about.

A very different application for their cleverness is warfare, and warfare also throws some light on other, hitherto covert aspects of *paxalmamo*. This is also the site where the issue of the Kara's small population is most reflected upon. To summarize an argument made elsewhere (Girke 2008), over the last three decades, the intermittent violent conflicts with the Nyangatom have become more sustained and bitter. Periods of peace seem to be growing shorter and shorter. Since the time I started my fieldwork in 2003, the numerically far inferior Kara have managed to inflict considerably higher casualties on the Nyangatom than vice versa. They do not see this as accidental. In their book, this was achieved by their cleverness and skill, especially in guerrilla warfare, as well as the ritual powers of their *bitti*. To be ruthless in defending themselves, whatever the odds, is imperative for the Kara. So if a Kara is killed, retribution is usually not long in coming, and then there is little interest in balancing the scales in any numerical way. From the cases I collected, the Kara tend to kill several Nyangatom for each of their own dead. Pursuing such a calculus of retribution is one thing, but in order for it to be effective, one needs to make it known.

Talking about one of these cases with a group of friends, they narrated the following story with grim satisfaction: 'The anger of the Kara is no joking matter. Everybody knows this, the Hamar as well as the Nyangatom. When M.'s wife was shot [by a Nyangatom in early 2006], the Nyangatom across the river were laughing, dancing and celebrating. At some point, though, [a certain man] admonished them. "Shut up", he said, "I grew up over there, I know them. You better stop laughing now, those Kara, they don't play around." The next day, some [Kara] men went, crossed the river at Kopriya [a place further north], and killed seven Nyangatom.' It is possible to imagine that this conversation might have reached the ears of the Kara, maybe via a Moguji; it may also have been made up. But the facts of the initial killing and the counterattack are well-established – the Kara did strike in this way, indiscriminately firing their AKs at a Nyangatom settlement. This story, as it was told afterwards, served to highlight the narrators' opinion that one needs to display resolve.

But, one might ask, where is the cleverness here? Responding to violence in kind hardly seems the mark of the superior intellect. The cleverness, as seen from the Kara point of view, is in always having the last word, or the last laugh, never allowing an opponent to outmanoeuvre them, to always make an enemy's victory a Pyrrhic victory, or to spoil it altogether. The shiftiness and elusiveness of *mētis* and *paxalmamo* also lies in being able to hurt 'the bigger guy', who the Nyangatom undoubtedly are. Many Kara have verbalized their awareness that they are playing with high stakes: in 1973, the Nyangatom killed more than one hundred Kara at the site of today's irrigation project as revenge for a previous massacre. Considering the small population of the Kara, such a loss is difficult to imagine. But not striking back, not seeking a restitution of the balance of power would constitute (as suggested by the Wheel of Autonomy) a near-surrender, a resigned abandonment of claims to self-determination and autonomy. Agency, here in the guise of insolent cunning, needs to be displayed, and the interests of the polity are well-served by a reputation for fierceness (compare Beidelman 1964: 45). Much of the work of David Turton (especially 1999) on Mursi warfare seeks to reconcile more materialist with such political and symbolic explanations.

As a final arena, similarly competitive but less physically violent, there are the numerous meetings, for which *gubai* (a loanword from the Amharic *guba'e*) is the most general term. The Kara speech genre of 'meeting talk' (compare Strecker 1976b) and the interactional aspects of the various formats of meetings as they are convened by government, NGOs or merely among the Kara are big topics in themselves. Here, I only discuss how they are relevant for Kara claims of cleverness, and my analysis is restricted to the sort of *gubai* convened by the local or regional administration. Many of these take place in Dus, Korcho or Labuk, but also in the market villages of Turmi and Dimeka up in the mountains. For meetings outside Kara country, it has been common over the last few years that cars are sent to collect a set number of elders and the occasional token woman. In some cases, per diems are paid. There are some people who always seem to be at meetings, and a look at a list of delegates reveals a good deal about political jockeying within Kara. At such meetings, the conveners will usually be placed at some sort of table, while the attending Shank'illa will be sitting on their *borkotto* headrests or on students' benches in schoolhouses, more or less looking up at the chairmen and minute-takers. The various groups attending take turns in that a delegate will give a speech. Often, these speeches are constantly interrupted for translation into Amharic or any other language required.

The topics of such meetings range from peace-making over capacity building and education to rangeland management and wildlife protection, and often involve other actors too, such as NGO representatives. Note that the structure of such meetings presumes that the Kara delegates will represent 'the Kara', a fundamentally problematic basis: the delegates can really only ever speak their mind, but can in no way commit 'the Kara' to a given course of action, save in the rare cases where they have been given explicit instructions by the *zersi* or the *borkotto bitti* before their departure. But even where there is nothing they can

Figure 8.1 A Kara elder at the height of his influence and competence (March 2008). Photograph by Felix Girke.

decide, the Shank'illa who have been called to a meeting can hardly afford not to attend, for fear of being stigmatized as unmutual.

During meetings, Shank'illa know that it is often detrimental to one's position to speak one's mind too frankly: either one is branded a liar or one is accused of being uncooperative. Looking closer at these instances, it becomes painfully obvious that it is not only the Shank'illa who are under a number of constraints. The administrators who run the meetings have usually been sent on these errands by their higher-ups, closer to the centre, and strive at all costs to avoid having to report bad news, unresolved complaints or fresh worries. This is why at several meetings that I attended, the Habesha conveners stated explicitly that 'we do not want to talk about the grievances of the past today, just about what we can do to avoid such problems in the future'. The hierarchies involved extend invisibly far beyond the storehouses, schoolrooms or shade trees where the meetings are commonly held.[13] In a recent example, it was quite understandable that right off the bat, the administrators could not let the initial, rather non-negotiable Kara contention stand. The Kara demand of 'there will never be peace unless the Nyangatom withdraw from the western bank of the Omo River' (see Girke 2008) could hardly be a basis for a peace conference, as the administrators simply did not have the capacity for resolving such major issues, even less to enforce a verdict at that scale. The only option that is reliably available to them is to stall voiced grievances in an attempt to wear down the petitioners.

Kara recognize the nature of such meetings well: they are mostly epiphenomenal effects of processes taking place elsewhere and not so much policy-oriented projects in themselves. Ripples of a splash far away. This contingent aspect of the agendas precludes that speakers will develop great emotional commitment. It is unsurprising that with such a heavy mortgage, meetings rarely have well-defined outcomes and that as often as not, style comes to hold the audience's attention much better than the substance, so to speak. If one cannot achieve anything of material importance in a meeting, speakers see it as a second priority to leave an impression, either by behaving exactly as they are supposed to or by subverting the occasion through off-record talk (Hendry and Watson 2001). Rhetorically, this comes out in the pattern that statements aiming to persuade are complemented by phatic jokes and aggressive provocations, intended to unsettle the competition, with speakers scoring points either against some specific (if absent) opponent or just by displays of cleverness and wittiness. Additionally, as if mentally marking off well-memorized boxes, a Shank'illa speaker to a Habesha audience often will try to hit certain buzzwords, commonplaces that elicit satisfied nods and encouraging scribbles of pencils on paper. Consider these examples:

- 'Do we have one father, or two?' (The reference is to the government that, through its administration, is seen to act biased and unfairly, thus like two fathers where there should be one.)
- 'We should marry one another, and then we shall have peace!'
- 'We took the words from the last meeting and brought them home, telling all the people what had been decided. But they, they did nothing of the sort, and this is why the trouble started again!'

Hardly any meeting in which war and peace between South Omo groups were negotiated went by without somebody putting forward these three modular utterances; others could be listed. These phrases are remarkable in that each reflects some 'official values' that are eternally propagated by the Habesha representing the state in any interaction with Shank'illa: equality and citizenship, solidarity and cooperation, and accountability. This is called an 'echoic' function, which is seen by some scholars as a defining feature of irony as such (Sperber and Wilson 1995: 240). It is not farfetched to assume that the speakers who use these arguments are fully aware from whence they came. Goiti-imba's speech given at the beginning of the chapter is a case in point: he knew exactly the way to return the ball, confronting the young official with a definition of the situation that entailed that the standards demanded from people on the periphery were hardly fulfilled by the centre itself.

In many meetings, it is likely that whatever is being debated will never be implemented or that its eventual implementation will be wholly independent of whatever was debated. The Kara have learned not to invest too much stock in delayed gratification. Still, meetings present an opportunity to make a display of Kara cleverness, which in turn feeds autonomy and agency 'even as it is being denied, attaining a form of political participation amid alienation' (Obadare 2009: 251).

To sum up, in education, the Kara find their claims to cleverness affirmed by their own behaviour and by others' reception of it. In tourism, they realize that they earn as much money and more posing for pictures as some city folk earn from a regular job. In warfare, they find that despite their numerical inferiority, they have up to now always been able to strike back, and very consciously cultivate a reputation as unreasonably fierce and audacious. In meetings, they emphasize their cleverness by not letting anybody else dictate the terms of an agreement, or even the frame of talk, and by having the last word whenever possible. But despite the fact that the Kara can find public confirmation of their claims to cleverness in all these arenas, it would be a most surprising ethnographic fact if people were able to constantly talk about their own cleverness and not realize the absurdity of issuing such claims. After all, does not everybody think that they are the smartest?

Such a sense of self-recognition is a fertile breeding ground for irony, a stance that always reflects itself and other views, and that plays with the interpretation of reality as much as it questions proclamations of sincerity, truth and morality. Already in the preceding discussion, I have repeatedly described ironic moments that spring from the rhetorical practice of cleverness, such as the practice of habitually feigning ignorance. The immanent relation between the practice of *paxalmamo*, 'doing "being clever"' as conversation analysts or ethnomethodologists might say (see Sacks 1984), and an ironic stance towards issues of power and values, is discussed in the following section.

Irony and Cleverness

My reflection on the rhetorical practice of *paxalmamo* as I encountered it in the field and have (re-)created it here led me inevitably to irony, the trope that deals in the unresolved ambiguity of statements and stances. That in Kara there is probably no word that directly corresponds to our notion of irony should not be offputting: the Odyssey is replete with irony long before *eironeia* became a staple of Sophistic rhetoric. Already Fernandez has suggested that as irony is fairly common in our life-worlds, 'how much more common must [it] be in the societies studied by anthropologists which are proverbially reliant upon indirection and analogy rather than upon direct analysis' (1977: 101). I would concur: no other trope is so cognisant of the tensions and contingencies of social relations. Below, I quote some scholars' reflections on how to grapple with irony. This compilation serves to avoid having to offer an inevitably problematic definition and still throws much light on the examples I provide throughout the chapter.

Kirsten Hastrup suggests that '[i]rony treats the world as inherently contingent, and it therefore comes closer to experience than those categories that are normally used to describe it' (2007: 203). This statement serves to reduce any reservations one might initially hold towards interpreting ethnographic material in these terms. For the user of irony, an acceptance of contingency is enabling, as it offers 'ways of dealing with the prospect of living without radical alternatives and coping with only partially improving conditions' (Torres 1997: 19). This need not lead to surrender of ideals, or blatant cynicism, but preserves 'a potential for social criticism, because [irony and humour] reinforce the skepticism that makes us see everything as less divine and more human. Therefore there is no enduring evil and all empires must fall' (1997: 188) – but of course, they must not.

Ironists recognize their own entrapment as part of the human condition, recognizing that social life inevitably entails manifest incongruities between 'is' and 'ought'. Thus, one can go on and be sceptical about the truth claims one encounters, without discarding the idea that people should keep on seeking truth. This leads to the recognition that irony is always social, an echoic commentary, an interpretation of another interpretation. Linda Hutcheon, arguing that irony comes 'with an edge', suggests that it '*explicitly* sets up (and exists within) a relationship between ironist and audiences (the one being intentionally addressed, the one that actually makes the irony happen, and the one being excluded)' (1994: 17, emphasis in original). This attention to the question of audience(s), of how they are constituted in the act of either recognizing an irony or feeling excluded from understanding, returns us to the social practice of *paxalmamo*. There, just as much, the question of who does what, for whose (doubtful) benefit, remains open, but in the use of cleverness and an appreciation of it, identities can become tangible.

As we become aware of the ironic aspect of proclamations of cleverness, the question whether the Kara 'really' think they are cleverer than others in their cultural neighbourhood loses relevance. To ask this question – and I did ask myself occasionally, in the field – indicates blindness to irony. The trap laid by the ironic aspect of the Kara claims of cleverness is triggered: the moment one considers it possible, the moment one starts assessing the evidence for or against their cleverness, one is caught in the snare of irony. The difficulty here is similar to the predicament of writing (about) stereotypes: during fieldwork, I have often been on the receiving end when Kara quite successfully demonstrated to me their personal cunning and elusiveness, and I also became implicated in situations where I colluded in Kara displays of cleverness vis-à-vis yet another audience. Writing about this now, it is difficult to extricate myself from this discourse. To describe *paxalmamo* can only mean to describe claims to *paxalmamo*, which, however, purport to be *paxalmamo*. While this is methodologically clear, it is still semantically awkward and invites misunderstanding. But there is no other way than to discuss the rhetorical practice of claiming comparative cleverness for oneself as a local 'language of claims', the notion introduced in Chapter 1. With this, the sticky web loosens somewhat: one can now trace how people unfold claims in their situational emergence. Thus, we realize that the problem is not the anthropologist's alone. Irony (and such claims as *paxalmamo*) poses exactly the same problems for the participants in a situation as for an observer bent on re-description and interpretation.

To talk about a 'language of claims' alerts us to attempts to define situations for often quite pragmatic goals. *Paxalmamo* in particular could be seen to establish a reputation, which sustains self-esteem and in turn engenders respect in others with all the attendant benefits. Not all Kara are constantly ironical in their assertions. Their responses to the vicissitudes of their lives are, as everywhere, heterogeneous (Torres 1997: 1). Some Kara might even have come to 'believe' in their own cleverness, as even blatantly invented traditions sometimes gain plausibility and naturalness (Fernandez 1986: 20). But the intensity with which interlocutors elaborated their reflections indicates that they held an attitude akin to my methodological stance: they understood well that in order to reap the benefits of a reputation for cleverness, it is sufficient if others believe or, more humbly, if others take such claims seriously. This entails that the Kara never need to decide for themselves which side of the fence to come down on. Acting in a way that indicates that yes, one perhaps does believe one's own tall tales, is fundamentally sufficient to define situations in this way.

The essence of irony, in Kenneth Burke's words, lies in just such awareness that 'the greater the *absolutism* of the statements, the greater the *subjectivity* and *relativity* in the position of the agent making the statements' (1945: 512, emphasis in original). To embrace their own relativity and contingency frees actors to engage in languages of claims that can be as absurd as positing their own cleverness to surpass everyone else's. In this, irony is 'possibly the most powerful trope' (Friedrich 1989: 305).

Paxalmamo, just as much as the ancient Greek *mētis* (Harrison 1986: 16f; Detienne and Vernant 1978: 27), is such an alluring stance to take in interaction precisely because of its fluid nature and because it can hide behind words, hint at itself and be gone before one can grasp it. The following episode exemplifies how a claim substitutes for 'the real thing', thus opening a site for ironical reputation management.

Sitting down with a Bashada man one day, he told me all sorts of terrible stories about the Kara, well aware that I was doing my research there. The narratives hardly bear out repeating, but they stereotyped the Kara as incredibly ruthless and amoral, casual to the utmost with the lives of others, for example, practising rituals requiring human sacrifice. He also insinuated that the Kara were extremely prone to secrecy, because if the truth about all their nefarious customs was to reach the outside, the outrage would be great. I felt and professed mild disbelief; he insisted on the literal truth of his words. Upon returning to Kara later, I confronted my friend Oita with those tales of terror. With a satisfied grin, he expressed his unreserved contentment over the idea that the Bashada might really believe these things: 'Let them think that, it's all good.' He contextualized the tales by hinting that there might have been some basis to them 'in the olden days' (*ana*), but since then, the Kara had become less callous: 'He talks like this because we do not tell our secrets to others. They do not know anything about us, while we know all about them.' This was in a way a pithy expression of the *paxalmamo* charter as such: a claim to total knowledge of the outside while being nontransparent and elusive towards all outsiders. If this had the effect that close neighbours such as the Bashada discussed the Kara in hyperbolic stereotypes, this counted as something positive for my friend. It mattered little that there was slander and scandal involved in the Bashada man's telling. So, for the clever Kara like Oita, there was no 'bad publicity'; the more people talked about them, the better. Hinting to me that their customs might have been more transgressive in the past is just an extension of this practice. In turn, my analysis of *paxalmamo* hardly gives the game away now. If the Bashada, who have intensive contact with the Kara, stereotype them in such a way, then my writing is unlikely to change that.

Oita demonstrates that at least some Kara are aware that their 'cleverness' exists largely as a social claim and that it is impossible to falsify such a claim in interaction. People greatly enjoy the provocation and challenge that they issue to others by styling themselves as always being a step ahead. They relish being insolent and audacious. But is this why they have adopted the charter of cleverness? Merely to annoy others?[14] This would be too simple an explanation, as it ignores the shifting nature of irony yet again. Maybe there is no irony, maybe all this is done out of cold calculation and the Kara have simply come to the conclusion that being known as clever and fierce saves them much trouble from would-be challengers in the future. Or maybe they all are utterly convinced of their superiority. The Kara's assertions of their *paxalmamo* truly set intersubjectivity in motion, in that they deny the hearer the certainty of sincerity.

What the discussion of the rhetorical practice of *paxalmamo* has revealed so far is that this charter can be sustained precisely because it is fundamentally impossible to pin down any claims as sincere, hyperbolic, provocative or outright lies. They might be any, none or all of these, even simultaneously. The true cleverness of the Kara lies in their highly aware audacity to claim cleverness, and their rhetorical skill in playing with the expectations of and responses by others to their individual and collective presentations of self.

Again I want to go back to my little vignette about the visiting official. Goiti-imba's statement about how there was no talk of subversion in Kara is fairly dripping with irony. But is it? To call some instance of behaviour 'irony' does not explain it. But to recognize the aspect of irony provides a richer context for the interpretation of the corresponding sequences of behaviour (Torres 1997: 21). To diagnose such actions as ironical is an attempt to do justice to their ambiguity, rather than eliminating it from the ethnographic record or trying to flush out the 'real meaning' behind some hidden transcript.[15] To weave together the methodological threads started earlier, I employ Linda Hutcheon's cogent argument that irony comes into being less through a speaker's intention and more through a hearer's internal unfolding of a statement (e.g. Hutcheon 1994: 151). This is in line with my general performative and audience-centred approach to the analysis of interaction, and with other inferential models of communication (Sperber and Wilson 1995: 24; see also Strecker 1988). A speaker might try to mark their stance as ironical, but we can never be certain that our interpretation matches their intention. What we do know is that we find ourselves seduced by suspicion, turning a statement over in our heads, unfolding it, looking for 'the unsaid' behind 'the said'. The ironic effect occurs not when we unveil 'what somebody really means' (for example, the Kara when they claim cleverness), but it emerges in our mental oscillation between what is said and what remains unsaid.[16]

The young official, then, might have understood the elder Goiti-imba to be telling him something along these lines: 'Come on, what do you expect? We will play your little games as far as necessary, but spare us these silly inquiries which we would never answer truthfully anyway. And you could not make us, either. You know that, really; you poor guy, they sent you here and made you ask such pointless questions. Now, I have provided you with a straight (if barbed) answer which you can take home to your superiors who know even less of us than you do.' Admittedly, writing this in such a linear form imposes order and structure where there are only inchoate hints, allusions, historical context and evocation. But I think the official could hardly avoid realizing that people found his attempt to define the situation in terms that would put the Kara on the defensive quite presumptuous. He was not lecturing schoolchildren, but savvy elders, who had seen many people just like him come and go before, literally over decades. At any rate, to paraphrase Scott, where 'humility and deference' are not convincingly performed, the display of 'haughtiness and mastery' required for domination is hard to sustain (1990: 11).

This incident is neither atypical, nor are such encounters rare. As mentioned above, *gubai*, 'meetings' of various kinds, have come to be one of the most important sites of Kara–Habesha interaction.[17] They always embody the key feature of the relationship between the peripheral lowlanders and the highlanders: power imbalance. Inequalities in power or, which is more accurate for the Kara case, unresolved, antagonistic claims to power provide a fertile ground for irony. Where such incongruous languages of claims as entailed by the Habesha–Shank'illa opposition are also involved, it is unsurprising when either or both sides take recourse to irony in order to better be able to bear the contradictions and tensions (see e.g. Capurro (1990) on Schlegel; Hutcheon (1994: 7) on Canada). Staying on the fence, as it were, allows people to not resolve the situation in one final way or other, when to do so would be individually problematic or even dangerous.

How such situated encounters as meetings between officials and elders come to be near-defining generative contexts of the wider Kara–Habesha relationship is discussed as the question of potential and actual power in the following chapter, which also presents the required structural frame by turning the discussion to the relationship between the Kara (and other Shank'illa) and the Ethiopian state.

Notes

1. Anthropological perspectives of that phase of Ethiopian history are well represented in the volume *Remapping Ethiopia* (James et al. 2002); for the Derg in particular, see Donham (2002b: 3–5).
2. I also discuss this case in Girke (2015).
3. I never got round to systematically recording these folktales, as they were referred to only rarely in everyday discourse. I only ever got to sit in on one 'natural' session where various people recited these apparently well-known tales, which seem all in all very typical animal fables of the gruesome nature. The narrators and audience were all adults, both men and women. The various animals besides the squirrel apparently have some stereotypical traits, but the kinship relations between them seemed contingent, i.e. it was not always the case that A was the MB of B. In general, the squirrel occupied the position that 'hare' has in Kaguru folk tales, for example, 'the shrewed, roguish manipulator of others' (Beidelman 1980: 29).
4. Nikolaus Schareika (2005) describes a very similar imagery from the Wodaabe of West Africa, who also explicitly link the squirrel with evasive political rhetoric.
5. It is also used for livestock that grows well and to prodigious dimension. Susanne Epple has suggested that *paxala* derives from *pak'*, an ideophone used in the HBB cluster indicating (visual) brightness. In this sense, the association with cleverness would translate

decently into English, since we also might say 'she's a bright person', but then lose the somewhat shady aspects always inherent in *paxala*.
6. There is also *dägamo*, which I learned to use as 'weakness' and 'incompetence'. I was told later that it was Amharic in origin. However, it is not clear from which Amharic term it might have been derived other than *däga*, which refers to 'the highlands' themselves.
7. They are not really sandals, but pieces of cowhide maybe 12 cm long, roughly cut into a shape of a sole.
8. Marshall Sahlins has pointed out that today's invented traditions (Hobsbawm and Ranger 1983) and yesterday's mythic charters (Malinowski 1992) are 'virtually the same thing' (1999: 403). Today, I would add 'cultural heritage' to the pile.
9. The Omo River water has proverbial qualities: if children among the Hamar suffer from a stutter, they should drink Omo water. The imagery translates easily: some speech flows like a stream; some is stagnant and obstructed as in a well. The flipside of the medal is found in the Hamar idiom 'he has drunk Kara water', which I found applied to myself when I once lost my temper over a perceived deception. Some source domains can be put to metaphorical work to express both attraction and repulsion.
10. Consider also the episode reported by Ivo Strecker, in which a Hamar friend of his replies to the query whether he also heard a truck approaching through the night: 'Brother-in-law, my ear is bad, it hears only the truth, it hears whether someone is going to live or die' (1988: 197). Strecker interprets this boastful and yet self-deprecating conversational turn as a bid for power through claims to knowledge. I would add that it was probably quite funny as well.
11. The best-known literature on Konso is Watson (1998) and still Hallpike (1972), but there is also much more recent research (e.g. Poissonnier 2009). The Kara know little factual information about the Konso, and many of the people they call 'Konso' would self-identify as Gawada, a population neighbouring the Konso.
12. The films by Ivo Strecker, mostly *Der Herr der Ziegen* (1984a) and *Tanz in der Savanne* (1984b) are celebrations of this lifestyle. The herdsmen appear here as effortlessly superior, confident and competent. They are the true masters of their land as it appears in these films, which of course pre-date current worries about tourism, the state's influence on societal change, economic transformations, capacity building, etc.
13. It was particularly disconcerting for me when at a meeting in Turmi, attended by Kara, Nyangatom, Dassanech and Hamar, the Hamar elders (and only the Hamar elders) raised their hands when they wanted to be excused for following nature's call. I could not tell whether this signal was an ironic commentary as well or whether it was indicative of a certain way governmental(ity) meetings were held in Hamar.
14. The moral merit of Socratic irony has been challenged on these very grounds: 'Der Dialektiker *depotenziert* den Intellekt seines Gegners. Wie? ist Dialektik nur eine Form der *Rache* bei Sokrates?' (Nietzsche 1922). F.G. Bailey, with verve, calls it 'bare-knuckle stuff, rhetorical assault and battery, intended to wear opponents down, to exhaust their capacity for logical combat, to knock all ideas out of their heads and thus make space for an implantation of "the truth" that Socrates, all the time protesting his own perplexity (and patently dissembling), professes not to know. In these circumstances the verb *persuade*, with its etymology of sweetness, would, as when a handgun is called a "persuader", itself be an irony' (2003: 167, emphasis in original).
15. Brown offers for a cutting criticism of those anthropologists who endeavour to seek out a truth behind any public statements. He argues that attempts to flush out 'hidden transcripts', based on the assumption that 'they are hiding something', is a typical aspect

of domination (1999: 13). In fact, under such scrutiny, it is likely that duplicity will emerge as a 'cultural form', which has the potential to make officials and anthropologists quite nuerotic (Evans-Pritchard 1940: 13).

16. In a more speaker-centred approach to rhetorical irony, one could distinguish between a 'speaking subject', who issues a sincere statement, and an 'actual subject', who is aware of the deception (Hirsch, Jr. 2001: 1708).
17. It is possible that increasing exposure to Amharic speech situations has also influenced the notion of *paxalmamo* as I discuss it here. The 'great Amhara virtue' *guabaz* (Levine 1965: 244) is used in a similar way to *paxala*. Whereas in *guabaz* Levine emphasizes the aspects of 'bravery, fierceness, hardihood, and a general male competence' (ibid.), I found that Amharic-speakers praised people as 'guabaz' in situations in which a Kara might approvingly comment on somebody's cunning and foresight.

Chapter 9

Seeing Like a Tribe

The imperial Abyssinian conquest, while still insufficiently described for this specific region (Strecker 1994; Donham 2002a), has fundamentally shaped what today is South Omo. Some groups were incorporated into the Empire more, others less brutally, but there can be no doubt that even those who escaped the worst ravages were well aware of what was going on elsewhere. In the wake of conquest, a colonial situation was established by the soldier-settlers (*neftenya*) who received land grants and were aptly called the 'landlords with guns' (Pausewang 1990: 42). The vanquished populations were forced to pay tribute, their land was occupied, their social order discredited. They were subject to slavery and abduction, to punitive expeditions, and a wide variety of prohibitions and rules and laws were imposed on them. The most vivid account of these times for South Omo proper is *Berimba's Resistance* by Ivo Strecker (2013), which presents 'The life and times of a great Hamar spokesman' as reported by his son, Baldambe (compare Lydall and Strecker 1979b). Not many other sources give more than passing insight into the relations at the time – their authors were either transient travellers (Stigand 1969; Neumann 1994) or very much implicit in the Abyssinian imperial adventure (Bulatovich 2000).

For the groups of South Omo (then Gamo-Gofa), it was fairly unambiguous that those who did all the slaving and imposing were others, others who brought with them a new social and political order, which by hook or by crook was imposed on the new subjects. This invader called them by the name Shank'illa, 'black slaves', and marked himself as Habesha, the 'red master'. One needs to understand that while this basic situation is in many ways similar to the way in which European colonies in Africa were both acquired and administrated, there was never a postcolonial moment in these southern marches of Ethiopia.[1] So even as the Kara readily state that things were worse under the Emperor as well as under the Derg regime, there is still a substantial divide between 'them' and 'us'. In many utterances, the word for 'Highlanders' (*jumpana*)[2] is used synonymously with *mengist*, the government. The Habesha and the state are, similarly to other peripheral places in Ethiopia (see Dereje 2009: 124), hard to keep separate in Kara semantics. I will not document the repetitive ways in which the Kara experienced their integrations into first the Abyssinian Empire, the nation as it was remapped by the Derg/Worker's Party of Ethiopia (1974–87/91), and the Federal Democratic Republic of Ethiopia since. There is next to no data on the imperial times, and precious little on the period since. Despite the proclaimed differences in political philosophy and specific mode of organization, and even notwithstanding the recent policy of ethnic federalism (Vaughan 2006), for the numerically insignificant groups of South Omo, there was always continuity: their rulers were Habesha, intrusive and often extractive (compare Abbink 2006: 393; Markakis 2011: 4). The discussion instead traces how this strict separation has come to be sustained – still, one has to say. The way forward is, then, to address the relations between such larger categories of belonging. The legacies of the past still come in at various points.

In Chapter 6, I discussed in detail the various categories and criteria of Shank'illa-ness from the Kara perspective. What about the Habesha-ness? Observing Kara and Habesha in interaction, and cross-checking this with internal Kara discourse, it turns out that it makes little difference beyond the folkloristic for a Kara whether a given Habesha is a Tigre, an Amhara, or even an Oromo or yet something different again (see Taddesse 2006: 222; Dereje 2009: 123). This is fundamentally a segmentary, stereotyping transposition, mirroring the way in which the Ethiopian centre has stereotyped and generified the people at its periphery for so long. The following table is an illustration of this double taxonomic reduction.

The Shank'illa are not unaware that there are differences within the overarching category of Habesha, and that elsewhere these categories are as exclusive and can be as relevant there as the local ethnic categories are for the cultural neighbourhood

Table 9.1 Segmentation in the imperial encounter

Amhara				Kara
Tigre	Habesha	IMPERIAL ENCOUNTER	Shank'illa	Hamar
Oromo				Aari
...				...

here. But for the interactions taking place in South Omo, this differentiation plays no role as of now.³ This is a simple reversal. Most times, an imperial centre will care little what different monikers the 'barbarians' down in the lowlands will affect – they are barbarians, and this designation is sufficient to frame and legitimize domination. That the barbarians also have little use for the specificities of the categories of the centre already carries the tangy taste of irony, as it relativizes the power to define that one might assume to lie predominantly with the centre.

For my overarching frame of ethnicity and group relations, this throws up a few questions. Primarily, how is it helpful to consider interaction between Kara and those Ethiopians who do not belong to any of the groups in the cultural neighbourhood as 'interethnic'? And if so, between members of which categories? John Galaty offers the 'working hypothesis' of 'ethnicity as a natural relationship between groups', just as kinship links individuals and clanship connects individual and group (1982: 2). Schlee has suggested that ethnicity entails the recognition not only that one belongs to an ethnic group oneself, but also the expectation that others belong to similar such formations (2008: 99). How different in scale, then, can the respective formations (or groups or categories) be to satisfy this criterion? A Kara might have to wear the mantle of Shank'illa in interaction with a Habesha, but for a person being classified in these ways, Kara and Shank'illa are very different sorts of identity categories: one shapes individual personhood in all its aspects, the other is a vague label people agree to be subsumed under for situational convenience, even as they know that it comes with negative connotations.

This is obviously a complex problem, which should not be discussed too abstractly. Thus, imagine being a Kara. When would you think of yourself in terms of your Shank'illa-ness? Would you ever 'feel Shank'illa' or would you merely acknowledge the pragmatic (even heurisitic) use value of the label? I have collected instances when Kara (and others) made sweeping statements in terms of 'we Shank'illa…' about their allegedly shared features and the predicaments they and their neighbours both suffer from. These were often more descriptive than affective, as people used the category to talk – frequently with a degree of self-deprecation – about stereotypical attitudes or abilities: 'Oh, it's always the same with us Shank'illa, the squabbling among us never stops.'⁴ But as I have indicated above, there were also recurrent situations where people from all over South Omo preached the benefits of Shank'illa unity. These I saw as first steps towards a positively connoted politicization of this category. This mirrors Torres' description of Mexican Tomato workers, who 'give themselves derogatory labels with an ironic twist in order simultaneously to convey acceptance of their status and challenge its premises' (1997: 17). In this respect, the division seems more class-based than ethnic or cultural.

Still, it might be possible to construct an argument in favour of retaining the ethnic distinction here. At this categorical scale, where people from the Lower

Omo encounter Highlanders, the intimacy of interaction is so low that stereotypical ascriptions are even more vague and generalized than those discussed in previous chapters. Hence, one could explore how experience, affect and forced classification come together in the emergence of the proactive Shank'illa identity claim. Such an argument, however, might obscure the truly distinguishing feature of the relation, which is of a different quality altogether: at the level of group relations within the cultural neighbourhood, the Kara can somehow argue an equivalence between the local groups, whose Wheels of Autonomy palpably grind against one another. A similar process might be happening in some other complex interplay far away in the Ethiopian centre, as suggested by the table above. Both sets of relationships might be helpfully called interethnic. But the Kara can impossibly sustain such an imagination in the face of these millions and millions of Habesha. Millions and millions of imagined Habesha, that is, who – as others – are 'more other' than any putative pastoralist even in Kenya or beyond.[5] Such a difference in scale precludes horizontal relations and at this vertical distance, the Wheels of Autonomy work differently.

Following up on my earlier discussion, I suggest that the strongest factor in the constitution of the boundary between the Shank'illa and the Habesha is the question of participation in the Ethiopian state, of inclusion and exclusion. Even today, there are those who conquered and those who were conquered, those who are (at) the centre and those who are (at) the periphery. While these abstract positions are subject to numerous negotiations and recontextualizations, which I will come to in the next section, the day when *mengist* will become something other than an other for the Kara is far off. The counter-argument that today there are a number of Kara men who have taken up administrative duties and that the state could accordingly no longer be such an other is hard to support. It defers the challenging question of how the Kara themselves deal with the recognition of their situation – because, of course, they do recognize this development. One common attitude is to react by casting doubt on the loyalty of the individuals enlisted in this way. By becoming part of *mengist*, one consequently becomes less Kara and less Shank'illa. From this, the general assumption that whoever becomes an administrator will also become loyal to the administration, or to themselves only, is quickly derived. The Kara are constantly tracking and evaluating the behaviour of their young men who work as clerks in the administration, and wonder which one of them will be the first to go away, 'become Habesha' and turn his back on Kara country for good. The state-induced process of local elite formation has hardly begun in South Omo.

The difference that makes the Habesha more different than other others is rather abstractly understood than practically problematic, as there is hardly any co-residence, and very little multiplex or even sustained interaction between Kara and Habesha. This suggests a modification of the Barthian model of ethnic groups and their boundaries. Typically, two discrete units are assumed, busy

Figure 9.1 The hearth inside the huts blackens the wooden girders, which have to be replaced regularly (January 2007). Photograph by Felix Girke.

with the upkeep of their joint boundary by signalling 'cultural stuff' (Barth 1969) at one another. This, however, does not seem to catch the inequality of the relation. In a way, only the Kara actively engage in the upkeep of the boundary, whereas most Habesha do not know (or care) that the Kara exist. So due to the difference in scale, the cultural stuff and the mutual negotiation of a boundary are not what people are concerned with. They worry about who tells them what to do, about the immanent transformations of their lives and livelihood, and the nagging question just how many decisions regarding their own lives they will still be able to make in the future. This is the question of power and agency. This is what looms large over all interaction between individuals from both sides.

As I outlined above, for the Kara as well as their neighbours, experience of 'state', quite irrespective of how we might want to define the notion, is conflated with the initial appearance and the subsequent spread of the Ethiopian Highlander throughout their life-world. Whatever the state is, it is an arena where the Highlander holds sway, an arena that holds the keys to money, development, law, force, education, and other hopes and fears. It is something one gains insight into, and maybe even some clandestine footholds, but anything more than that would require (and entail) a transformation of the very notion of Shank'illa. The groups of the cultural neighbourhood of South Omo see themselves as *a priori* excluded from the machinations of power going on in the national centres. This exclusion, then, is the fifth criterion that marks the groups of the cultural neighbourhood (from Chapter 6): they also belong and are alike by virtue of not belonging to the state in any convincing way.[6]

The idea that power derives from the state apparatus is not detachable from the Habesha, the Highlander. When Shank'illa, as individuals or as a body politic, do manage to set the state apparatus in motion in their favour, it is a subversive anomaly. Such is the abstract model of power relations between the state and the cultural neighbourhood, as it is largely enacted by both sides of the Habesha–Shank'illa divide. In practice, the model takes on particular cultural forms and becomes an object of rhetorical struggles in itself. To reiterate: my point is not that one could apply any old centre–periphery model to the relationship between Kara and the Habesha and find some matching facts; this is hardly surprising. Instead, I explore what problems a clearly (self-)defined and bounded population such as the Kara encounters in their dealing with a centre in terms of the Wheel of Autonomy, and how a group well-versed in the struggles of the interethnic arena can apply these skills in a different game, with slower moves and often unclear but possibly higher stakes. I argue that the Kara negotiate the centre–periphery relationship on their own terms and carry the habit of displaying their agency vis-à-vis their cultural neighbours into this larger arena just as much.

In the next section, I offer a comparison of Kara and their historical trading partners, the Aari, using the material on the latter provided by Alexander Naty. This will serve to highlight the variation in stances Shank'illa groups assume towards the Ethiopian state. The periphery is far from homogeneous, and the centre–periphery relations turn out differently in different places. Following up on this, the arguments turns to the question of how 'power' is negotiated between Kara and Habesha in interaction proper.

Aari and Kara: Two Divergent Responses to Conquest

> A harmless and docile people, these Schankella. I never encountered them in any other way and I have never been quite able to believe the scare stories that the Abyssinians told me about these 'cruel' negro tribes. Rather do I think that the 'cruelty' of the negroes was only concocted by the Abyssinians to have a pretext for covering the land with war.[7]
> —The traveller G. Escherich in Aari, from *Im Lande des Negus*

The settlements of Kara and Aari are not far apart in terms of linear distance: about 70 kilometres. Considered only in these terms, it is not obvious why the Kara should occupy a different position vis-à-vis the Habesha in comparison to the Aari. A closer look at the map reveals that the Aari are found in the highlands, around 1,300 metres and above, while the Kara reside in the much hotter and drier Omo valley proper, at around 400 metres, and the steep escarpment separating the two settlement areas makes for rough passage. This surely had an influence on the conquest itself that affected various parts of the land to varying degrees. Also, while the administrative efforts over the last century were not equally intense in all places, might one still not expect similar responses to the incorporation into the Ethiopian Empire?[8] This is clearly not the case: various groups have engaged with the challenges of *mengist* in significantly different ways. One example is found in Turton's presentation of the Mursi. Faced with the arrival of the Abyssinian armies, the Mursi quite suddenly found that their previously 'Mursi-centric' worldview had become untenable (2004: 15ff). For decades, the Mursi went on to pursue a 'strategy of avoidance – amounting almost to denial' (2004: 16) towards the Ethiopian state, struggling to maintain their view of themselves at the centre of their world, and of the world in their terms.

This was sustainable during the imperial period, as the interaction with the Habesha was restricted to being sporadically raided and/or taxed, and only began to fail when the Derg military government extended administrative control to the South Omo periphery through its peasant committees. Today, Turton adds, such avoidance is clearly 'counter-productive' (ibid.), as the current government began to give recognition to ethnic groups and boundaries and still allocates resources and access accordingly. Jon Abbink's account on the neighbouring Suri (see Map 0.1), a population rather similar to the Mursi, already diverges somewhat from this template. He describes with caustic detail how the revolutionary Derg activists were initially stalled and largely disregarded by Suri elders (2002: 163). Even though the Suri have by now achieved some representation and access to administrative positions, they still hold an 'ingrained perception of the encroaching Ethiopian state as an imposition and a threat' (2002: 168).[9]

These scholars, as well as others, provide us with narrow windows on the localized Shank'illa–Habesha relations, but the brief accounts only superficially address the cultural terms in which the Mursi or Suri word their position today. In the work of the late Alexander Naty, who has left us two significant texts on the 'culture of powerlessness' among the Aari (1992, 2002), I have found an approach that invites comparison with my Kara material.[10] In a nutshell, the Aari and the Kara ways of dealing with the Habesha and the problem of power relations could hardly be more different. I will first provide a summary of Naty's interpretation of his Aari material and will then go on to elaborate the Kara case.

What Naty pithily calls the 'culture of powerlessness' is for him 'an historically conditioned social-psychological dimension of unequal power relations between the state and a local people' (1992: 12). Faced with the immense capabilities of Empire, the Aari chose the path of acquiescence instead of open resistance. The soldier-settlers (*neftenya*; see Naty 2002: 60) who took their farms from them 'shattered Aari images of themselves as masculine and bellicose people' (Naty 1992: 271). The Aari were reduced to serfdom for their new tribute-extracting lords, who derisively called them Shank'illa. They could hold on to neither their land nor to their families: 'Aari men were not able to defend their women and children from slavery' (ibid.). Under the guise of a 'civilizing mission' (1992: 95–99, 115f), the settlers set up a highly stratified social order, in a way simply replacing earlier hierarchies with a new one, collecting tribute and forcing people into labour.[11] This subservient position was briefly inverted during the Italian invasion when the Aari collaborated with the European forces and took the chance to get revenge, rising against their landlords.

After the Italians' retreat, though, the Aari suffered yet harsher retributions from the Ethiopian side. They were also branded as 'ignorant' by the soldier-settlers for their failure to be loyal to the Ethiopian side (1992: 129, 307). In contrast, their 'pastoralist' neighbours, who had supported the Ethiopian loyalists when the latter retreated into their lowland territories, were called 'smart'. In more recent times, the Aari again failed to assert their autonomy through displays of agency – for example, they could not prevent 'the imposition of state policies such as collectivization and military conscription' (1992: 274). This perpetual experience of domination thus bridged the imperial and Derg periods, and, as Naty diagnoses, found an outlet in metaphorical expression. Prominent source domains from which imagery was drawn to evoke the Aari position versus the Ethiopian state were 'livestock' (i.e. sheep) and 'femininity' (1992: 12). Both domains offer a rich idiom to express hierarchy, subservience and powerlessness: 'Informants often remarked that their situation under these states [the imperial and socialist regimes] was similar to a marital relationship in which the husband assumed a dominant status in relation to his subordinate and subservient wife' (Naty 2002: 72). The status of being a wife in Aari is mirrored by the status of a serf in that both cannot hold property, are excluded from sites of power and have no control over their own lives. The Aari men felt emasculated, as they were prevented from going to war for their local chiefdoms. This is also reflected in metaphors that equated them with oxen, castrated for fattening, to be slaughtered at their owners' whim. Even as they are used to denounce the state of affairs, these metaphors not only draw on images of masculinity, but simultaneously perpetuate them and the vision of hierarchy they entail (1992: 275). Naty's Aari did not have a problem with hierarchy and domination as such, they were just despondent because they – king, men, women, all – were the ones being dominated.

The image of the 'castrated male animal' provides the link to the metaphorical practice that likened the Aari to livestock, particularly to sheep. The following quote is representative for the numerous statements Naty cites: 'We are like the sheep to its owner. The owner of a sheep puts a rope around its neck and drags it wherever he wants' (2002: 258). Note the aptness of the metaphor: it would not be as evocative to refer to goats, as goats have an independent and insolent streak in their character (at least compared to sheep) that makes them quite unsuitable as an image of powerlessness.

Naty's interpretation of 'the culture of powerlessness' proceeds with deliberation. He emphasizes that public quiescence, even over a long period, does not constitute a 'cultural trait' (1992: 12). Allowing that passivity can be a 'reasonable human mechanism of survival' (ibid.), Naty does not fall prey to delusions of ideological hegemony. His Aari act strategically and tactically. While their metaphors of powerlessness might seem to naturalize (and, inevitably, legitimize) their subservient position, Naty sees this as a case of 'pragmatic resignation' (Scott's term in Naty 1992: 24; see Simmel 1964: 113). The various metaphors listed above are hardly noncommittal descriptions, but articulations of 'historical and contemporary power relations between the Aari people and the Ethiopian state' (1992: 274). Even in highlighting this element of critique, Naty makes sure to point to the double nature of the self-deprecating claims to powerlessness. On the one hand, they 'condition Aari attitudes toward the state and its agents [and this discourse] stifles the Aari spirit of resistance' (1992: 275). On the other hand, by their 'sullen but silent opposition' (2002: 59), they challenged the legitimacy of their domination by the Habesha and the extant power relations. In this tension between collision and collusion, the central issue is encapsulated in a turn of phrase borrowed from Michael Lerner (1986: 3, in Naty 1992: 305f) – 'surplus powerlessness'.

To even write down this collocation points to the uncomfortable question of whether the Aari really were as powerless as they claim they were (compare Bourdieu 1991: 164). Were they colluding in their own domination? Were they actually supporting the definition of the situation as imposed by the Habesha? What might have persuaded them to stop spinning the Wheel of Autonomy, if that is a helpful description of what happened? What were the actual and potential differences in power? Naty chooses not to answer these questions, and so the analysis arrives at a sociological conundrum, the 'ambiguity of "passive agents"' (Torres 1997: 217; see also Schnepel 2005). Talking about a similar dilemma in the field of medical illness, Meneley offers the possibly applicable notion of 'ironic vision', which enables 'individuals ... to actively resign themselves to their fate' (2004: 35). Naty himself seeks no such methodological escape, but remains on the fence regarding whether the Aari were as powerless as they claimed, not wanting to indulge in untenable mindreading (1992: 312). We only have his interpretations, and it would be problematic to reread his texts in an attempt to get at 'better' answers.[12] Still, the questions listed above are directly generated from the lacunae he left, and I will pursue them in the next section.

From my reading of his texts, which are littered with references to the work of Scott on 'weapons of the weak' (1985) and 'the arts of resistance' (1990), it is especially surprising that Naty's Aari are so straightforward: there seems to have been little ambiguity in their claims about their situation. Did the Aari approach something like 'zero irony', as Paul Friedrich called the moment of traumatic (or in fact ecstatic) speechlessness (2001: 229f)? At any rate, the Aari 'culture of powerlessness' is sociologically interesting in that it encapsulates the victims' disclaimer of their own agency. In Naty's text, the Aari appear to be (too) sincere in their accounts, as if they 'meant' their own metaphors. So while doubts remain as to whether Naty has not possibly underestimated the duplicity of the Aari, or the performativity of their trauma narratives, for the sake of argument I will proceed in my argument with the image of the Aari as Naty presented it: despondent and quiescent when dominated, vengeful and violent given half a chance, always in one of these binary off/on states, but never shifty or elusive.

Now consider again the case of the official who visited Kara, whose example was given at the start of Chapter 8. I have so far argued that this episode was fairly typical of the particular way the Kara dealt in various arenas with individual Habesha who were representing state and government. This Kara stance is characterized by deliberate displays of elusive 'cunning intelligence' and by a general irreverence that they only spuriously veil. I have been reticent in asserting motives behind this behaviour, other than pointing out Kara attempts to define various situations. With the Aari case as a comparison, it is better possible to formulate the Kara stance as an alternative to a second 'culture of powerlessness'. One might call this the 'culture of cleverness', to indicate how the Kara themselves portray their stance towards the Great Ethiopian Other.[13]

Fundamental to the Kara attitude is the explicit recognition of their peripheral location. While in the mythic past (of the mid nineteenth century) the entire Lake Turkana Basin might have shaken in fear of the mighty Kara, it is quite obvious today that their position, both geographically as well as within the administrative space of the Ethiopian state, could hardly be more marginal. Their response to this recognition, though, is far from simple. The *a priori* negative connotation of 'periphery' comes to be denied in a perspective from Kara, and their peripheral location is instead revalued in positive terms.

As a first aspect, the distance from the Ethiopian centre is relativized: if even the rich tourists come despite the long and arduous journey, they really must want to see South Omo and especially the Kara very badly, goes the local understanding. The desires and opinions of some white *ferenji*, although they may be merely tourists, are praised as a surer guide to one's real – global – significance than merely national(ist) discourses.

Second, there is at least by now a sense that Ethiopia itself is peripheral in a wider context. 'Why is it', asked me an elder once, 'why is it that all these others, the Dassanech, the Turkana, even the Toposa, that all of them speak English and we don't?' I told him what I knew about the colonial history of the Sudan and Kenya, assuming he had actually wanted an answer – he might have, but he was also making a subtle statement that the Habesha were deficient in not 'speaking English' either and accordingly could not teach Shank'illa such as him.

Finally, the attraction of the centre comes to be denied. The *katama*, the city, a term applied to the local market villages as well as to larger, more distant towns, is described as a dirty, violent, immoral place, where 'everything costs money, no-one will give you anything for free'. The fact that in return their own lowlands are seen as highly inimical by Highlanders is also known well. How could it not? Most Habesha who come to Kara make no secret of it that they seek to depart as quickly as possible.

These three factors combine in the reimagination of the peripheral location of Kara and of South Omo within Greater Ethiopia. The Kara claim that they could live happily largely autonomous and undisturbed in the land of the forefathers. While people will travel when expedient, and while it is even a stereotypical inclination of young men to roam widely, it appears that there is little need for a shift towards the centre: numerous others – tourists, organizations, researchers, all – come to Kara of their own volition. Anthony Cohen calls such an awareness 'peripheral wisdom', a 'mode of knowledge on the periphery' that inverts the given imbalance by conceptualizing 'itself as central, and the putative centre as remote, inept, peripheral to its own essential values', and he – which is relevant for the figurative/rhetorical analysis – explicitly highlights the formal structure of such a reversal (2000: 12). An additional, less spatial aspect of the Kara attitude vis-à-vis the Habesha is that there exists, in stark contrast to the Aari, no dominant narrative about the trauma of the conquest. I could elicit little of the history of conquest beyond the plain and unembellished accounts of how the Kara had fled from their lands and spent some time hiding in a dense forest up north. While some elders could put names to people and places, most young Kara were unclear about where, when and for how long this had been. This in itself is telling. When I prompted them, people would agree that there had been raiding and abuse and unfair taxation, but this topic had no conversational relevance today. Instead, my interlocutors preferred to turn to exciting narratives of the late 1930s, of how their parents' generation, in alliance with fugitive Ethiopian loyalists, were adventurously ambushing Italian forces. I also found no accounts of a 'first contact' situation, narrations about the first white men who came to the Lower Omo. This is not entirely surprising, though, considering the insolent casualness with which the Dassanech greeted the Teleki and von Höhnel expedition in 1888 (Girke 2006), which was in fact their 'first contact (with Europeans)' event. Some groups apparently have a wider alterity horizon than others.

So even if the conquest itself was experienced as brutal and transgressive at the time, the generation of Kara just dying out today (some of whom claimed to remember seeing Italians), whose parents, in turn, were contemporaries of the conquest, do not talk about it in such terms. This nondramatic view is supported by the traveller Stigand, who in the early twentieth century found an 'Abyssinian post' at Kara (his 'Kerre'; Stigand 1969: 231). From his descriptions, one gains a sense of perfectly relaxed co-existence. Even then, apparently, the Habesha were unsuccessfully trying to get the Kara to abolish the *kumbassa* practice (Stigand 1969: 234).[14] This seems to have been the only intervention Stigand, who was curious and rather observant, noticed. Still, he reports that when he visited Dassanech, some people used the by now familiar idiom of powerlessness, dramatic in its metaphors: 'We have become as donkeys and beasts because of these [Highlanders], who have taken over our country' (1969: 226). From Stigand's description and the material Naty presents on the matter of the *neftenya* soldier-settlers who took over Aari land, it seems plausible to assume that while the Kara certainly got a good idea of the capabilities of the Habesha, they were never at the receiving end of the northern civilizing mission as much as the Aari. Accordingly, their self-image was possibly never as 'shattered' in the way that Naty claims happened to the Aari (1992: 271), and the Kara way of dealing with the power difference between them and the Habesha today reflects this.

But there were instances when the Kara, just as Stigand's Dassanech interlocutors, used the idiom of powerlessness themselves. During the time I spent there, I heard exclamations such as 'we have become the wife of the Highlander!' maybe three or four times in total. It never occurred to me to interpret these metaphors as evidence of acquiescence to domination and acknowledgement of the superior power of the Habesha. The frame was wrong. These statements were made with an air of exasperation, annoyance, feigned or exaggerated anger, and rather than resigned reflections on a sorry state of affairs, they were rallying cries to spur the audience on towards a reassertion of their self-esteem (see Strecker and Lydall 2006). 'We have become the wife of the Highlander!' always implied an explication such as 'because we were too lazy' or 'too complacent' or 'not clever enough', and a conclusion along the lines of 'and now this needs to stop'. In other words, in situations in which the Kara found themselves subordinated to the Habesha, unable to assert their autonomy, they presented the situation to themselves (and to me, and to any other audience) as contingent rather than necessary. The question of the power differential between them and the Habesha is apparently not considered closed by the Kara, as it seems to be in the Aari case, but kept unresolved. One would assume that the 1,400 Kara cannot possibly think that they could assert themselves vis-à-vis state authorities, but they act as if they did think just that. This attitude is inextricably connected to the claims to cleverness I have discussed above, empirically as well as methodologically. It seemed as if the Kara could not possibly be sincere in their claims about *paxalmamo*. The answer to this open question of power relations, I suggest, can be found in the same notion – irony (compare Girke 2015).

Potential and Actual Power at the Edge of Empire

In his account of the dynamics of engagement between the Suri of southwestern Ethiopia and the Ethiopian centre, Jon Abbink provides us with a penetrating vision of the situation, which connects to and expands upon my discussion from the last section:

> For local society, the Ethiopian state continued to figure as an external, impermeable framework of power and hegemony, led by elites located outside local arenas of interaction. In the decades of contact between Suri and state agents, the conflictual dynamics of Suri-state relations in their various forms were shaped by the unresolved competition of cultural models of the nature and construction of political power, space and sociality. State representatives … and local (Suri) society, all had different notions about the specific hierarchical power structure in Ethiopia. (Abbink 2002: 158)

The paragraph remains perfectly valid if we substitute the name of any of the groups of South Omo for 'Suri' here. The description of the unresolved tensions between the different models of power applies to all or – *pace* the Aari – did at least at some time.

I suggest that Abbink's 'competition of cultural models of political power' is central for an understanding of the Kara's approach to the Ethiopian state and the Habesha. The state has grown and encompassed them, and it demands their allegiance and civility, but the Kara act in a way that denies the inevitability of their subordination. I present a number of ethnographic examples of where Kara more or less subtly acted in disregard of the demands made by state agents. The argument is that only attention to the interaction between the Kara and the Habesha can give any indication of how the Kara, in their peripheral wisdom, perceive of and deal with what is for them 'the state'. For such a constellation, as suggested by Fernandez and Huber, irony is a suitable lens, since 'irony can be expected in situations of unequal power when discourses, interests, or cultures clash' (2001: 4) and, more generally, since 'ironies have to do with contacts between peoples greatly unequal in power and wherewithal: people in the center and margins of history' (Fernandez 2001: 85; Friedrich 2001: 229).

A Kara youth one day surprised me with the news that down at the road towards Kangaten (see Map 0.2), some men had intercepted a truck bound for Nyangatom, fully loaded with coffee. Inquiring further, I got confirmation and further details: the truck had been ambushed, and armed Kara had made the driver turn around and head to the Murule safari camp. There, they had deposited the owner of the coffee, a Nyangatom man. Then they directed the truck to nearby Korcho, unloaded the coffee (purportedly one hundred sacks) and let the driver go. The Kara who told me this were laughing slyly, and when I asked about the police, they just shrugged their shoulders. When I discussed this with Teddy, a Habesha who oversaw the Kara irrigation site at the time, he shook his head and said that this was sure to get a response from the dreaded Federal Police. So, Kara country waited and wondered about what sort of reaction was to be expected. Only weeks later did the owner of the sacks of coffee come to Korcho, accompanied by some district policemen. I was not present, but this is the story

I was told: when the police asked around for the coffee, the Kara said they would not return it. After all, had not the Nyangatom stolen last year's harvest from the fields of the western bank of the Omo?

They had, in a way: in a much-appreciated bout of cooperation, Kara and Nyangatom had been jointly cultivating the Kara's farms. Then, one day, a young Kara had shot two Nyangatom herding boys on the western bank, thus taking revenge for the killing of his wife some years before by a Nyangatom sniper. Immediately, all the Kara withdrew from the western banks. With baited breath, people waited whether the event would escalate into a hot war. Eventually, the Nyangatom collected the ripe grains from the fields on the western bank and carried them off, and the Kara had to resign themselves to the harvest from the eastern bank. This is what the Kara told the police and, so the narrative proceeded, the police agreed, and returned to whence they had come. The trader was left impoverished, and in the southern part of Kara country people were commenting that they were drinking *bume bunno* ('Nyangatom coffee') for months.

The deed itself was audacious. Not only did it disrupt trade and involve Habesha (the drivers of the truck), but it also sent a clear message to the Nyangatom and the regional administration: Kangaten, the entry point into southern Nyangatom territory and intended seat of administration for the district, the one site where everybody and everything has to cross the river, could be cut off from outside access by the Kara if they waylaid cars on the single feeder road. While no physical violence occurred, this act necessitated an official response – but when it came, it was too little, too late. The policemen who arrived at Korcho were merely from the local district. The coffee was nowhere and everywhere, and no individual perpetrators could be identified. Instead of attempting the impossible, they accepted the Kara justification and so could go home without an even more spectacular loss of face.

Another case concerns the individual mentioned above, the man who took revenge for the death of his wife. His identity was known from the moment of the deed. All Kara and probably many Nyangatom also knew who he was and what his motives had been. Also on this occasion, eventually, the police had come to Dus. He, however, had taken his rifle and disappeared into the forest as soon as the nature of the visitors had become clear. When again policemen came to Dus and demanded his surrender, the assembled elders washed their hands of the affair: 'He will shoot us, too, if we try to catch him. If you want him, you will have to get him yourself.' The police departed, unwilling to track a desperate man through unknown territory. Over the next few months, I could observe the man drifting away from the village whenever cars came into sight and returning once it was safe to do so. A few years have gone by since, and the Kara estimate that soon enough, this will blow over too, so that he can even go to towns like Jinka again.

The list could be continued. No case can be considered as a separate incident. Each one contributes to the dossier on the actual power of the police and, concomitantly, the state administration. In an ironic twist, the hesitancy of individual police (and their superiors in the district) to escalate in such a conflict is not discursively praised as restraint. Instead, it offers an occasion for people to say that 'the Habesha are all liars'. To first loudly impose laws and rules, and then to not enforce adherence to them sends a very clear message about agency and power. I have hardly encountered even one incident where justice was meted out in the way prescribed by laws and regulations.

The Kara, aware of the predicaments of police who hardly feel secure in pressing an issue in the face of the well-armed Shank'illa, and of the low- to mid-level administrators, who can hardly make far-reaching decisions on the spot, have understood that they can get away with a lot (compare Abbink 2006). How far can they push it? This, of course, is contingent and unknowable, but every case in which they manage to escape retribution despite their transgressions is again another precedent. It is clear that too blatant a humiliation of the administration or too gory an act of violence will be crossing the line, Scott's 'cordon sanitaire' (1990: 19). But this line has not been drawn very clearly in recent times. Almagor's analysis (2002) of the relations between the Dassanech and the Habesha (he uses 'Amhara') in the mid twentieth century describes such a system of checks and balances well: the regional governor insisted on collecting tax (in livestock) from the Dassanech. But while the governor could never extract as much tax as desired, the Dassanech also never totally refused to pay.

What does this say about power relations? In such situations on the internal periphery of the Ethiopian state, power is not only analytically more a potential than an actual faculty; the actors themselves are aware that they are negotiating claims. All sides involved are thus trying (like the governor of Dassanech) to get at least a little bit of what they demand, and thus avoid losing face over being unable to follow through with an exaggerated claim. Such elusive performances do not make the subordinates 'opaque to elites' (Scott 1990: 132). The main effect of Kara displays of cleverness and ironic reversals is that the elites have to realize that they are not as superior as they assume – or wish. 'If someone misbehaves, send him to Gamo-Gofa [an earlier name for South Omo]' goes an old Amharic saying (quoted in Naty 2002: 61). Nobody voluntarily transfers to South Omo and it must not be assumed that this common Habesha disdain of the lowlands has remained obscure to the Shank'illa.

Irony, as this section has suggested, allows one to acknowledge others' claims to power over oneself as inevitable, even where they appear unfounded and untenable. In turn, the ironical Kara realize that their opposites, the representatives of government or large institutions, are subject to similarly unreasonable structures. The Kara claims to cleverness as well as their ironical stance towards others' demands are not marked by cynicism, but instead reveal an empathetic awareness of the affinity between self and other. Janice Boddy has suggested that:

> In colonial situations in which a dominant group seeks to replace an indigenous regime with its own, the subordinates' contemplative agency is constrained. So, too, is that of the colonizers, whose vision prevails as truth and their subjects' as its foil: 'superstition', 'backwardness', 'barbarity'. (2004: 61)

On reflection, I would say that it is largely the second part that seems to be applicable to Kara. This offers a spark of hope against what Achille Mbembe calls the 'mutual zombification' of dominant and dominated that looms in the postcolonial situation (1992: 2): on the Omo, the zombification seems hardly mutual.[15] David Graeber's comments on 'imaginative identification' come closer to the mark: 'The victims of structural violence invariably end up spending a great deal of time imagining what it is like for those who benefit from it; the opposite rarely occurs' (2007: 405). This is corroborated by observation: the Kara, and likely other groups (such as Abbink's Suri), empathize with the specific individuals who are sent to negotiate with them, who are outcasts from the centre themselves, but the Kara nevertheless seek to endlessly defer the final resolution of the power question through their shifty behaviour. That is why I am reluctant to identify the Kara's ironic behaviour as a 'weapon of the weak', because the powerful are evidently weak themselves.

The Limits of Irony: Korcho's Disease

'*Korcho-sa choki zerbo deidina* – Korcho has a very bad illness', said Mirja-imba, a decisive and respected elder, in one of the discussions held on the riverside, near the small villages of Chelläte and Gurdo (see Map 0.2), during the early months of 2007. After finishing a hard day's work, the men regularly met in one household's shade and shelter, occasionally over *parsho* beer, and discussed current issues. It had been known for some time that these two hamlets would be administratively assigned to the village of Korcho, to form what was to become the third *kebele* of Kara land.

One of the crucial issues in these debates seemed to be the question of the *kabin* (a Kara-ized version of 'cabinet', via the Amharic), the administrative functionaries of each *kebele*.[16] At this time, it was known that there would be four positions to be filled and to each of them would be attached not only some vague clout (and accountability), but more centrally a salary.[17] The Kara from Chelläte and Gurdo, many of whom felt closer to Dus than to Korcho in this divide of southern Kara country, were worried that they might be totally left out of the distribution of these prestigious and attractive positions. Most members

Figure 9.2 The Kara erect shelters in their exposed fields to rest, share food and coffee, and talk (January 2007). Photograph by Felix Girke.

of this new *kebele* lived in Korcho proper, and so could imaginably just assign the jobs according to the village's internal factional structure. In this context, another (albeit short-lived) rumour emerged: the people of Gurdo and Chelläte, largely belonging to the Nyuwaya section of Dus, were seeing indications that the Nyuwaria, who make up the vast majority of Korcho households, wanted to carry their dominance over into the *kebele* structure by keeping the Nyuwaya out of the *kabin* posts.

In addition, there was a worry among those present, largely true Kara but not exclusively so, that the above-mentioned *choki*, the illness, could manifest itself through the machinations of the Moguji of Korcho, again a sizeable minority. Two discourses had emerged on how to go about the distribution of the *kabin*; I call them 'meritocratic' and 'proportional'.

Meritocratic: this is what the true Kara I spoke with were proposing – they demanded that the indubitably best speakers should be nominated and should be the ones to 'watch the land' and go to meetings with the Habesha. Accordingly, one should be ethnicity-blind and select four respected people with reputations of eloquence and prudence, and install them. If they turned out to not live up to expectations, one would replace them with other candidates, who would for now be waiting in the wings. This model, it was suggested, was good for the wellbeing of the country, for all its inhabitants. That no Moguji would be suggested on these grounds, as they always commanded limited respect regardless of their actual oratorical skills, a glass ceiling of sorts, was hinted at in various degrees of mirth by true Kara. The meritocratic motion also fit well with the general demand of ethnicity-blindness as I have presented it above in the context of *ädamo*.

Proportional: this procedure was suggested by the Moguji, who constituted a significant minority in southern Kara, especially as there were at this point no Gomba or Bogudo elders in Dus or Korcho. While several Nyangatom-Kara families belong to Korcho and while there are respected elders among them, they also did not figure in the public discussion. This is not untypical: I have never learned of an instance when Nyangatom-Kara acted as a corporate group. At any rate, they are immigrants and not 'of' the land. The Moguji, however, in order to ensure that the *kabin* always reflected the demographic set-up of the land, demanded that one of the *kabin* positions should in perpetuity be assigned to the Moguji. The true Kara, in their internal discussions, denied that there was even one Moguji qualified for the task and that it would create a danger to the land if an incompetent buffoon was given so much responsibility just because one *kabin* post had to be a given to the Moguji for proportional reasons.

As I spent little time in Korcho, I do not know to what degree these issues were publicly worked out at any point. I assume that in fact they were not. In the end, four true Kara were installed, young and old, two of them in fact from Gurdo and Chelläte. There is a very fine irony here in the sense that the people of Gurdo and Chelläte had – in effect – been arguing a proportionalist agenda as well, in that they insisted that some of them should be among the *kabin* while simultaneously denying that there was any value to proportional representation when the Moguji raised their claim. This only became apparent to me when writing up my data.

However, bitterness as well as vague worry remained. The true Kara were troubled about this issue, since they suspected that there was, in fact, seditious talk among the Moguji, that they might all move away and become Nyangatom, or conspire against the land in some other way, a clear revival of the fears of the past (see Chapter 5 on the 'schism'). What was going on? In my interpretation, the Moguji's move to emancipate themselves by demanding representative rights brought up memories of the 'divisive practices' that the true Kara had sought to remedy before. This was taken as a threat to the status quo of the land, in that not only did the Moguji think they could represent Kara, but that they were actually quite clever about it. No true Kara admitted this cleverness to my face, but the argument of proportionality was well understood by people and, as they loudly denied its applicability due to the dearth of qualified candidates, they might have grudgingly acknowledged that the cleverness of the argument in and of itself was proof of the opposite.

They were, then, very unironical about this kind of *paxalmamo*, directed against their definition of the situation. Unlike the ironic adaptation of the narrative about the 'Trail of the Red Bull' that I discussed before, in this arena, there were real stakes to be struggled over. The relevance of these events for my overarching interest in *ädamo* is clear. Everybody in Kara country is supposed to accept the *primus intra pares* claim of the true Kara without challenge and without pointing out the little fact that there is even such a thing as a 'true Kara' political position. But this is exactly what the Moguji demand was all about: by offering their definition of what was right and proper, they in no unclear terms suggested that they had specific interests as Moguji and that they dared to voice their opinion that these were not safeguarded. In the face of this challenge, the true Kara of Korcho (with the tacit approval of the Nyangatom-Kara) still pulled through, as they distributed the *kabin* as they saw fit. But it was quite apparent that they had won this victory not due to their superior Kara cleverness, but through their numbers.

Ironically into the Future?

In this chapter, I have argued that while the Kara recognize that they are marginalized, just as all the Shank'illa groups are, they deal with this situation on their own terms. It is not merely that they put up a dividing line between 'us' and 'them' or that they engage in resistance and 'insubordination' (Herzfeld's (2001) substitute term). Pursuing their charter of cleverness, they not only sustain their self-esteem in times of immanent change, but also recognize the incongruities implicit in the civilizing mission of the state (and other actors), and the predicament of people different from themselves.[18] There is another gain: in 'causing power to face up to its own grossness, the subaltern attains an incomputable but nevertheless tangible moral victory' (Obadare 2009: 249).

As Ivo Strecker graphically illustrates, the problem is not new: already in the early decades of the twentieth century, the Shank'illa were challenging the position of the low-level officials. Berimba, a great Hamar spokesman, attempted to gift two lion cubs that he had caught to the Ethiopian Emperor in person. Strecker develops the symbolism of the lion in Ethiopia: the Emperor himself is a lion and also fights like a lion, but he does not actually go out and fight against real lions, as Berimba did. Strecker's explanation as to why the local administrators could not allow this venture to succeed is convincing: 'If the Shankilla were allowed to feel themselves to be equal or even superior to the Ethiopian aristocracy and the Emperor, then the basis of the administrators' social status would vanish, and with it their power, economic base, and also their pride and self-esteem' (2006a: 183). The sophisticated Emperor and his court, Strecker surmises, would probably have appreciated the irony of the gesture and the cleverness of Berimba (see further Strecker 2013).

Regarding future developments, what will happen with the Kara's charter of cleverness? The enthusiasm for schooling, one of its most visible manifestations, will not be broken any time soon. As the security situation is developing now, with the Nyangatom *ante portas* and a gigantic hydroelectric dam preventing the natural flooding of the Omo, their subsistence-oriented livelihood – a foundation of their aspirations to autonomy – is no longer as feasible as it was in the past. The sheer number of students striving for education bespeaks the awareness that there is currently a range of alternatives to pursue, both as an individual and as a community. Still, it is impossible to know now which decision will turn out right. Even sending kids to school creates problems galore, as there are well-known examples of young men who went to town to study and instead became drunks and louts when they failed to find gainful employment, but were already alienated from the fields of their home. So while there are opportunities, no obvious solution to the problems is at hand.

The philosopher Richard Rorty differentiates between two perspectives on the world:

> The metaphysician, in short, thinks that there is a connection between redescription and power, and that the right redescription can make us free. The ironist offers no similar assurance. She has to say that our chances of freedom depend on historical contingencies which are only occasionally influenced by our self-redescriptions. (1989: 90)

In this terminology, the Kara tend to the ironists' side: they do their best to keep up with current developments, but they are always aware that there is much they can never influence. The following exchange occurred between two Kara elders during an informal discussion on some demands made by an administrator some days before: 'Enough! Leave me alone with this! Let's not bother ourselves with these annoying questions, let's just go home and be farmers!' – 'That's right! You spoke well! And there is not even a government!'

These utterances together provide a vivid example of just such an ironical stance as posited by Rorty, as one counterfactual claim is stacked on top of another: to just be farmers, and simply cultivate their gardens, both elders know, is simply no longer an option, even if one's agency to affect the administrative matters at hand and in general is unreliable at best.

In addition to all the other unpredictable developments looming, recently some certainty has been added, in that the longstanding rumours about a huge dam and hydroelectric project some hundreds of kilometres upriver have become consolidated. The Gibe III Dam was completed in 2016, and without getting too technical here, I just want to state the main effect that this has already had on the Lower Omo Valley: the Omo floods have been stopped and will – in a best-case scenario – eventually resume by means of regulated releases.[19] Just this is enough to destroy the entire basis of the Kara subsistence production and along with it their system of landholding, and the local calculus of exchange and status. It used to be that a man who owned many plots along the river was a desirable son-in-law. When they were growing old, men used to exchange some of their goats, or a gun, or money even, for some plots to leave to their sons. No more. Already years before the dam had been constructed, people stopped buying plots. 'It is just going to be soil, not a field – why should I buy it?' was what one man said to the other Kara with whom he had been in negotiations over the purchase of a field for a long time. Without the Omo floods, which make the Kara system of cultivation so very efficient (see Matsuda 1996), everything will change. To add some grim irony, with the unpredictable and sometimes massive Omo floods about to be stopped, which puts paid to the local productive system, much of Kara country has been designated as a feasible site for industrial irrigation, with two farms already in operation at the time of writing. This has massively transformed the hinterland of the Kara settlements already now, and mid-term and long-term consequences of this comprehensive transformation are hard to guess at this point. Already in 2006 it was reported to me that officials had visited the Kara regarding this prospect. When the visitors asked the latter something along the lines of 'so, if the floods stop, what would you like to do instead? Irrigation maybe?', according to my informants, the Kara said 'why yes, thank you': *eh-e*. The hardly positive experiences the Kara have had with irrigation were mentioned above. With both the dam project and the industrial irrigation in place, the Kara's prospects appear dire. They might be offered employment as unskilled labourers and some plots to work for themselves, or they might simply be resettled elsewhere at some point.

When I visited Kara in early 2008, two items dominated the daily conversations: first, there were yet again violent conflicts with the Nyangatom; and, second, the news of the planned industrial irrigation site was spreading. Accordingly, there was much talk about the future in general, what had to be expected, what people worried over and where they saw the potential for action. At some point, Wujo, a vigorous elder, spat and disgustedly said: 'Oh, I hope those *ferenji* [the foreign-run farms] come soon to take our land. Then at least the trouble with the Nyangatom will stop.'

This comment is so condensed that it is a fitting capstone to my argument: Wujo knows that there is little he or anyone can do to halt the dam project. So even as he is fundamentally distraught in the face of this drastic transformation, which I suppose he is, he simultaneously relativizes the situation the Kara have now been in for a long time. Wujo does not conjure up an idealized state, an idyllic autonomy that is now threatened by the most recent developments. Instead, he acknowledges that there are always vicissitudes in life one has to cope with as they appear, such as the decades of struggle to halt the Nyangatom's encroachment. In Rorty's terms, he offered an ironical re-description of the situation. While irony does not provide any solutions for the Kara's very material problems, 'it can make the powerless feel good' (Bailey 2003: 179), as they recognize that presumptions of power are much easier to issue than to fulfil and that history never proceeds quite according to anyone's plan.

This, then, is how a 'tribe' sees the state: as an awesome force in principle, which can be quite brittle up close and that one should only antagonize with deliberation and skill so as to avoid an actualization of its potential power. This makes for an interesting variation on the Wheel of Autonomy, as autonomy and agency are measured differently, and distinction can be achieved in different ways: The Aari's shared tale of collective victimhood contributes to a sense of Aari-ness as the Kara's pursuit of cleverness facilitates feeling 'Kara'. It is clear to the Kara that dealing with the state and the transformations of their life-world ordered by the distant centre will be the decisive arena of the future, but it is not clear to them whether their cleverness will help them to preserve the autonomy that has been the cornerstone of Kara-ness.

Notes

1. This brutal war has found its apologists in academia, who claim that it only formalized an already-existing factual connectedness of centre and periphery (Levine 2000; see the formal criticism in Schlee 2008: 73–74). Markakis (2011) identifies the southern lowlands as a direct consequence of these historical burdens as one of the 'last frontiers' of Ethiopia, frontiers here to be taken as areas still resistant to national, cultural and economic integration.
2. This is the definite plural of the generic noun *jumpa*. A singular definite Highlander would be called *jumpita*. The etymology of *jumpa* is unclear, but phonetically similar words exist throughout South Omo. To avoid confusion, I stick with the Amharic term Habesha, which forms a dialectic dyad with Shank'illa.
3. Many people identifying as Oromo would reject inclusion in the Habesha category. But the distinction matters little when viewed from the Lower Omo – excepting, of course, the familiar Borana, whose pastoral lifestyle and historical entanglement especially with the Arbore and Hamar at least vaguely qualifies them as Shank'illa, as seen from Kara.
4. As regards bodily features, the opposition came to be extended to Ferenji like me as well. After a somewhat gruelling hike, Haila admonished other Kara to go slower next time, as 'he is not a Shank'illa!' That is, I was not used to heat and presumably physical exertion as such.
5. Kara use the term 'Shank'illa' when talking about faraway lands as well. It is plausible that they subsume non-Ethiopian yet familiar groups such as the Turkana or Toposa under Shank'illa: the understanding that one has much in common is reasonable. When the conversation turned speculative, though, I found that the term was used to refer to very different sorts of categories. While some groups were labelled as Shank'illa on the basis of phenotype, others (even if European or Asian) could be included as long as they were pastoralists or belonged to the periphery of their respective nations. In the case of Kenya, for example, it took some sorting out until Kara interlocutors accepted that the contemporary rulers of that country were as 'black' as they were.
6. While the title of this chapter invokes a reversal of Scott's analysis (1999), I clearly have not pursued this systematically here (cf. Girke 2013).
7. Original quote: 'Ein harmloses, gutmütiges Volk, diese Schankella. Ich habe sie nie anders kennen gelernt und habe die Schauermärchen, die mir die Abessinier von diesem 'grausamen' Negerstamme erzählten, nie recht glauben können. Ich denke wohl, dass die

"Grausamkeit" der Neger erst von den Abessiniern ersonnen wurde, um einen Vorwand zu haben, das Land mit Krieg zu überziehen.' (Translation: F. Girke)

8. See Donham (2002b: 34) on the 'unevenness of *encadrement*' during the Derg time.
9. The Suri population is much larger than either that of the Mursi or Kara, and thus benefits from quotas set for political participation. In addition, foreign missionaries have been very active in advancing literacy and general education (Abbink 2002: 169f).
10. The sad fate and eventual death of this Eritrean who studied the Ethiopian periphery is recalled by Abbink et al. (2004).
11. The full Amharic name of this institutionally imposed serfdom is *gebbar sirat* (see Naty 2002: 60f). The 'civilizing mission' is of course carried out in an utterly unironical way, even though the underlying contradictions (namely, that one version of freedom is extinguished in the name of another in the nation-building process) invite an ironical stance (Capurro 1990; see also Fernandez (2001) on development discourse).
12. Turton (2003) has suggested that the Aari response might already look different now than during the time when Naty did his research in the late 1980s: in a conflict with the Mursi in 1999, they apparently pressured the local administration into action from a position of relative political weight.
13. It would be interesting (but would go beyond the argument pursued here) to compare these Ethiopian cases with the Latin American peasantry as discussed by Eric Wolf, who used terms like 'defensive ignorance' or 'rejection pattern' to characterize their reaction to state incorporation (1955: 459).
14. Despite his overall competence, Stigand probably got it wrong when he against all evidence persisted in his understanding that Kara always killed their firstborn and not only illegitimate children (Cerulli 1956: 60). The *kumbassa* practice was discussed at length before. It is one of the main 'harmful traditional practices' governmental and nongovernmental activists have been trying to urge the Kara to drop.
15. Mbembe notes that humorous engagement or disengagement by the periphery vis-à-vis the centre does not do 'violence to the *commandement's* material base'. Obadare counters this by his remark that there might well be long-term erosive effects of the centre's legitimacy project (2009: 248).
16. The four positions were named and in a consensus reached through nonobvious means were assigned to the four candidates according to what people thought best fit their understanding of what these positions were all about. I list them here with the Amharic name, the Kara version and a literal translation of the Kara expression: (1) *Astetader* – 'pe shedeia', the watcher of the land; (2) *Hizb aderjajet* – 'zersi putsheia', the one who assembles the people; (3) *Matawaka* – 'delak' bokisseia', the one who reminds the people of previous discussions; and (4) *Tsatitaserf* – 'shauki mareia', the one who wards off war. I hypothesize that the new Korcho *kabin* were selected so as to fill the positions with people somewhat similar in character to those already installed in their positions for the Dus *kebele*: I found that both 'reminders of talk' (of Dus and Korcho, that is) were comparatively young and vigorous men; chairmen were middle-aged men with a reputation of competence and calm manner; and the 'war wardens' were in both cases the respectively eldest men of this committee.
17. The *astetader*, as chairman, received a little more money than the rest, ETB 200 vis-à-vis ETB 150 for the rest. This seems typical for Ethiopian standards and presents a worthwhile income in Kara at least. These numbers can safely be expected to change occasionally. I thank Fekadu Adugna for providing some context and spelling advice.
18. The ironical stance of the Kara is also very visible in their interaction with NGO workers.

The potential for irony springing from the incongruities and internal contradictions of the developmental project, which in South Omo is strikingly cyclical instead of cumulative, have been recognized well (Fernandez 2001; Marcus 2001; Rottenburg 2002: 3f, 11–14; Yurchak 2006).
19. Currently, this is a very visible topic, with vociferous international protests (compare Girke 2013) clashing against the counterarguments of the dam's defenders.

Conclusion

So is this 'how they do it'? Is this a satisfactory analysis of how the Kara have managed up until now to remain Kara, not only as members of a category, but also as a bounded, corporate, to some degree autonomous group, with a palpable reality for its members? Have the previous chapters managed to tease out their reasons for doing so? Does it also answer the question of 'Who are the Kara' in the first place? (*pace* Michael Moerman 1965; Girke forthc.a).

I believe so. To recapitulate: in my ethnographic chapters, I have explored the ways in which Kara act in their aspect as members of this and other categories in their relations to various others, and how these relations gain tangibility and plausibility in their enactment through rhetorical languages of claims: the various actors' struggles both symbolic and material in the arenas within and without sustain the very idea of Kara and, concomitantly, the other politico-territorial groups of the region. Central is the shared worry over the possible dissolution of the community and all that it enables, a worry that is never too far from people's minds. Below, I review the main dynamics explored throughout this book with an eye on the guiding notion of *ädamo*.

The Bogudo, intrinsically joined to the whole of the Kara body politic and ritual, were refused the right to unilaterally modify the ritual proscriptions they had been subject to. When some decided to abolish the *yekinta* ritual and thus allowed themselves to bear out otherwise illegitimate and polluting pregnancies, the true Kara recategorized them as Gomba. To recall, Gomba are not nearly as 'good' Kara as the true Kara are – there are marked commensality taboos between them. 'Bogudo', as it turned out, is not exclusively or at least not in each instance a descent-based ethnic category – when the drama I recounted in Chapter 3 occurred, the true Kara treated adherence to the *yekinta* ritual as the one feature that effectively defined the Bogudo. Without it, they simply became ritually inferior Gomba.

The interaction between members of different ethnic categories in Kara is to a large degree predicated on the unspoken assumption that to have many restrictive rituals is a sign of positive distinction. To have few, or none, is a sign of inconsequentiality, of lacking commitment to the idea of human sociality as such. That those Bogudo voluntarily relinquished the most distinguishing ritual there is, the *yekinta*, subverted this principle. This principle of correspondence between strict ritual duties and general worthiness also serves as the great saving lie that legitimizes the true Kara's position as the dominant group within the community. So the true Kara reasserted the point that to surrender rituals must correspond to loss of status and thus re-established their power to define. In this example, *ädamo* came up only in a negative sense: the Bogudo's decision was taken as a challenge to the way things work – but the way things work is how the true Kara want them to work. It is part of the social contract, as it were, to not challenge this political arrangement or its ritual expressions, and to not even doubt the true Kara's proclaimed goodwill vis-à-vis the members of all the other ethnic categories of the population.

The Bogudo's singular challenge, though, was nothing compared to the existential problem presented by the Moguji. I have discussed this relation, so fraught with tension and taboo and enshrined in myth, in terms of its metaphoric construction in Chapter 4. The Moguji, half inside Kara and half outside, are a problem precisely because they are so close to the Kara, with their histories entwined and even mutually constitutive. To justify the mythic origin story about the Trail of the Red Bull, which recalls their arrival to the Lower Omo Valley, the true Kara need to radically 'other' the Moguji. For a long time, it seems, the Kara were also successful in disaggregating the Moguji as a corporate group, limiting their access to land and dispersing them throughout the country by tying up individual families in patronage relations. The Moguji were politically dominated and economically constrained, and in a rhetorical shift, their low ritual status was legitimized through the principle stated above: because they perform hardly any life-path rituals in comparison to the true Kara.[1] This debasement is mirrored in the metaphors of the Moguji, which deny them all that the true Kara consider important for themselves: the human qualities of decency, productivity and sophistication.

This, then, is how the ethnic category of 'Moguji' matters in social practice: the Moguji's place within Kara is entangled with the issue of land-ownership. Not only is this material issue fundamental for how 'Moguji' is conceptualized, but it has also led to the past upheavals and the more recent and still current political discomfiture in Kara country. My data were collected in the contemporary context of a politicization of the Moguji ethnic category, and this is what makes the case above all distinct from the Bogudo example, which discursively remained within the ritual realm. The analysis, in general, aimed to unravel how personal bonds are caught up in symbolism, in questions of access, property, materiality and structural differentiation, and which discursive and rhetorical forms the negotiation of various interests takes in practice.

However, at least one Moguji faction, in the wake of the Ethiopian policy of ethnic federalism since the 1990s, seems to have found ways to act in concert, with their own interests in mind. Some have left Kara, triggering a violent reprisal, while others have remained, but many have become more assertive and self-conscious. This, too, presents a problem for *ädamo*: much more than the few renegade Bogudo, the Moguji challenge the publicly voiced assertions of 'we are all Kara'. They know full well that some people are more equal than others, and seemed less and less reluctant to voice that awareness, which reliably triggered reprisals from the true Kara. Such reprisals resulted less, I felt, from a sense of indignation, as it had been in the case of the Bogudo, but with very real worries that a splitting off of the Moguji from the Kara (whether to join the Nyangatom or to pursue a putatively anomic existence in the 'forest') would create concrete existential dangers for the very survival of Kara as a polity as well as for people's lives. Methodologically, the cases are comparable: the true Kara's power to define situations, as for example manifested in the system of land tenure and the ritual order, was challenged through these attempts to change the status quo. As I have argued and illustrated throughout this book, the participants in such dramas on the Lower Omo act with the sense that if a challenge to an established power claim goes unanswered, this power is necessarily diminished. The true Kara react as they do in each of these cases in order to prevent precedents from being established – *pour encourager les autres*. They also always painted their actions as reactions, suggesting that others had violated the moral demands of *ädamo* first. Such violations can simply be the near-unspeakable act of pointing out that the specific (and corporate) interests of the ethnic subgroups within Kara even exist.

Beyond these internal arenas, 'the Kara' and their neighbours as politico-territorial groups are alike in being taxonomically encompassed by the overarching category Shank'illa, and all belong to each other's cultural neighbourhoods. This relationship is where the Wheel of Autonomy model can be most clearly demonstrated. While there is, as I argued, a fundamental understanding of equivalence between the groups, their relations are still marked by constant struggles. Their ability to compete in these struggles, in a way, makes them 'groups' in the first place. Each time people defend their autonomy, display their agency and underline specific differences to various others, they communicate – and the most basal fact they communicate is 'we exist'. This is true for wars, territorial encroachment and very real competition over scarce resources. In the case of Kara, the stakes of the struggle are the access to the Omo River and the fertile riverbanks. This is what they fight over with the Nyangatom, and this is part of the reason why their allies and friends, the Hamar and their massive cattle herds, inch closer and closer every year. It has now come to the point where the Kara feel beleaguered from all sides. *Ädamo*, in this predicament, is reflected in how Kara try to define these various relations by manipulating claims of distance and closeness. None of these social relations are entirely pre-given, but are instead subject to rhetorical manipulation. I have reported that the Kara emphatically deny any descent-based relations to the Hamar (which would make them *äda*), even as they by and large try to cultivate amiable relations with these neighbours who are culturally and linguistically so similar to them. Nothing would be more historically plausible than to assume that the Kara are simply an adventurous offshoot of the Hamar, and maybe they once were. Today, though, the Kara vociferously deny any such assumptions, which might be detrimental to their continued existence as an autonomous group.

The relation to the Nyangatom appears obverse: the Nyangatom are not particularly similar to the Kara in these respects and over the last few decades, the relationship has been marked more by conflict than by cooperation. Still, the Kara respect the Nyangatom and are fond of their culture and their language. They would want to live in peace with them. This is difficult today, so I designated the Nyangatom as a 'respected enemy'. In this context, *ädamo* emerges from of the will to get along, as the two groups apparently did better before the 1970s: a good number of my Kara age-mates have Nyangatom mothers or grandmothers. Finally, the Arbore and Dassanech are distinctly others in terms of language and culture, but somehow they are claimed to be the ancient true relatives of the Kara, *äda*, of one blood. I suggest that no matter what historical origins this notion might have had, it has to be interpreted as a situated rhetorical claim: by persistently emphasizing this descent today, it is much easier to deny the much more likely descent from the Hamar.

Thus, within the cultural neighbourhood, one can observe 'how they do it', how the Kara negotiate and construct their various relations. They never sever all ties of *ädamo* with any of their neighbours, but constantly assert their autonomy and display their agency precisely by denying kinship here (while cooperating economically), preserving amity there (even in the face of perpetual conflict) and invoking shared ancestry yet elsewhere (in a *prima facie* counterfactual manner). Stereotyping and mutual comparison are important aspects of this, as they help in lending the various populations a *gestalt*, a coherence and a (conditional) predictability, all of which are essential elements for narrating and imagining them as collective actors.

Finally, I explored how the Kara question their putative insignificance at the outmost periphery of the great nation of Ethiopia (see Chapters 8–9). *Ädamo* can hardly be identified as an aspect of group relations at this scale. The 'groups' involved are much too different for this – 1,400 Kara here and millions upon millions of Habesha there, this overarching category of people so strongly conflated with the state. But interaction takes place between individuals, and

Figure 10.1 The young men of the Ologuita age-set prepare for their initiation (October 2004). Photograph by Felix Girke.

even as this was the most asymmetric encounter, within this we can trace elements of *ädamo* in a very humanistic sense: the Kara recognize well that officials who are sent to the Lower Omo are also marginalized in relation to the centre. These administrators are supposed to represent the state and its power, but they in fact have very limited capabilities to enforce their policies and demands. This is what allows the Kara, in turn, to deny their own powerlessness in word and deed.

So while the Kara regularly react to these officials' claims and impositions with irony, a stance that constantly questions the final vocabularies of nationhood and development, they are not overly cynical or aggressive towards the respective individuals. Celebrating their own cleverness, the Kara are unflagging terms of in finding ways to sustain their self-esteem, and often succeed in seducing others to – inadvertently – confirm these claims. Their ironic posturing is pragmatic and tactical as much as aesthetic. As it undercuts grand narratives and subverts truth claims, it naturalizes the contingency of history and social categories and their relationship, and thus frees the individual – alongside their discursive community – to fashion themselves. This fashioning includes the capacity to establish *ädamo* according to one's own desires and needs, and many young Kara schoolboys seem set to take on the Ethiopian adventure on their own terms.

In summary, this is how the different differences and the links that they afford between the groups play out: the populations of the cultural neighbourhood pursue 'groupness' and autonomy. This enables them to maintain orderly relations, which in turn are based on the recognition that they all belong to a larger category of Shank'illa, a recognition that very strongly emerges from the way they talk to each other about each other. These relations are politically dissimilar from the metaphorical Othering of the Moguji, whose very existential status is ordained by the relationship between them and the true Kara. These relations are also dissimilar vis-à-vis the Kara's evasive and ironical take on the Habesha. Still, all these relations, even that to the Habesha, have an ethnic component in that people are divided into categories with assumed shared characteristics. In conclusion, the ethnic relations within the cultural neighbourhood provide a useful baseline for the understanding of other group relations. This is true for my analysis as well as for the Kara themselves. All the other dynamics I investigate can be insightfully described by assessing just how they diverge from this baseline. Ethnicity, then, is not a monothetic category, but much rather polythetic: every single one of its features is 'neither essential ... nor sufficient to define to allocate an item to a group' (Ellen 2006: 33). In Wittgenstein's terms, ethnicity is but a family resemblance of a wide range of different claims through which actors attempt to define the situation. Neither descent, nor cultural similarity, nor ritual practice, nor ontological equivalence – not one of these features is decisive for all of the cases I describe (compare Galaty 1982). But there is an ideal type for the inhabitants of South Omo, and that is the agentic, storytelling, bounded group, with a range of typical paradigmatic institutions, and much effort is invested in making these formations plausible and tangible by means of ethnic differentiation. Ethnicity serves as a means to maintain meaningful differences, which in turn are necessary for the maintenance of collectives: the protagonists of the region's meaning-generating narratives. Thus, ethnicity remains an essential aspect of the South Omo life-worlds, inextricable from everyday life, even as observation of everyday interactions reveals the rhetorical work necessary to translate this implicit understanding of different kinds of people into collective action and corporate identity. In political speech, ethnicity is a prime explanation and legitimation of action. People's conscious and often even articulate attempts to define situations reveal the different ways in which significance is established between social actors.[2]

The ways in which the different differences between the Kara and other stabilized collectives, between the various types of Kara, and between the Kara and the Habesha play out show a wide spectrum of rhetorical strategies that allow people to deal with difference and to generate difference, difference that seems necessary to actors because they have agreed (in a silent consensus) to see ethnicity as a natural feature of the world. The Wheel of Autonomy models this achievement of mutual significance (more on that below), even as the churning of the gears requires the establishment of others, others who do not get to have Wheels of their own. They are not allowed autonomous action, cannot tell their own story and are constrained to remain a category rather than aggregating in a polity.

The rallying cry 'We, the Shank'illa', occasionally heard today when representatives of South Omo polities come together in political meetings, is a segmentary response to the experiences first of conquest by the Ethiopian empire and to the subsequent confrontation with the facts of state encroachment and the increasing contact with the Habesha highlander. Cognitively, two classificatory processes can be diagnosed in this process: 'taxonomic particularizing' (Sapir 1977: 18), which focuses on the differences between the ethnic groups of South Omo, and 'taxonomic generalizing' (1977: 17), which substitutes genus for species, if you will, the category for its members. The latter, a pursuit in which both insiders and outsiders engage, subsumes all the groups of South Omo as 'these/we pastoralists' or 'Shank'illa'. This in turn supports the concomitant emergence of an emic region-wide ethnicization, an 'ethnic common sense' (Brubaker 2004: 9): both talking about one's neighbours with the aim of achieving distinction and talking with the aim of confirming analogy give sharper contours to the sense of a group-self, a collective with shared features and joint interests.

I mentioned earlier that I did not plan to return to the notion of 'tribe', but what is, the reader might well ask, the concrete difference between the 'politico-territorial groups' described here, whose central activity is in the assertion of their distinction and autonomy from other, similar groups, and earlier considered understandings of 'tribe'? As must be clear by now, in my understanding of the cultural neighbourhood, the polities of South Omo are not primordially 'given'. Even as individuals are born into categories and are socialized into a naturalized taxonomy of labels, the groups themselves are the product of people's efforts to band together, politically, to secure a certain ecological niche and to maintain by now distinct lifestyles. This has the side-effect that many of the populations discussed here are rather heterogeneous within – even if the Kara with their numerous subcategories are likely to be an extreme case. These are internally differentiated, politically organized groups that need rhetorical guidance to maintain any semblance of cohesion and coordination, and part of that guidance consists in the social fiction of ethnicized collectives that are on some level considered equivalent in their qualities, if different in the details. Therefore, it remains valid and helpful to use an expression such as 'Kara culture', especially in reference to people's experience, because there is simply so much knowledge along with connected practices that only matters (or is even understood) among people who self-identify as Kara. Cultural detail serves as a boundary marker, but as a contingent one: differences emphasized at one point might well be downplayed only a few years (or even a few meetings) later. The exact demarcation of boundaries is always fuzzy here; even people do drop in and drop out – but 'the Kara' go on in their constant ongoing differentiation from others. They go on, as I elaborated above, until either the ecological conditions that provide the shared base of the group change beyond recognition or internal differences arise that can no longer be reconciled. Either condition would force a change in narrative and a reduction in the Kara's ability to define their collective situation. This would likely lead to a looser sort of Kara ethnicity, less tightly constrained by ritual and categorical hierarchy, less tribal and better suited to a dispersing population trying to hold on to some sort of shared heritage. Then, the set of porcupines would change as well – and the maintenance of a relevant sense of being Kara would require finding new others to be rhetorically recognized as equals, both similar and different, and complimented by other others whom one could yet again dismiss as unworthy, dependent and not proud movers of a Wheel of Autonomy.

With this contingency of the boundary markers, the main function of ethnicity on the Lower Omo becomes apparent: talking in ethnic terms conjures up a world of actors and narratives into being that provide the fundamental incentive for individuals to think of themselves in terms of membership, of belonging to a distinct, coherent and autonomous group – and not any other.

I addressed the question of 'How do they do it?' by way of illustrating how the internal differences within Kara significantly contribute to a tangible experience of community. This has been recognized since Bateson's work on schismogenesis: differentiation can have centripetal effects, and even violent conflict can be diagnosed as having integrative effects on various levels, interpersonal as well as structural.[3] But despite the triumph of their community, Kara also lends itself to demonstrate the opposite, more expected outcome: how antagonistic talk, arguments or fights can be dysfunctional, as they put pressure on social faultlines that are only stable due to either immense rhetorical efforts or communal collusion in ignoring their very existence. Claims of and demands for *ädamo* can be used to great effect to shut down these dynamics, but a significant part of the appeal of *ädamo* as a strategic tool is the actors' awareness that dissolution and anomy are never far away. Conflict can do the work of integration, but it is also commonsensical that it does not always do that. What has interested me throughout regarding this empirical question is, as always, the emic perspective, people's reflection about how what they do (or do not do) impacts their communal project. Where do they see the dangers? How do they feel they can influence the state of affairs? When do they decide to rather not spin the Wheel of Autonomy quite as decisively as they could? The answers to these questions (and a good number were provided throughout this book) indicate the central concerns today current among Kara, which provide a baseline for future research.

Coda

Identity and distinction, corporate groups and social categories, stereotypes and interaction, performance and power, metaphors and ironies, agency and differentiation: this book has touched upon a good number of classical and still current anthropological subjects. The Wheel of Autonomy provided a useful heuristic to think these through, and clearly lends itself to wider adaptation and even modification. Crucially, it seeks to preserve the one lesson that fieldwork with the Kara has again and again driven home to me: the academic anthropologist is tasked with connecting their work with a larger corpus and history of thought, but their informants often think about the same issues without the same baggage. It still pays today to literally sit on the village square for a year and learn how people model their own worlds, how they compare, how they abstract, how they generalize and especially how they reflect their own practices. On the Lower Omo, where the Kara are surrounded by so many neighbours, there is ample source material for such reflections. In its simple triadic structure, the Wheel of Autonomy grew out of fieldnotes, and while there are no clear translations of 'autonomy', 'distinction' and 'agency' in the Kara language, the social circumstances these notions refer to are rather concrete issues for people. They regularly rear their conceptual heads in discussions public and private, and I find it evident that many Kara have considerable practical knowledge regarding the sociologically relevant dynamics found in their everyday lives.

This is especially true for the problem of the collective as an 'actor' that I have pursued here. Rather consistently, individual Kara seem to take the existence of the Kara and the Hamar and the Mursi for granted, but it is their way of talking about them and of acting as if they existed that supports the continuous existence of such entities. At times, though, I could witness actions and claims that revealed possibly underlying ethnosociological ideas and schemata for how groups work: that ethnicity must be policed, practically by controlling marriages and landholding, symbolically through prohibitions and a hierarchical ritual order that needs to be defended against challenges and always through maintaining distinctions. The 'autonomy' of the Wheel can be rendered as a kind of 'authority' as well: the authority to author narratives, to define the collective self rather than being defined by others – that perpetual state of deprivation that the Moguji seek to escape. In closing, I want to emphasize that the Wheel of Autonomy is not about ethnicity as such. Ethnicity surely can matter a great deal if it is the idiom through which distinction is pursued and the idiom in which the resulting autonomy of a population is rendered. The Wheel of Autonomy, though, really models how actors are generated in interaction – other actors as well as selves. It is a subjectivation engine, as it were, as it allows subjects to understand and speak of themselves and others. In mutuality or in contestation, people seek to stabilize patterns in their social world, patterns that aggregate, patterns that segregate, and patterns that remain in tension.

So 'how do they do it?' I started off with the question of how the Kara sustain themselves; this was a material matter, a question of geography and diplomacy. Along the way, I shifted towards the question how the Kara manage to be the Kara – a symbolic and affective and cognitive matter. But in the end, both questions have the same answer: the Kara manage to sustain themselves, to contend with the encroachments from all sides, by actively cultivating their sense of self and their relations with others, and by rhetorically manipulating closeness and distance. The very same processes are at work in the micro-situations I discuss, the social dramas through which faultlines become visible while contributing to the experience of Kara-ness at the same time. Their rhetorical efforts at identification, at narrating, at communicating with their audiences in the Omo Valley, and be it through ruthlessly defending their territory and reputation, were in effect their way of getting through the twentieth century.

The Kara are clearly not a collective actor in the sense that the collective acts just like an individual might, with a clear strategy of self-preservation and a monolithic sense of purpose, a hive mind with 3,000 arms and legs. I am also unable to probe this question in great historical depth – we simply have no strong data that can tell us about either 'the Kara' in – say – the eighteenth century or more generally what was going on in the place where Labuk, Dus and Korcho are now at that time (pending more and better archaeology). My analysis is strictly focused on the last few decades, but even so, it was possible to draw out some patterns in how ethnicity allows populations to regulate their interaction. Primarily, this comes back to the rhetorical creation of difference, to the rich and complex narrative delineation of 'Kara' and 'Hamar' that is so unproblematic in South Omo. People talk about the world in a way that makes 'the Kara' and 'the Hamar' protagonists or antagonists, and this helps members of these entities to keep imagining themselves collectively, more so than any distinct diacritical marker or 'cultural difference'. Throughout, I explored the various ways these stories come to be persuasive – or, where the persuasion is lacking, how they can be protected from contestation. Because if populations lose the wherewithal to talk themselves into being, by demonstrating to others that they need to be reckoned with, they step off as the main actors on the stage of the cultural neighbourhood and are relegated to bit parts. In that sense, I would identify as a main feature of a group its ability to speak – to itself, to others like it and to others quite unlike it. There is a wider point to be made here how nation-building in general effectively seeks to drown out a million voices in favour of one, and with the ongoing environmental and infrastructural transformations and destructions in the Omo Valley, it is not at all clear what the future will look like. But if the Kara can maintain or reclaim their subsistence production (at least to a degree), hold their territory (or at least some of it) and allow cultural change to occur on their own terms, they can keep telling stories and pride themselves on their cleverness and the reassuring sense that they are, in fact, autonomous.

Notes

1. Ritual depends on a ritual economy. That the Moguji at the margins of society, people who are economically deprived already, are symbolically denounced partly because they have no means to participate in this ritual economy seems unjust. But looking at modern Western societies, the practice of blaming victims of structural conditions for implied weaknesses or individual failure is surely quite common.
2. Already in the mid 1990s, Hermann Amborn discussed the case of the Burji in a way that contrasts starkly with the South Omo material. He states that while Helmut Straube in 1955 could plausibly speak of the Burji as a 'tribe', today many Burji think of their own ethnicity as rarely as (in a rather German simile) a church-taxpayer thinks of his or her religious affiliation – which is to say, not very much at all (1998: 349). He sees social change and dispersal of integrated settlements as the main causes for this loss of relevance.
3. This, of course, is the central hypothesis for the 'Integration and Conflict' Department of the MPI for Social Anthropology in Halle, led by Günther Schlee, out of which this very book series emerged.

Glossary of Non-English Terms

Abba	term of address and reference: 'my father'
Abba-pe	the land of my father
äda	kin, people in a relationship of significance and familiarity
ädamo	kinship, amity, positive relationships in general
ana	before, in the past
anza	girl, unmarried female in general
arti	sorcerer
asaabamo	term for cleverness (rare)
ashko	sorcery
atsi	teeth
baasal	mostly: the personalized calabash of a male elder
baiss	in-law, often used vaguely
ball'	(1) an open ground in a settlement used for council sessions or dancing; (2) the organizational division of Dus and Korcho into two vaguely separate factions (see Nyuwaya and Nyuwariya below)
bärgi-ed	'people of the rainy season', a cohort of men during their initiation towards marriage
bärgitamo	the period of initiation towards marriage
bariyo	blessing, wellbeing, creator, also Christian god
baski	partnership between a widow and a man, as a rule economic as well as sexual/reproductive
bel	term of address and reference: 'bondfriend'
beltamo, belmo	Kara and Moguji terms respectively for 'bondfriendship'
benta	grains kept safe for seeding in the next year

bersha	male adolescent, usually unmarried
bittamo	being spiritually in charge of land, people or ritual
bitti	spiritual leader of the country, often metaphorically used for other leadership positions
borkotto	stool and headrest (see *kara borkotto*, *yedda borkotto*)
borkotto bitti	council of spokesmen and political leaders
bunno	coffee, in Kara usually brewed out of coffee husks rather than beans
chaachi	'roots', a kin relation indicating marriageability
chip	ideophone indicating being crowded in (see *ənch*)
choki	an illness, a disease
dägamo	laziness
d'ebbi	(somebody who is) indebted, mostly for a violation of conduct rules vis-à-vis kin or age-mates
d'ebbamo	a morally-laden debt, usually purged through sacrificing small stock or another payment
doya	scout
duriye	(Amharic) rascal, ne'er-do-well, petty criminal (usually in an urban context)
edi	'people', sometimes in the sense of 'socially relevant people'
eh-e!	expression of assent ('yes, you are right/I feel you')
ənch	ideophone indicating being crowded in (see *chip*)
gaggi	dug-out canoe, by extension other watercraft
gaita-märsha	annual ritual for blessing digging tools
galmar	(Oromo) see *marmar*
garro-delak	aggravating and trouble-inducing talk
gebbar	(Amharic) serfdom in the context of the conquest
gemeri-ed	'the mountain people', i.e. the Hamar, Banna and Bashada
gilo	ritual, in extension sometimes 'habitual custom' or even 'personal habit'
gilo-ed	'ritual-person', i.e. somebody who is tasked to perform a ritual
gind'o	mythical sleeping sickness that decimated the Kara in the past
gubai	(from Amharic) meeting, council session
hariya	term of reference and address: 'age-mate', also used by women towards their husbands' age-mates
hizb	(Amharic) population at large
imba	father, often used metaphorically for owner or prime specimen
irsha	irrigation, usually referring to a specific site outside of Dus
ishemo	elder brother, often used for the (directly) senior age-set
jumpa	people from the Ethiopian highlands (generic form)
k'aissamo	serfdom, in general the duty to perform dependent and low-status activities for somebody else

k'aiss	taboo
k'aissi	slaves, servants, often used mockingly
k'ambi	'gathered-up one', i.e. orphan
k'andi	specific notches cut into the ears of goats and other livestock to indicate ownership by a person belonging to a specific subsection of a clan
kantsi	instigation, often in reference to warfare
kantsi-ed	instigator, somebody who makes two other people fight
kabin	(from Amharic) members of the government-sanctioned community council (see *kebele*)
kaido	annual ritual to inaugurate the sorghum harvest; in line of seniority, household heads within one lineage have to chew and spit out some sorghum kernels
kanna	younger brother, often used for the (directly) junior age-set
kara borkotto	stool and headrest for adult males with one solid foot, only to be used by members of an initiated age-set
katama	(Amharic) 'the city'
kau	bush, forest, occasionally used metaphorically
kebele	(Amharic) originally 'peasant association', today the smallest administrative unit
kelta	highly costly ritual performed before a wife who was born as an eldest daughter can become pregnant
kogo	grandfather
kogo-ed	ritual fire-maker who once a year kindles a new flame that is carried from house to house to light the hearths
kogo-nana	a man's classificatory granddaughters who are the furthest degree of kinship that is not marriageable; this relation entails joking behaviour
kumbassa	a ritually nonsanctioned pregnancy that demands termination or infanticide; numerous reasons can make a pregnancy *kumbassa*
lematt	(Amharic) development
maassi	'blood', sometimes refers to the spoilt relationship between the lineage of a killer and that of his victim
mahaber	(from Amharic) a cooperative that pools money for collective purposes
malgimi	weak, scrawny
malgintamo	weakness (of body and purpose)
maltamo	mischievous cleverness
malti	mischievously clever
marmar	the elder's ritual house, a massive wooden structure located in Dus (see also *galmar*)

mengist	(from Amharic) 'the government', often used in reference to any or all state institutions, bureaucracy, repressive apparatus
mingi	ritual uncleanness in general; often used similarly to *kumbassa*, even though there are specific differences
mirt	celebratory ritual for a killer of big game or people; usually entails the slaughter of livestock, feasting and a praise song, among other elements
moro	(1) lineage; (2) the area of a settlement
motalla	a go-between or mediator, used for many negotiations and rites of passage
muutsi	salty soil gathered on the western bank of the Omo River near Mt. Lokulan, valued as a source of salt for livestock
nechauleh	a demand from Nyangatom-Kara fathers (and their age-mates) to receive a punitive payment from men who impregnate their daughters
neftenya	Amharic/highlander soldier-settlers who occupied the Ethiopian South in the wake of Menelik II's conquest
oida	'to be hot', to be popular
olo	clan
osh	deliberative meeting of male elders, usually connected with a meat feast
parsho	alcoholic gruel brewed from sorghum, also beer
paxala	clever
paxalmamo	cleverness
pe	land, territory, home
pehssa ashka	'fixing of the land', i.e. settling problems
rukunti	'guts', kin, i.e. people underlying the incest taboo
saxa-pe	'land of tomorrow', i.e. the future
selli	a white pigment made from clay, often used to decorate the skin for a party, dance or ritual; a part of a new age-set's initiation is known as 'buying the *selli*'
sherka	calabash
siamo	'badness', a problem, a current concern demanding resolution
sudima	deception
sugsug	spear shaft, probably from the *sugai* tree
sünn-ed	'just there person', a man of no consequence
terbi	the only drum in Kara, used once a year in a ritual
woh	edible green leaves growing near the riverside fields
woreda	(Amharic) a district comprising several *kebele*
yedda	to take hold of; also a euphemism for 'rape'
yedda borkotto	simple three-legged stool cut from a bush with curved branches; can be used by anybody

yekinta	regular ritual performed by two spouses and the husband's mother that legitimates a pregnancy
yeti	particularly close personal friend
yihr-ed	'person of significance', i.e. somebody whose eldest son has married
zersi	(1) the elders; (2) the population at large
zonza	an elder, technically a married man

Glossary of Places and People

Aari	a largely agriculturalist population living in the hill areas northeast of Kara, around the zonal capital Jinka
Aiba	a Nyangatom settlement area on the western bank of the Omo River; also 'Aeba'
Arbore	a population living near in the Woyto Valley north of Chew Bahir, claimed by the Kara as ancient kin; also 'Hoor'
Atula	a Kara term for the Banna
Banna	a population in the hill ranges northeast of Kara, part of the Hamar-Banna-Bashada (HBB) cluster
Banno	a Kara term for the Bashada
Bashada	a population in the hill ranges east of Kara, part of the Hamar-Banna-Bashada (HBB) cluster
Bitolo	a small Kara clan
Bogudo	a very small ethnic subsection of the Kara, with two distinct branches in the north (Labuk) and south (Korcho); especially in the South, the Bogudo hold large tracts of fields
Bume	exonym for the Nyangatom
Chelläte	small village between Dus and Korcho; for the farming season, several families move from Dus to Chelläte as their riverbank fields are conveniently accessed from there; 'home' of the ethnographer
Dangarr	a small Kara clan that provides the *bitti* for Dus; it forms an exogamous unit with Garshima and Eshiba

Glossary of Places and People 267

Dassanech	a large population in and around the Omo River delta, claimed by the Kara as ancient kin
Derg	(Amharic) colloquial term for the military regime that ruled Ethiopia from 1974 to 1991
Diba (also Lake Diba)	a large depression south of Korcho that is occasionally flooded by the Omo River and provides opportunities for agriculture as the water evaporates
Dimeka	a small market town between Hamar and Banna with a regular market and schools; centre of the Hamar district
Dingolo	a small Kara clan, often grouped together with Ongosula
Dirtta	a small Kara clan
Doro	an area on the western bank of the Omo River
Dus	the largest and ritually most important Kara village
Duyu	a section of the Moguji, seen as descendants of the aboriginal inhabitants of the Omo Valley; mostly located today in the area around Kuchur
Eshiba	a Kara clan that forms an exogamous unit with Garshima and Dangarr
Ferenj (also Parang)	European, foreigner, white person
Galeba	exonym for the Dassanech
Galgidda	an area on the western bank of the Omo River
Gamo-Gofa	old name for an administrative district roughly equivalent to South Omo
Garchi	(1) a population decimated by the inhabitants of Dus, likely in the early twentieth century; only a few Garchi lineages are counted among the 'true Kara'; (2) the name of a largely uninhabited stretch of land between Dus and Labuk
Garshima	a large Kara clan that forms an exogamous unit with Eshiba and Dangarr
Gomba	an ethnic subsection of the Kara, nearly exclusively in Labuk
Gorrente	stretch of fields along the riverside, close to Chelläte
Gorsbolo	a large Kara clan; clan of the ethnographer
Gurdo	a small village similar to and a little north of Chelläte
Habesha	(Amharic) term used in Kara to refer to all 'highlanders', forms a semantic dyad with Shank'illa
Hamar	a large population in the hill ranges southeast of Kara, part of the Hamar-Banna-Bashada (HBB) cluster
Ihaddik	(Amharic) colloquial term for the party that has ruled Ethiopia since 1991 (EPRDF)

Jinka	capital of the South Omo zone, site of the South Omo Museum and Research Centre
Kadokochin	an important area on the western bank of the Omo River, formerly the site of a major Kara settlement
Kangaten	administrative centre of the Nyangatom district
Kara	a small population on the eastern banks of the Omo River; main focus of this book
Karo	exonym for the Kara
Kibish	also 'Nakwa', a settlement and region west of Kara towards the Kenyan and South Sudanese borders
Kizo	a deep wadi between Hamar and Kara
Koegu	alternative spelling of Kwegu
Kogo	a Kara clan
Konso	a large population to the East of South Omo, mostly characterized as labourers
Kopriya	an area on the western bank of the Omo River
Korcho	the southernmost village of Kara above Lake Diba
Kuchur	a village inhabited by the Moguji, northwest of Labuk
Kundamma	name of a wooded area due west of Dus around which the Omo River loops; site of the *irsha* and a massacre of the Kara by the Nyangatom
Kwegu	alternative name for the Moguji, especially among the Mursi
Labuk	northernmost village of Kara
Lapa	an area on the western bank of the Omo River
Lokulan	a hill with hot springs on the western bank of the Omo River, across from the *irsha*; source of *muutsi*; allegedly home of spirits
Lorianta	a Kara age-set, three levels junior to that of the ethnographer
Loxode	an area on the western bank of the Omo River
Maale	a population far northeast of Kara
Mago River	a waterway feeding into the Omo River just north of Kara; lends its name to the 'Mago National Park'
Moguji	an ethnic subsection of the Kara, and the mythical first-comers to the Omo Valley (see Duyu); often derided as hunter-gatherers, fishermen, and bad agriculturalists; some members seek greater autonomy either among the Nyangatom or by reclaiming territory acquired by the Kara (see Worba)
Muguji	alternative spelling of 'Moguji'
Muina	dismissive variation of 'Moguji'

Glossary of Places and People 269

Mursi	a population northwest of Kara, with the self-designation 'Mun'
Murle	also 'Omo Murle'; a formerly autonomous population that was probably decimated during the nineteenth century and now forms a section of the Nyangatom
Murule	a privately owned safari lodge south of Lake Diba; also 'Naumur'
Nakwa	see Kibish
Nacheput	a small village similar to and a little south of Chelläte; was abandoned at some point around 2007/8
Nokere	also 'Nokure', a wide savannah between Hamar and Kara (see Kizo), marked by high termite mounds
Numurtuin	mythical 'forest Mursi' who migrated through the Omo Valley
Nyangatom	a large population west of the Omo River with a complex relationship to the Kara
Nyichekapus	a Kara age-set; one level senior to that of the ethnographer
Nyikuamong	a Kara age-set; two levels senior to that of the ethnographer
Nyinyankot	a Kara age-set; one level junior to that of the ethnographer
Nyiramalai	a Kara age-set; age-set of the ethnographer
Nyuwaya	(1) an age-set active in the early twentieth century; (2) one of the two *ball'* of Dus (see Nyuwariya)
Nyuwariya	(1) an age-set active in the early twentieth century; (2) one of the two *ball'* of Dus (see Nyuwaya)
Ologuita	a Kara age-set; two levels junior to that of the ethnographer
Omo Rate	town on the Omo River south of Kara in Dassanech territory
Omo River	here mostly in reference to the lowest stretch of the river before it flows into Lake Turkana; the major perennial river in the region, with a distinct seasonal change in level
Ongosula	a Kara clan, often grouped together with Dingolo
Shank'illa	formerly an epithet referring to the 'black' inhabitants of the Ethiopian lowlands; forms a semantic dyad with Habesha
South Omo zone	an administrative unit of the SNNPRS (Southern Nations, Nationalities and Peoples' Regional State); includes settlement areas of many ethnically differentiated populations
Suri (also Surma)	a population northwest of Kara, with many similarities to the Mursi
Tsamai	a population in the Woyto Valley north of Arbore
Turmi	a small market town in Hamar, due south of Dimeka; the beginning of the road to Kara

Worba	a section of the Moguji, not seen as the descendants of the autochthonous inhabitants of the Omo Valley
Woyto (also Weyto)	a river bordering Maale territory in the North and then flowing southwards through Tsamai and Arbore, east of the Hamar hills

References

Abbink, J. 2002. 'Paradoxes of Power and Culture in an Old Periphery: Surma, 1974–98', in W. James, D.L. Donham, E. Kurimoto and A. Triulzi (eds), *Remapping Ethiopia: Socialism and After*. Oxford: James Currey, pp. 155–72.
———. 2006. 'Ethnicity and Conflict Generation in Ethiopia: Some Problems and Prospects of Ethno-Regional Federalism', *Journal of Contemporary African Studies* 24(3): 389–413.
———. 2015. 'Extensions of the Self: Artistry and Identity in the Headrests and Stools of Southwest Ethiopian Peoples', *African Arts* 48(4): 46–59.
Abbink, J., C. Ybarra, D.L. Donham, T. Woldemikael and J. Woldemikael. 2004. 'Obituary: Alexander Naty', *Anthropology Newsletter (AAA)*, February, 24–40 (shorter version in *Ethiopian Journal of Social Sciences and Humanities* 2(1): 89.
Albert, E. 1964. '"Rhetoric", "Logic", and "Poetics" in Burundi: Culture Patterning of Speech Behavior', *American Anthropologist* N.S. 6(2): 35–54.
Almagor, U. 1978. *Pastoral Partners: Affinity and Bond Partnership among the Dassanech of Southwest Ethiopia*. Manchester: Manchester University Press.
———. 2002 [1986]. 'Institutionalizing a Fringe Periphery: Dassanetch-Amhara Relations', in D.L. Donham and W. James (eds), *The Southern Marches of Imperial Ethiopia: Essays in History and Social Anthropology*. Oxford: James Currey, pp. 96–115.
Alvarsson, J.-Å. 1989. *Starvation and Peace or Food and War? Aspects of Armed Conflict in the Lower Omo Valley*. Uppsala Research Reports in Cultural Anthropology, vol. 8.
Amborn, H. 1990. *Differenzierung und Integration: vergleichende Untersuchungen zu Spezialisten und Handwerkern in südäthiopischen Agrargesellschaften*. Munich: Trickster.
———. 1998. 'Die zerfranste Ethnie: Zum analytischen Umgang mit komplexen Gesellschaften', *Anthropos* 93(4/6): 349–61.
Anderson, B. 1983. *Imagined Communities: Reflections on the Origin and Spread of Nationalism*. New York: Verso.
Appadurai, A. 1995. 'The Production of Locality', in R. Fardon (ed.), *Counterworks: Managing the Diversity of Knowledge*. New York: Routledge, pp. 204–25.
Asmarom Legesse. 1973. *Gada: Three Approaches to the Study of African Society*. New York: The Free Press.

Ayalew Gebre. 1995. *The Arbore of Southern Ethiopia: A Study of Inter-ethnic Relations, Social Organization and Production Practices.* Addis Ababa: Addis Ababa University Press.

Bailey, F.G. 1960. *Tribe, Caste, and Nation.* Manchester: Manchester University Press.

———. 1969. *Stratagems and Spoils: A Social Anthropology of Politics.* Oxford: Blackwell.

———. 1973. *Debate and Compromise: The Politics of Innovation.* Oxford: Blackwell.

———. 1977. 'The Definition of Factionalism', in M. Silverman and R.F. Salisbury (eds), *A House Divided? Anthropological Studies of Factionalism.* Toronto: University of Toronto Press, pp. 21–36.

———. 1978. 'Tertius Gaudens aut Tertius Numen', in F. Barth (ed.), *Scale and Social Organization.* Oslo: Universitetsforlaget, pp. 194–214.

———. 1983. *The Tactical Uses of Passion: An Essay on Power, Reason, and Reality.* Ithaca, NY: Cornell University Press.

———. 2003. *The Saving Lie: Truth and Method in the Social Sciences.* Philadelphia, PA: University of Pennsylvania Press.

———. 2009. 'The Palaestral Aspect of Rhetoric', in M. Carrithers (ed.), *Culture, Rhetoric and the Vicissitudes of Life: Studies in Rhetoric and Culture*, vol. 2. New York: Berghahn Books, pp. 107–20.

Barth, F. 1969. 'Introduction', in F. Barth (ed.), *Ethnic Groups and Boundaries: The Social Organization of Culture Difference.* Oslo: Universitetsforlaget, pp. 9–38.

———. 2000. 'Boundaries and Connections', in A.P. Cohen (ed.), *Signifying Identities: Anthropological Perspectives on Boundaries and Contested Values.* London: Routledge, pp. 15–36.

Bassi, M. 2011. 'Primary Identities in the Lower Omo Valley: Migration, Cataclysm, Conflict and Amalgamation, 1750–1910', *Journal of Eastern African Studies* 5(1): 129–57.

Bateson, G. 2000 [1972]. *Steps to an Ecology of Mind*, with a new introduction by M.C. Bateson. Chicago, IL: University of Chicago Press.

Bauman, R., and C.L. Briggs. 1990. 'Poetics and Performance as Critical Perspectives on Language and Social Life', *Annual Review of Anthropology* 19: 59–88.

Beidelman, T.O. 1964. 'Intertribal Insult and Opprobrium in an East African Chiefdom', *Anthropological Quarterly* 37(2): 33–52.

———. 1980. 'The Moral Imagination of the Kaguru: Some Thoughts on Tricksters, Translation and Comparative Analysis', *American Ethnologist* 7(1): 27–42.

———. 1989. 'Agonistic Exchange: Homeric Reciprocity and the Heritage of Simmel and Mauss', *Cultural Anthropology* 4(3): 227–59.

Benjamin, G. 2002. 'On Being Tribal in the Malay World', in G. Benjamin and C. Chou (eds), *Tribal Communities in the Malay World: Historical, Cultural and Social Perspectives.* Singapore: ISEAS/IIAS, pp. 7–76.

Berntsen, J.L. 1976. 'The Maasai and their Neighbours: Variables of Interaction', *African Economic History* 2: 1–11.

Beyer, J., and F. Girke. 2015. 'Practicing Harmony Ideology: Ethnographic Reflections on Community and Coercion', *Common Knowledge* 21(2), Symposium 'Peace by Other Means, Part 3': 196–235.

Blok, A. 1998. 'The Narcissism of Minor Differences', *European Journal of Social Theory* 1(1): 33–56.

———. 2000. 'Relatives and Rivals: The Narcissism of Minor Differences', in H. Driessen and T. Otto (eds), *Perplexities of Identification: Anthropological Studies in Cultural Differentiation and the Use of Resources.* Aarhus: Aarhus University Press, pp. 27–55.

Boddy, J. 2004. 'Barbaric Custom and Colonial Science: Teaching the Female Body in the Anglo-Egyptian Sudan', in M. Lambek and P. Antze (eds), *Illness and Irony: On the Ambiguity of Suffering in Culture*. New York: Berghahn Books, pp. 60–81.

Boon, J.A. 2001. 'Kenneth Burke's "True Irony": One Model for Ethnography, Still', in J.W. Fernandez and M.T. Huber (eds), *Irony in Action: Anthropology, Practice, and the Moral Imagination*. Chicago, IL: University of Chicago Press, pp. 118–32.

Bourdieu, P. 1984. *Distinction: A Social Critique of the Judgment of Taste*. Cambridge, MA: Harvard University Press.

———. 1991. *Language and Symbolic Power*. Cambridge, MA: Harvard University Press.

Brandstetter, A.-M. 2006. 'Anthropological Approaches to the Study of Cultural Contact: A Short Overview', in I. Strecker and J. Lydall (eds), *The Perils of Face: Essays on Cultural Contact, Respect and Self-Esteem in Southern Ethiopia*. Berlin: Lit, pp. 19–35.

Brandstetter, A.-M., I. Strecker, S. Epple and C. Meyer. 2004. 'Zur rhetorischen Analyse von Kulturkontakt: Eine ethnologische Perspektive', in W. Bisang et al. (eds), *Kultur, Sprache, Kontakt. Kulturelle und sprachliche Kontakte*, vol. 1. Würzburg: Ergon, pp. 83–120.

Broch-Due, V., and D.M. Anderson. 1999. 'Poverty and the Pastoralist: Deconstructing Myths, Reconstructing Realities', in V. Broch-Due and D.M. Anderson (eds), *The Poor Are Not Us: Poverty and Pastoralism in Eastern Africa*. Oxford: James Currey, pp. 3–19.

Brown, D.J.J. 1983. 'The Kwegu' (letter), *RAIN* 55: 12.

Brown, K. 1999. 'Marginal Narratives and Shifty Natives: Ironic Ethnography as Anti-Nationalist Discourse', *Anthropology Today* 15(1): 13–16.

Brown, P.[aula] 1964. 'Enemies and Affines', *Ethnology* 3(4): 335–56.

Brown, P.[envelope], and S. Levinson. 1987. *Politeness: Some Universals in Language Use*. Cambridge: Cambridge University Press.

Brubaker, R. 2004. *Ethnicity without Groups*. Cambridge, MA: Harvard University Press.

Brubaker, R., M. Loveman and P. Statmatov. 2004. 'Ethnicity as Cognition', *Theory and Society* 33(1): 31–64.

Brüderlin, T. 2005. 'The Incorporation of Children into the Society: Pre- and Postnatal Rituals among the Hamar of Southern Ethiopia', MA thesis. Mainz: Faculty of Social Sciences, Johannes Gutenberg-University.

Bulatovich, A. 2000. *Ethiopia through Russian Eyes: Country in Transition 1896–1898*, trans. and ed. R. Seltzer. Lawrenceville: Red Sea Press.

Burke, K. 1945. *A Grammar of Motives*. Berkeley, CA: University of California Press.

Callon, M. 1986. 'Some Elements of a Sociology of Translation: Domestication of the Scallops and the Fishermen of St Brieuc Bay', in J. Law (ed.), *Power, Action and Belief: A New Sociology of Knowledge?* London: Routledge & Kegan Paul, pp. 196–233.

Capurro, R. 1990. 'Ironie. Begriffsgeschichtliche Erörterung einer menschlichen Grundstimmung', unpublished manuscript. Retrieved 12 February 2018 from http://www.capurro.de/ironie.html.

Carlson, M. 1996. *Performance: A Critical Introduction*. New York: Routledge.

Carrithers, M. 1992. *Why Humans Have Cultures: Explaining Anthropology and Social Diversity*. Oxford: Oxford University Press.

———. 2005a. 'Why Anthropologists Should Study Rhetoric', *Journal of the Royal Anthropological Institute* (N.S.) 11: 577–83.

———. 2005b. 'Rhetoric? Culture? Rhetoric Culture! A Report', *Durham Anthropological Journal* 13(2). Retrieved 12 February 2018 from http://www.dur.ac.uk/anthropology.journal/vol13/iss2/index.html.

Carrithers, M., L.J. Bracken and S. Emery 2011. 'Can a Species Be a Person? A Trope and its Entanglements in the Anthropocene Era', *Current Anthropology* 52(5): 661–85.
Cerulli, E. 1956. *Peoples of South-West Ethiopia and its Borderlands*. London: International African Institute.
Chock, P.P. 1987. 'The Irony of Stereotypes: Toward an Anthropology of Ethnicity', *Cultural Anthropology* 2(3): 347–68.
Clifford, James 1986. 'Introduction: Partial Truths', in J. Clifford and G. Marcus (eds), *Writing Culture: The Poetics and Politics of Ethnography*. Berkeley, CA: University of California Press, pp. 1–26.
Cohen, A.P. 1985. *The Symbolic Construction of Community*. London: Tavistock.
———. 2000. 'Introduction. Discriminating Relations: Identity, Boundary and Authenticity', in A.P. Cohen (ed.), *Signifying Identities: Anthropological Perspectives on Boundaries and Contested Values*. New York: Routledge, pp. 1–13.
Colby, B.N., J.W. Fernandez and D.B. Kronenfeld. 1981. 'Toward a Convergence of Cognitive and Symbolic Anthropology', *American Ethnologist* 8(3): 422–50.
Colson, E. 1974. *Tradition and Contract: The Problem of Order*. Chicago, IL: Aldine.
De Certeau, M. 1984. *The Practice of Everyday Life*. Berkeley, CA: University of California Press.
Degu Tadie, and A. Fischer. 2013. 'Hunting, Social Structure and Human–Nature Relationships in Lower Omo, Ethiopia: People and Wildlife at a Crossroads', *Human Ecology* 41: 447–57.
Dereje Feyissa. 2009. 'The Ethnic Self and the National Other: Anywaa Identity Politics in Reference to the Ethiopian State System', in Bahru Zewde (ed.), *Society, State and Identity in African History*. Addis Ababa: Forum for Social Studies, pp. 123–153.
———. 2011. *Playing Different Games: The Paradox of Anywaa and Nuer Identification Strategies in the Gambella Region, Ethiopia*. New York: Berghahn Books.
Detienne, M., and J.-P. Vernant 1978. *Cunning Intelligence in Greek Culture and Society*. Brighton: Harvester Press.
Distefano, J.A. 1990. 'Hunters or Hunted? Towards a History of the Okiek of Kenya', *History in Africa* 17: 41–57.
Donham, D.L. 2000. 'On Being "First": Making History by Two's in Southern Ethiopia', in J. Abbink (ed.), *Cultural Variation and Social Change in Southern Ethiopia: Comparative Approaches. Northeast African Studies* (N.S.) 7(3): 21–34.
———. 2002a [1986]. 'Old Abyssinia and the New Ethiopian Empire: Themes in Social History', in D.L. Donham and Wendy James (eds), *The Southern Marches of Imperial Ethiopia: Essays in History and Social Anthropology*. Oxford: James Currey, pp. 3–48.
———. 2002b. 'Looking Back on the Projects of the Socialist State, 1974–91', in W. James, D.L. Donham, E. Kurimoto and A. Triulzi (eds), *Remapping Ethiopia: Socialism and After*. Oxford: James Currey, pp. 33–36.
Ellen, R. 2006. *The Categorical Impulse: Essays in the Anthropology of Classifying Behaviour*. New York: Berghahn Books.
Epple, S. 2003. 'Bäšada', in S. Uhlig (ed.), *Encyclopedia Aethiopica*, vol. III. Wiesbaden: Harassowitz, pp. 490–92.
———. 2007. 'Ritual und Rollendifferenzierung bei den Bashada in Südäthiopien', Ph.D. dissertation. Mainz: Faculty of Social Sciences, Johannes Gutenberg-University.
Eriksen, T.H. 1991. 'The Cultural Contexts of Ethnic Differences', *Man* (N.S.) 26(1): 127–44.
———. 2001 [1995]. *Small Places, Large Issues: An Introduction to Social and Cultural Anthropology*. London: Pluto Press.

Escherich, G. 1921. *Im Lande des Negus*. Berlin: Georg Stilke.
Evans-Pritchard, E.E. 1940. *The Nuer: A Description of the Modes of Livelihood and Political Institutions of a Nilotic People*. Oxford: Clarendon.
Ferguson, R.B., and N.L. Whitehead (eds). 2000. *War in the Tribal Zone: Expanding States and Indigenous Warfare*. Santa Fe, NM: School of American Research Press.
Fernandez, J.W. 1977. 'The Performance of Ritual Metaphors', in J.D. Sapir and J.C. Crocker (eds), *The Social Use of Metaphor: Essays on the Anthropology of Rhetoric*. Philadelphia, PA: University of Pennsylvania Press, pp. 100–31.
———. 1986. *Persuasions and Performances: The Play of Tropes in Culture*. Bloomington, IN: Indiana University Press.
———. 2001. 'The Irony of Complicity and the Complicity of Irony in Development Discourse', in J.W. Fernandez and M.T. Huber (eds), *Irony in Action: Anthropology, Practice, and the Moral Imagination*. Chicago, IL: University of Chicago Press, pp. 84–102.
Fernandez, J.W., and M.T. Huber (eds). 2001. 'Introduction: The Anthropology of Irony', in J.W. Fernandez and M.T. Huber (eds), *Irony in Action: Anthropology, Practice, and the Moral Imagination*. Chicago, IL: University of Chicago Press, pp. 1–37.
Ford, C.M., and red. 2003. 'Aari Ethnography', in S. Uhlig (ed.), *Encyclopedia Aethiopica*. Wiesbaden: Harassowitz, pp. 2–3.
Fortes, M. 1969. *Kinship and the Social Order: The Legacy of Lewis Henry Morgan*. London: Routledge & Kegan Paul.
Fortes, M., and E.E. Evans-Pritchard (eds). 1940. *African Political Systems*. Oxford: Oxford University Press.
Freeman, D., and A. Pankhurst. 2003. *Peripheral People: The Excluded Minorities of Ethiopia*. London: Hurst.
Fried, M. 1975. *The Notion of Tribe*. Menlo Park, CA: Cummings.
Friedman, J. 1992. 'The Past in the Future: History and the Politics of Identity', *American Anthropologist* 94(4): 837–59.
Friedrich, P. 1989. 'Language, Ideology, and Political Economy', *American Anthropologist* N.S. 91(2): 295–312.
———. 2001. 'Ironic Irony', in J.W. Fernandez and M.T. Huber (eds), *Irony in Action: Anthropology, Practice, and the Moral Imagination*. Chicago, IL: University of Chicago Press, pp. 224–52.
Gabbert, E.C. 2010. 'Introduction', in E.C. Gabbert and S. Thubauville (eds), *To Live with Others: Essays on Cultural Neighborhood in Southern Ethiopia*. Cologne: Rüdiger Köppe, pp. 13–28.
———. 2012. 'Deciding Peace: Knowledge about War and Peace among the Arbore of Southern Ethiopia', PhD thesis. Halle/Saale: Martin Luther University Halle-Wittenberg.
———. 2014. 'Songs of Self and Others in Times of Rapid Change: Music as Identification among the Arbore of Southern Ethiopia', in F. Girke (ed.), *Ethiopian Images of Self and Other*. Halle: Universitätsverlag Halle-Wittenberg, pp. 105–20.
Gabbert, E.C., and S. Thubauville (eds). 2010. *To Live with Others: Essays on Cultural Neighborhood in Southern Ethiopia*. Cologne: Rüdiger Köppe.
Galaty, J.G. 1982. 'Being "Maasai"; Being "People-of-Cattle": Ethnic Shifters in East Africa', *American Ethnologist* 9(1): 1–20.
Gezahegn Petros. 1994. 'The Karo of the Lower Omo Valley: Subsistence, Social Organization and Relations with Neighbouring Groups', MA thesis. Addis Ababa: Addis Ababa University.
Girard, R. 1977. *Violence and the Sacred*. Baltimore, MD: Johns Hopkins University Press.

Girke, F. 2002. 'Die theoretischen Entwicklungen im Werk von FG Bailey: Handlung, Politik und Rhetorik', *Working Paper of the Department Anthropology and African Studies* No. 8. Mainz: Johannes Gutenberg University.

———. 2006. 'Respect and Humiliation: Two "First Contact" Situations in Southern Ethiopia', in I. Strecker and J. Lydall (eds), *The Perils of Face: Essays on Cultural Contact, Respect and Self-Esteem in Southern Ethiopia.* Berlin: Lit, pp. 109–49.

———. 2008. 'The Kara-Nyangatom War of 2006-07: Dynamics of Escalating Violence in the Tribal Zone', in E.-M. Bruchhaus and M.E. Sommer (eds), *Hot Spot Horn of Africa Revisited: Approaches to Make Sense of Conflict.* Berlin: Lit, pp. 192–207.

———. 2010. 'Bondfriendship in the Cultural Neighborhood. Dyadic Ties and Their Public Appreciation in South Omo', in E.C. Gabbert and S. Thubauville (eds), *To Live with Others: Essays on Cultural Neighborhood in Southern Ethiopia.* Cologne: Rüdiger Köppe, pp. 68–98.

———. 2011. 'Plato on the Omo: Reflections on Decision-Making among the Kara of Southern Ethiopia', *Journal of Eastern African Studies* 5(1): 177–94.

———. 2013. 'Homeland, Boundary, Resource: The Collision of Place-Making Projects on the Lower Omo River, Ethiopia', *Max Planck Institute for Social Anthropology Working Paper* No. 148. Halle/Saale.

———. 2014a. 'Ethiopian Images of Self and Other: Essays on Identification and Stereotype', in F. Girke (ed.), *Ethiopian Images of Self and Other.* Halle: Universitätsverlag Halle-Wittenberg, pp. 11–31.

———. 2014b. 'Metaphors of the Moguji: Self-Defining Othering in Kara Political Speech', in F. Girke (ed.), *Ethiopian Images of Self and Other.* Halle: Universitätsverlag Halle-Wittenberg, pp. 147–69.

———. 2015. 'The Uncertainty of Power and the Certainty of Irony: Encountering the State in Kara, Southern Ethiopia', in R. Hariman and R. Cintron (eds), *Culture, Catastrophe, and Rhetoric: The Texture of Political Action. Studies in Rhetoric and Culture*, vol. 7. New York: Berghahn Books, pp. 168–93.

———. 2018. 'The Triangle of Orality: On Language, Culture, and Fieldwork in South Omo', *Aethiopica* Special Issue "Oral Traditions in Ethiopian Studies", ed. by A. Meckelburg, D. Bustorf and S. Dege. Wiesbaden: Harassowitz, pp. 267–92.

———. forthc.a. 'Ethnisieren als Praxis', in C. Meyer, E. Schüttpelz and M. Zillinger (eds), *Anthropologie der Praxis.* Stuttgart: Metzler.

———. forthc.b. 'Establishing Ethos: The Rhetorical Work of Bondfriendship', in J. Abbink and S. LaTosky (eds), *Rhetorics and Social Relations: Studies in Rhetoric and Culture*, vol. 8. New York: Berghahn Books.

Girke, F., and S. Köhn. 2007. *Morokapel's Feast: The Story of a Kara Hunting Ritual*, film. Göttingen: IVE.

Girke, F., and C. Meyer. 2011. 'Introduction', in C. Meyer and F. Girke (eds.), *The Rhetorical Emergence of Culture: Studies in Rhetoric and Culture*, vol. 4. New York: Berghahn Books, pp. 1–32.

Girtler, R. 1995. *Randkulturen: Theorie der Unanständigkeit.* Vienna: Böhlau.

Gluckman, M. 1973. *Custom and Conflict in Africa.* Oxford: Basil Blackwell.

Gluckman, M. (ed.). 1964. *Closed Systems and Open Minds: The Limits of Naivety in Social Anthropology.* Edinburgh: Oliver & Boyd.

Gordon, R.G., Jr. (ed.). 2005. *Ethnologue: Languages of the World*, 15th edn. Dallas: SIL International.

Graeber, D. 2007. *Possibilities: Essays on Hierarchy, Rebellion, and Desire.* Edinburgh: AK Press.

Granovetter, M.S. 1973. 'The Strength of Weak Ties', *American Journal of Sociology* 78(6): 1360–80.
Groys, B. 2000. *Unter Verdacht: Eine Phänomenologie der Medien*. Munich: Carl Hanser.
Gudeman, S. 2001. *The Anthropology of Economy: Community, Market, and Culture*. Malden, MA: Blackwell.
Gulliver, P. 1971. *Neighbours and Networks: The Idiom of Kinship in Social Action among the Ndendeuli of Tanzania*. Berkeley, CA: University of California Press.
Hallpike, C.R. 1972. *The Konso of Ethiopia: A Study of the Values of a Cushitic People*. Oxford: Clarendon.
Harrison, R.P. 1986. 'The Ambiguities of Philosophy', *Diacritics* 16(2): 14–20.
Harrison, S.J. 1993. *The Mask of War: Violence, Ritual, and the Self in Melanesia*. Manchester: Manchester University Press.
———. 2002. 'The Politics of Resemblance: Ethnicity, Trademarks, Head-Hunting', *Journal of the Royal Anthropological Institute* 8(2): 211–32.
———. 2006. *Fracturing Resemblances: Identity and Mimetic Conflict in Melanesia and the West*. New York: Berghahn Books.
Hastrup, K. 2007. 'Performing the World: Agency, Anticipation and Creativity', in E. Hallam and T. Ingold (eds), *Creativity and Cultural Improvisation*. New York: Berg, pp. 193–206.
Hayward, R.J. 2009. 'What's Been Happening in Omotic?', *Journal of Ethiopian Studies* 42(1–2): 85–106.
Helander, B. 2003. *The Slaughtered Camel: Coping with Fictitious Descent among the Hubeer of Southern Somalia*. Uppsala: Uppsala University Library.
Helm, June (ed.). 1968. *Essays on the Problem of Tribe*. Seattle, WA: American Ethnological Society.
Hendry, J., and C.W. Watson (eds). 2001. *An Anthropology of Indirect Communication*. London: Routledge.
Heritage, J. 2004 [1984]. *Garfinkel and Ethnomethodology*. Cambridge: Polity.
Herzfeld, M. 1984. 'The Significance of the Insignificant: Blasphemy as Ideology', *Man* N.S. 19(4): 653–64.
———. 1998. *The Social Production of Indifference: Exploring the Symbolic Roots of Western Bureaucracy*. Chicago, IL: University of Chicago Press.
———. 2001. 'Irony and Power: Towards a Politics of Mockery in Greece', in J.W. Fernandez and M.T. Huber (eds), *Irony in Action: Anthropology, Practice, and the Moral Imagination*. Chicago, IL: University of Chicago Press, pp. 63–83.
———. 2003. 'The Unspeakable in Pursuit of the Ineffable: Representations of Untranslatability in Ethnographic Discourse', in P.G. Rubel and A. Rosman (eds), *Translating Cultures: Perspectives on Translation and Anthropology*. New York: Berg, pp. 109–34.
Hieda, O. 1991. 'Koegu Vocabulary, with a Reference to Kara', *African Studies Monographs Supplement* 14: 1–70.
———. 1996. 'Multilingualism in Koegu: Interethnic Relationships and Language', in S. Sato and E. Kurimoto (eds), *Essays in Northeast African Studies*. Senri Ethnological Studies 43. Osaka: National Museum of Ethnology, pp. 145–61.
———. 2003. 'Kwegu-Muguǧi', in S. Uhlig (ed.), *Encyclopedia Aethiopica*, vol. III. Wiesbaden: Harassowitz, pp. 463–64.
Hill, J.H., and J.T. Irvine. 1993. 'Introduction', in J.H. Hill and J.T. Irvine (eds), *Responsibility and Evidence in Oral Discourse*. Cambridge: Cambridge University Press, pp. 1–23.
Hinton, P.R. 2000. *Stereotypes, Cognition and Culture*. Hove: Psychology Press.

Hirsch, E., Jr. 2001 [1960]. 'Objective Interpretation', in V.B. Leitch (ed.), *The Norton Anthology: Theory and Criticism*. New York: W.W. Norton, pp. 1684–709.
Hobsbawm, E., and T. Ranger (eds). 1983. *The Invention of Tradition*. Cambridge: Cambridge University Press.
Huizinga, J. 1994 [1938]. *Homo Ludens: Vom Ursprung der Kultur im Spiel*. Hamburg: Rowohlt.
Hutcheon, L. 1994. *Irony's Edge: The Theory and Politics of Irony*. New York: Routledge.
Izikovitz, K.G. 1969. 'Neighbours in Laos', in F. Barth (ed.), *Ethnic Groups and Boundaries: The Social Organization of Culture Difference*. Oslo: Universitetsforlaget, pp. 135–53.
James, W., D.L. Donham, E. Kurimoto and A. Triulzi (eds). 2002. *Remapping Ethiopia: Socialism and After*. Oxford: James Currey.
Jenkins, R. 1997. *Rethinking Ethnicity: Arguments and Explorations*. London: Sage.
Jensen, A.E. (ed.). 1959. *Altvölker Süd-Äthiopiens*. Stuttgart: W. Kohlhammer.
Kenny, M.G. 1981. 'Mirror in the Forest: The Dorobo Hunter-Gatherers as an Image of the Other', *Africa: Journal of the International African Institute* 51(1): 477–95.
Konings, P., and D. Foeken (eds). 2006. *Crisis and Creativity: Exploring the Wealth of the African Neighbourhood*. Leiden: Brill.
Kopytoff, I. (ed.) 1989. *The African Frontier: The Reproduction of Traditional African Society*. Bloomington, IN: Indiana University Press.
Kratz, C.A. 1994. *Affecting Performance: Meaning, Movement and Experience in Okiek Women's Initiation*. Washington, DC: Smithsonian Institution Press.
Kurimoto, E. 1998. 'Resonance of Age Systems in Southeastern Sudan', in E. Kurimoto and S. Simonse (eds), *Conflict, Age and Power in North East Africa*. Oxford: James Currey, pp. 29–50.
Kurimoto, E., and S. Simonse (eds). 1998. *Conflict, Age and Power in North East Africa*. Oxford: James Currey.
Lakoff, G., and M. Johnson. 2003 [1980]. *Metaphors We Live by*, with a new afterword. Chicago, IL: University of Chicago Press.
Lambek, M. 2004. 'Introduction: Irony and Illness – Recognition and Refusal', in M. Lambek and P. Antze (eds), *Illness and Irony: On the Ambiguity of Suffering in Culture*. New York: Berghahn Books, pp. 1–19.
LaTosky, S. 2006. 'Reflections on the Lip-Plates of Mursi Women as a Source of Stigma and Self-Esteem', in I. Strecker and J. Lydall (eds), *The Perils of Face: Essays on Cultural Contact, Respect and Self-Esteem in Southern Ethiopia*. Berlin: LIT, pp. 371–86.
———. 2014. 'Images of Mursi Women and the Realities they Reveal and Conceal', in F. Girke (ed.), *Ethiopian Images of Self and Other*. Halle: Universitätsverlag Halle-Wittenberg, pp. 121–45.
Latour, B. 1986. 'The Powers of Association', in J. Law (ed.), *Power, Action and Belief: A New Sociology of Knowledge?* London: Routledge & Kegan Paul, pp. 264–80.
Law, J. 1986. 'Editor's Introduction: Power/Knowledge and the Dissolution of the Sociology of Knowledge', in J. Law (ed.), *Power, Action and Belief: A New Sociology of Knowledge?* London: Routledge & Kegan Paul, pp. 1–19.
Leach, E. 1964. *Political Systems of Highland Burma: A Study of Kachin Social Structure*, reprint with introductory note. London: Athlone.
———. 2000 [1964]. 'Animal Categories and Verbal Abuse', in S. Hugh-Jones and J. Laidlaw (eds), *The Essential Edmund Leach. Volume 1: Anthropology and Society*. New Haven: Yale University Press, pp. 322–43.
Lerner, M. 1986. *Surplus Powerlessness: The Psychodynamics of Everyday Life and the Psychology of Individual and Social Transformation*. Amherst, NY: Humanity Books.

Levine, D.N. 1965. *Wax and Gold: Tradition and Innovation in Ethiopian Culture*. Chicago, IL: University of Chicago Press.

———. 2000 [1974]. *Greater Ethiopia: The Evolution of a Multiethnic Society*. Chicago, IL: University of Chicago Press.

Lévi-Strauss, C. 1966 [1962]. *The Savage Mind (La Pensée Sauvage)*. London: Weidenfeld & Nicolson.

Lewellen, Ted. 1983. *Political Anthropology: An Introduction*. South Hadley, MA: Bergin & Garvey.

Lewis, J., and J. Woodburn (n.d.). 'Final Narrative for the Christensen Fund Grant 2256680', unpublished document.

Loimeier, R. 2011. 'Die Rinderpest 1887–1898 in Afrika', in R. Loimeier (ed.), *Themenschwerpunkt 2011: Seuchen in der Geschichte Afrikas. Periplus. Jahrbuch für außereuropäische Geschichte*. Hamburg: LIT, pp. 83–114.

Lydall, J. 1982. 'Review of "The Kwegu" (Film)', *RAIN* 50: 22–24.

———. 2002. 'Having Fun with Ideophones: a Socio-linguistic Look at Ideophones in Hamar, Southern Ethiopia', in Baye Yimam et al. (eds), *Ethiopian Studies at the End of the Second Millennium: Proceedings of the 14th International Conference of Ethiopian Studies, November 6–11, 2000*. Addis Ababa: Addis Ababa University, Institute of Ethiopian Studies, pp. 886–911.

———. 2005. 'Hamär Dialect Cluster', in S. Uhlig, (ed.), *Encyclopedia Aethiopica*, vol. II. Wiesbaden: Harassowitz, pp. 983–84.

———. 2010. 'The Paternalistic Neighbor. A Tale of the Demise of Cherished Traditions', in E.C. Gabbert and S. Thubauville (eds), *To Live with Others: Essays on Cultural Neighborhood in Southern Ethiopia*. Cologne: Köppe, pp. 314–34.

Lydall, J., and I. Strecker. 1979a. *Work Journal: The Hamar of Southern Ethiopia I*. Hohenschäftlarn: Klaus Renner.

———. 1979b. *Baldambe Explains: The Hamar of Southern Ethiopia II*. Hohenschäftlarn: Klaus Renner.

Mackenzie, W. 1978. *Political Identity*. Manchester/Harmondsworth. Manchester University Press/Penguin.

MacKie, M. 1973. 'Arriving at "Truth" by Definition: The Case of Stereotype Inaccuracy', *Social Problems* 20(4): 431–47.

Malinowski, B. 1992 [1926]. *Magic, Science and Religion*. Prospect Heights, NY: Waveland.

Marcus, G.E. 2001. 'The Predicament of Irony and the Paranoid Style in Fin-de-Siècle Rationality', in J.W. Fernandez and M.T. Huber (eds), *Irony in Action: Anthropology, Practice, and the Moral Imagination*. Chicago, IL: University of Chicago Press, pp. 209–223.

Markakis, J. 2011. *Ethiopia: The Last Two Frontiers*. Woodbridge: James Currey.

Masuda, K. 2003. 'Banna', in S. Uhlig (ed.), *Encyclopedia Aethiopica*, vol. I. Wiesbaden: Harassowitz, pp. 466–67.

Matsuda, H. 1994. 'Annexation and Assimilation: Koegu and Their Neighbours', in K. Fukui and J. Markakis (eds), *Ethnicity and Conflict in the Horn of Africa*. Oxford: James Currey, pp. 48–62.

———. 1996. 'Riverbank Cultivation in the Lower Omo Valley: The Intensive Farming System of the Kara, Southwestern Ethiopia', in S. Sato and E. Kurimoto (eds), *Essays in Northeast African Studies*. Osaka: National Museum, pp. 1–28.

———. 2002. 'Political Visibility and Automatic Rifles. The Muguji in the 1990s', in W. James, D.L. Donham, E. Kurimoto and A. Triulzi (eds), *Remapping Ethiopia: Socialism and After*. Oxford: James Currey, pp. 173–84.

———. 2003. 'Kwegu-Muguǧi Ethnography', in S. Uhlig (ed.), *Encyclopedia Aethiopica*, vol. III. Wiesbaden: Harassowitz, pp. 464–65.

———. 2007. 'Kara', in S. Uhlig (ed.), *Encyclopedia Aethiopica*, vol. III. Wiesbaden: Harassowitz, pp. 340–41.

Mbembe, Achille. 1992. 'The Banality of Power and the Aesthetics of Vulgarity in the Postcolony', *Public Culture* 4 (2): 1–30.

Meneley, A. 2004. 'Scared Sick or Silly?', in M. Lambek and P. Antze (eds), *Illness and Irony: On the Ambiguity of Suffering in Culture*. New York: Berghahn Books, pp. 21–39.

Meyer, C. 2005. *'Mahnen, prahlen, drohen…' Rhetorik und politische Organisation amerikanischer Indianer*. Frankfurt: IKO.

———. 2008. 'Persuasive Interaktion und soziale Beeinflussung. Zur Mikrophysik der Macht in einem Wolof-Dorf Nordwest-Senegals', *Paideuma* 54: 151–72.

———. 2009. 'Precursors of Rhetoric Culture Theory', in I. Strecker and S. Tyler (eds), *Culture and Rhetoric: Studies in Rhetoric and Culture*, vol. 1. New York: Berghahn Books, pp. 31–48.

Meyer, C., and F. Girke (eds). 2011. *The Rhetorical Emergence of Culture: Studies in Rhetoric and Culture*, vol. 4. New York: Berghahn Books.

Middleton, J., and D. Tait (eds). 1970. *Tribes without Rulers: Studies in African Segmentary Systems*. London: Routledge & Kegan Paul.

Moerman, M. 1965. 'Ethnic Identification in a Complex Civilization: Who are the Lue?', *American Anthropologist* 67(5): 1215–30.

Moore, S.F. 1987. 'Explaining the Present: Theoretical Dilemmas in Processual Ethnography', *American Ethnologist* 14(4): 727–36.

Naty, A. 1992. 'The Culture of Powerlessness and the Spirit of Rebellion among the Aari People of Southwest Ethiopia', Ph.D. dissertation. Stanford, CA: Department of Anthropology, Stanford University.

———. 2002. 'Memory and the Humiliation of Men: The Revolution in Aari', in W. James, D.L. Donham, E. Kurimoto and A. Triulzi (eds), *Remapping Ethiopia: Socialism and After*. Oxford: James Currey, pp. 59–73.

Needham, R. 1970. 'Introduction', in R. Needham (ed.), *A.M. Hocart. Kings and Councilors: An Essay in the Comparative Anatomy of Human Society*. Chicago, IL: University of Chicago Press.

Neumann, A.E. 1994 [1898]. *Elephant-Hunting in East Equatorial Africa: Being an Account of Three Years' Ivory-Hunting under Mount Kenia and among the Ndorobo Savages of the Lorogi Mountains, Including a Trip to the North End of Lake Rudolph*. New York: St Martin's Press.

Nietzsche, F. 1922: *Götzen-Dämmerung*. Nietzsches Werke Taschenausgabe, vol. 10. Leipzig: Alfred Kröner.

Obadare, E. 2009. 'The Uses of Ridicule: Humour, "Infrapolitics" and Civil Society in Nigeria', *African Affairs* 108(431): 241–61.

Otto, T., and H. Driessen. 2000. 'Protean Perplexities: An Introduction', in H. Driessen and T. Otto (eds), *Perplexities of Identification: Anthropological Studies in Cultural Differentiation and the Use of Resources*. Aarhus: Aarhus University Press, pp. 9–27.

Pankhurst, A. 1999. '"Caste in Africa": The Evidence from South-Western Ethiopia Reconsidered', *Africa* 69(4): 485–509.

———. 2006. 'A Peace Ceremony at Arbore', in I. Strecker and J. Lydall (eds), *The Perils of Face: Essays on Cultural Contact, Respect and Self-Esteem in Southern Ethiopia*. Berlin: LIT, pp. 247–67.

Pausewang, S. 1990. '"Meret al arrashi" Land Tenure and Access to Land: A Socio-historical Overview', in S. Pausewang (ed.), *Ethiopia: Options for Rural Development*. London: Zed Books, pp. 38–48.
Petrollino, S. 2016. *A Grammar of Hamar: A South Omotic Language of Ethiopia*. Cushitic and Omotic Studies, vol. 6. Cologne: Rüdiger Köppe.
Plessner, H. 2002 [1924]. *Grenzen der Gemeinschaft: Eine Kritik des sozialen Radikalismus*. Frankfurt: Suhrkamp.
Poissonnier, N. 2009. *Das Erbe der 'Helden': Grabkult der Konso und kulturverwandten Ethnien in Süd-Äthiopien*. Göttingen: Universitätsverlag.
Potter, J. 2004. *Representing Reality: Discourse, Rhetoric and Social Construction*. London: Sage.
Quinn, N. 1991. 'The Cultural Basis of Metaphor', in J.W. Fernandez (ed.), *Beyond Metaphor: The Theory of Tropes in Anthropology*. Stanford, CA: Stanford University Press, pp. 57–93.
Radcliffe-Brown, A.R. 1952. 'The Comparative Method in Social Anthropology', *Journal of the Royal Anthropological Institute* 63: 15–22.
Rapport, N. 2000. 'Community', in A. Barnard and J. Spencer (eds), *Encyclopedia of Social and Cultural Anthropology*. London: Routledge, pp. 142–45.
Rapport, N., and J. Overing. 2007. *Social and Cultural Anthropology: The Key Concepts*, 2nd edn. London: Routledge.
Rorty, R. 1989. *Contingency, Irony, and Solidarity*. Cambridge: Cambridge University Press.
Rottenburg, R. 2002. *Weit hergeholte Fakten: Eine Parabel der Entwicklungshilfe*. Stuttgart: Lucius und Lucius.
Sacks, H. 1984. 'On Doing "Being Ordinary"', in J.M. Atkinson and J.C. Heritage (eds), *Structures of Social Action: Studies in Conversation Analysis*. Cambridge: Cambridge University Press, pp. 413–29.
Sagawa, Toru. 2010. 'Local Potential for Peace. Trans-ethnic Cross-cutting Ties among the Daasanech and Their Neighbors', in E.C. Gabbert and S. Thubauville (eds), *To Live with Others: Essays on Cultural Neighborhood in Southern Ethiopia*. Cologne: Rüdiger Köppe, pp. 99–127.
Sahlins, M. 1968. *Tribesmen*. Englewood Cliffs, NJ: Prentice Hall.
———. 1999. 'Two or Three Things I Know about Culture', *Journal of the Royal Anthropological Institute* 5(3): 399–421.
———. 2004. *Apologies to Thucydides: Understanding History as Culture and Vice Versa*. Chicago, IL: University of Chicago Press.
———. 2013. *What Kinship Is – and Is Not*. Chicago, IL: University of Chicago Press.
Sapir, J.D. 1977. 'The Anatomy of Metaphor', in J.D. Sapir and J.C. Crocker (eds), *The Social Use of Metaphor: Essays on the Anthropology of Rhetoric*. Philadelphia, PA: University of Pennsylvania Press, pp. ix–xi.
Schareika, N. 2005. 'Exploring Wodaabe Political Rhetoric and Reality', *4th International Rhetoric Culture Conference 'Rhetoric in Politics and Economics', Mainz, 16–20 July 2005*. Mainz: Johannes Gutenberg-University.
Schlee, G. 1994a. *Identities on the Move: Clanship and Pastoralism in Northern Kenya*. Nairobi: Gideon S. Were.
———. 1994b. 'Ethnicity Emblems, Diacritical Features, Identity Markers: Some East African Examples', in D. Brokensha (ed.), *A River of Blessings: Essays in Honor of Paul Baxter*. Syracuse, NY: Maxwell School of Citizenship and Public Affairs, pp. 129–43.
———. 1994c. 'Kuschitische Verwandtschaftssysteme in vergleichenden Perspektiven', in T. Geider and R. Kastenholz (eds), *Sprachen und Sprachzeugnisse in Afrika*. Cologne: Köppe, pp. 367–88.

———. 1997. 'Cross-cutting Ties and Interethnic Conflict: The Example of Gabbra, Oromo and Rendille', in K. Fukui, E. Kurimoto and M. Shigeta (eds), *Ethiopia in Broader Perspective: Papers of the 13th International Conference of Ethiopian Studies*. Kyoto: Shokado, pp. 577–96.

———. 1998. '*Gada* Systems on the Meta-Ethnic Level: Gabbra/Borana/Garre Interactions in the Kenyan/Ethiopian Borderland', in E. Kurimoto and S. Simonse (eds), *Conflict, Age and Power in North East Africa*. Oxford: James Currey, pp. 121–46.

———. 2005. 'Forms of Pastoralism', in S. Leder and B. Streck (eds), *Shifts and Drifts in Nomad-Sedentary Relations*. Wiesbaden: Reichert, pp. 17–53.

———. 2008. *How Enemies are Made: Towards a Theory of Ethnic and Religious Conflict*. New York: Berghahn Books.

Schlee, G. (ed.). 2004 [2002]. *Imagined Differences: Hatred and the Construction of Identity*. Münster: LIT.

Schnepel, B. 2005. 'Zur Dialektik von *agency* und *patiency*', *Paragrana: Internationale Zeitschrift für Historische Anthropologie* 18(2): 15–22.

Schütz, A. 1982 [1971]. *Das Problem der Relevanz*. Frankfurt: Suhrkamp.

Scott, J.C. 1985. *Weapons of the Weak: Everyday Forms of Peasant Resistance*. New Haven, CT: Yale University Press.

———. 1990. *Domination and the Arts of Resistance: Hidden Transcripts*. New Haven, CT: Yale University Press.

———. 1999. *Seeing Like a State: How Certain Schemes to Improve the Human Condition Have Failed*. New Haven, CT: Yale University Press.

———. 2009. *The Art of Not Being Governed: An Anarchist History of Upland Southeast Asia*. New Haven, CT: Yale University Press.

Seymour-Smith, C. 1986. *Macmillan Dictionary of Anthropology*. London: Macmillan.

Simmel, G. 1950. *The Sociology of Georg Simmel*. New York: Free Press.

———. 1964 [1923]. *Conflict and the Web of Group-Affiliations*, with a foreword by E.C. Hughes. New York: The Free Press.

Smidt, W. 2010. 'Šanqəlla', in S. Uhlig (ed.), *Encyclopaedia Aethiopica*, vol. 4. Wiesbaden: Harrassowitz, pp. 525–27.

Sobania, N. 1980. 'The Historical Traditions of the Peoples of the Eastern Lake Turkana Basin c. 1840–1925', Ph.D. thesis. London: University of London, School of Oriental and African Studies.

Sperber, D. 2002 [1986]. *Explaining Culture: A Naturalistic Approach*. Oxford: Blackwell.

Sperber, D., and D. Wilson. 1995. *Relevance: Communication and Cognition*, 2nd edn. Oxford: Blackwell.

Stauder, J. 1971. *The Majangir: Ecology and Society of a Southwest Ethiopian People*. Cambridge: Cambridge University Press.

Stigand, C.H. 1969 [1910]. *To Abyssinia through an Unknown Land: An Account of a Journey through Unexplored Regions of British East Africa by Lake Rudolf to the Kingdom of Menelik*. New York: Negro Universities Press.

Strathern, M. 1988. *The Gender of the Gift*. Berkeley, CA: University of California Press.

Streck, B. 2000 (ed.). *Wörterbuch der Ethnologie*, 2nd edn. Wuppertal: Peter Hammer.

Strecker, I. 1976a. 'Traditional Life and Prospects for Socio-economic Development in the Hamar Administrative District of Southern Gamu Gofa: A Report to the Relief and Rehabilitation Commission of the Provisional Military Government of Ethiopia', unpublished manuscript.

———. 1976b. 'Hamer Speech Situations', in M.L. Bender (ed.), *The Non-Semitic Languages of Ethiopia*. East Lansing: African Studies Center.

———. 1979. *Sprung über die Rinder: Ein Initiationsritus der Hamar in Südäthiopien*, film. Production in cooperation with the Institut für Wissenschaftlichen Film (IWF). Göttingen.

———. 1984a. *Der Herr der Ziegen: Opfer und Weissagung in Hamar*, film. Baden-Baden: SWF.

———. 1984b. *Tanz in der Savanne*, film. Baden-Baden: SWF.

———. 1988. *The Social Practice of Symbolization: An Anthropological Analysis*. London: Athlone Press.

———. 1994. 'Glories and Agonies of the Ethiopian Past', *Social Anthropology* 2(3): 302–12.

———. 2005. 'Hamär Ethnography', in S. Uhlig (ed.), *Encyclopedia Aethiopica*, vol. II. Wiesbaden: Harassowitz, pp. 984–86.

———. 2006a. 'A History of Pride and Confrontation in South Omo', in I. Strecker and J. Lydall (eds), *The Perils of Face: Essays on Cultural Contact, Respect, and Self-Esteem in Southern Ethiopia*. Berlin: LIT, pp. 151–84.

———. 2006b. '"Face" as a Metaphor of Respect and Self-esteem. Lessons from Hamar', in I. Strecker and Jean Lydall (eds), *The Perils of Face: Essays on Cultural Contact, Respect and Self-Esteem*. Berlin: LIT, pp. 83–103.

———. 2011. 'Tenor in Culture', in C. Meyer and F. Girke (eds), *The Rhetorical Emergence of Culture: Studies in Rhetoric and Culture*, vol. 4. New York: Berghahn Books, pp. 137–54.

———. 2013. *Berimba's Resistance: The Life and Times of a Great Hamar Spokesman*. Münster: LIT.

Strecker, I., and J. Lydall. 2006 (eds), *The Perils of Face: Essays on Cultural Contact, Respect, and Self-Esteem in Southern Ethiopia*. Berlin: LIT.

Strecker, I., and A. Pankhurst. 2003. *Bury the Spear!*, film. Watertown: DER; Göttingen: IWF.

Swartz, D. 2003. *Culture and Power: The Sociology of Pierre Bourdieu*. Chicago, IL: University of Chicago Press.

Taddesse Berisso. 2006. 'The Pride of the Guji-Oromo: An Essay on Cultural Contact and Self-Esteem', in I. Strecker and J. Lydall (eds), *The Perils of Face: Essays on Cultural Contact, Respect, and Self-Esteem in Southern Ethiopia*. Berlin: LIT, pp. 207–24.

Tadesse Wolde Gossa. 2000. 'Entering Cattle Gates: Trade, Bond Friendship and Group Interdependence', in J. Abbink (ed.), *Cultural Variation and Social Change in Southern Ethiopia: Comparative Approaches. Northeast African Studies* (N.S.) 7(3): 119–62.

Taylor, L.J. 2001. '"Paddy's Pig": Irony and Self-Irony in Irish Culture', in J.W. Fernandez and M.T. Huber (eds), *Irony in Action: Anthropology, Practice, and the Moral Imagination*. Chicago, IL: University of Chicago Press, pp. 172–87.

Tedlock, D. 2001. 'Ideophone', in A. Duranti (ed.), *Key Terms in Language and Culture*. Malden, MA: Blackwell, pp. 113–15.

Ten Have, P. 2004. 'Ethnomethodology', in C. Seale et al. (eds), *Qualitative Research Practice*. London: Sage, pp. 151–64.

Todorov, T. 2001. *Life in Common: An Essay in General Anthropology*. Lincoln, NE: University of Nebraska Press.

Tornay, S. 1979. 'Armed Conflict in the Lower Omo Valley, 1970–1976: An Analysis from within Nyangatom Society', in K. Fukui and D. Turton (eds), *Warfare among East African Herders*. Osaka: National Museum of Ethnology, pp. 97–117.

———. 1981. 'The Omo Murle Enigma', in M.L. Bender (ed.), *Peoples and Cultures of the Ethio-Sudan Borderlands*. East Lansing: African Studies Center, pp. 3–60.

———. 2001. *Les fusils jaunes: générations et politique en pays Nyangatom (Éthiopie)*. Nanterre: Société d'Éthnologie.

———. 2007. 'Murle Ethnography', in S. Uhlig (ed.), *Encyclopedia Aethiopica*, vol. III. Wiesbaden: Harassowitz, pp. 1077–78.

———. 2009. 'Modernization in the Lower Omo Valley and Adjacent Marches of Eastern Equatoria, Sudan: 1991–2000', in G. Schlee and E.E. Watson (ed.), *Changing Identifications and Alliances in North-East Africa. Volume 1: Ethiopia and Kenya*. New York: Berghahn Books, pp. 77–86.

Torres, G. 1997. *The Force of Irony: Power in the Everyday Life of Mexican Tomato Workers*. New York: Berg.

Tosco, M. 2005. 'Ɖáasanač Ethnography', in S. Uhlig (ed.), *Encyclopedia Aethiopica*, vol. II. Wiesbaden: Harassowitz, pp. 2–3.

Turner, E. 1985. 'Prologue: from the Ndembu to Broadway', in V.W. Turner, *On the Edge of the Bush: Anthropology as Experience*, ed. E. Turner. Tucson, AZ: University of Arizona Press, pp. 1–15.

Turner, V.W. 1966. 'Ritual Aspects of Conflict Control in African Micropolitics', in M.J. Swartz, V.W. Turner and A. Tuden (eds), *Political Anthropology*. Chicago, IL: Aldine, pp. 239–46.

———. 1967. *The Forest of Symbols*. Ithaca, NY: Cornell University Press.

———. 1974. *Dramas, Fields, and Metaphors: Symbolic Action in Human Society*. Ithaca, NY: Cornell University Press.

Turton, D.A. 1973. 'The Social Organisation of the Mursi: A Pastoral Tribe of the Lower Omo Valley, South West Ethiopia', Ph.D. thesis. London: University of London.

———. 1980. 'The Economics of Mursi Bridewealth: A Comparative Perspective', in J.L. Comaroff (ed.), *The Meaning of Marriage Payments*. London: Academic Press, pp. 67–92.

———. 1982. 'The Kwegu', *RAIN* 51: 10–12.

———. 1993. '"We Must Teach Them to Be Peaceful": Mursi Views on Being Human and Being Mursi', in T. Terje (ed.), *Conflicts in the Horn of Africa: Human and Ecological Consequences of Warfare*. Uppsala: Department of Social and Economical Geography/EPOS, pp. 164–80.

———. 1994. 'Mursi Political Identity and Warfare: The Survival of an Idea', in K. Fukui and J. Markakis (eds), *Ethnicity and Conflict in the Horn of Africa*. London: James Currey, pp. 15–32.

———. 1999. 'Warfare in the Lower Omo Valley, Southwestern Ethiopia: Reconciling Materialist and Political Explanations', in S.P. Reyna and R.E. Downs (eds), *Deadly Developments: Capitalism, States and War*. Amsterdam: Gordon & Breach, pp. 133–52.

———. 2002a [1986]. 'A Problem of Domination at the Periphery: the Kwegu and the Mursi', in D.L. Donham and Wendy James (eds), *The Southern Marches of Imperial Ethiopia*. London: James Currey, pp. 148–72.

———. 2002b. 'The Same Only Different: War and Dueling as Boundary Marking Rituals in Mursiland, Southwestern Ethiopia', in T.J. Cornell and T.B. Allen (eds), *War and Games*. Woodbridge: Boydell Press, pp. 171–92.

———. 2003. 'The Politician, the Priest and the Anthropologist: Living beyond Conflict in Southwestern Ethiopia', *Ethnos* 68(1): 5–26.

———. 2004. 'Lip-Plates and "the People Who Take Photographs": Uneasy Encounters between Mursi and Tourists in Southern Ethiopia', *Anthropology Today* 20(3): 3–8.

———. 2007. 'Mursi', in S. Uhlig (ed.), *Encyclopedia Aethiopica*, vol. III. Wiesbaden: Harassowitz, pp. 1078–80.

Tuzin, D. 1989. 'The Organization of Action, Identity, and Experience in Arapesh Dualism', in D. Maybury-Lewis and U. Almagor (eds), *The Attraction of Opposites: Thought and Society in the Dualistic Mode.* Ann Arbor, MI: University of Michigan Press, pp. 277–96.

Tyler, S. 1978. *The Said and the Unsaid: Mind, Meaning, and Culture.* London: Academic Press.

Van der Geest, S. 2003. 'Confidentiality and Pseudonyms: A Fieldwork Dilemma from Ghana', *Anthropology Today* 19(1): 14–18.

Van Zwanenberg, R.M. 1976. 'Dorobo Hunting and Gathering: A Way of Life or a Mode of Production?', *African Economic History* 2: 12–21.

Vaughan, S. 2006. 'Responses to Ethnic Federalism in Ethiopia's Southern Region', in D. Turton (ed.), *Ethnic Federalism: The Ethiopian Experience in Comparative Perspective.* Oxford: James Currey, pp. 181–207.

Von Höhnel, L. 1968 [1891]. *Discovery of Lakes Rudolf and Stefanie: A Narrative of Count Samuel Teleki's Exploring and Hunting Expedition in Eastern Equatorial Africa in 1887 and 1888.* London: Frank Cass.

Watson, E.E. 1998. 'Ground Truths: Land and Power in Konso', Ph.D. thesis. Cambridge: University of Cambridge.

Werbner, R.P. 1984. 'The Manchester School in South-Central Africa', *Annual Reviews in Anthropology* 13: 157–85.

Wimmer, A. 2008. 'Elementary Strategies of Ethnic Boundary Making', *Ethnic and Racial Studies* 31(6): 1025–55.

Wolf, E. 1955. 'Types of Latin American Peasantry: A Preliminary Discussion', *American Anthropologist* 57(39): 452–71.

———. 1966. 'Kinship, Friendship, and Patron-Client Relations', in M. Banton (ed.), *The Social Anthropology of Complex Societies.* London: Tavistock Press, pp. 1–22.

Wood, J.C. 2000. 'The Similarities of Difference: Symbolic Reversals among East Africa's Gabra and Their Neighbors', in J. Abbink (ed.), *Cultural Variation and Social Change in Southern Ethiopia: Comparative Approaches. Northeast African Studies* (N.S.) 7(3): 59–84.

Woodhead, L., and D. Turton. 1982. *The Kwegu: The Mursi Trilogy Part 2*, film. London: Royal Anthropological Institute.

Yurchak, A. 2006. *Everything Was Forever, Until It Was No More: The Last Soviet Generation.* Princeton, NJ: Princeton University Press.

Zijderveld, A. 1995. 'Humor, Laughter, and Sociological Theory', *Sociological Forum* 10(2): 341–45.

Index

A
actors, action, 5, 8, 18, 24n12, 26–28, 31–33, 36–43, 45nn3–4, 46–50, 63, 74, 76–77, 83, 86, 90, 94, 98–99, 107, 116, 124, 132, 145, 156, 163, 172, 176, 186, 188, 198–202, 209–11, 215, 220–21, 240, 248n12, 255, 257–58
  social, collective, 5, 7–8, 13, 18–19, 26, 30–34, 36, 39–42, 44, 47–48, 50–51, 60, 65–66, 74, 79, 84, 93, 96, 99, 109, 116, 122–23, 133, 149, 151–55, 159–60, 162–64, 166, 185–86, 190–91, 196, 204, 206, 246, 250, 253, 255–56, 258–59
äda, 6, 10–11, 60, 80n18, 81n28, 110, 112–13, 128, 129n16, 130n17, 132, 136–37, 157, 169, 173, 176, 184, 186, 253
ädamo, 4–9, 11, 14, 20, 22, 25–26, 28, 59, 73–75, 78–79, 82n39, 88, 93, 97, 99–101, 107, 116–17, 119, 125–28, 133–39, 140–41, 144, 146n13, 175–76, 179, 185–86, 188–91, 210, 243–44, 250–55, 257
administration, 34, 53, 71, 138, 150, 158, 170, 182, 186, 194–95, 202, 208, 210, 213, 215, 217, 229, 239, 240, 248n12
affect, 6, 27, 40, 50, 59, 68, 73, 124, 136, 144, 150, 163, 228, 229, 232, 259

age-sets, 7, 9, 11, 13, 16, 38, 46, 49, 52, 55, 58, 62–67, 69, 71–72, 79n6, 81nn24–27,29, 88, 105, 107–108, 130n22, 139–42, 152, 157, 181, 183, 254
agency, 19, 21, 28–29, 31–34, 36, 39–41, 49, 51, 73–75, 79n4, 121, 133, 152, 159, 176, 190–91, 192n6, 201, 210–11, 215, 218, 230–31, 233, 235, 240–41, 245, 247, 252–53, 258
agon, 34–35, 42, 44, 47, 50, 57, 68, 71, 74, 78, 79n1, 84, 141, 201, 223
ambiguity, 8, 61, 83–84, 92, 169, 203, 219, 222, 234
amity, 6, 11, 59, 107, 135–36, 164, 176, 253
anonymity, 14, 16, 67, 163
Arbore, 21, 81n20, 82n35, 128n3, 130n21, 146n13, 156, 159, 165n11, 170, 173–77, 184–88, 191, 192nn8,9,11, 193nn17–18, 194, 207, 211–12, 247n3, 253
arena, 5, 7, 13, 35, 37, 46, 48, 50–78, 79n1, 82n40, 88, 96–97, 107, 115, 127, 144, 148–49, 168–70, 180, 188, 196, 203, 206–7, 210–18, 230–31, 235, 238, 243–44, 247, 250, 252
'as if', 10–12, 26–27, 36, 41, 84, 114–15, 162, 204, 217, 235, 237, 258

ascription, 19–20, 36–37, 39, 41, 61, 121, 123, 126, 162–63, 200, 229
assimilation, 1, 74, 87, 100, 131n26, 133, 146n11
audience, 6, 9, 27, 35, 37, 42, 47, 50–51, 86, 104, 149, 155, 159–60, 185, 190, 200, 202, 208–9, 217, 219–20, 222, 223n3, 237, 259
autonomy, 18–21, 28–36, 39, 40, 44, 45n3, 49, 68, 75, 119–20, 126, 142–43, 149, 152, 155–56, 158–59, 163, 176–77, 178, 190–91, 211, 215, 218, 233, 237, 246–47, 252–53, 255–56, 258–59

B

Bailey, Frederick George, 4–5, 26–27, 39, 42–43, 45nn6–7, 51, 79n1, 101, 115, 189, 198, 202, 224n14, 246
Banna, 1, 2, 54, 87–88, 91, 129n16, 130n19, 155–56, 167–73, 174, 187, 192nn4–5, 207
Barth, Fredrik, 29–31, 38, 41, 73, 155, 176, 182, 190, 229–30
Bashada, 1, 82nn34,40, 83, 87–88, 91, 105, 128n2, 129n16, 144, 167–74, 187, 192n4–5, 207, 221
beatings, 62, 65, 80n13, 108–12, 130n22, 139–40
Beidelman, Thomas O., 34–35, 40, 42, 149–50, 154, 184, 208, 215, 223n3
belonging, 8, 10–11, 19, 41, 47, 49, 57, 78, 84, 89, 94, 99, 127, 137, 145n6, 152–53, 188, 227, 231, 242, 257
beltamo, bel. See under bondfriendship
bitti, 52–55, 61–63, 81n20, 156, 172, 174, 193n13, 214
  borkotto bitti, 62–66, 75, 77–78, 81n22, 82n40, 139, 141, 186, 215
Blok, Anton, 29–31, 45n3
Bogudo, 20, 51–52, 61–62, 79, 79n5, 83–101, 106, 114–15, 125–26, 132, 144, 148, 152–53, 203, 243, 250–52
bondfriendship, 6, 10, 12–13, 135–37, 145n8, 151, 167, 175
  borkotto, 11, 62, 65–67, 70, 81n23, 108–12, 115, 129n5, 194, 206, 215
boundaries, 1, 6, 8, 21, 23n9, 26, 34, 38–41, 72–73, 81n19, 105–6, 114, 116, 143–44, 152, 154–55, 158–59, 168, 190, 229, 231–32, 250, 255, 257
bridewealth, 58, 69, 112, 115, 120

C

Carrithers, Michael, 22n1, 41, 153, 163
categories, 7, 10–11, 13–14, 19–21, 31–32, 36–39, 41–42, 44, 46–51, 58, 61, 68, 73, 75–76, 79, 80n14, 84, 90–93, 99, 106–7, 122, 127, 131n25, 135, 139, 142, 161–62, 167–68, 177, 189, 192n11, 196, 212, 219, 227–28, 247n5, 250, 255–56
  ethnic categories, 4, 6–7, 14, 23n9, 34, 37–39, 44, 81n19, 83, 88, 90–91, 94, 97, 99–101, 125–27, 137, 151, 160, 163, 165n7, 227, 251
  social categories, 7, 11, 14, 20, 26, 28, 30, 36–37, 40, 42, 46–49, 74, 83, 108, 128n4, 160, 162, 164, 189, 255, 258
cattle, 2, 54, 69, 80n12, 102n2, 104, 121, 130n19, 141–42, 146n16, 167, 170–71, 173–74, 181, 186, 192n3, 204, 210, 252–53
centre-periphery, 154, 158, 231
challenges, 11, 13, 26, 37, 39–40, 42–44, 47, 50–51, 61, 63, 68, 74, 92, 98, 101, 107, 128, 138, 142, 144–45, 149, 189–90, 202, 232, 258, 259
claims, 5, 8, 20, 22, 25, 26, 33, 36–38, 40, 42–44, 46–51, 59, 63, 65, 72–74, 78–79, 98–99, 105–7, 114, 119–20, 123–24, 126, 129n13, 130n19, 135, 148–49, 152, 159, 162, 165n12, 169, 172, 176, 179, 185, 188, 191, 192n7, 196, 219, 221–23, 224n10, 234, 240, 253–55, 257–58
  identity claims, 4, 20, 26, 47, 63, 65, 73, 79, 97, 99, 102n6, 106, 116, 119, 122–23, 127–28, 128n4, 137, 145n5, 175, 185, 195, 199–200, 204–206, 211, 213, 215, 218, 220, 229, 237, 240
  language of claims, 26, 28, 39–40, 44, 49–50, 220–21, 223, 250
clans, 7, 11, 13–14, 34, 46, 50, 57–62, 81n21, 87, 89–90, 92, 100, 102n6, 105, 115, 120, 129n7, 130n23, 142, 145n1, 152, 157, 174, 177, 192n7, 193n17, 228

classification, 26, 36–41, 107, 119, 127, 155, 229
  systems of classification, 26, 28, 39, 43–44, 47, 49
cleverness, 1, 3–4, 21–22, 62–63, 116–17, 121, 130n18, 169, 194–223, 235, 237, 240, 243–44, 247, 255, 260
commensality, 39, 58, 60, 72, 79n3, 91–93, 105–7, 112, 115, 117, 143, 250
  food taboos, 13–14, 97, 107, 117, 124, 250
  meat, 55, 80nn13,16
communication, 16, 195, 202, 222
community, 14–18, 25, 31, 41, 43, 48–50, 53, 57, 60, 65, 71–72, 76, 78, 82n40, 87, 106, 122, 138–40, 150, 154, 158, 165n11, 175, 182, 189, 197–98, 245, 250–51, 255, 257
  communal life, 28, 40
  discourse community, 17, 98, 150
  face-to-face community, 16, 18, 28
  triumph of community, 72–76, 78, 257
comparison, 52, 80n17, 120, 141–45, 150, 164n5, 167, 176, 201, 207, 211, 214, 231–32, 235, 251, 253
conflict, 4, 16, 27, 46, 47–48, 50–53, 55, 57–60, 64–67, 69, 72, 76, 134, 136, 142, 145n3, 149, 151, 154, 170–71, 179–80, 183, 185–86, 189, 193n14, 214, 238, 240, 246, 248n12, 253, 257
conquest, 22, 130n24, 187, 190–91, 204, 226, 231–37, 256
cross-cutting ties, 3, 34
cultivation, 2–3, 10, 56–57, 59, 71, 81n21, 94, 105–06, 115, 122–23, 125, 130nn20,24, 137, 155, 157, 167, 177, 201, 246
cultural neighbourhood, 3, 6, 21, 76, 136, 144, 148–64, 164n1, 175–76, 187–91, 192n2, 193n18, 195, 203, 206–11, 213–14, 220, 227–31, 252–53, 255–56, 259
  membership in the cultural neighbourhood, 21–22, 150, 152, 154, 157, 191
culture, 1, 3–4, 10, 18, 27–28, 76, 126, 164, 164n5, 165n7, 167–68, 180, 183, 195, 204, 232, 234–35, 238, 253, 257

D
dams, 22, 244–46
dancing, 13, 57, 60, 109, 174, 214
Dassanech, 21, 77, 79n9, 128n3, 137, 158, 170, 173–77, 179, 183–86, 188, 192nn8–9, 192n11, 193n17, 199, 204, 207, 224n13, 235–37, 240, 253
definition of the situation, 5–8, 11–12, 18–19, 22, 26, 36–37, 39, 42–44, 45n6, 46, 48–49, 59, 63, 74, 79, 97, 106–7, 119, 126, 151, 160–61, 177, 202, 211, 218, 220, 222–23, 234–35, 243–44, 252, 255–57
demography, 106, 174, 186
descent, 6, 23n2, 55, 57, 60, 90, 93, 169, 178–79, 185, 188, 250, 253, 255
development, 21–22, 34, 56–57, 72, 82n36, 96, 123–24, 133, 158, 170, 208, 210, 229–30, 244–46, 248nn11,18, 254–55
diacritical markers, 39–40, 92–93, 105–6, 259
difference, differentiation, 3, 6–8, 13–14, 20–21, 24n12, 25–26, 29–31, 34, 36–37, 39–40, 43–44, 46–51, 55, 63–64, 73–74, 76, 78, 81n25, 84, 87, 100, 107, 112–13, 119, 121, 125–26, 130n22, 139, 141, 143–44, 146n19, 148–49, 152, 154–56, 161–62, 168–69, 176, 184, 188–89, 192n5, 193n16, 195, 197, 227–30, 234, 237, 252, 255–59
Dimeka, 14, 52, 69, 170, 172, 212–13, 215
displays. *See under* performance
distinction, 19, 24n12, 28–29, 31–32, 34, 36, 39–40, 42, 44, 49, 57, 59, 61, 65, 93, 96–97, 100, 107–8, 119, 125, 136, 145n2, 146nn17,19, 155–58, 165n7, 168–69, 176–77, 190–91, 195, 228, 247, 251, 256, 258–59
divisions, 6–7, 13–14, 20–21, 25, 29, 39, 41, 46, 48, 51, 53–55, 57–58, 64, 76–77, 105, 114, 130n22, 132, 136–37, 143, 145n5, 152, 156–57, 174, 182, 189, 202, 227–28, 231, 241, 244, 255
domination, 8, 14, 22, 44, 83, 87–88, 93, 98, 107, 113, 115, 117, 119, 124, 126–27, 129n9, 135–36, 142–44, 149, 154, 189–90, 195–96, 207, 223,

domination (*cont.*)
224n15, 228, 233–34, 236–37, 241, 251
Dus, 9, 14, 20, 51–58, 60–63, 76, 79nn6–7, 80nn10–11, 81n21, 87–88, 90, 102n3, 112–113, 116, 122, 129n10, 132, 134–36, 139–40, 167, 172, 181, 193n13, 194, 214–15, 239, 241–43, 248n16, 259
duties, 6, 59, 62–63, 68–69, 71, 143, 156, 229, 251

E

edi, 6, 68, 88, 115
education, 34, 52, 71, 146n12, 203, 207, 210–13, 215, 218, 230, 245, 248n9
egalitarianism, 78, 101, 137, 145, 148, 175
elders, 11, 13, 17–18, 40, 50, 52, 54, 57–58, 61–71, 77, 79n4, 81nn21,30, 87, 91, 105–6, 108–10, 117, 139–40, 178, 182–83, 185–86, 194, 208, 210, 212–13, 215, 223, 224n13, 232, 236, 239, 243, 245
equality, 25, 195–96, 218
escalation, 7, 35, 47, 50, 59–60, 64–65, 69, 96, 140, 193n14, 239–40
Ethiopia, 1–2, 14, 16, 21, 23nn2,4,7, 77, 143, 145n5, 146n19, 147n20, 150, 173, 194, 226, 227, 235–38, 244, 247n1, 253
Ethiopian state, 3, 21–22, 25, 34, 76, 127, 223, 227, 229, 231–35, 238, 240, 253, 259–60
ethnicity, 4, 6, 14, 20, 25, 30, 37–38, 41, 44, 73, 75, 83–84, 106, 108, 117, 132, 137, 144, 151, 154–55, 164, 228, 255–59, 260n2
 constructivism vs. primordialism, 23n2, 94, 144, 147n20
 ethnic categories (*see under* categories)
 ethnic differences (*see under* diacritical markers)
ethnomethodology, 27, 153, 218
exchange, 25, 33–35, 69, 130n21, 150–51, 167, 174–75, 187, 208, 245
exclusion, 7–8, 49, 51, 97, 107, 117, 142, 144, 164, 229–31
exogamy, 58, 60–61, 84, 105, 120, 145n1, 157

F

factionalism, 7–8, 51, 58, 80, 152, 198, 242, 252
fieldwork, 1, 8–9, 17, 25, 34, 47, 50, 53, 69, 76, 83, 96, 106, 136, 145n5, 159, 164n1, 166, 182, 193n15, 206, 214, 220, 258
figuration, 4, 119, 128, 144, 236
film-making, 17, 102, 129nn7,10, 224n12
fishing, 20, 105, 113, 121–22, 125, 132,143-44, 146n10, 173
framing, 7, 26, 33, 40, 42, 44, 49, 53, 76, 86, 96, 98–100, 116, 148–49, 151, 200, 206, 218, 223, 228, 237
freedom, 202, 245, 248n11, 255
freedom from imposition, 33, 153
friends, friendship, 10–11, 13–14, 16, 23n7, 25, 50, 63–65, 78, 81n28, 92, 99, 105, 108, 112, 119–20, 124–25, 128, 129n16, 130n19, 139, 143, 146n12, 157, 173, 175, 177, 181, 183–84, 188, 206, 208–11, 214, 221, 224n10, 252–53
frontier, 3, 16, 247n1

G

gender, 16, 40, 51, 60–61, 66, 69, 84, 89–90, 117, 121, 162, 179, 182, 194, 233
gerontocracy, 63, 66, 72
Gezahegn Petros, 75, 79n5, 81n27, 82n34, 87–88, 91, 106–7, 128n1, 130n19, 129, 136, 169
goats, 11, 58, 63, 65–66, 69, 71, 93, 113, 121, 130n18, 139–40, 167, 172, 175, 178, 181, 233, 246
Gomba, 20, 51–52, 79n5, 84, 87, 89–100, 102n6, 107, 112, 114–15, 118, 125–27, 132, 144, 148, 152–53, 193n12, 203, 243, 250–51
group
 group size, 3, 14–18, 22, 24n11, 48–49, 150, 205 (*see also* demography)
 groupness, 36, 255
 interest groups, 3, 5, 6–7, 21–22, 25–28, 33, 38–39, 48, 50, 59, 71, 73–74, 79, 98, 134, 153–54, 157, 163, 191, 215, 238, 244, 252, 256

H

Habesha, 21–22, 148–49, 154, 164n6, 167, 187–88, 190–91, 194–97, 202–3, 206, 208–9, 212, 217–18, 223, 226–32, 234–40, 242, 247nn2–3, 253–54, 255–56

Hamar, 1, 10, 21, 52–53, 68, 79n9, 80n17, 81n20, 82n40, 87, 91–92, 100, 102n5, 129nn8,12,16, 130n19, 137–38, 141, 143, 145n5, 155–57, 159, 162–63, 165n11, 167–76, 179, 183, 185–88, 191n1, 192nn3,7, 193n17, 194, 207, 209–14, 224nn9–10, 224n13, 226–27, 244, 247n3, 252–53, 258–59

Hamar-Banna-Bashada cluster, 67, 80nn14,18, 143–44, 167–68, 169, 174, 176, 183, 223n5,

harmony ideology, 7, 82n39

Harrison, Simon, 29–33, 44n1, 126, 149, 201, 221

headrests. See under *borkotto*

heartland, 2, 16, 102n3

herding, 11, 69, 71, 104, 110, 121, 130n18, 134, 142–43, 157, 170–72, 181, 184, 210–12, 224n12, 239, 252

Herzfeld, Michael, 8, 28, 48, 160, 163, 165n12, 190, 244

Hieda, Osamu, 117, 128n3, 130nn19,21, 134, 136, 138

hierarchy, 7, 39, 65, 79n3, 88, 93, 127, 155, 196, 208, 217, 223, 233, 238, 257–58

highlands, highlanders, 1, 21, 71, 89, 100, 105, 148, 154, 167, 177, 194–95, 223, 224n6, 227, 229–31, 236, 237, 247n2, 256

history, 13, 17–18, 45n2, 59, 65, 69, 74, 90, 92–94, 106, 114, 116–17, 125, 130n21, 145n5, 149, 152, 154, 166–67, 179, 193n16, 202, 217, 221, 223n1, 227, 235–36, 238, 243, 246, 251, 255, 258

historical accounts, 7, 46, 54, 58, 79n5, 94, 102n6, 104–5, 114, 144, 153, 174, 235

history of the Kara, 17–18, 46, 54, 58–59, 65, 74, 79n5, 83, 87, 90, 94, 104, 114, 117, 127, 174, 179, 188, 204, 208, 221, 235

households, 6, 51–52, 57–59, 87, 90, 92, 110, 112–13, 115, 129n16, 136, 143, 146n9, 150, 178–79, 182–84, 212, 241–42

hunting, 8, 11, 16, 20, 50, 66, 68–69, 72, 81nn24,28, 82n32, 106, 112–13, 119, 122, 125, 132, 142–44, 145n5, 146nn16,18,19, 175, 179, 197, 199, 210

I

ideology, 19–20, 37, 47, 82n39, 107, 124, 127, 129n9, 142–44, 175, 180, 210, 234

ädamo as ideology, 7–8, 25–26, 28, 136, 144

identification, 17, 30–31, 35–36, 39, 41, 47–49, 65, 71, 73, 80n16, 84, 87, 93–96, 100, 121, 131n28, 134–35, 141–44, 149, 152–53, 157–58, 161–62, 165nn7,14, 175–76, 179, 184–85, 195–97, 201–4, 209, 211, 219, 224n11, 228–29, 241, 247n3, 255, 257, 258–59

inclusion, 7–8, 49, 65, 81n24, 117, 144, 155, 164, 173, 188, 197, 229, 247n3

independence, 33, 36, 106–7, 136, 168, 188

individual interests, 5–6, 25, 27–28, 38, 48, 75, 201, 210

initiation, 4, 11, 52, 59, 67–68, 71, 80n13, 81n30, 88, 92, 120, 129n12, 157, 165n7, 178, 184, 254

institutions, 14, 20, 34, 44, 46, 48, 62–63, 75, 78, 81n20, 157, 167, 187, 240, 255

integration, 4, 9–11, 13, 21, 34, 46, 49, 53, 59, 65–66, 86–87, 106, 133, 139–41, 158, 168, 179–80, 185, 191, 227, 247n1, 257

interactionalism, 28, 42–43, 49

interdependence, 3, 33, 150, 180

intermarriage, 13–14, 25, 39, 89, 112, 143, 150, 174, 177, 179, 185, 189

interpretation, 5, 14, 27, 76, 82n31, 96–101, 124, 129n12, 133, 140, 160, 190–91, 198, 202–3, 218–20, 222, 232, 234, 243

intersubjectivity, 32, 222

I

intimacy, 6, 8, 16, 22, 29, 32, 35–36, 50, 53, 59, 64, 77, 81n28, 90, 112, 129n7, 150, 163, 170, 174, 180–83, 185–86, 188, 191n1, 193n12, 211, 229, 251, 253, 259
irony, 22, 195–96, 200, 202, 203–4, 209, 218–23, 224n14, 225n16, 228, 234, 237–38, 240–47, 248n18, 254
irrigation/Irsha, 15, 55–57, 215, 238, 246

J

Jinka, 10, 14, 52, 69, 88, 110, 114, 164n4, 181, 187, 207, 212, 239
justification, 7, 13–14, 17, 39–40, 48–49, 110, 113, 116–17, 119, 125, 127, 204, 239, 251

K

Kara
  true Kara, 14, 20, 25–26, 51–52, 55, 67, 68, 83–84, 87–101, 105–108, 114–21, 124, 125–28, 129n16, 132, 137, 139, 141, 143–44, 145n2, 169, 177–79, 182, 189, 196, 203, 242–44, 250–52, 255
kebele, 52–54, 57–58, 61, 134, 137, 202, 241–42, 248n16
killing, 68–69, 77, 86, 94, 102n8, 146n13, 171–72, 176, 179–81, 214
kinship, 6, 10, 12, 49, 60–61, 84, 93, 112–13, 125, 135, 146n13, 157, 168, 174–76, 180, 185, 223n3, 228, 253
knowledge, 16–17, 28–29, 48, 69, 86, 100, 120–21, 130n19, 130n21, 159, 167, 174, 182, 190, 200–1, 205–6, 211, 221, 224n10, 236, 257–58
Korcho, 14–15, 20, 51–54, 57–58, 62, 79n9, 80n10, 89, 108–10, 112–13, 122–23, 137, 139–40, 146n10, 175, 185, 214–15, 238–39, 241–44, 248n16, 259
Kratz, Corinne, 119, 153–55, 165n7, 190
kumbassa, 86, 90–94, 96, 100, 101n1, 116, 120–21, 236, 248n14
Kundamma, 55–57, 84, 181. *See also* Irsha

L

Labuk, 14–15, 20, 51–55, 58, 61–62, 70, 78, 79nn6–7, 80n11, 81n25, 84, 89–90, 93–94, 102n6, 112, 129n7, 181, 193nn12–13, 215, 259
Lake Diba, 80n10, 89, 137–39
land, 33–34, 52, 54–55, 57, 61–62, 73, 78, 80n15, 87, 90, 100, 105, 110, 122, 126–28, 136, 138, 144, 169, 171–72, 181–82, 192n7, 193n14, 203, 208, 210, 224n12, 226, 231–32, 236–37, 241–43, 246, 248n16, 251–52
  arable land, 113, 134, 137, 187
  land ownership, 7, 83, 99, 113–19, 137, 157, 251
language, 1, 3, 10, 14, 33, 80nn15,17, 87, 105–6, 119–20, 128n3, 130n21, 131n27, 132, 159, 161, 168, 173–74, 177, 180, 182, 184, 192n5, 193n19, 205, 215, 253. *See also under* claims
  Kara language (*kar'appo*), 41, 106, 131n27, 132, 135, 166, 178, 181–82, 206, 258
leap across the cattle, 52, 81n30, 87–89, 92, 97, 99, 117, 129n12, 157, 168, 178
legitimacy, 28, 43, 89, 91, 127, 130n24, 144, 179, 191, 198–99, 228, 234, 248nn14,15, 250–51, 255
lineages, 48–49, 55, 59–60, 62, 67, 72, 80nn15,16, 84, 87, 89–90, 99, 102n8, 115, 129nn7,10, 169, 173, 182
lowlands, 10, 21, 145n5, 158, 228, 236, 240, 247n1
Lydall, Jean, 10, 21, 23n6, 80n14, 81nn20–21, 91, 129n8, 143–44, 169, 173, 187, 192nn5,7, 226, 237

M

maalo. *See under* boundary
Mago River, 11
marginalization, 20, 51, 119, 125, 141–44, 146n18, 147n19, 164n6, 195–96, 235, 244, 254
marriage, 11, 13, 16, 50, 52, 55, 58, 60–61, 66–69, 71, 80n18, 81nn19,24, 84, 86, 88–95, 102nn5,8, 105, 110, 112–13, 115, 120, 129nn12,16, 130n17, 140, 168–69, 178–79, 189, 192n6, 214, 233, 237, 239, 258

materiality, 1, 3, 20–21, 31, 40, 43–44, 59, 93, 105–106, 110, 123–27, 130n21, 132, 142, 144, 150, 152, 165n7, 176–77, 180, 183–84, 188, 191, 200, 211, 213, 217, 231, 246, 248n15, 250, 251–52, 259
Matsuda, Hiroshi, 10, 87, 119, 121–22, 126, 128n3, 130nn19–20, 132–37, 145n4, 198, 202–3, 246
mediation, 7, 67, 78, 105, 112–13, 135, 174
membership, 7, 11, 21, 40, 46, 49–50, 52, 57–59, 81n24, 113, 152, 157, 191, 257
metaphor, 20–22, 30, 60, 86, 94, 106, 119–26, 127, 129nn14–15, 135, 142–43, 148, 160, 162, 169, 181, 186, 233–35, 237, 251, 255, 258
methodology, 4–5, 8–9, 11–12, 18, 26–27, 40–43, 79, 86, 107, 161, 165n7, 190, 196, 202, 220, 222, 234, 237, 252
mētis, 198–99, 201–202, 215, 221
metonymy, 16, 119, 161, 209
migration, 3, 9, 81n20, 87, 94, 102n6, 106, 113–14, 125, 127, 128n4, 130n24, 132, 143, 152, 169, 173, 175, 190–91, 232, 251
mimesis, 3, 29, 31, 89, 151–52, 164n5, 184, 188–89
mingi, 69, 96, 101n1
models, 6–7, 18–19, 26, 31–32, 37–38, 40, 42–43, 48–52, 75–76, 84, 86, 89, 94, 98, 100, 129n15, 151, 154, 162, 180, 190, 222, 229, 231, 238, 242, 252, 256, 259
modernity, 22, 172, 195, 205, 210, 260n1
Moguji, 20–22, 33, 51, 52, 80n13, 82n38, 83–84, 89, 91, 93, 94, 97, 99–100, 104–28, 128nn1, 3, 4, 129nn6, 11, 14, 16, 130nn17, 19–20, 22–23, 132–45, 145nn4–6,8, 146n13, 148, 152–53, 157, 160, 162, 181, 184, 191, 196, 202–4, 207–11, 214, 242–44, 251–52, 255, 258, 260n1
morality, 47, 50, 55, 62, 99–100, 122, 125, 127, 130n22, 131n28, 141, 153, 157, 159, 175, 182, 198–99, 201–2, 204, 209, 218, 221, 224n14, 236, 244, 252

mountain people, 91, 129n16, 167–73, 175–76, 179–80, 185, 188, 191, 192n11, 210. *See also* Hamar, Banna, Bashada
multiplex, 16, 29, 43, 60, 74, 90, 127, 211, 229
Mursi, 21, 23n6, 33–34, 36, 41, 79n9, 80n15, 89, 100, 102nn3,6, 105, 115, 128n3, 133, 142, 145nn3,5,8, 152–53, 155–56, 158, 164n6, 165n7, 177–86, 188, 192n11, 193nn12,13, 207, 212, 214–15, 232, 248nn9,12, 258
mutuality, 6, 8, 17, 29, 36, 48, 50, 52–53, 55, 58–59, 65, 81n24, 88, 93, 107, 113, 117, 120, 131n26, 135, 150–51, 163, 167, 176–77, 183, 185–86, 196, 216, 230, 241, 251, 253, 256, 259
myth, 20, 55, 104, 106, 114, 122, 126–27, 137, 168, 203–4, 251

N

names, naming, 12, 16–17, 44, 55, 58, 63, 65–68, 77, 80n15, 81n25, 170, 183, 199, 206, 236
narcissism of minor differences, 29, 45n3
narrativity, 9, 14, 19, 21–22, 36, 41, 48, 54–55, 65, 74, 87, 94, 104, 120, 127, 128n4, 130nn22,24, 132–33, 135, 137, 139, 141, 150–55, 159–64, 166, 169–70, 174–75, 189–91, 192n7, 200, 204–5, 208, 210, 214, 221, 223n3, 235–36, 239, 243, 253, 255, 257–59
Naty, Alexander, 100, 187–88, 231–35, 237, 240, 248nn11–12
NGOs/non-governmental organizations, 34, 51, 53–54, 56, 77, 110, 123, 138, 171, 176, 210, 212, 215, 248n18
normativity, 6, 9, 26, 33, 40–42, 47, 73, 78, 148, 189, 200
Nyangatom, 1, 20–21, 23n6, 33, 79n5, 80n16, 81n27, 83, 89–90, 99–100, 103n10, 106, 110, 113, 121, 126, 130n23, 133–35, 137–41, 145nn5–6, 146nn11–12, 152–53, 155–56, 158–59, 165nn7,10, 166, 170–73, 175–86, 188–89, 191, 192n11, 193nn13,16, 204–5, 207–12, 214–15, 217, 224n13, 238–39, 244–46, 252–53

294 *Index*

Nyangatom-Kara, 51–52, 84, 89–91, 93, 97–99, 103n10, 145n3, 193n13, 203, 243–44

O

Omo River, 1, 3, 10, 18, 51, 80n10, 104, 109, 135, 146n10, 170–71, 181–82, 205, 210, 217, 224n9, 252
oracle, 92–93, 96
ostentation, 51
othering, 3, 5, 8, 12, 18, 20–22, 23n9, 25, 30–31, 33–37, 39, 44, 72, 76, 92, 99–101, 119, 125–28, 135, 142, 148, 150, 154–61, 166, 181, 186–88, 190–91, 194–96, 207, 211, 226, 228–29, 235, 240–41, 251, 253, 255–57

P

participant observation, 13, 16–17, 36
patron-client relations, 87, 110, 115, 121, 127–28, 129n9, 135, 142, 145n8, 251
peace, 12, 22, 25, 80n16, 108, 109–10, 113, 138, 141, 165n11, 172, 175, 181, 182–84, 186, 193n13, 214–15, 217–18, 253
performance, performativity, 12, 37, 47, 51, 86, 106, 107, 159, 165n7, 186, 199–200, 235, 240, 258
personhood, 5–6, 14, 17, 27, 32, 35–36, 43, 52, 55, 61, 68, 78, 79n7, 88, 92, 95, 101, 146n18, 168, 189, 228
persuasion, 4–5, 7, 8, 12–13, 18–19, 26, 36–44, 45n7, 47, 49, 60, 63, 73–75, 94, 124, 161, 166, 190, 202, 217, 224n14, 234, 259
plausibility, 7, 28, 41–42, 46–47, 49–50, 54–55, 73–75, 151, 154, 156, 164, 176, 199, 220, 237, 250, 253, 255
plot, 41, 106, 114, 152, 160–66, 182, 189–91, 200
political project, 22, 74, 78, 204, 217, 248n15
politico-territorial groups, 4, 34, 100, 148, 158, 168, 170, 186, 204, 250, 252, 256
polities. *See* politico-territorial groups
populations, 1, 3, 13–14, 16, 18–21, 23n6, 25–26, 29, 32–34, 37, 39, 41, 46, 49, 52, 57, 72, 75, 77, 79, 83, 86–88, 90–91, 93, 98–99, 102n2, 106, 122, 129n16, 132–33, 135, 142–44, 146n17, 148, 150–51, 153, 155, 157–58, 160, 165n9, 167–68, 174, 176, 183, 190, 192n7, 198, 203, 205, 214–15, 224n11, 226, 231–32, 248n9, 251, 253, 255–57, 259
porcupines, 29–30, 32, 34–36, 42–43, 45n4, 156, 257
Potter, Jonathan, 27, 162, 200
power, 14, 19–22, 25–26, 28, 32–33, 36–37, 40, 42–44, 45n4, 51, 59, 61, 63, 73, 78, 84, 97–98, 106, 127, 133, 144, 149–50, 154–56, 161–62, 165n14, 190–91, 194–97, 201–2, 206, 214–15, 218, 223, 224n10, 228, 230–34, 237–41, 244–47, 251–52, 254, 258
precedents, 7, 18, 97, 107, 145n3, 240, 252
pride, 6, 16, 51, 54, 65, 77–78, 124, 208–9, 213, 244, 257, 260
privileges, 6, 24n10, 63, 69, 83, 94, 97, 100–101, 144

R

Rapport, Nigel, 73–74, 76, 149, 152–53, 159–60, 166, 204
recognition, 17, 22, 23n6, 30–31, 35–36, 45n4, 50, 54, 57, 66, 69, 72, 101n1, 115, 150, 154, 185, 190–91, 204, 218–19, 228–29, 232, 235, 244, 255
reflexivity, 6, 23n2, 76, 78, 161, 196, 198, 203–4, 206–7, 214, 218, 220, 237, 257–58
regionalism, 29, 144, 150, 155–59, 186, 188, 191, 194, 211
relationships. *See* social relations
resistance, 44, 149, 152, 154, 164n5, 191, 196, 202, 226, 232, 234, 244, 247n1
responsibility, 26, 52–54, 56, 62, 64, 68, 71–72, 78, 92, 110, 113, 116, 128, 243
Rhetoric Culture Theory (RCT), 22n1, 45n7
ritual practice, 20, 25, 33, 39–40, 52, 58–61, 63–64, 71, 80n16, 81n21, 86, 88, 91–100, 101n1, 102n5, 106, 113–117, 129n7, 135, 137, 143–44,

146nn10,13, 157, 168, 178, 183, 193n12, 221, 250–52, 255
riverbanks, 50, 57, 114, 126, 127, 134, 204, 211, 252

S
sacrifice, 65, 102n1, 112, 116, 221
saving lie, 101, 202, 251
schismogenesis, 76–78, 107, 151, 257
Schlee, Günther, 3, 16, 34, 48–49, 60, 80n17, 150, 153, 168, 177, 185–86, 190, 191n1, 193n17, 195, 228, 247n1, 260n3
schools, 14–15, 69, 71, 183, 207, 209, 211–13, 245
Scott, James C., 98, 165n9, 201, 206, 223, 234, 240, 247n6
segmentation, 37–38, 48–49, 57, 227, 256
self-esteem, 22, 149, 220, 237, 244, 255
settlements, 3, 6–7, 10–11, 14–15, 18, 20, 46, 49–54, 57, 59, 61, 66, 69, 72–73, 79n3, 82n40, 83, 102n8, 106, 112, 114, 121, 124, 129nn10,16, 133, 136–37, 140–41, 145n3, 146n18, 157, 165n10, 169–71, 178, 181, 205, 212, 214–15, 231–32, 235–36, 241, 246, 260n2
Shank'illa, 21–22, 148–49, 154–55, 164n6, 167, 188, 191, 195–96, 202–5, 210, 212–13, 215–18, 223, 226–32, 235, 240, 244, 247nn2–5, 252, 255–56
similarity, 3, 21, 29, 84, 119, 128n3, 149, 151, 156, 163, 165n7, 167–69, 173, 175–76, 179–80, 183–86, 188–89, 192n5, 193n17, 195, 199, 202–3, 255
Simmel, Georg, 29, 31–32, 149, 167, 175, 234
size. *See* group size
social drama, 20, 47, 76, 83, 86, 128n4, 259
social organization, 3–4, 46, 57–61, 86, 180, 208
social relations, 6, 9, 11–12, 16, 18, 20–21, 26, 28–29, 31, 34–37, 43, 49–50, 54, 60, 78, 84, 86, 88, 97, 99, 104, 106–7, 112–13, 115, 119, 126–27, 130n17, 134, 136–37, 142–44, 148–50, 152, 160–61, 174–76, 181, 184–86, 188, 191–92, 192n11, 193nn16–17,

194–96, 211, 219, 223, 228–29, 231, 233, 252–53, 255
solidarity, 6, 12, 52, 59, 64, 75, 112–13, 167, 185, 218
sorghum, 2–3, 30, 59, 106, 122, 130n21, 138, 167, 177, 204, 208
South Omo, 1–3, 6–7, 12, 16, 19, 21–22, 23nn6–7, 32, 33–34, 37, 41, 56, 74, 79n9, 87, 110, 121, 130n21, 131n28, 142, 144, 145nn3,5, 148–52, 154–59, 162–64, 164n1, 165n11, 166–91, 191n1, 192n7, 193nn17–18, 195, 203, 205, 208, 211, 218, 226–29, 232, 235–36, 238, 240, 247n2, 248n18, 255–56, 259, 260n2
South Omo Museum and Research Centre (SORC), 10, 23nn4–5, 129n5
status, 16, 20, 32, 41, 44, 46, 48–49, 52, 54, 61, 69, 71–72, 77–78, 84, 87, 91, 93–94, 97, 99–101, 139, 142, 144, 145n5, 150, 165n11, 178, 181, 191, 209, 228, 233, 243–45, 251–52, 255
stereotypes, 21, 23n9, 33, 39, 41, 44, 106, 144, 149–50, 152, 155, 159–64, 165n12, 166, 169, 175, 183–84, 187–90, 204, 206–7, 209, 211, 220–21, 227–29, 236, 253, 258
Strecker, Ivo, 4, 10, 22n1, 23nn4,6, 52, 77, 80n14, 81nn20–21, 82n40, 87–88, 91, 100, 101n1, 125, 129nn8,12, 137, 143, 164n1, 167, 169, 176, 187, 191n1, 192n7, 215, 224nn10,12, 226, 237, 244
subordination, 75, 106, 134, 141, 195–96, 238
subsistence, 2–3, 10, 33, 69, 142, 155, 157, 207, 245, 260
symbolic interactionism, 30, 86, 94, 161, 211
synecdoche, 163

T
taboo, 7, 13–14, 25, 59–62, 67, 80n18, 86, 88, 92, 97, 100, 107, 112, 117, 124, 129n11, 133, 146n13, 157, 171, 176, 191, 226, 250–51, 258
terms of address, 10–11, 38, 60, 66, 68, 81n27, 135, 145n8, 184

territory, 3, 10, 14, 20, 33–34, 41, 52, 54, 126, 134–36, 151–52, 155, 157, 170, 172, 174–75, 181, 192n4, 199, 212, 239, 259–60
'the third', 27–28, 35, 37, 42, 47, 50–51, 62, 86, 88, 92, 98, 104, 115, 149, 155, 160–61, 179, 185, 188, 190, 200, 202, 208–9, 217–22, 223n3, 237, 259
tourism, 34, 53–54, 71, 79n9, 123, 151, 181, 208, 210, 212–14, 218, 224n12, 235–36
translation, 8, 28, 41, 43, 45n7, 144, 145n8, 182, 215, 248n16, 258
tribalism, 34, 131n26, 145n5, 149, 154, 195, 209, 226, 231, 247, 256–57, 260n2
Turmi, 14, 52, 69, 110, 170, 172, 182–83, 212, 215, 224n13
Turner, Victor, 28, 47–48, 61, 86, 152
Turton, David, 23n6, 33–34, 41, 69, 80n15, 115, 129nn9,13, 133–34, 142, 144, 145nn3,8, 152, 177, 181, 193n13, 215, 232, 248n12
Tyler, Stephen A., 4, 8, 22n1

W

war, 6, 12, 22, 25, 33, 55, 60–61, 67, 72, 77, 81n24, 82n33, 107, 134, 140, 145n3, 150, 158, 167, 169–72, 175, 177, 180–82, 189, 193nn13,15, 204–5, 214–15, 218, 231, 233, 239, 247n1, 248n16, 252
weapons, 12, 37, 60–62, 65, 70, 78, 133–34, 136, 145n3, 158, 165, 165n10, 181, 205
Wheel of Autonomy, 18–21, 28–43, 45n3, 49, 73–74, 79, 126, 132–33, 139, 144–45, 148, 152–53, 156–57, 159, 163, 176–77, 181, 188–89, 191, 211, 215, 229, 231, 234, 247, 252, 256–59
Wood, John, 131n28, 175, 188–90

Y

youths, 14, 52–53, 65–66, 69, 71, 81n23, 107–108, 112, 128n3, 169–70, 182, 213

Z

zersi, 52, 67–68, 79n4, 86, 110, 112, 139–41, 215, 248n16
zonza, 11, 17, 57–68, 71, 77, 81n21, 87, 91, 105–10, 112, 115–17, 150, 178, 182–83, 186, 203, 208, 210, 215, 223, 224n13, 236, 243

Integration and Conflict Studies
Published in Association with the Max Planck Institute for Social Anthropology, Halle/Saale

Series Editor: Günther Schlee, Director of the Department of Integration and Conflict at the Max Planck Institute for Social Anthropology

Editorial Board: Brian Donahoe (Max Planck Institute for Social Anthropology), John Eidson (Max Planck Institute for Social Anthropology), Peter Finke (University of Zurich), Joachim Görlich (Max Planck Institute for Social Anthropology), Jacqueline Knörr (Max Planck Institute for Social Anthropology), Bettina Mann (Max Planck Institute for Social Anthropology), Stephen Reyna (University of Manchester)

Assisted by: Cornelia Schnepel and Viktoria Zeng (Max Planck Institute for Social Anthropology)

The objective of the Max Planck Institute for Social Anthropology is to advance anthropological fieldwork and enhance theory building. 'Integration' and 'conflict', the central themes of this series, are major concerns of the contemporary social sciences and of significant interest to the general public. They have also been among the main research areas of the institute since its foundation. Bringing together international experts, *Integration and Conflict Studies* includes both monographs and edited volumes, and offers a forum for studies that contribute to a better understanding of processes of identification and intergroup relations.

Volume 1
How Enemies Are Made: Towards a Theory of Ethnic and Religious Conflict
Günther Schlee

Volume 2
Changing Identifications and Alliances in North-East Africa
Vol.I: Ethiopia and Kenya
Edited by Günther Schlee and Elizabeth E. Watson

Volume 3
Changing Identifications and Alliances in North-East Africa
Vol.II: Sudan, Uganda, and the Ethiopia-Sudan Borderlands
Edited by Günther Schlee and Elizabeth E. Watson

Volume 4
Playing Different Games: The Paradox of Anywaa and Nuer Identification Strategies in the Gambella Region, Ethiopia
Dereje Feyissa

Volume 5
Who Owns the Stock? Collective and Multiple Property Rights in Animals
Edited by Anatoly M. Khazanov and Günther Schlee

Volume 6
Irish/ness Is All Around Us: Language Revivalism and the Culture of Ethnic Identity in Northern Ireland
Olaf Zenker

Volume 7
Variations on Uzbek Identity: Strategic Choices, Cognitive Schemas and Political Constraints in Identification Processes
Peter Finke

Volume 8
Domesticating Youth: Youth Bulges and their Sociopolitical Implications in Tajikistan
Sophie Roche

Volume 9
Creole Identity in Postcolonial Indonesia
Jacqueline Knörr

Volume 10
Friendship, Descent and Alliance in Africa: Anthropological Perspectives
Edited by Martine Guichard, Tilo Grätz and Youssouf Diallo

Volume 11
Masks and Staffs: Identity Politics in the Cameroon Grassfields
Michaela Pelican

Volume 12
The Upper Guinea Coast in Global Perspective
Edited by Jacqueline Knörr and Christoph Kohl

Volume 13
Staying at Home: Identities, Memories and Social Networks of Kazakhstani Germans
Rita Sanders

Volume 14
'City of the Future': Built Space, Modernity and Urban Change in Astana
Mateusz Laszczkowski

Volume 15
On Retaliation: Towards an Interdisciplinary Understanding of a Basic Human Condition
Edited by Bertram Turner and Günther Schlee

Volume 16
Difference and Sameness as Modes of Integration: Anthropological Perspectives on Ethnicity and Religion
Edited by Günther Schlee and Alexander Horstmann

Volume 17
Bishkek Boys: Neighbourhood Youth and Urban Change in Kyrgyzstan's Capital
Philipp Schröder

Volume 18
The Wheel of Autonomy: Rhetoric and Ethnicity in the Omo Valley
Felix Girke

www.ingramcontent.com/pod-product-compliance
Lightning Source LLC
Chambersburg PA
CBHW051529020426
42333CB00016B/1842